Scouting in the Santa Clara Valley

THE SEVENTY YEAR ADVENTURE

1920 - 1990

THE HISTORY OF THE SANTA CLARA COUNTY COUNCIL
BOY SCOUTS OF AMERICA

SAN JOSE, CALIFORNIA

Researched and Assembled by
Council History Task Force
James P. Sturrock, Chairman

Edited by Mardi Bennett

Published by
Santa Clara County Council
Boy Scouts of America
P.O. Box 28547
San Jose, California 95159
1990

ISBN 0-9628133-0-3

Printed in the USA by
      Rosicrucian Press
      P.O. Box 908
      San Jose, California 95106

Typesetting by
      Hilary Graphics
      1450 Koll Circle, Suite 109
      San Jose, California 95112

"Years of Decision"
Paul and Nessie Chesebrough with Tiger Cub Glenn B.B. Penner, Pack 61
Camp Chesebrough, 1983   Photo: Mat Weingart

THE SCOUT BUGLE

VOLUME I   SAN JOSE CALIF., APRIL 23, 1926   NUMBER 4

Annual Patrol Leaders Conference, San Jose High School, April, 1926
with nearly 150 Scouts and adult leaders attending from San Benito, Santa Clara and Santa Cruz counties. The upper picture shows all of the lads attending the session. The lower picture shows the eagle scouts and adult leaders in charge of the conference and school. Those in the photograph are, left to right—front row, George Buchanan, Eason Monroe, Wallace Biddle, Alvin E. Rhodes, H.E. Rhodes, H.E. White, Robert Schulenberg and Rev. L.P. Walker; rear row, William G. Sweeney, W.H. Norman, Caldwell Hansen, George Wihelmy, Wilbur Fair, Elmo Stevenson and Rodney Capps.

Dedication

This history is dedicated to the thousands of Scouters, both volunteer and professional, who have worked together in a unique partnership since 1920 to make the programs of the Boy Scouts of America available to the youth of Santa Clara Valley.

BOY SCOUTS OF AMERICA

Table of Contents

Flag Ceremony, Camp Hi-Sierra

Foreword

Growing up today is more difficult than when we were boys, as it was more difficult for us than for our fathers. Opportunities grow greater which often bewilder today's youths, while the simple yet profound values of Scouting remain the same. In fact, change has occurred so rapidly in this world center of high technology that only now have we paused to compile the record of Scouting in Silicon Valley.

From the seasons of orchards to the time of computers, Scouting values have been transmitted painstakingly by parents, friends and leaders, by example and through shared experience. The lessons of serving others, making ethical choices and achieving full potential continue today as before. It is fitting that we look back over the past seventy years to trace the progress, rejoice in the successes, bridge over the disappointments, and thereby gain renewed strength for the fresh challenges that belong to the boys of today.

This book attempts, for the first time, to recall, collect and present aspects of Scouting for boys and their leaders here in the valley. As in most things in life, the path is uneven, the story incomplete, and always more words can be written and photographs printed.

However, a rich and colorful heritage emerges of purposeful youth, dedicated leaders and fond memories of shared adventures.

Jim Sturrock and his hard working committee of veteran Scouters have provided the leadership in this project. Mardi Bennett has ably extracted data and edited the manuscripts, while Leonard McKay has applied the printer's art to the book. As always, Brian Allen has served as the focal point to keep it all together and honor the calendar with its dates.

The same fundamental values expressed in the Scout motto, oath and law are just as relevant today in this valley of rapid change, now, at the end of this century as they were at the beginning. In this book, we will be reminded how much the implementation has changed.

Browse, read, reflect and enjoy. This is a celebration of being a boy in this century, in this valley called Santa Clara.

Glen McLaughlin
President, 1986-87
Santa Clara County Council, BSA

Scoutmaster Conference

James P. Sturrock
Chairman, Council History Task Force

Glen McLaughlin
Council President, 1986–1987

Acknowledgments

In 1987 the idea of writing a history of the council to commemorate its 70th anniversary in 1990 was given serious consideration and, after favorable review, a decision was made to proceed with the project. In August, 1987, President Glen McLaughlin directed Jim Sturrock to organize and head a group to prepare and publish a comprehensive history of the Santa Clara County Council.

The Council History Task Force held its first meeting in October, 1987, and continued meeting monthly for two years to outline the history, collect data and conduct extensive interviews of prominent council Scouters. The following retired veteran Scouters, all holders of the Silver Beaver, performed outstanding service as members of the task force:

William J. Adams; Executive Board Member. Bill specialized in the areas of Awards and Recognitions and Council Statistics.

Walter D. Chronert; Executive Board Member. Walt specialized in the area of Council Properties and has been of tremendous help in digging up "ancient history."

Stephen H. Goodman; Executive Board Member. Steve concentrated on the histories of Organizations and Special Programs within the council. In addition he made several important interviews of key Scouters.

Charles Orr; International Scouter and Woodbadge trainer. Charlie helped with unit histories, photography and the interviews.

James P. Sturrock; Advisory Committee Member and Chairman of the Council History Task Force.

In addition, invaluable support was provided by:

Brian L. Allen; Council Scout Executive. Brian gave much appreciated direction, advice and moral support.

Nessie Chesebrough; Council Benefactor, Foundation Member and Executive Board Member. Nessie served as chief conscience, critic and proof reader.

Doris Hambrick; Council Development Director. Doris was always the cheerful helper, go between and "provider of everything else." She was especially helpful in obtaining valuable historical records from the National Council Office.

By the summer of 1989 the task force had completed the data-gathering phase of the project and was ready to proceed with the editing and publishing activities. One of the board members agreed to provide up front funding which enabled the project to proceed.

In August a professional editor, Mardi Bennett, was engaged to take the accumulated material, condense it and put it in narrative form for the book. In 1980 Mardi founded Marben Associates which provides consultant services in Historic Preservation, Community Relations and Governmental Affairs. Ms Bennett has written books and articles on local history and in 1987 she published a history of the Los Gatos, Saratoga and Monte Sereno area called *Images of Long Ago.*

In addition, a veteran printer and publisher volunteered to oversee publishing the book. Leonard McKay, a former Scout in Troop 501, has retired from a printing and publishing career where he produced numerous history books. He is the co-owner of Memorabilia of San Jose, a firm specializing in books on Santa Clara County and California history.

The following people not individually recognized, have generously provided photographs for this history: William Adams, William Balch, Walter Chronert, Burton Corsen, Steven Goodman, Albert Mason, Charles Orr, Pat Reilley, Bill Sheldon, Albert Smith, and James Sturrock. Also, many photographs of unknown origin have been utilized. In addition, Clip-art provided by Kevin Reeve has been used extensively.

Finally, the assistance of several divisions in the National Office of the Boy Scouts of America is gratefully acknowledged. Their efforts have provided historical records of the early years of this council which no longer were available locally.

Mardi Bennett
Editor

Council History Task Force and Escorts—at Mess Hall Site, former Camp Arroyo Sequoia, March 1989.
L. to R.: Charlie Orr, Glen McLaughlin, Bill Adams, Al Smith, Walt Chronert, Steve Goodman, Ken Robison, and Brian Allen.

Lord Baden-Powell of Gilwell

Introduction

The Scouting Movement Begins

Lieutenant General Sir Robert S.S. Baden-Powell founded the Boy Scout movement in England in 1908. This evolved from his experiences as an Army officer during the Boer War in South Africa.

Toward the end of the 1800s, while serving as adjutant of his English regiment, Baden-Powell realized that the soldiers were lacking in the knowledge of basic social values as well as in the ability to care for themselves. He wrote a training manual in 1883 and instigated training programs to instill in the soldiers the characteristics of dependability, initiative and resourcefulness as well as the basic skills of survival in the field.

In 1899 Baden-Powell wrote and published *Aids to Scouting* based upon his training experience and to emphasize military reconnaissance skills. The book was used to great advantage in training soldiers and boy messengers during the long siege of Mafeking in 1899 and 1900 where Baden-Powell commanded the defending troops. Also, the book sold well and was widely read in England as the public followed the progress of the war.

When Baden-Powell returned to England as a hero in 1903, he found, to his great surprise, that his soldiers training manual had been adapted and used in schools for boys. The school officials enthusiastically urged him to put the philosophy of the book into a workable program for young boys, which he agreed to do.

During these same years, across the Atlantic, men of vision felt the same needs and responded to them in similar ways. A Canadian, Ernest Thompson Seton, had established a reputation as a naturalist, wildlife artist, author and lecturer. In 1898 he moved to Cos Cob, Connecticut, and began to put into practice his concern for the large numbers of city boys who had no opportunity to interact with the great outdoors.

Seton invited neighborhood youths to camp on his property and soon was teaching them camping skills. They learned about trees and wildlife, and about their predecessors, the American Indians. Out of Seton's camp for boys came the first tribe of Woodcraft Indians in July 1902, at the Fresh Air and Convalescent Home for slum children in Summit, New Jersey.

While Englishman Baden-Powell and Canadian Seton were working out their concepts for training boys, Daniel Carter Beard, of the United States, was developing a similar program. Beard, also an author and illustrator of note, founded, in 1905, the Society of the Sons of Daniel Boone which became the biggest boys club in the United States.

Seton and Beard, both living in the Northeast section of the United States, attracted a total of nearly 4,000 boys to their programs.

Still another group in the United States, called the Young Men's Christian Association (YMCA), had fifty years of experience working with boys before the turn of the century. It had been operating summer camps since 1885.

In 1906 Seton visited Baden-Powell in London. Following their meeting Baden-Powell drew up a plan entitled "Boy Scouts—A Suggestion" and sent copies to those he felt might be interested and the response was enthusiastic. The next step was a field test.

To put into practice his ideas Baden-Powell, recruited 12 boys from the upper income class and nine boys from the working class districts of Poole and Bournemouth. In August of 1907 the first Boy Scout camp was held on Brownsea Island in Poole Harbor for two weeks with Baden-Powell as the Scout Master.

In those days nobody in England "went camping," only the Army camped when required to during training exercises. The four boys' patrols lived in Army tents and were fed by Army cooks. The experiment was a resounding success and led Baden-Powell to the writing of the first Boy Scout manual, *Scouting for Boys,* published in 1908. This book became an instant success and thus the world wide Scouting movement was launched.

Scouting Comes to America

Chicago publisher William Dickson Boyce had been introduced to the Boy Scout program when on a business trip to London. It seems Boyce was lost in particularly dense fog when trying to find the office of a business associate. A young Boy Scout appeared out of the fog and helped him get to his destination. To Boyce's astonishment, the young man refused a tip

William D. Boyce
Instigator and Financier (1910)

Edgar M. Robinson
Organizer and Executive Board (1910–1914)

Colin H. Livingston
President (1910–1924)

Dr. James E. West
Chief Scout Executive (1910–1943)

Ernest Thompson Seton
Chief Scout (1910–1914)

Daniel Carter Beard
National Scout Commissioner (1910–1941)

Founders of the Boy Scouts of America

for his assistance. Boyce was so impressed he decided to find out more about these Boy Scouts and paid a visit to Lord Baden-Powell to learn about them first hand. William Boyce, with Baden-Powell's approval, filed incorporation papers for the Boy Scouts of America. This was completed in Washington, D.C., on February 8, 1910. Since Boyce employed about 25,000 boys to sell his publications in the East and Midwest, his purpose was to do something worthwhile for his boys.

The YMCA saw the Boy Scout program as an asset to their training methods and offered their help to Boyce. Edgar M. Robinson of the YMCA, with expenses underwritten by Boyce, opened a Boy Scout office in New York City. Robinson achieved the seemingly impossible task of bringing the several established boy membership organizations, and the independently organized Boy Scout groups, together under the name of the Boy Scouts of America. Soon a group of influential leaders was convened to plan a permanent organization. The organizing committee appointed a Washington lawyer, James Edward West, as the first Chief Scout Executive. Dr. West served in that capacity for 32 years and helped build the Boy Scouts of America into a national institution.

Much credit is due both Seton and Beard for sublimating their own established organizations in order to strengthen the formation of the fledgling Boy Scouts. They both went on to serve the new organization in influential positions; Seton as the first Chief Scout, wrote the original handbook; and Beard served as the National Scout Commissioner for 31 years.

Establishing an Organization

A Federal Charter was enacted by Congress on June 15, 1916, which granted permanent protection to the name, purpose, uniform and insignia of the BSA. The national council was now secure but the organization had a long way to go to provide the necessary support to Scout troops which were springing up all across the country. Scouts were demanding handbooks, training material, uniforms and insignia which simply were not available in the early months.

Gradually these items became available, and local councils were organized in each state to administer to the needs of the troops in their communities. These councils were manned by volunteer local citizens interested in the success of the new youth program. As sufficient funds became available a council would hire a full time professional Scout Executive and thus become a First Class Council.

Lone Scouts or Troops organized in territories not serviced by a local council were registered individually with the National Council. This was still the situation when Scouting began in Santa Clara Valley.

This history begins with the earliest known Scouting activity in Santa Clara Valley in 1915, records the beginning of the council in 1920, and continues through the exciting story of seventy years of Scouting's organized growth and prosperity in the Santa Clara Valley. It attempts to document the events and activities which have occurred and to recognize the units and leaders who have made it happen.

James P. Sturrock
Chairman, Council History Task Force

The Baden-Powell Stone on Brownsea Island

Andrew J. Bonfield, 1979, 1980

Jan W. Passmore, 1981, 1982

General Robert E. Huyser, 1983–1985

John B. Lochner, 1988, 1989

Recent Council Presidents

Carl E. Cookson, President 1990–

Brian L. Allen, Scout Executive 1982–

Chester D. Bartlett, 1946–1958

Raymond J. Ewan, 1958–1974

Randolf B. Kohl, 1975–1977

Robert N. Allexsaht, 1978–1982

Recent Council Scout Executives

Albert B. Smith
President, Memorial Foundation, 1984–

Opening Ceremony at Camp Hi-Sierra   Photo: Pat Reilley, circa 1960

I. The Santa Clara County Council, 1920-1990

Prologue: Pre-Council Activity

The First Boy Scouts in Santa Clara County

Scouting activity is known to have existed in Santa Clara County as early as 1915 when Troop 1 in Los Gatos was first chartered by the National Council. This was followed in 1918 by Troop 2, Los Gatos, which is still active today as Troop 501, the oldest troop in the council. Also, there is reference to a Troop 6 being active in Saratoga in 1915.

Reverend Frank J. McLain, minister of the Westminister Presbyterian Church, started the first Boy Scout troop in San Jose in 1916. Other troops were formed and by 1920 there were nine troops in San Jose and six more in the county.

During World War I Scout troops worked diligently to support the war effort. They helped plant Liberty Gardens, distributed patriotic literature, and sold Liberty bonds.

After the war, Troop 1 was meeting at 59 Julian Street every Friday. The San Jose Evening News reported on August 2, 1920, that Troop 1 spent a weekend hike at the home of Everis Hayes, the publisher of the News. His home, called Edenvale, was located on the Monterey Road on 28 acres. Ernest Savliere, the father of one of the Scouts, treated the troop to a watermelon feed.

Eight other troops were meeting regularly in the cities of Santa Clara, Campbell, Los Gatos and Palo Alto.

On August 11 the San Jose Evening News mentioned that DeForest Jones, Scoutmaster of Troop 94, New York, and Joseph Farrell, hiked into San Jose on a Boy Scout tour to promote the Boy Scout Movement. The News later reported on August 19 that an address at the San Jose Rotary Club by Charles B. Miller, National Boy Scout Commissioner, had prompted the group to pledge themselves to give $5,500 to get a Boy Scout Council started in San Jose. They hoped to have a membership of 500 boys.

In late August the same paper announced that the Rotary Club planned to launch a two week campaign for funds. The Rotarians planned to offer associate memberships at a cost of $10 which would be subscribed by adults, and would finance one Boy Scout

for a year. The publicity and membership committees were comprised of several public spirited men representing different areas of the county. (listing in Insert, Reprint, San Jose Evening News, August 1920)

1915
ARCH BROLLY

In 1915, when I was about 14 years old, I joined Troop 6 in Saratoga. The Rev. J.A. Emerich was the Troop Leader. He was the minister of the Christian Church on Big Basin Way, where the Mere Michele Restaurant is now. He contacted the boys and asked them to join.

We met in the lumber storage yard, which used to be right in the center of town where the Memorial Arch is now. We used to sit on the lumber. Quite often two or three of the boys weren't there because they'd rather be up in the mountains hunting squirrels.

Youngsters back then were a freewheeling lot. We had one camping trip that the Assistant Scoutmaster went on—and the minute he got back, he resigned.

1918
ERIC THORSEN

I've been in this valley off and on since 1918, that's when my dad came and bought the first ranch through Will Weston. I can remember when Saratoga Avenue had a trolley line on it that went on up to Congress Springs. You could go from San Jose clear to Palo Alto on Stevens Creek Boulevard on a trolley.

Of course, I grew up in the days when we had the ferry boats from Berkeley and Oakland to San Francisco, and then they built the bridges. Some of my school mates who lived in Berkeley commuted to San Francisco; in fact, one commuted from Walnut Creek. He came over the hill in a car and picked up the Key System at the Claremont Hotel.

It really wasn't a long commute (for my Dad) because he said he could leave his home and he could be in the office in San Francisco in an hour and twenty five minutes. My dad commuted for better than forty years from Berkeley. We lived up next to the University of California stadium near the International House. He only had a block to walk down to College Avenue to pick up the street car which took him down to where it connected with the big trains which took him out to the mole where it connected with the ferry.

1919
LESTER STEIG

Many of the soldiers, on returning to the states after the war, offered their uniforms to the Boy Scouts. I was one of the boys who accepted their offer, as did many others, and we proceeded to wear them to the meetings. I had joined the Scouts in 1916, but later when we registered with the Boy Scouts of America, we discontinued wearing Army uniforms.

The Council is Organized

In 1990 a civically active person who gets things done is called "a mover and a shaker." In 1920 three such people, from the San Jose Rotary Club, came together to organize the official San Jose Council of the Boy Scouts of America.

John D. Crummey, President of Bean Spray and Pump Company (later called Food Machinery Corporation), Robert I. Bentley, Jr., President of Muirson Label Company, and Archer Bowden a San Jose attorney, convened a group of businessmen on August 20th, 1920, who elected the first Council Officers. They were president, Robert I. Bentley, Jr.; first vice-president, Archer Bowden; second vice-president, Charles L. Snyder; third vice-president, Dr. J.L. Pritchard; secretary, J. Derrol Chace; treasurer, A.B. Post. One order of business was to complete and sign the original charter application.

With the financial support of Crummey and the Rotary Club, and a charter from the National Council of the Boy Scouts of America, the San Jose "First Class" Council was in business. However, its jurisdiction extended to the San Jose city limits only.

In 1922 a charter revision permitted a name change to Santa Clara County Council, with permission to administer the program for the entire county. Jurisdiction over San Benito County was added in 1923, over Monterey and Santa Cruz counties, in 1927.

The Council was incorporated in 1923, and in 1924 the National Council officially designated it "Santa Clara County Council, #55, San Jose, California."

Dr. Lester Steig — 70 year Veteran Scouter

SCOUTING HISTORY - JAMES WEST,
The Early Days
Ken Curzon

James E. West was born in Washington, D.C., on May 16, 1876.... He was appointed Executive Officer of the Boy Scouts of America in October, 1910, and began service January 2, 1911, later becoming Chief Scout Executive. There is probably no single man in America so intimately associated with the early days of Scouting in this country. From the very beginning, Mr. (Dr.) West interested himself actively in every phase of Scout work. He was a member of the Committee on the Scout Oath and Law, and it was owing to his personal interest that the twelfth Law (point), which is an addition to the English Laws, was included in our American code.

Mr. (Dr.) West was a delegate to the International Scout Conferences in (the twenties). He ... addressed conferences of educational and civic bodies.... Since 1924 he served as Editor of *Boys Life* and carried on his duties actively until his death in 1948. He was awarded the Silver Buffalo for Distinguished Service to Boyhood in 1926....

(Reprint: Santa Clarion, 6/79)

The Early Years, 1920-1930

Introduction

The early years were a time for establishing a viable program, getting funding sources in place, and reaching out from the San Jose headquarters to the neighboring communities and nearby counties.

From the meeting on August 20, 1920, which the San Jose Rotary Club had initiated under the leadership of John Crummey, many dedicated men and women worked together to give the Boy Scout program a firm foundation. During the early years the Council operated under a standard Constitution and By-laws recommended by the National Council.

Council Presidents of the first decade were Robert I. Bentley, Jr., Archer Bowden, Walter Bachrodt, Wendell Thomas, Andrew Mortensen and Judge Harry Lucas. They were assisted by able Scout Executives Julius Rainwater and Harrison White, and Council Commissioners Edmund Richmond, Dr. J.L. Pritchard and John Hansen.

Soon after J.H. Rainwater arrived from Chicago on September 22, 1920 as the first Scout Executive at a monthly salary of $250, the first Scout Office was occupied by taking advantage of the generous offer of 100 square feet of space donated by the Chamber of Commerce. Council's address was Room 518, Growers Bank Building, First Street, San Jose. By 1923 they had 300 square feet, half of it was increased to 396 square feet, completely paid for by the Council. It was Council Headquarters until 1930.

Goals and their Implementation

The aim of the Scouting program was straightforward and simple: physical fitness, citizenship training and character building for all boys.

During the first couple of years the Council emphasis was on getting the program organized. However, by 1922 there was concern that some of the older boys appeared to be losing interest in Scouting.

Scout Executive Julius Rainwater felt strongly that many of the problems could be traced to, "Inefficient leadership ... boys entering High School imitate older boys, pursue girls and leave Scouting. (They also are) working after school and evening." In order to strengthen leadership, the Council initiated a Scoutmasters Troop for "training and recreation."

Keeping up the momentum, the Council, in 1926, was pleased to have a certified training course for 43 Scoutmasters, and a specialized training course for 62 Troop Committeemen, plus a training course for Patrol Leaders.

In 1925 Courts of Honor had been held "to provide recognition before the Scouts' parents and friends of the achievements of advancement (which would) further dignify Scouting to the individual Scout as well as the public at large."

The Charter renewal application signed by Council President Andrew Mortensen in early 1927 set forth these outstanding needs:
- "• To bring closer contacts with the smaller communities to the program.
  - That there be a more thorough understanding of civic relationships.
  - There should be a development of a more positive understanding of real leadership on the part of the leaders and the boys.
  - Better camping and more of it for the boys. Putting the 'out' in Scouting.
  - Fixing in the minds of the volunteer leaders that (their) services ARE (sic.) appreciated."

That same year the Council actively promoted good reading and cooperated with public libraries, bookstores, schools and troops.

Following the addition of San Benito, Monterey and Santa Cruz Counties to the area served by the Santa Clara County Council, the Council's goal was to involve the new territory by having their representatives on the Executive Board. They also insured proportionate time and services of the Scout Executive and staff.

Troop 2, Los Gatos, at Big Sur circa 1926
Lyndon Farwell's Buick Roadster

Troop 2, Los Gatos at Big Basin, circa 1928
Scoutmaster Marc Vertin, Assistant Scoutmaster Cecil Dickenson, Cook Joe Espinosa

Council Operations

In August of 1920 the Rotary Club of San Jose decided to assist with the organization of a Boy Scout Council and to provide the council's operating expenses for the first year. Rotarians were members of the organizing committee and many went on to become leaders in the new council.

The first order of business for the newly established committee was to file the "Application for Charter for Local Council" with the National Council of the Boy Scouts of America. This application was for the "San Jose City Council" with jurisdiction over San Jose, California. The form was signed by Council President R.I. Bentley, Jr. and the Council Secretary J.D. Chace on August 20, 1920.

The Local Council Registration Fee was for $25 and there was an additional quota for the National Field and Extension Service of $435.

Evidently, Mr. Chace managed the council's affairs as interim Scout Executive until Julius H. Rainwater took over as the first Scout Executive in November,

1920. The first "Application for Renewal of Charter for Local Council" was signed on February 21, 1921, by Scout Executive Rainwater and the Council President for 1921, Archer Bowden.

In 1922 the council's name was changed to "Santa Clara County Council" to reflect increased territorial responsibilities. At this time the council was organized into 7 districts. Also, its finances were given a boost when the Community Chest added the council to its list of beneficiaries.

The council was enlarged again in 1924 when its southern neighbor, San Benito County, was added to its territory. The name then became "Santa Clara and San Benito Counties Council." About 6500 individuals were contributing to the operating expenses of the council by then and an automobile expense of $614 was listed for the first time. Also in that year, the council was assigned Number 55 by the National Council.

Still further expansion occurred in 1927 when the adjacent coastal counties of Monterey and Santa Cruz were added to the territories administered from San Jose. The council title became even longer: "Santa

Clara, San Benito, Monterey and Santa Cruz Counties Council." That title did not change until 1933 when the three neighboring counties split off to become the "Monterey Bay Area Council" and the remaining territory (Santa Clara County) reverted to its former name the "Santa Clara County Council." That title has remained unchanged since 1933.

In 1928 the Districts became known as Administrative Centers, each of which accepted responsibility for their share of the council finances. Twelve of these centers were established in order to cover the expanded-county council territory.

LITTLE KNOWN FACTS ABOUT COUNCIL NUMBERS

The National Council assigned numbers to all local councils in 1924, although these numbers did not appear on the charters or come into common usage until two or three years later.

Councils existing in 1924 were numbered in the following manner:
- States were listed alphabetically;
- Councils were listed alphabetically within each state;
- Numbers were assigned consecutively, 1 through 640;
- Overseas councils in Panama, Tokyo and Peking were assigned numbers 641, 642 and 643.

Many councils existing between 1910 and 1924 were never numbered because they had merged with other councils, or had ceased to exist prior to the numbers being assigned. The numbers for councils which ceased to exist after 1924 were often reassigned to newly organized councils, however, this practice was discontinued in later years.

In this manner Santa Clara County Council was assigned the number 55. It is interesting to note that the Monterey Bay Area Council was later numbered 25 and the Stanford Area Council was numbered 31 because previous numbers had been reassigned.

(information source: National Council office, BSA, Irving, Texas)

NEWS NOTES

DeForest Jones, Scoutmaster of Troop 94, New York, and Joseph Farrell hiked into San Jose on a Boy Scout tour to promote the Boy Scout movement.

(Reprint: San Jose Evening News, August 11, 1920)

ROTARIANS PLAN BOY SCOUT MOVE

Following an address by Charles B. Miller, National Boy Scout Commissioner, the San Jose Rotary Club yesterday went on record of pledging themselves to give the sum of $5,500 for the inauguration here of a Boy Scout movement which will have an ultimate membership of at least 550 boys. While San Jose has had about 9 Boy Scout Troops heretofore there has never been any unity between them because of the fact that there has been no Boy Scout Council here.

(Reprint: San Jose Evening News, August 19, 1920)

ROTARIANS WILL START DRIVE FOR BOY SCOUT AID

With two important committees appointed and everything set the Rotary Club will tomorrow launch a fifteen day campaign to place the San Jose Boy Scout movement upon a firm basis. With a 15 acre tract allotted by the city above Alum Rock Park for the camp and hundreds of boys anxious to reap the benefits which go with the membership in the organization, there is little doubt but that the $5500 goal will be reached.

The committees are: A Publicity Committee of J.R. Chance, E.K. Johnson, H.L. Baggerly, Jay McCabe, Roscoe Wyatt. A Membership Committee of H.C. Dunlap, H.L. Austin, Earle Barthwell, Joseph DeBrutz, Leon Jacobs, W.C. Lean, Louis Normandin and O.H. Speciale.

The financial end of the local Boy Scout movement will be handled largely through associate memberships. These will cost $10, will be taken out by adults and each one will be sufficient to finance one boy for one year. 550 boys are provided for in the plan. It is expected that all civic bodies and citizens will get behind the movement which will mean so much to San Jose youngsters.

(Reprint: San Jose Evening News, August 1920)

THE BOY SCOUTS OF AMERICA— A MEMBERSHIP ORGANIZATION CHARTERS

The Boy Scouts of America does not operate the Cub Scout packs, Boy Scout troops, Varsity Scout teams, or Explorer posts. These are the units through which youth members receive the program and training offered by the Boy Scouts of America (BSA). The BSA charters organizations to use the program as a resource for children, youth and families.

Following its incorporation in 1910 in Washington, D.C., the Boy Scouts of America became increasingly popular across the United States. Congress recognized Scouting's potential as an educational resource and, in 1916, granted a federal charter to the BSA to make the program available to boys through community organizations. Under the aegis of its Congressional mandate, the BSA, in turn, issues two kinds of charters:

• One charter grants to a local Scouting council the authority and responsibility to provide services to community organizations, enabling them to use the Scouting program for their youth. There are more than 400 local councils throughout the United States...,

• The other charter is issued to a community organization granting it the use of the Scouting program, operated under its own leadership, to serve the children, youth and families for which it has a concern.

(Excerpt: National Council Tract: "Chartered Organization — Relationship and Growth")

Troop 2, Los Gatos, Big Sur Camp 1926

The first committees organized by the Council were: Executive, Associate membership, Court of Honor, Publicity, Extension, Examinations and Tests, Finance, Camping, Inspection and Supervision. In 1921 Civic Service, Troop Organization, and Leadership Training Commmittees were added. Twelve men served on the Executive Board.

By 1922 membership of the Council included 35 men, the majority of them businessmen, but including civic, educational and religious leaders as well. New interests and programs were addressed by three new committees in 1926: the Reading Program, Sea Scouting and Rural Scouting.

As noted in the Charter application of 1928, Council committees were kept very busy. The frequency of meetings listed during the year: Council, 2; Executive Board 9; District Committees 62; Courts of Honor 72. A Health and Safety Commmittee joined the other active committees.

In 1929, with A.M. Mortensen of San Jose as President, the Council Executive Board reflected the participation of representatives from the outlying areas, i.e. Vice Presidents: W.L. Bachrodt, San Jose; Dr. H.G. Watters, Watsonville; Judge H.C. Lucas, Santa Cruz; W.C. Meacham, San Juan Bautista; J.E. McDowell, Los Altos; and Treasurer, C.L. Snyder, CPA, San Jose; Secretary, G.F. Shaner, Los Gatos. The Deputy Commissioner for Lone Scouts was Hans Iverson from Santa Cruz.

Membership

When the San Jose Council was organized in late summer of 1920 there were already several Boy Scout Troops functioning. The Charter application stated there were 107 Boy Scouts listed in 7 troops. By the end of December of that year there were 279 registered Scouts aged 12-20. At that time there were 11 public schools, 2 parochial schools and 2 private schools in San Jose.

In 1922 when the Council requested the National Council for a larger jurisdiction, and for permission to be renamed the "Santa Clara County Council," registered Boy Scouts were divided into communities, i.e. San Jose, 370; Palo Alto, 40; Los Altos, 38; Saratoga, 12.

San Benito County was added to the Scouting jurisdiction of the Council in 1923 and the joint Council was serving an estimated population of 100,000. A districting plan was developed so that each city was a district. Registration continued to increase and by the end of 1923 there were 826 Boy Scouts in 36 troops.

Troop 2, Los Gatos, Big Sur Camp 1926

In 1924 there were six district committees with their Deputy Commissioners as liaison to the Council.

The Santa Clara and San Benito Counties Council encompassed such diverse communities as Hollister, Gilroy, San Jose, Los Gatos, Palo Alto, Mountain View and Sunnyvale. It was estimated that 35% of the youth in these cities were foreign born, with the predominant ancestry being Italian, Portuguese and Japanese.

By the end of 1927 there were 1585 Boy Scouts in 78 troops and 215 Scouters. Also listed were 2 Lone Scouts. By the end of the decade the totals were 1507 Scouts in 79 troops and there were 5 Lone Scouts.

These were hard-working boys. As early as 1921 the Council proudly boasted 2 Life Scouts, 2 Star Scouts and 1 Eagle Scout. By 1924 there were 17 Life Scouts, 17 Star Scouts and 18 Eagle Scouts.

The Council served all boys in the various programs and in 1928 referred to them in the categories of "Land, Sea, Cub and Lone Scouting."

Scoutmaster Marc Vertin Troop 2, Los Gatos,
Big Sur Camp 1926

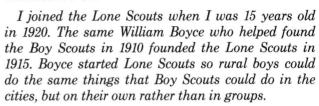

1920
THERON FOX

I joined the Lone Scouts when I was 15 years old in 1920. The same William Boyce who helped found the Boy Scouts in 1910 founded the Lone Scouts in 1915. Boyce started Lone Scouts so rural boys could do the same things that Boy Scouts could do in the cities, but on their own rather than in groups.

The key to the thing was the Lone Scout Magazine that Boyce published in Chicago. He accepted letters and articles written by boys. They even gave merit badges for the boys' journalistic efforts. I received a Bronze badge for mine.

We were here but did not attract very much attention. One of the main activities was corresponding with members in other parts of the country, and the world, for that matter. Say, come to think of it, that was probably what started my interest in stamp collecting. Of course, I've always been a stamp collector.

In that time of my life it was very important. The Lone Scouts got names of other Lone Scouts from the magazine. I must have corresponded with twenty people, one of them was the son of a Mexican doctor who had escaped the Mexican Revolution of 1914, and fled to Los Angeles. I still correspond with a fellow whom I first wrote to in 1924, so friendships started then have often lasted through the years.

Somehow it seems that Lone Scouts went into certain careers. They mostly all became printers, newspapermen, college professors or politicians. Take the bunch from San Jose and their professions: Joe Bonacina, attorney; John Brundage, banker; Bob Felton, printer; Lloyd Gravatt, machinist; Willard Loughlin, printer; Phil Richards, Librarian at San Jose State College; and myself, who was a newspaperman.

We had a Lone Scout who became a Superior Court Judge in San Rafael. Then there was Governor Faubus of Arkansas, U.S. Senator Rush Holt from West Virginia and another State Senator in Rhode Island. And then there was that member from India who attended one of our reunions.

Editor's Note: Before the Lone Scouts merged with the Boy Scouts in 1924, 523,470 boys had joined in its ten year span of existence.

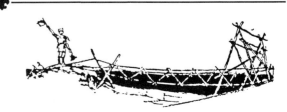

1929
CARL McCLELLAND

Troop 10 began with twelve unkempt, all too lively urchins with little or no home training. These undisciplined boys let all the air out of Louis Larson's tires. I had brought special refreshments of cider and doughnuts, which they promptly dunked, and heaved out the windows.

As a result of their attitude, we were asked to leave the (newly constructed) Salvation Army Building.

Editor's Note: Walter Bachrodt, Superintendent of the San Jose Schools, and former 2 term president of the Santa Clara County Council, offered the Scouts the use of an unused basement storage area at Lowell School, at Seventh and Reed Streets. This became the Troop 10 meeting place.

Outdoor Activities

One of the first orders of business for the new Council in 1920 was to have fifteen acres in Alum Rock Park set aside for the exclusive use of the Boy Scouts.

$3200 was budgeted for "Camp Property" in 1925 when Camp Swanton, near Davenport, was leased from the University of California.

The next year, even though 412 boys participated in camping activities, Scout Executive Harrison White felt that there should be, "Better Camping and more of it for the boys." He was anxious to put the "out" in Scouting. By 1928 he was able to run a 6-week summer camp, a spring camp had been initiated, and several overnight hikes were held annually for troops and patrols.

1922
ALBERT HERSCHBACH

I joined the Scouts in 1922. Our troop, Troop 2, met at Willow Glen School. William Forsythe was the Scoutmaster. He would really get mad when we called him "Bill."

First we met in the basement of the school. Then we would take the streetcar and go to Los Gatos. Then we would hike up the railroad tracks and camp. We also took the streetcar to Congress Springs. We would hike from Congress Springs to Castle Rock ... That was a good hike.

We never had a pack like they have now, we had a blanket roll that we put everything in and tied it over our shoulder and tied it down. We carried our food and cooked stew and eggs and steak and bacon bread. No tents.

During the day we played games and had skills going on. We took up bow and arrows and shot at a target. We learned how to build a fire, had races, sack races, and tug of war.

Hike to Big Basin Park, early 1930's

Depression and War—
Survival Years, 1931-1950

Introduction

The Depression Years from 1931 to about 1934, were marked by a determination on the part of the Council to hold the ground they had gained during the first ten years.

An example of the hard times that beset Santa Clara County Council was the $700 debt owed to the National Council at the end of 1932, and the request of the local Council that a credit of $250 be extended for Supply Service in 1933. All debts were cleared in 1933.

An adjustment in the composition of the Council's jurisdiction and financial structure was necessary when the coastal counties separated to form the Monterey Bay Area Council in 1933 and no longer needed the services of the Santa Clara County Council.

Some of the less hardy groups of Scouts dissolved. All of the earlier experimental Cub Packs were inactive by the end of 1933.

The next year the Council, as a non-profit organization, applied for and received their incorporation papers at the state level. The Council also revised and resubmitted ammendments to their Constitution and By-Laws in 1934, which were finally adopted in 1936.

By 1934 the term "Districts" was used again for subdivisions of the council territory instead of "Administrative Centers."

In the mid-thirties the mainstream wage earners had begun to make progress once again and life reflected their optimism. There was time to think of, and put energy into, endeavors such as the Scouting Program. The Cub Scouts were reactivated, joining the other boys in programs designed for their special interests such as Sea Scouts, Explorer, Rover Crew and Neighborhood Patrol programs.

Adults were found whose leadership enabled the boys to participate in Camporees, Agricultural Fairs, Boy Scout Week and troop special events.

During 1939 another group of Scouters separated from the Council in order to apply for Charter jurisdiction over the northern section of Santa Clara County, namely the cities of Palo Alto, Mountain View and Los Altos. This became the Stanford Area Council in January, 1940.

Council Presidents who persevered during this difficult decade were Andrew Mortensen, San Jose; H.G. Watters, Watsonville; Almon Roth, Palo Alto; and H.H. Hallin, Theo Wright and Dr. Ernest Abbott all of San Jose. Scout Executive Duncan McKinley served the Council dependably until 1941. Field Executives were Lester Quinley and Egbert Rozeboom.

In 1931 the Council headquarters had been moved to 213 Bank of America Building at the corner of First and Santa Clara in San Jose. Sometime in 1941 or 1942 the Council moved again, this time to 315 Security Building in San Jose.

1941
KEN ROBISON

(When Oscar Matthews was Scout Executive) our office was in the Bank of America Building. They rented three rooms on the second floor to the Council. The Court Offices were right across the way and (Judge) Marshall (Hall) would call up and say, "I need a witness right away." So I would rush across the street to his office and act as a witness for some federal infraction. Everybody who served as a witness got paid $10 a day. That was pretty good pay for a half hour of your time."

In late 1941, just as the Scouting Programs were solidifying their ability to attract and hold the attention of Santa Clara County boys, World War II was declared. The decade of the forties became another story of dedicated people doing their best in the face of tremendous odds.

History repeated itself, finding the Boy Scouts involved with the home front efforts as they had been twenty odd years before during WWI. The government requested Boy Scout service for distribution of defense bonds and stamp posters; collection of aluminum and wastepaper; victory gardens and cooperation with the Red Cross.

At the end of 1941 the Council was in debt, $630 to the National Council and $139 to the National Supply Service. The operating budget was $11,510. They were also in debt in 1942 but were able to clear it with an operating budget of $14,538. About that time membership was on the increase and monetary contributions were also on the rise.

During the remaining two years of the war, Boy Scout troops continued to distinguish themselves in salvage drives, food production and conservation of the country's resources.

In the mid-forties, fathers and brothers came home at the end of World War II, and life in Santa Clara County began to return to normal.

The late years were devoted to increasing membership and training opportunities for both Boy Scouts and their leaders.

The Scouting Program of this decade was fortunate in having unusual continuity. Two San Jose judges with consecutive terms, Judge Marshall Hall and Judge William James were Council Presidents from 1941-48 when Marc Vertin, a former mayor of Los Gatos, became President for the last two years of the decade. Oscar Matthews and Chester Bartlett split the decade in half as Scout Executives, and Milton Ryder was Scout Commissioner from 1940 through 1949.

A well-dressed Scout in the 30's

CHALLENGING "GOOD TURNS"

Three nationwide "Food Conservation" Programs are under way to help combat the threatened World Famine. We are advised ... that without help millions may die. Our Government is now calling on us Americans to produce abundance, to conserve, and to share. Here is our chance to put into action a part of the Scout Oath "To help other people at all times."

Start plans now to have your Scouts "do something" about the following:

- **1. Emergency Food Collection Campaign:**

A national drive, headed by Secretary of Commerce Wallace, to obtain contributions of food canned in tin, or money to buy food. Find out who heads this worthwhile campaign in your community and offer to help.

- **2. Share the Bread Campaign:**

Americans called upon to eat 40% less cereal foods and 20% less fats and oils. Scouts can help publicize this effort and observe the request in their own home. One ounce saved a day by each registered man and boy in Scouting would mean 125,000 pounds daily from the Scout group alone.

- **3. "Victory Gardens" for '46:**

As proved in the War years, the Scout Family with a garden needs less from the store shelves. Urge Scouts to develop their own gardens and to continue livestock projects and help on farms when practical....

"SHIRTS OFF OUR BACK"

Have you turned in the clothing collected? If not, bring to Scout Headquarters or to the collection department announced by your Scoutmaster....

(Excerpt: The Dispatch Rider [Leadership Bulletin] 4/46)

Goals and their Implementation

One of the aims of the Scouting Program of the thirties was to provide service and counsel to the coastal counties of San Benito, Monterey and Santa Cruz. This goal was implemented by electing representatives from those counties to the executive board. Council Presidents from these outlying areas were Judge H.C. Lucas from Santa Cruz (1930) and Dr. H.G. Watters from Watsonville (1933).

Another more basic goal was to build youth registration while maintaining the Boy Scouts already in troops. In order to do that, the leaders tried to make Scouting interesting and challenging. Renewed energy and commitment was put into the camping program, and more emphasis into health and safety training.

In the mid-thirties both Rural Scouting and Cubbing were started. Rural Scouting was a new category for "Boys and units in villages under 2,500 population and open country." At the end of 1935 there was no figure available for the number of Rural Scouts but there were 79 Cub Scouts. The Council's goal for 1936 was to enroll 35 Cub Scouts. They exceeded their expectations by attracting 112 Cub Scouts to the program.

The goal uppermost in most minds during the first half of the forties was to be of service to the war effort. With World War II a dominant factor in the life of American families, an outlet for young boys' energies was to help with General Eisenhower's Wastepaper Campaign, grow food for the General Douglas MacArthur Medal, and work diligently in the Air Scout and Sea Scout programs.

WWII expanded the horizons of the Boy Scouts of America and local boys became aware of Scouting in other parts of the world. A new goal developed which emphasized a better understanding of Boy Scouts overseas. Due to the wartime devastation and postwar economies, "The Shirts Off Our Back" campaign was inaugurated to help Scouts abroad. In 1947 the sixth World Jamboree was held in Moisson, France which brought together 32,000 Scouts from 38 countries.

Council Operations

Sometime in 1930 or 1931 council headquarters was moved from 515 Growers Bank Building to 213 Bank of America Building at First and Santa Clara Streets in San Jose. In 1930 the council had five employees: Scout Executive Duncan McKinley, Field Executives Lester Quinley and Egbert Roseboom, Secretary Valeria Perry and Stenographer Mary Cronquist.

The council registered 120 members in 1932, 26 of whom were on the Executive Board. That year only three committees were reported as functioning well while 10 others were reported as not functioning well.

In 1936 comments on committee records were: **Advancement,** "Very outstanding"; **Organization,** "No lapsed troops during the year"; **Training,** "Best training record we have had"; **Civic Service,** "Very good — a hard job"; **Cubbing,** "Excellent for first year."

In November of 1939 the Santa Clara County Council gave approval to leaders in Palo Alto, Los Altos, Mountain View and Stanford University to apply for

a charter as a separate council. In January, 1940, a charter was issued to this group as the Stanford Area Council, thus removing those north county communities, which had been the North District, from the jurisdiction of the Santa Clara County Council.

The charter application for 1941 required information in the following areas: The Council, Finance, Organization and Extension, Camping and Activities, Leadership Training, Advancement, Health and Safety, and Reading Program.

For the first few years of the decade the net operating expenditures were listed; in 1940 they were $13,578. In 1943 they were $14,538. Beginning in 1945 dollar amounts were no longer reported on the charter applications.

Camp Arroyo Sequoia Pool (in 1989)

1932
JACK COX

At that time I met the Scout Executive who was Duncan McKinley, and he was a great guy. Before I met him, one night at troop meeting this young man came into the meeting and he had a pair of britches on and a tan jacket. He sat down while I was doing some instruction or something, and when I finished, I went over to him and introduced myself. He told me his name was Les Quinley. Well, the name didn't mean much to me, and I said, "Are you interested in Scouting?" He said, "Yes, very much." I said, "That's fine because I was looking for a helper." And then he said, "I am the Field Executive for Santa Clara County Council." Then I said, "Oh, that's great." What ever that was! He was a real pro....

Council Trip to Death Valley, 1940   Photo: Al Smith

In 1942 and 1943 the Health and Safety Committee insisted on the inspection of all meeting places, and also that "All boys in Junior and Senior High Schools were subject to Physical Exam yearly." In 1944 the committee report stated, "Schools have complete examination—health check-up, annually." Medical examinations of new Scouts have not been given since that time.

The Organization and Extension Committee of 1943 stated that 8 new Cub Scout Packs had been formed. In 1944 the Camping and Activities Committee held regional and sectional regattas for the Senior Scouts, plus helping the older Scouts to assist in what was termed "Agricultural Cooperation" for the war effort.

As the Council acquired more property, it realized that a more businesslike approach would be necessary and it established a Memorial Foundation as a separate entity. Its charge was to "hold title to all Council properties and to secure funds ... for the maintenance of these properties and for other needs of the Council."

The 1946 charter application contained a rather terse report on the 1945 committees: "Apparently the Operating Committees were not too active during the past year. An attempt will be made to carry on Council Program through active committees during 1946." The council appeared to have reflected the preoccupation of local families with the last crucial battles of WWII, and the difficult period of adjustment as servicemen returned home to resume more normal lives.

After the war the council committees bounced back from the transitional year of 1945 and functioned well.

Besides noting the religious preference of the council committees the National Council was anxious to have representatives from a broad spectrum of interests. In 1949 the Council included men from the religious, educational, labor, civic, business and farm segments of the community.

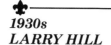

1930s
LARRY HILL

While I was teaching in Willow Glen, somehow or other I inherited a troop of kids out in East San Jose. We met on a kind of tent platform in the middle of a mud flat area. Their homes were around in the same area and we had a good troop. They were nice kids, and they liked the program, and we did a lot of things; a lot of handiwork of one kind or another, and we also learned to march.... We did everything a Scout Troop should do.

Well, they had a parade in San Jose and the Scouts were taking part. These kids wanted to be in the parade and the Scout Executive wouldn't permit it because they didn't have full uniforms. They just had jeans, a few of them had shirts. They couldn't afford them, they couldn't afford anything. I got a few shirts donated, that was about the best I could do.

Well, because they weren't fully uniformed, he wouldn't let them in. The kids were crushed, they didn't want to be Scouts any longer, and I resigned, not only from that, but from Scouting for maybe, I guess for, about ten years.

Outdoor Activities

In 1931 the Council promoted an all year round Camping Program. The 6 week Summer Camp at Swanton was attended by 12% of the total Scout membership. Camp Swanton was on the Pacific Coast 16 miles north of Santa Cruz. Scout Executive Duncan McKinley was the resident Camp Director. A Cub Scout Camp was planned for a week at Big Basin in 1931, as well.

Winter Camp was in its second year at Camp Curry in Yosemite. It drew 3% of Scout membership.

In 1934 the Council reported that they promoted an Activities Program. Many of the featured events were outdoors, i.e., the Camporees, special troop events and the vacation program in addition to camping. These activities still continue today.

In 1935 the proposed first National Jamboree was cancelled because of an infantile paralysis epidemic that was sweeping the country.

In 1937 the first National Jamboree was rescheduled and was held in Washington, D.C. at the invitation of President Roosevelt. Some representatives from the Santa Clara Conty Council attended but there is no record of their names.

In 1940 15% of the troops and 12% of the Scouts were in camp for at least one week under their own leadership. In 1941 the percentages were 20% and 23% respectively. In 1943 only 10% of the troops did no camping of any kind.

In August 1944 Reginald Stuart, and his wife, Grace, gave 80 acres of their ranch property in the foothills of Saratoga to the Council for use as a Boy Scout Camp. That year 56% of the troops participated in at least one week of camping.

About that time boating became a Senior Scout activity and sectional and regional regattas were held.

In 1949 the Council was given a 100 acre parcel by Edward Jenness. (He actually charged them $10 for it!) It is located south of the Sonora Pass Highway midway between Longbarn and Pinecrest. It was named Camp Hi-Sierra, and it replaced the San Lorenzo Scout Ranch which had not proved suitable for camping.

The Council insisted that a varied daily program be offered. Some of the outdoor activities were woodcraft and handicraft, hiking, nature study, water sports, and the development of skill in archery, marksmanship, photography, outdoor cooking and Scout advancement.

Throughout the thirties and forties individual troops participated in one day hikes and overnight camping activities, and scheduled excursions to interesting destinations.

1933
MICHAEL ANTONACCI

Well, our City Manager at the time was a pillar of the Westminister Presbyterian Church, right down here on the Alameda, and they had lost their Scoutmaster ... so he asked me if I would take it for a few months. That lasted almost two years.

I never will forget that first night when I went to the church. They were in a large rectangular room upstairs with doors on both sides. The youngsters of the troop, called Troop 3, were from the more affluent families along the Alameda, and they were raising all sorts of noise. As I stood at one door, I could see, through the opposite door, the choirmaster trying to hush them.

I looked at them and counted seventeen boys out of the three patrols. I said to myself, "Well, you little rascals, you may be three patrols of a Boy Scout Troop, but you are going to be three squads of a military unit. So, I went in and introduced myself, got them in the order of size, and at attention, as you would in a military unit. One youngster spoke up and said, "You are mixing up the patrols." And I said, "You are at attention."

About eight months later, Walter Bachrodt, our Superintendent of Schools, presided and gave out the awards at a Court of Honor. I shouldn't brag about this, but it was a record. Those youngsters took more merit badges than any two troops there. But I worked them. I tried to use on one hand, the general paternalistic hand of the father, and on the other, a little bit of the military.

As I followed several of them later, they turned out to be very fine people. I know this, no youngster can help but be better by being a Scout, particularly by being an Eagle Scout.

1934-38
AL SMITH

When we camped here (Camp Swanton) we hiked to a lot of places. There were troop hikes, study hikes, overnight hikes, hikes to Indian burial grounds, the fish hatchery, the deserted village, the dam, Water Snake Lake, and to the ocean.

And another thing, about the Indian burial grounds, at Ano Nuevo Island where the elephant seal are, the Indian calendar didn't have the same things as our calendar with lots of months with "R"s in it. Now, if you have a month with no "R" in it you don't eat shellfish. But the Indians ate shellfish the year around. Every now and then a Red Tide would get them and they (the Indians) would be buried out there, just covered with sand. Ano Nuevo is a State Park today. It is an island and we used to go down the other side and walk along the beach.

Camp Arroyo Sequoia Gateway, circa 1933

Troop 13 at the Pinnacles, 1949

Membership

In December of 1930 there were 1655 Boy Scouts in 87 troops. 407 were First Class, 400 Second Class and 848 were Tenderfoot. At the end of 1931 there were 75 Sea Scouts in 5 Ships and 1 Patrol.

A new emphasis for the Cub Scouting program was launched by the local council in 1931 when 45 Cubs were listed in 3 Cub Packs led by 15 adults. In 1935 they grew from 79 Cubs in 2 Packs with 12 Cubbers to 160 Cubs in 6 Packs with 30 Cubbers in 1936.

1933 saw a drop in registration of Boy Scouts which reflected the withdrawal of the membership from San Benito, Santa Cruz and Monterey Counties. Total Scout membership rose to 1361 the next year. 1280 were Boy Scouts; 81 were Sea Scouts. Thirty-five units were transferred to the new council including 32 Troops and 3 Sea Scout Ships.

In 1933 President Franklin Roosevelt became honorary president, and former President Hoover, honorary vice president of the Boy Scouts of America. Boy Scouts in Santa Clara County responded to a 1934 radio broadcast by President Roosevelt to do a "Good Turn." They joined Boy Scouts nationwide in collecting clothing, household furnishings, foodstuffs, and supplies for the distressed and needy victims of the Depression.

In 1935 the Silver Jubilee of Scouting was celebrated with nationwide membership passing the one million mark. In Santa Clara County there were 1359 Boy Scouts and 150 Sea Scouts which included 17 Scouts holding dual membership in Troops and Sea Scout Ships. Signaling and Mapping were popular courses for the Senior Scouts. In 1937 the Explorer Scouts Program was initiated.

When the Stanford Area Council was formed in January, 1940, fifteen units left the council including 2 Cub Packs, 10 Scout Troops, 2 Sea Scout Ships and 1 Explorer Troop.

The Boy Scouts of America were ready and willing to assist wherever needed in their own cities' war effort when the United States was drawn into World War II. Many of the Scouts' fathers had worked in the earliest troops to help during World War I.

The national drive to collect 30 million pounds of rubber in two weeks was very successful. Local Boy Scouts conducted salvage drives based on the Government issued pamphlet called, "Scrap and How Scouts Collect It." Scouts worked on victory gardens, farms and in harvest camps, and were Government dispatch bearers.

The total number of Scouts in the Santa Clara County Council in 1942 decreased to 907. This included 66 Sea Scouts, 59 Explorer Scouts, and 185 Cub Scouts. The loss was attributed to the north county forming their own Council and to the uncertainties of the first year at war. The total number of Boy Scouts increased to 1003 in 1943. Membership was on the rise again in 1944 with 1209 registered, including 48 Sea Scouts, 14 Air Scouts and 671 Cub Scouts.

Keeping up with the times, long pants and the Scout cap were made an official part of the Scout uniform in 1943.

Age levels were lowered in 1949 so that now Cub Scouts were to be 8 through 10, Boy Scouts, 11 through 14 and Explorer Scouts, 14 and up. That year the names of the Sea and Air Scouts were changed to Sea Explorers and Air Explorers. Important new guidelines were also adopted for incorporating handicapped boys into Scouting.

1938
LEONARD McKAY

It was during the Depression thirties when Troop 2, now Troop 501, Los Gatos, made our 14-mile hike to Mt. Umunhum. Following CCC-cut* fire trails, we first overnighted at Cypress Ranch. Here grizzled trapper Peter Rogers had a cabin and pack of hunting hounds. Pete scratched out a living collecting the bounty on coyotes, an occasional mountain lion, and sometimes a bob cat—for which the town of Los Gatos was named.

Pete regaled our group with mountain stories while we stood encircling him, straining to catch every word. The Wagner boys, Phil and Jim, Big Jim Powell, Bob (Horse) Board, Louie (Red) Morton, Scoutmaster Gil Becker, and I were all outclassed by a young blond giant, Dave Anderson. Dave, dressed in Scout shirt, neckerchief, shorts, and knee-high boots with gray woolen socks, had been the star fullback at Los Gatos High School, and later at UC Berkeley.

As Pete talked, his dogs circled our group until one male decided that Dave must have been a tree, lifted his leg, and marked Dave as his territory. It wasn't until the warm liquid trickled down his leg that Dave realized what had happened, and by then the rest of us were rolling on the ground in uncontrollable laughter.

*Civilian Conservation Corps

1943
ERIC THORSEN

(I was Scoutmaster of Troop 49 in Santa Clara) and there was also a Troop 47. I was a Protestant and I originally had 24 boys and they were all Catholic, but that didn't make any difference to me. Our meeting place was in the Catholic Church, in the basement. It just happened that way. Santa Clara was very heavily Catholic at that time.

Lots of them were Portuguese fellows. I had one Spanish boy whose father was section foreman on the Southern Pacific. I finally got down to a steady troop of about 18 which were three patrols. When the troop finally broke up 13 years later, we had three Protestants in the troop, the rest of them were all Catholic.

... When they used to come out to the ranch and camp, Sunday morning would come, they would put on their uniforms. I would take them from our ranch up to Milpitas to the Catholic Church in the truck, sit outside and wait for them to come out.

When we had a Camporee in the hills, here off of Stevens Creek Boulevard, I used to take a whole group of them from camp down to the Catholic Church on Lawrence Station Road.

So, as far as religion was concerned, I honored their status and never made any comment. Their religion was theirs and I didn't impose on it one way or the other, nor did I curtail them in any way.

Troop 41 Band, 1949   Photo by Stelling

1930s
HAROLD HALLIN

My father, H.H. Hallin*, was influential in starting the Sea Scout program in the Santa Clara County Council. He even talked the Navy at Mare Island into supplying whale boats for the Sea Scouts down here to use.

I remember going up to the Dumbarton Bridge with my father on Ray Wilkins yacht and we towed a bunch of whale boats back to Alviso. That was when Alviso was 12 feet higher, of course.

*H.H. Hallin was Council President in 1935 and 1936.

1944-51
ERIC THORSEN

I had quite a few good boys. Eddie Panelli was in my troop (T-49) and Bookie Castro, who is related to the Acronico family, who has the maraschino cherry place (processing plant) in Santa Clara. Of course, Panelli is in Sacramento as a State Supreme Court judge and Castro is teaching chemistry in a Southern California university. I just seemed to have an awfully congenial clicking of boys in my troop. I would have been perfectly willing to take them any place.

I had a troop that you might say were orphans, because I'd have 12 or 14 of them out at the ranch over Easter vacation with no parents, and not a parent would call. My wife would say they didn't know whether I was on the end of a bottle, or not.

These kids would make up their menu and bring their food. We had a big refrigerator and, so, they could come in and out the house when they were getting ready for meals. They did their own cooking. At one time our troop had the highest record of camping in the whole council. Every time there was a vacation period these kids would know it was coming, and they would ask if they could come out to the ranch and camp. That made it an awfully nice situation. I had 63 acres and there was about an acre and a half of open ground just south of my house, and a grove of trees which made it just fine for them. They could camp down there 150 feet away from the house, and they were more or less by themselves.

Post-War Expansion 1951-1970

Introduction

The beginning of the new year and a new decade was a good time to take stock:

- 1950 was the 40th anniversary of the Boy Scouts of America. 1950 also marked the Second National Jamboree at Valley Forge.
- The people of California were becoming accustomed to the rapid influx of new residents who had started to arrive on their doorstep immediately following the end of World War II. Many of these were service men from other states who had been stationed in California.
- Schools, housing, transportation, government services—all felt the strain of providing more of everything to accommodate the newcomers.
- The economy was booming as more goods were needed, and even the U.S. involvement in the Korean War in 1950 did not seem to slow the pace.

The Council was experiencing the same growth in Boy Scout registrations. They went from 3,033 in 1950 to 6,136 in 1955, doubling in five years. By the end of the decade registration had increased to 9,846 boys with 2186 Scouters, including Den Mothers, to lead them.

Council Presidents, who guided the expanded programs during the fifties, were Marc Vertin of Los Gatos, Clark Bradley, San Jose, Larry Hill, Campbell, and Bill Nicholson, Santa Clara. Scout Executive Chester Bartlett's tenure lasted from 1946 through 1958. He retired in April 1958 and was succeeded by Raymond Ewan. Harold Alexander was the Assistant Executive, and Milton Ryder served as Scout Commissioner throughout the fifties and into 1961.

In the 1950s, the Council had been trying to keep up with the population explosion in Santa Clara County, one of the most popular destinations in the state. In the 1960s, there were many new challenges and many new directions for the Council.

Economic production soared, and with it came increased purchasing power. New methods of fund raising to finance Scouting expenses became crucial.

Troop 10 on hike to Siverts Ranch, 1959

In science, new personnel and new laboratories made their debut. The new products and services they contributed liberated Californians from many manual tasks and helped develop new habits and life styles. These new forms of business and services demanded specialized skills for which the education system had to be reprogrammed.

With new affluence and more leisure time, larger numbers of people became interested in the environment. College students and other activists became alarmed with the rapid consumption of California's natural resources and rallied to popular causes such as fighting pollution of the atmosphere, oceans, lakes and streams.

These rapid changes in everyday life were reflected by a Council Executive Board with the flexibility to effect change in its programs and policies. Throughout the fifties and sixties, new committees were appointed to stimulate the troop leadership. Their primary aims were to promote troop concerns about the environment, and to increase their awareness of socio-political issues.

The strategy was proven successful as Scout registration continued to climb during the sixties from 10,745 in 1960 to 16,500 in 1966. Once again, continuity of good leadership was an ingredient that assured this progress. The Council had three multiple term presidents, Bill Nicholson, Bill Powell and Robert Morris, and one Scout Executive, Ray Ewan. Milton Ryder finished up a 21 year tenure as Council Commissioner and was succeeded by Greg McGregor in 1962 and Robert Morris in 1965.

1960 was a banner year for Boy Scouts throughout the country with gala celebrations marking Scouting's Golden Jubilee Year. The U.S. Postal Department issued a commemorative stamp. Nationwide, membership in the BSA was 5,160,958. Another milestone was reached in 1965 when the 500,000th Eagle Scout Badge was presented. In 1967 an updated Cub Scout program was launched that established a Webelos Scout program. Long-term camping reached an all time high with almost 65% of troops in the United States providing about 800,000 Scouts a first-hand experience with Nature by the end of the sixties.

In the sixties a monthly "Council Bulletin" was the latest of several efforts through the years to communicate with the units, however, it did not cover District activities. Before long an expanded newsletter, dubbed the "Santa Clarion" replaced it. As far as is known the first issue came out in September 1964. It carried the "Half Circle" Council logo on its masthead.

Bill Nicholson and R.I. Bentley, Jr., First Council President, circa 1960

Goals and their Implementation

The main goal of the fifties was to service the districts with leadership training for the expansion that was occurring so rapidly. Recruitment of good leaders was a never-ending pursuit. Fortunately, many of the new residents had been involved in Scouting in their former locations and wanted to become involved again.

The goal of having its own building for the Council Headquarters was realized in February, 1954. Its relatively central location away from the congested downtown business district of San Jose was helpful for Scouters. The new headquarters were a boon to the Council Executive Board and the Scout Executive. They finally had enough room for staff to be able to operate more efficiently.

In a move to increase effectiveness, the Council realigned district boundaries from the former districts: North (1), South (2), Campbell (3), West Valley (4), Los Gatos/Saratoga (5), South Valley (6). In October, 1959, the districts were assigned new names and numbers: Ponderosa (100), Mene Oto (200), Pioneer (300), Polaris (400) and Redwood (500).

The main Council goal of the sixties was to develop viable and exciting programs that would be relevant to all boys. All three programs, Cub, Scout and Explorer, were competing for the attention of boys who were in school and church athletic programs and other youth organizations such as the YMCA and Police League.

Secondarily, money to finance the Council operation and the camp facilities was becoming harder to find. Creative new ways to interest corporations and companies in investing in Scouting were developed during these years, among them the President's Club, the Distinguished Citizen Dinner and the Golf Tournament. They have proven successful and are still serving the Council's budgetary requirements.

Council Operations

In the spring of 1954 the Council moved its headquarters from 315 Security Building in downtown San Jose to their newly completed building at 2095 Park Avenue. The mailing address was still San Jose, but its location at the corner of Park Avenue and Newhall street brought it fairly close to the City of Santa Clara boundary.

The annually elected Councilmembers still had a roster of 121 men representing six districts in 1950, and met twice a year. The Executive Board of 34, was comprised of the Council Officers, District Chairmen and additional key Scouters. It met 4 times that year and was functioning well, as were the Committees on Organization and Extension, Leadership Training, Advancement, Camping and Activities, Health and Safety and Finance.

The organizational and/or institutional sponsor continued to be an integral part of the local support of the Scouting program. In 1950 they were called "Chartered Institutions," and there were 84 such groups which sponsored one or more Scouting units. In 1955 there were 121 sponsors. Each had a representative on the Council.

By 1959 the Council had trimmed down to 85 members, and the Executive Board numbers had been maintained at 35.

The National Council had requested a clarification of the boundaries separating the Stanford Area Council from the Santa Clara County Council, and the latter attempted to respond with more definitive boundary lines in 1957.

In September, 1959, the Executive Board authorized the formation of an Eagle Scout Association for adult Eagle Scouts.

The sixties demanded an even more active Council. It provided regular Commissioner service in 1960 to 270 units out of a total 292 units. Each of the 5 districts had functioning district committees. By 1966 a Council-wide conference attracted 55 commissioners.

At the end of December in 1960 there were 203 Chartered Institutions; in 1967, their total was 334. The sponsor roster continued to be made up of local churches, schools, PTAs, service clubs and other youth-oriented organizations. Each assisted the Scouting program in its own way.

In 1968 a long-range plan was being developed that would project needs in the areas of finances, membership, land and facilities. The Council served 7 districts by 1969 when the former five districts were joined by the new Sierrra and South Valley districts.

Boy Scout Membership

By December 31, 1950 there were 3033 boys in 54 units. 295 were Explorers, 1013 Boy Scouts and 1573 Cub Scouts. In that year no Rovers or Air or Sea Explorers were reported to be registered. The total adult members of the Scouting program were 1137.

At the end of 1955 there were 6136 boys in 175 units. 358 were Explorers, 1738 Boy Scouts and 3878 Cub Scouts. Total number of adult leaders was 2391.

The National Council-sponsored 3-year crusade called "Strengthen the Arm of Liberty" ended in 1951. It had accounted for a 33% gain in membership nationwide. A new 3-year program, initiated in 1952, was called "Forward on Liberty's Team." It included distributing posters and Liberty Bell doorknob hangers in a Get-Out-the-Vote campaign. Scouts in the mid-fifties also secured blood-donor pledges, collected clothing for worthy causes, and assisted in conservation projects and civil defense.

In 1958 the new Exploring program was started and in 1959 the sixth edition of the *Boy Scout Handbook* was published by the National Council.

It was probably not even imagined by the first Boy Scouts in 1920 that forty years later, in 1960, there would be 10,745 boys in Scouting in this county. Of that number there were 6811 Cub Scouts, 3526 Boy Scouts and 408 Explorers. The total number of adult leaders was 3999.

Beside the opportunity to enjoy the companionship of other boys when getting out into the woods on hikes and camping trips, there were unexpected dividends for being a Scout. The San Jose Bees baseball team had a "Boy Scout Day" when all Scouts and Cubs in uniform were admitted free to a game, and their fathers were admitted for $1. Half of the gate receipts for that day were donated to the Boy Scouts.

Near the end of the sixties (1968) the Scout Executive Ray Ewan compared the growth in membership over the past ten years of his tenure in that office. In comparing 7579 boy members in 230 units to the 1968 totals of 19,581 boys in 553 units, membership had grown 160% in boys and 140% in units. In order to train leaders for these boys, training courses increased from 132 in 1958 to 424 courses in 1968.

Marc Vertin, President 1949-1952

1950s
AUSTEN WARBURTON

We had some outstanding young people, including Bill Wilson, Sr., who established the Wilson's Jewel Bakery in Santa Clara. We had Bruce Eberhardt, who was a descendant of the Eberhardt cannery family in Santa Clara, and a number of other young people like that, who were tremendously interested in the program, and did a great deal....

In the case of Bill Wilson, when he grew up, he graduated from the University of California and took over his father's business running the bakery in Santa Clara. (He) got married to Rosalie Gangi and had two sons. One of his sons he named Ken, after Ken Robison. They are applications as to how relationships affect people and ... Ken had (made) such an impression upon him, in the work, and things that Ken had been doing.

Ed. note: Austen Warburton was an advisor to Explorer Post 77 in Santa Clara. Ken Robison was an Assistant Scout Executive.

Council Officers, 1964: Fred Hilton, Vice President;
Judge Marshall Hall, Past President; Bill Powell, President;
Eric Thorsen, National Representative.

Outdoor Activities

The Scout Troops' activities were limited only by their leaders' creativity, courage and troop budget.

Since the very beginning of the Santa Clara County Council, troops had scheduled their own hikes, overnighters, and weekend trips at their convenience. Hike-O-Rees were taken to Uvas Dam just north of San Martin. Fifty mile backpackers went to all points of the compass. All were fascinating destinations such as the campsite above the Hetch Hetchy Reservoir.

Overnighters frequently ended up in places like Berkeley's beautiful Tilden Park and the awe inspiring Big Basin State Park in the Santa Cruz Mountain redwoods.

More ambitious trips involved more than one troop. Frequently, several would combine forces to work out transportation costs and logistics. These included trips to Yosemite, the Grand Canyon, Pacific Grove and Big Sur.

Each of the established Council camps was popular, and each continued to improve its facilities for handling more campers with more amenities such as the new swimming pool which was installed at Camp Stuart in 1967. Camp Stuart, south of Saratoga, and Camp Hi-Sierra, near the Sonora Pass, ran close to capacity all summer, with extensions into both Spring and Fall. Winter camping was scheduled during school vacation times.

In the Golden Jubilee Year of 1960 three troops of Council Scouts attended the Fifth National Jamboree in Colorado Springs, Colorado. During the sixties Santa Clara County Council representatives attended National Jamborees at Valley Forge, the first World Jamboree to be held in the United States at Farragut State Park in Idaho in 1967, and other encampments throughout the country.

1950s (early)
ERIC THORSEN

After a week on the Tuolumne River we moved and went over to Yosemite and were at Camp #9 in Yosemite Valley and we spent seven days there.

The kids had an experience. We had these great big metal boxes about 24 inches wide and about 5 feet long. All the perishable stuff like sugar, syrup and everything else was kept in them. It made it easy because you could stack three of those on the truck.

One night there was an awful rattling and banging going on; the bears had found us! The bears could smell the sugar and the syrup in there, and here they were rolling a couple of these boxes around. One of the boys got to talking to one of the rangers about it. The ranger said if it happens again, turn on your flashlights and make a lot of noise.

Well, the next night along side of each kid's pillow was a stack of rocks. I had 14 boys with me and sure enough, about two'clock in the morning there was a rattling and banging. The flashlights went on and when they spotted the bear, oh, boy, what a raining of rocks he got!

1950s
AUSTEN WARBURTON

We were encouraged to take longer pack trips out of the Hi-Sierra Camp with our Explorer Scouts. We did some exploring up there with Ken (Robison). Some of my Explorers, for example, went down the stream, checking the area for historic spots.

We found an old Indian campsite where the bark of the Incense Cedar trees had been used to make a little shelter for themselves. But, somewhere along the line the trees had fallen on top of the shelter, but it was still there. The fire pit was there with the smoke impregnated in the bark.

We found an old carved expression in one of the granite boulders downstream, perhaps a half-mile or a mile below the dam at the camp. I said, we found it accidentally, because we were just sitting here enjoying the view and everything we could drink in with our eyes and senses. And someone scraped some of the debris, the leaves, that had fallen on top of this rock several inches deep, and it appeared there was writing. We scraped it all off and found that there was written the expression, "Granite, passive love endureth."

We don't know who put it there, we don't know when it was put there, but it had been there for quite some time.

Innovation and Outreach, 1971-1990

Introduction

The decade of the seventies was memorable as a time for proud reflection on the past and for optimistic projections for the future. The Council celebrated its own 50th anniversary in 1970, and joined the nation in observing its 200th anniversary, in 1976.

Special preparations were made for several exciting events in 1970, among them the Golden Anniversary Dinner which honored John Crummey, a prominent founder of the Santa Clara County Council, chartered in 1920 by the National Council of the Boy Scouts of America. Another memorable event was the gigantic rally, with over 5,000 boys in attendance held in the Redevelopment section of downtown San Jose near Park and Almaden Avenues.

The nationwide celebration of our country's bicentennial in 1976 stimulated a new interest in history, and an intensified feeling of patriotism that had not evidenced itself for several years. The Council's observation of this milestone in history took several forms. However, the high point of the year was the Bicent-O-Ree at the Frank Bernard's Ranch near Hollister which attracted approximately 2,500 Scouts and Webelos.

In addition to these observances, the Council continued to maintain all its other programs, each of which required the same amount of planning, funding and manpower as they had in former years. One example was the long deferred renovation of the Scout Service Center which had been constructed in 1954. A dedicated volunteer crew completed the job in December of 1975.

Another example was the unexpected, but much appreciated, gift of 413 acres of undeveloped forest land from Nessie and Paul Chesebrough. This former logging company land was in the Santa Cruz Mountains just north of Big Basin State Park. This large project needed effective Council leadership in administration of funds, and distribution of volunteer labor to prepare the primitive area for use. By 1977

Camp Chesebrough became available for Scout weekend excursions the year round, and has been used frequently for Troop Leader Development and Wood Badge Training Courses.

Throughout the seventies and eighties the Council followed through on many National Council programs such as "Boypower '76," the 8-year long-range plan for improving the effectiveness of Boy Scout programs on the local level, and Project SOAR (Save Our American Resources). Local Scouts participated in the first annual "Keep America Beautiful Day" in June 1972, with 2 million other Scouts and Scouters. Working together they cleaned up over 200,000 miles of highways and waterways, and 400,000 acres of land, as more than a million tons of litter were collected.

Council Presidents who directed these forward steps in the seventies were Robert Morris, Frank Bernard, Charles Munger, Blair Egli, Donald Allen, and Andrew Bonfield. Their Scout Executives were Ray Ewan, Randolf Kohl and Robert Allexsaht. Dr. John Cox and James Sturrock filled the post of Council Commissioner during those years.

In the eighties an experienced and knowledgeable Executive Board understood the critical need to provide a positive influence for young people in today's stressful society.

Campfire Ceremony, Camp Hi-Sierra, 1967

With illiteracy and unemployment still factors in the workplace; with the assimilation of new immigrant populations; with substance abuse of drugs and alcohol in both urban and suburban families; the young people often needed help from outside their family circle.

The Executive Board's policy of promoting self-reliance and self-esteem continued to develop decision-making skills, educational abilities and healthful activities. These programs were carried out through the community-based programs of the Cub Scouts, Boy Scouts and Explorers, and the school-based programs of In-school Scouting, Junior High Varsity, and Career Awareness.

Some of the major activities that were scheduled for Scouts and Scouters were the National Scout Jamborees attended by contingents from the Santa Clara County Council; Councilwide Camporees; and the annual Scout-O-Ramas. In addition there are several special activities such as the annual Eagle Scout Recognition Dinner, Order of the Arrow ceremonies, and Courts of Honor at the unit level.

Add to those the Executive Committee Meetings, Leadership Training Courses and fund raising events, and you found a very busy group of Scouters in the eighties. In charge, during the eighties, were Council Presidents Jan Passmore, General Robert Huyser, Glen McLaughlin and John Lochner. Carl Cookson was

Scout-O-Rama, 1972. Sheriff James Geary, Council Commissioner Dr. Jack Cox, Assemblyman Dominic Cortese.

elected Council President for the 70th anniversary year of 1990. Scout Executive Robert Allexsaht was succeeded in 1982 by Brian Allen, who has continued in his position to the present (1990). The Council Commissioners were James Sturrock, Richard House, Brent Dickson and Darrel Jensen.

Explorer Booth at Scout-O-Rama, 1963

Goals and their Implementation

The challenge for the Santa Clara County Council Executive Board during the next to last decade of the twentieth century was the same as it had been from its earliest beginnings: to provide programs that serve the needs of the youth of the valley, and to make those programs relevant and exciting.

A flyer written in 1988 could just as easily have been written in 1923—neither the challenges nor the values of Scouting had changed in sixty-five years. It said, "Scouting gives opportunities for youth to develop leadership skills, to set tasks and follow through to their completion, and to recognize that people working together and cooperating accomplish more than they accomplish alone."

However, when the flyer enumerated the types of activities the Scouting Program utilizes in order to enable young Scouts to develop those skills, some of the subjects would have been offered before the seventies, and some would not. It stated, "Scouting provides a place where youth can learn about their world through ecology, environmental science, geology, botany, conservation, government, computers, health, safety and careers."

The stage was set for a renewed emphasis on conservation when the Council was notified in April 1970 that they had won the 1969 U.S. Department of Agriculture Green Seal Conservation Award for Region 12.

Realizing that new ground must be covered in areas like computers and careers, the Council of the seventies also knew the value of continuity, so they relied on the "tried and true" basic premise to achieve this goal that had successfully withstood the test of time: community sponsorship and involvement, volunteer commitment, and youth and adult education.

Council Operations

After experiencing the growing pains of the tremendous expansion of membership and its dire need for services, the Council Executive Boards of the seventies and eighties knew they must provide innovative new ways of raising funds to be able to afford those services. Several of the funding methods had been initiated in earlier years. The Council felt it necessary to augment them with new scenarios to finance the costs of the enlarged operation.

An aggressive committee to work on the Sustaining Membership campaigns had continued to be effective since its inception. The Memorial Foundation, started

---

YEAR-END REFLECTIONS
Raymond J. Ewan, Council Scout Executive

- 1971 marked the 51st year of service by the Santa Clara County Council to youth. It witnessed the full registered participation of girls in the Explorer program and a continued large increase in career-interested Explorer Posts, attracting hundreds of additional young men between the ages of 15 to 20 years.

- 53,000 people attended the largest Scout-O-Rama in the Council's history.

- Older Scouts and Explorers participated as delegates in 3 great national conferences: The Knights of Dunamis (Eagle Scouts) conference in West Point, New York; the National Explorer President's Conference, Washington, D.C.; and the National Order of the Arrow (camp honor and service organization) conference at University of Illinois.

- 33 selected Scouts and Explorers participated in the World Jamboree in Japan, under the capable leadership of Scoutmaster Jack Howay, assisted by John Espinoza and Jerry Millon. They presented an 8-foot diameter redwood tree slab to the Jamboree and also redwood seeds to San Jose's sister city, Okayama.

- 96 Scouts participated in the Council's annual JLIT program for one week at Camp Hi-Sierra—the largest group of Junior Leaders yet to be trained at this event.

(Reprint: Santa Clarion, 1/72)

Archery, Camp Hi-Sierra, circa 1970

Waterfront Fun

by former Council President Marshall Hall and others in 1945, was reactivated in 1977 to secure contributions and bequests for the Endowment Fund of the Foundation. The Executive Club, launched in 1968, was renamed The President's Club in 1975. Its mission was to recognize present investors and encourage additional investors in the Boy Scout programs.

In 1975 the first annual "Distinguished Citizen" Award was made at a gala fund raising dinner, sponsored by the President's Club, for former Council President and Scout Benefactor, Frank Bernard. This proved to be a good public relations project as well as an excellent funding source. In 1981 the first annual Boy Scout Pro-Am Golf Tournament was held at the Saratoga Country Club. Its success lay in the winning combination of involving individuals and businesses in Scouting, while having fun doing it.

In 1970 the Santa Clara County Council's operating income was $257,761. Its percentage quota fee was $3,050. In 1979, income was $787,514, its quota, $10,230. The figures demonstrated how time and Council budgets had changed in seventy years from the 1920 quota fee of $435.

The primary emphasis for the Council Executive Board in the 1980s was the Outreach Program. Expanding on the Explorer Program, the board focused on guiding high school students through the confusing maze of job opportunities, helping to match both boys' and girls' interests and skills with appropriate careers.

Through the Career Awareness Program, schools with a high percentage of minority students were targeted. The goal of the program was to decrease the high dropout rate. Volunteers from industry such as Woody Williams and Stan Ogawa from General Electric, Jim Veny from Food Machinery Corporation, and Robert Dominguez, DDS, and Gary Silver, MD, from the health careers formed policy and direction for this unique program. Career Awareness reached over 14,000 students annually by 1990.

Through the In-School Scouting Program, Scouting was made more accessible to elementary school children on the San Jose Eastside. The Executive Board determined that the need in the schools was for science education, and hands-on-science classes have been taught weekly since 1983 to a growing number of children. By 1990, 8,000 children participated weekly, taught by part-time instructors who were hired and trained by the council.

Varsity Scouting provided a sports program for middle school youth in Eastside and San Jose schools. Role modeling, sportsmanship, skills and decision-making have been major features of this program.

Funding for the outreach programs in the eighties came from the Valley Foundation, The Luke B. Hancock Foundation, The Morris Stulsaft Foundation, The James Irvine Foundation and the United Way of Santa Clara County.

In 1979 Walter Chronert was named chairman of the new Scouting for the Handicapped Committee. Many excellent dividends came from this facet of the community outreach program.

The Executive Board, supported by the dedicated men and women who served on the President's Advisory Committee, the District Committees, the Memorial Foundation and the Women's Reserve, brought the Santa Clara County Council to the 1990s by carrying on the hard-working tradition of each succeeding Council's leadership of the last seventy years.

SCOUTING'S NEW MANAGEMENT CONCEPT

... The Council has had a study committee underway for several months. The committee's purpose has been to develop more equitable use of volunteer and professional manpower on the Council and District level. To this end, "service areas" have been set up which are designed to improve field service to Units and Unit Leaders.

A major step in this direction is the formation of an Exploring Division within the council, as requested by the National Council. All Explorer Posts of the council will be included in the division.

The Council Exploring Committee, under the chairmanship of Larry Hill, will be enlarged with additional volunteers from the Districts and will be responsible for organization, program and service. A Professional Exploring Executive will work with the division....

These improvements, which have been approved by the National Council ... (will be) put into effect during the start of the program year in September and October.

(Excerpt: Santa Clarion, 9/72)

SCOUTING PAYS OFF!

... A recent study of records of Scouts and former Scouts in high schools and colleges reveals that they are achievers who will someday bear a large share of the responsibility for what we expect of future generations.

- 89% of senior class presidents were Scouts;
- 80% of junior class presidents were Scouts;
- 71% of football captains, 65% of basketball captains were Scouts;
- 85% of student council presidents were Scouts;
- 75% of managers of school publications, 88% of school newspaper editors;
- 77% of editors of school annuals were Scouts.

Counted among the (Scout) alumni are:
- 64% of the graduates of the Air Force Academy;
- 68% of the graduates of West Point;
- 72% of the Rhodes scholars;
- 85% of the FBI agents;
- 90% of the astronauts presently in training.

(Excerpt: Santa Clarion, 2/83)

"A Scout is Reverent," Troop 478 at Stinson Beach, circa 1970

Scouts on the Trail

AMIGOMOBILE SCOUT RECRUITERS GO MECHANIZED

Scouting has always been a neighborhood oriented program here in the Santa Clara valley. The Santa Clara County Council will be taking Scouting into the small communities, migrant worker camps and low income areas via a Scoutmobile made possible by a grant from the James Irvine Foundation.

According to Dr. Frank Bernard, President of the … Council, the 25 foot "Amigomobile" will be used by members of the professional staff to organize new Cub packs and Scout troops in areas previously unreachable. The main purpose of the scoutmobile (or Amigomobile), which is a fully equipped mobile training and program center, will be to create an interest among young people and adults, to conduct training - programs, and to organize new units.

One of the prime purposes of the unit will be to expand Scouting among the migrant workers and the various ethnic neighborhoods within the council. Once the Scout unit and the leader are trained, experienced Scouters, will take the new Scouts on their first weekend camping experience with all the equipment being utilized out of the … (Amigomobile).

Hundreds of young people annually will have the opportunity to participate in Scouting as a result of the services provided by the Amigomobile. We are proud to have been selected as one of the councils in California to have received a "Mobile Scout Service Center."

(Reprint: Santa Clarion, 11/73)

GROWN-UP SCOUT DESIGNS NEW COUNCIL PATCH

Mark Deady, President of O'Deady and Associates, submitted his design for the new council patch to the Council Executive Committee March 25 where it received unanimous approval.

The patch depicting the valley with its agriculture base and electronics influence through a very simple design, was adapted from several designs received during the recent Santa Clarion contest.

Now in production, the patch will be available for Council Scouters by June 1.

Mark, an Eagle Scout and former member of Troop and Post 488, now heads his own marketing and creative design firm in San Jose. Mark recently joined the Council Marketing Committee and will be working to help strengthen the image of Scouting within the County.

(Reprint: Santa Clarion, 4/81)

(Editor's note: Shortly after the districts were renamed in 1959, a contest was held for the design of a Council patch. A half circle logo with symbols representing each district was adopted. The patch was worn on the right pocket of the uniform. Event segments could be added as they were earned.

Later, the BSA standard white on red shoulder patch was replaced with a colored patch based on the half circle logo. This design became obsolete as districts were changed or added.

In 1981 another contest developed the current council patch.)

Membership

In a report to all Scouters and Boy Scouts, Scout Executive Ray Ewan gave some facts and figures regarding membership in the January 1971 edition of the "Santa Clarion." He stated, "It is interesting to note that in its first year the Council had only 198 Scouts, 65 adult volunteers, 10 Units, 1 professional staff man and 1 office staff member. The budget was $6,068, a cost of $30.60 per boy.

"Today 50 years later—20,240 boys, 7,215 volunteers, 607 Units—but only 13 professionals and 8 office staff. Budget $286,000 ... (a cost of) $15 per boy."

The Santa Clara County Council, #55 has been assigned to Region 12 which included 53 other Councils. Ewan went on to say that it had maintained its position among the top ten councils in the Region due to the quality program of Scouting sponsored by the Council.

BOY SCOUTS GET NEW LOOK

Designer Oscar de la Renta unveiled on March 12, the design for the new Cub Scout, Boy Scout and Leader uniforms. The new contemporary-looking uniforms, made of more durable material, will be available beginning August 1, 1980 at your local distributors.

The Cub Scout uniform, styled in navy blue with new baseball style caps in appropriate colors, replaces the old Cub Scout visored cap. The new Boy Scout uniform will feature khaki tan shirts with long or short sleeves and olive drab green trousers, long or short pants, with cargo pockets. To complete the summer uniform, add green knee socks with contrasting cuffs.

This is the year Cub Scouting celebrates its 50th Anniversary, Santa Clara County Council celebrates its 60th Anniversary and the Boy Scouts of America celebrates its 70th Anniversary, so it seems very appropriate to start the new decade with a new style of uniform.

The new design uniforms being available in the near future by no means makes the present uniforms obsolete. They can be worn as long as they are serviceable. The Boy Scouts of America, who have not changed the style of their uniforms in 58 years, look forward to the new design of the '80s with their new contemporary looking uniforms.

(Reprint: Santa Clarion, 10/79)

THINK ABOUT IT

In your mind's eye take a look at any 100 boys who have recently joined Scouting—line them up in your imagination.

Of those 100 boys:
- Only rarely will one ever appear before a juvenile court;
- 12 of the hundred will receive their first church contact through Scouting;
- 5 of the hundred will receive church awards and one will enter the clergy;
- 18 will develop hobbies that will give them whole-life interest;
- 8 will find their future vocation through Merit Badge work and Scouting contact;
- 1 will use Scouting skills to save another person's life, and 1 will credit it with saving his own;
- 2 of the hundred will reach Eagle rank;
- 17 will become future Scout leaders and will give leadership to additional thousands of boys.

(Reprint: Santa Clarion, 9/79)

The 1990 Scouting program was working with a budget of $1,918,983 of which the United Way contributed 21%. On December 31, 1989 there were 32,500 youth, 4,600 adults, 500 units, 16 professionals, 2 camp rangers, and 6 office staff involved in the Council's Scouting program. Costs per boy were $55.

Additional new program costs were incurred to service 183 boys and girls in 8 handicapped units that were registered in the Scouting program.

During the seventies and eighties, boy members were not only on the receiving end of program services, they were inspired to make their own contributions.

Among the community service projects in which Boy Scouts were involved was the "Med Fly Swat Team" in 1981, a major Good Turn to their community. During the seventies and eighties countless individual Scouts did a Good Turn for someone else, and several individual Scouts were awarded recognition and honors for individual acts of bravery and heroism. Explorer Scouts assisted the financing of their own program in 1984 by having a "Gala Benefit Auction" of Scout memorabilia.

Many Scout troops and Explorer posts participated in emergency service activities following the October 17, 1989 earthquake which affected structures near the San Andreas Fault in the Santa Cruz Mountains, Los Gatos and Gilroy.

President Bill Powell and Past President Senator Clark Bradley, circa 1965

Outdoor Activities

The Cub Scouts had been increasingly active and were very involved in many activities. The Cub Scout Pow Wow was an annual training event that brought Den Mothers, Den Leaders, Webelos Leaders, Cub Masters and their assistants together. Everyone brought a bag lunch, shared new craft ideas, discussed solutions to common problems, and left the training sessions with new inspiration. The individual Cub Pack annual Blue and Gold Banquet became a highlight of every Cub Scout year.

Besides carrying on the well-established traditions of overnight hikes, weekend campouts, and other excursions, the Explorers had opportunities for training in survival skills, and enjoyed certain privileges reserved for the older Scouts. One such privilege was being eligible to go to Winter Camp. They were able to snowshoe into camp bringing their own food, clothing and sleeping equipment on their own backs.

Another challenge was the Explorer Olympic program. It was geared for both male and female Explorers and included events such as track and field, canoe races, archery, swimming, basketball, golf, a car rally, and even table tennis, chess tournaments and public speaking. Winning Post teams went to Fort Collins for the National Olympics. Those winners went to the World Olympics in places like Munich, Germany and Nippon, Japan.

The 1976 Bicent-O-Ree was the camporee to be remembered by Scouts and Scouters alike. It provided an outstanding camping experience for 2,500 Scouts

and Webelos in four activity-packed days at former Council President Frank Bernard's ranch near Hollister. Handicapped Units were included in the event schedules. The participants are still talking about what they called "the event of a lifetime."

Camp Stuart is used year 'round as it has been since it opened in the early forties and Camp Hi-Sierra has been in continual use since 1950. Camp Chesebrough, well-known as an excellent camp both for hiking and for learning wilderness training and skills, has grown in popularity since it was developed in 1977. These camps, which to several generations of Scouts and Scouters, seemed to just get better and better, generated the same feeling of exhilaration to the Scouts and Scouters of the seventies and eighties.

AS I SEE IT
Brian Allen

My first sixty days as your Council's Scout Executive have been most challenging, interesting and enjoyable as I become acquainted with the Scouters—both volunteer and professional— of the Council, its current programs, and opportunities for the future.

I have come to know a very competent professional and clerical staff at the Scout Service Center along with hundreds of dedicated and knowledgeable volunteers on all levels from the Council's Executive Board to the positions of unit leadership.

To better understand the depth and quality of the Council's program, I availed myself of the opportunity to visit the Council's Woodbadge practical, the Troop Leader Development course, the Blazer Day Camp, Cub Scout Day Camp, the Agnews Day Camp experience and Boy Scout Summer Camp at Camp Hi-Sierra. Each clearly showed a deep involvement of competent volunteer leadership and an excellence of program content.

For the past several months a group headed by Richard House, a member of the Board, has been addressing the task of charting the future of the Santa Clara County Council. The Council Long Range Plan is now being finalized and will chart the course of growth in the Council for the next several years.

If first impressions are lasting, and I believe they are, the Scouting program in the Santa Clara County Council is among the finest in the nation.

(Reprint: Santa Clarion, 9/82)

Council and District Organization

Introduction

Through the early years of Scouting in Santa Clara County, the governing council gradually expanded its territory. The first local council charter was approved by the National Council to offer the Scouting program to boys residing within the city limits of San Jose. Very quickly it was determined that there were many more boys in the other cities of the county, and in the unincorporated areas of Santa Clara County, that could benefit by having the opportunity to register as Boy Scouts.

Since the Boy Scouts had started as an organization which might be a partial solution to some of the problems facing a society as it moved from an agricultural mode into the twentieth century industrial world, expansion of the Scouting program was the logical answer.

The progression of names denoting changing jurisdictional responsibilities in the early era of the Council with headquarters in San Jose, were

1920 — San Jose City Council;
1922 — Santa Clara County Council;
1924 — Santa Clara and San Benito Counties Council;
1927 — Santa Clara, San Benito, Santa Cruz and Monterey Counties Council;
1933 — Santa Clara County Council.

In the period between World War I and World War II the counties served by the Council were still agricultural. The majority of the communities were not cities, they were simply small towns, separated by miles of fruit trees and fields of lettuce and tomatoes. During this era many boys came from ranches and farms and welcomed the chance to interact with boys their own age in a Scout troop.

Chronology

Over the last sixty years various factors have affected the numerous changes of size, shape and jurisdiction of the Districts. For example, the breaking away of the counties of San Benito, Monterey and Santa Cruz in 1933 to form their own council, caused the Santa Clara County Council districts to shrink from 8 in 1932 to 5 in 1933. A few years later, the number of districts were reduced from 6 in 1939 to 5 in 1940, when the Palo Alto District formed their own council called the Stanford Area Council.

The first years of World War II took their toll as reflected by the year 1941 which had no organized districts, and 1942, which had only 3 districts.

The following chronological list of districts reflect numbers of districts in the Santa Clara County Council and their name changes:

1934 — San Jose, Palo Alto, La Rinconada, Macon;
1935 — No. 1 Willow Glen, Nos. 2, 3, 4, 5 San Jose, No. 6 Palo Alto, No. 7 Los Gatos, No. 8 Sunnyvale;
1936 — Nos. 1, 2, 3, 4, 5 San Jose, Palo Alto District, Los Gatos District, Santa Clara District;
1937 — San Jose, Palo Alto, Los Gatos, Gilroy;
1938 — Nos. 1, 2, 3 San Jose, Palo Alto, Los Gatos, Gilroy;
1939 — Nos. 1, 2, 3 San Jose, 4 Los Gatos (including Alma), 5 Gilroy (including San Martin);
1940 — Nos. 1, 2, 3 San Jose, Los Gatos/Saratoga/ Alma, 5 Gilroy/San Martin;
1941 — Not reported;
1942 — Districts' names are not known for the years between 1942 and 1958. However, there were 3 districts in 1942; 7 or 8 from 1943 through 1947, and 5 or 6 from 1948 through 1965;
1958 — San Jose North, No. 1, San Jose South, No. 2, Campbell, No. 3, West Valley, No. 4 Los Gatos/Saratoga No. 5, South Valley No. 6.

In October 1, 1959, the districts were renamed replacing the previous system of numbers. There was also another minor realignment of district boundaries. During this change each district was assigned three digit unit numbers. The new district series number became a prefix for the former two digit unit number, i.e. former Saratoga Troop 63 being assigned to Redwood District 500 became Troop 563.

Council Presidents Charles Munger and Frank Bernard, Commissioner Dr. Jack Cox

The numbering of the new districts was Ponderosa-100, Mene Oto-200, Pioneer-300, Polaris-400 and Redwood-500.

From 1965 to 1990 the average of 5 to 7 districts has remained constant. Sample years:

1970 — Ponderosa, Mene Oto, Pioneer, Polaris, Redwood, Sierra, South Valley;

1973 — Mt. Hamilton, Mene Oto, Pioneer, Polaris, Redwood/South Valley;

1978 — Mt. Hamilton/Sierra, Mene Oto, Pioneer, Polaris, Redwood, Gavilan;

1982 — Mt. Hamilton, Mene Oto, Pioneer/Redwood, Polaris/Redwood, Gavilan;

1990 — Mt. Hamilton, Mene Oto, Pioneer, Polaris, Gavilan.

In general terms the areas the Polaris, Pioneer and Redwood districts encompass are called the West Service Area functioning in Santa Clara, Sunnyvale, Cupertino, Saratoga, Campbell and Los Gatos. Mt. Hamilton, Mene Oto and Gavilan districts encompass the East Service Area functioning in Milpitas, San Jose, Morgan Hill, Gilroy and San Martin.

In the early 1980s the East and West Service Areas, managed by Field Directors, were discontinued. Today each district is managed independently by its own District Executive who reports to the Assistant Scout Executive.

DISTRICT BOUNDARIES

Since 1959 the geographical boundaries of the districts have changed in the following ways:

1. The old North district, Ponderosa, gave up Santa Clara to Pioneer, and took over East San Jose formerly known as Mt. Hamilton/Sierra.

2. Growth of the South Valley area created a new district called Gavilan.

3. The former Redwood District was dissolved. Los Gatos was absorbed by Pioneer in the central Section. Saratoga was absorbed by Polaris in the west section.

REDWOOD DISTRICT TO MERGE

The Executive Board of the Santa Clara County Council, Boy Scouts of America, at its meeting on February 15, 1982, voted to merge Redwood with Polaris and Pioneer Districts, thereby reducing the number of districts within the council to five. Under this realignment, those units in Saratoga would become part of Polaris District and those in Los Gatos and the Saratoga Stake of the LDS Church would become part of Pioneer District. This realignment was done with the prior knowledge and approval of the Redwood District Chairman, Dr. Leo Berk and key volunteers.

The Executive Board felt that the Scout program in the Redwood District could be better served by this district realignment. We know ... that Redwood District has an old and proud tradition and (that) a friendly spirit has long existed between Redwood, Polaris and Pioneer Districts. We will make every effort to make the transition as easy as possible while following the best spirit of Scouting.

We anticipate few, if any, changes that will affect Redwood units directly, i.e. unit numbers will remain unchanged, etc. We are investigating locations that will permit us to move many of our district meetings ... farther south in order to be closer to the Los Gatos-Saratoga units. Over the next few weeks we will be working closely with Redwood District Scouters to insure the least interruption possible to your Scouting activities.

(Reprint: Santa Clarion, 3/82)

District Operations

The Districts operate as subdivisions of the Council with responsibility for servicing the units in their respective geographical areas. The Districts have similar committees to those at the Council level, but are fewer in number. The District committees are limited to those related to unit activities. The District leaders perform functions similar to the corresponding Council leaders.

The District Chairman chairs the District Committee and is responsible for the overall operation of the District. He represents the District on the Council Executive Board.

The District Commissioner is a member of the District Committee and is in charge of the District

Commissioner Staff. He represents the District as a member of the Council Commissioner's Staff.

The District Executive is the Professional Staff member who represents the Council Scout Executive at the District level.

These three District leaders are known as "The District Key Three." They work as a team to manage their District just as the "Council Key Three" manages the Council. Other District Committee members who chair the various operating committees within the District also serve as members of their respective Council Committees such as Advancement and Training.

The District Commissioner, through his staff of Unit Commissioners, is the direct link between elements of the Council and every unit in the District. The commissioner is usually a Scouter who has had considerable experience in all phases of the program so he may share his knowledge and counsel with unit leaders.

Council-District Relationships

The same relationship between Council and District organizations has existed from the earliest days, and similar relationships exist between leaders at all levels of Scouting. It has been found to be an effective way of getting standard Scouting policy and program information all the way from the National Council Executive Board to every unit committee in the country.

One unique aspect of this system is the special relationship that exists between the professional and the volunteer Scouters. They work in parallel at every level of Scouting where a specially trained professional executive is available to guide and assist his elected volunteer leaders. While the Council President and District Chairman are the executive officers, the Council and District Commissioners provide the unit service function. In the early days of Scouting the commissioner often was referred to as "the right arm of the Scout Executive." In fact, he often performed the executive's functions in small councils before they were able to hire a professional. At that time these councils were known as "Second Class Councils."

Council Commissioners

Fortunately for the Santa Clara County Council the Commissioners who have accepted this important post have served consecutive terms. One man, Milton Ryder, was Council Commissioner from 1940 to 1961. Commissioner Jack Cox served nine years during the seventies. This continuity exerted a stabilizing influence on the Council's operation at a time when many other aspects of the Scouting program were rapidly changing.

These Scouters have served as Council Commissioners:

1921-22	— Edmund N. Richmond
1923-24	— Dr. J.L. Pritchard
1925	— unknown
1926-29	— John O. Hansen
1930-40	— unknown
1940-61	— Milton Ryder
1962-64	— Greg McGregor
1965-68	— Robert B. Morris
1969	— unknown
1970-74	— Dr. John E. Cox, Jr.
1975	— none elected
1976-80	— Dr. John E. Cox, Jr.
1980-82	— James P. Sturrock
1983-86	— J. Richard House
1987-88	— L. Brent Dickson
1989-90	— Darrel D. Jensen

(information source
for the section on Districts: James Sturrock)

District Report

MENE OTO DISTRICT REPORT 1976-1980
(excerpts)

In 1976 Vern Kuhn was the district executive; Bill Foulk and Letitia Maldonado followed in 1977 and 1978. A normal, active Scouting operation was maintained by Ken Curzon, George Martin, Jared Jones, Bob Anderson, Charlie Orr, Larry Fletcher, Ed

"Scouts Own," Troop 233, Anderson Dam, 1968

Sheldon and many others. In 1978 the entire district committee was involved in goal-setting and event-planning for the first time.

As is common in most districts, there was a constant turnover in personnel. Many of the key people were promoted to council level positions and had to be replaced. Vern Kuhn was promoted to Field Director, Bill Foulk took over as District Executive. Scout Program Chairman Bob Quincy became Council Leadership Development Chairman. Scout Commissioner Bob Anderson took over Quincy's job, and Rich Evans became Scout Commissioner. Charlie Orr resigned as Scout Advancement Chairman and was replaced by John Compatore.

In order to know what was happening and to effectively communicate it to all members of the district committee, Mene Oto Scouters kept the following records:

- a district map with district boundaries and unit locations, school sites and units, and lapsed/inactive units;
- recharter status charts indicating date due, to whom issued, statistics;
- unit activity chart showing units, activities attended, SME participation;

- membership plan showing unit location, total available boys per school, potential unit locations, potential sponsors, priorities....

(information source: Burt Corsen)

1959
ROBERT RICHARDSON

Bob Chapman was District Executive. Ted Rogers was at the council level and he and Bob asked me to be the Activities Chairman. Vint Matthews took over as (District) chairman and our first task was to determine a name for the district.

One popular name was Mercury or Quicksilver for the mines in Almaden. Howard Campen was also on the committee. Dan Owen suggested that we go Indian in names. It was suggested it be named "Meke Mene Oto." They voted out the "Meke" part of it because it sounded like Mickey Mouse.

WHAT IS SEVENTY YEARS?

It could be marked as the time between man's first fledgling flights in aircraft of wood and canvas, to man's flight into the outer reaches of space. Or it could be counted as the time between a million deaths each year from smallpox to a time when that dread scourge no longer exists on the face of this earth. But, perhaps, it can best be seen as the span of a man's life, from birth to old age, with all the changes, all the successes, and all the failures inherent therein. Regardless of how we mark it, it has been a time that most of man's needs have undergone great changes.

For many organizations, seventy years has been more than a lifetime. Started with noble intent, they served the needs of the time, but as the needs changed, they failed. To Scouting, seventy years has only been a beginning, because man has certain needs that will never change, and it is these needs that Scouting serves. Oh yes! Scouting has changed. In 1910 the most common mode of transportation was the horse, and so Scouting taught boys how to stop a runaway horse. But even then, it was not stopping the horse that was most important, it was teaching boys that they had a duty, a responsibility to try to stop that runaway horse. Today we no longer teach Scouts how to stop a runaway horse, but we still teach them about duty and responsibility. America has no great demand for knot tiers, snake chasers or rope bridge builders, but America will always have need for men of character, and that will always be the purpose of Scouting. Today, as in 1910, Scouting is "A Better Way."

(Credit: The National Council, BSA, 1980)

II. Scouting Units

Introduction

During the Bi-centennial year of 1976 the National Council re-issued the *Handbook for Boys,* originally written in 1911. The book started out with a Preface and "A Message from Chief Scout Ernest Thompson Seton" written June 1, 1911. His conclusion: "... whether you be a farm boy or shoe clerk, newsboy or millionaire's son, your place is in our ranks, for these are the thoughts in Scouting; it will help you do better work with your pigs, your shoes, your papers, or your dollars; it will give you new pleasures in life; it will teach you so much of the outdoor world that you wish to know; and this Handbook, the work of many men, each a leader in his field, is their best effort to show you the way....."

The Preface describes the training of the Scouting Program, "In these pages and throughout our organization we have made it obligatory upon our Scouts that they cultivate courage, loyalty, patriotism, brotherliness, self-control, courtesy, kindness-to-animals, usefulness, cheerfulness, cleanliness, thrift, purity and honor. No one can doubt with such training added to his native gifts, the American boy will in the near future, as a man, be an efficient leader in the paths of civilization and peace...."

The handbook was enthusiastically received by parents and educators who recognized the Scouting Program as a good influence on "their boys." Laudatory accounts of the new youth organization appeared in newspaper editorials and articles, and in national publications such as Harpers Weekly and Good Housekeeping Magazine. In 1912 the National Council began publishing a boys' magazine called *Boys Life.* With all this attention it isn't surprising that "Scouting," which started on the East Coast, spread like wildfire across the United States.

Today, *Boys Life* continues to be an important aid to programming in every troop. Over the years the *Handbook for Boys* has become *The Boy Scout Handbook.* It is now in its 10th edition and has sold millions of copies.

SCOUTS NEW HANDBOOK
Dallas Morning News, Irving, Texas

The New Boy Scout Handbook goes beyond pitching tents and singing around a campfire. The glossy book still emphasizes the outdoors and adventure but now also addresses such modern problems as drug and child abuse.

"The goal is to empower young people to tackle new activities that will help them become more independent and improve their self-esteem," said a national spokeswoman for Boy Scouts of America, which is based in Irving, Texas.

Stores across the country carrying Boy Scout clothing and other materials will have the books in stock this month. More than 33 million copies of the first nine editions have been sold.

Camping trips and cookouts are still a big part of Scouting, but under new guidelines in the handbook, the Scouts will learn to be kinder to the environment. The rules teach youths to leave campsites "in even better condition than when they found them," she said. Scouts are being told to reduce the number of campfires, in an attempt to save wood, and to use outdoor stoves sparingly, to cut down on air pollutants.

One of the most significant changes is a 24-page section dealing with child abuse and drug abuse. The section can be removed by parents. In this section, youths are encouraged to talk to parents about how to spot child and drug abuse— and how to stop both.... A video on preventing drug abuse is also available to Scouts and their parents under the new program....

More than 4.3 million youths across the country are involved in Scouting. Membership has increased by 33 percent since 1979.

(Excerpt reprinted, S.J. Mercury News, 2/1/90

Scouting reached Santa Clara County in 1915 when Troop 1 was chartered by the National Council. Troop 1 was located in the town of Los Gatos and was sponsored by the Episcopal Church with the Rev. H.H. Gillies as Scoutmaster. It functioned for a few years and then did not continue. Troop 2, sponsored by the Rotary Club of Los Gatos, was chartered in April, 1918. Its history appears later in this section as Troop 501.

According to Historian Eugene Sawyer, who wrote a comprehensive *History of Santa Clara County* in 1922, the Rev. Frank J. McLain started the first troop in San Jose in 1916. Sawyer also stated that when the San Jose Council, Boy Scouts of America, charter was granted, there were nine troops in San Jose and six troops in the county.

All Boy Scout Troops, Cub Scout Packs and Explorer Posts with more than ten years service were invited to make a contribution to this history of Scouting in the Santa Clara Valley. Several units did contribute material, some outlines, some stories, some newsletters, and some personal recollections from both youth and adult members. The "histories" were written by whomever was brave enough to tackle the job in each unit.

This chapter on Scouting Units deals with the programs, the challenges and the achievements of these units, one or two of which were chartered longer than the Council itself. A few others are of quite recent vintage. All accounts however, reflect individual impressions of the fun and excitement of enjoying companionship and adventure in the fascinating world of Scouting.

And, lest we forget, running between the lines is the story of dedicated adults; the men and women who followed in Chief Scout Ernest Thompson Seton's footsteps. These are the unsung heroes who have burned kerosene lamps full of midnight oil, planning; who have spent hundreds of hours, executing; who have hiked, camped, driven, rowed, and even flown with "their boys." Many of the boys' stories reflect their admiration and acknowledge their debt to these leaders for their caring and inspiration.

At the end of December, 1989, 31,000 youth members in 500 units were being served by the Santa Clara County Council.

Waterfront, Camp Hi-Sierra, circa 1970

Troop Histories

Introduction

The organization of the Boy Scout program has gone relatively unchanged over the years. In 1949 the entrance age requirement was dropped one year for all programs to: Cub Scouting, 8, Boy Scouting, 11, and Exploring, 14. At the time Senior Scouts could not stay in a troop, but that rule was soon rescinded since it proved to be impossible to run a troop without the help of junior leaders.

Today, Scouting still teaches values that last a lifetime—honesty, reverence, helpfulness, respect and duty. It still teaches teamwork and preparedness, and promotes self-reliance and self-esteem. It still creates strong friendships. And, equally important, it still offers programs that are relevant to Scouts' daily lives.

A recent Santa Clara County Council brochure entitled "The Promise of Scouting," described membership in the Boy Scouts as a chance to achieve and to grow. It went on to say, "From age 11-17, Scouts discover that the words of the Scout Law: "Be trustworthy, loyal, helpful, friendly, courteous, kind, obedient, cheerful, thrifty, brave, clean and reverent." —are more than just words. They are a way of life!"

For all boys, regardless of rank, there is much to be gained. A universal truth that all Boy Scouts learn is that achievement requires hard work. Often, boys realize the fruits of their labors long after they have graduated from the Scouting program. All that hard work has produced unexpected dividends such as physical fitness, sound judgement, self-confidence, and having that good feeling of pride in a job well done.

SCOUT OATH

On my Honor, I will DO MY BEST
    To do my duty to God and my Country
And to Obey the Scout Law
    To help other people at all times
To keep myself Physically Strong,
    Mentally Awake and Morally Straight

Troops, 50 Years and Older

Troop 501, Los Gatos, 71 years of service

Boy Scout Troop 501 is the oldest troop of continuous operation in Santa Clara County. Troop 501 was originally Troop 2, chartered by the National Council of Boy Scouts of America, in April 1918. When the San Jose Council became the Santa Clara County Council in 1924, Troop 2 came under its jurisdiction.

In 1959 the Council renamed the districts. Los Gatos was in Redwood District, with units in the 500 series. Troop 2 was assigned the number 501.

The first sponsors of the Troop were a group of individuals; the meeting place was the carriage house on the Lyndon Farwell property.

The Rotary Club of Los Gatos has sponsored the Troop since 1924. Their first building, "The Boy Scout Hut," was built by the Rotary Club in 1948. It was located off Wood Road on land leased from Mr. Farwell by the club (address 55 Broadway). In 1968 the property was sold in order to construct a retirement center called Los Gatos Meadows. The San Jose Water Works gave the Troop permission to relocate the Scout Hut on their property behind the Los Gatos High School where it remains today.

The building was enlarged several times with volunteer Rotarian labor. In 1978 the building was renamed Eagle Lodge.

Tom Gleason, the present Committee Chairman, believes that, "If one were to look at the roster of Troop 501 from 1918 to the present, he would be impressed by the service Troop 501 and Eagle Lodge have been to the community. The same surnames will appear at different times; first as leaders, then a few years later as Scouts, then a few years later as leaders again. It is rewarding to see how Troop 501 and Eagle Lodge have served from generation to generation, and the part they have played in molding the character of our future leaders."

(information source: Tom Gleason)

WILLYS PECK, Troop 39 (539), Los Gatos, 1936

Where Pollard Road meets Winchester Boulevard in Los Gatos, there's a vacant overgrown lot beyond the railroad tracks where the emptiness gives no suggestion of the considerable activity that took place there.

Actually there were two activities. One was the Sewall S. Brown apricot-pit processing plant. The other was Boy Scout Troop 39....

I always thought of that place as the ideal Scout headquarters. It was out in the country, with all kinds of space and a collection of troop buildings that looked like something out of a Western movie.... Ranged in back of the main hall were the patrol cabins. (Three of them) had been built from old railroad ties when the Peninsular Railway interurban tracks were torn up....

Close by, there was a large field where we played Scouting's classic game, Capture the Flag, and even practiced close-order drill when a parade was coming up....

Camping was always a big thing with that troop. At that time (circa 1936) the Santa Clara County Boy Scout Council had its camp at Swanton, a former lumbering area about 20 miles north of Santa Cruz, and a couple of miles inland. It was pretty well covered with second-growth redwood, and one of the projects was building a log cabin on the site allocated to our troop. We did our own felling, peeling and cutting. No environmental impact reports.

I'll never forget my initial camping experience at Swanton, a three-day outing during Thanksgiving vacation. It was my first time away from home, with a bunch of kids I hardly knew, and the dismal, mournful tones of the foghorn at Point Ano Nuevo on the coast, echoing through the dripping woods at night, matched my mood perfectly. I was homesick. But it was the first and only time....

It was only a very few years later that I was doing a lot more camping, but this time it was with the added encumbrance of an M-1 rifle, and the woods weren't echoing to any friendly, if mournful, foghorns. The camping trips with Troop 39 served me well.

(Excerpts: San Jose Mercury News article, 10/12/82)

BUD BAUMGARDNER, Troop 3 (39, 539), Los Gatos

Troop 3 started in 1924 when Troop 2 became too large. I was one of the original seven boys in the troop. I can't remember all their names but I do recall that Morris Campbell, Jerry Erwin, Charlie Phillips and Maury Russ were among those first seven. Cecil Dickinson was our leader and we were sponsored by the Kiwanis Club.

Our first meetings were in a two story building on West Main street just west of the La Canada building.

We met in an old lodge hall room upstairs over a feed store. When we moved in we brought in brooms and pails of water and really gave that place a thorough scrub-down. Later we found out that our earnest cleaning efforts had been responsible for some of the feed and grain down below—sprouting!

KEN ROBISON, Troop 3 (39, 539), Los Gatos

... I became an Assistant Scoutmaster when I was eighteen, at that time it would have been 1929. (The troop was) Troop 39 in Los Gatos; it was Troop 3 originally ... the third troop established in Los Gatos. I was with it when it became Troop 39 because they organized on a Council basis. (Then) we were supposedly the 39th troop in the Council. When they broke up into districts they became Troop 539, which it still is....

Two troops meet in the community area in back of Los Gatos High School. Ours was the Kiwanis troop. Troop 2, which was the Rotary troop, was the second troop in Los Gatos. It is now called Troop 501.

Troop 55 (which was the first troop established in Los Gatos) had the first building down there. It was built from the old Wright's Hotel up the railroad (south of Los Gatos), and that was the American Legion troop, but it ceased to exist.

Our troop (539) has been continuous for a good many years (65). *(Ed. note: it has the second longest registration in the council.)*

New Scout Hall, Los Gatos — Reunion of Troop 2 Scouts (1918-1930) — May 6, 1950

Troop 13, San Jose, 51 years of service

Troop 13 was first chartered in 1939 when Ken Robison recruited Ric Wells as a "temporary Scoutmaster" until a permanent one could be found. Ric enthusiastically took on the job with 14 or 15 boys and began to build the Troop 13 tradition.

The first sponsor of the troop was the Dad's Club; later the First Presbyterian Church at Third and San Antonio permitted the troop to use a basement room.

One special project was helping with the war effort of World War II collecting scrap metal, newspapers, tinfoil, and old tires. A special event was the National Jamboree at Irvine Ranch in Southern California. Ric was Scoutmaster of the troop from Santa Clara County Council. The troop was designated "Troop 13" and contained 13 Eagle Scouts from Ric's own troop. The "Prune Bowl of the World" tents, still occasionally used by the troop, came from this Jamboree.

Ric continued as Scoutmaster for 27 years, retiring in 1966 due to ill health. Bob Fox took over the troop with Ron Hagelin as Assistant Scoutmaster. Both were former troop members. In 1969, John Alden became Scoutmaster, assisted by his older sons Jack and Jerry.

In 1989, John Alden was succeeded by Don Turpin, who merged his own troop with Troop 13 and kept their number.

In the 50 years of its existence, Troop 13 has had approximately 300 boys as members and produced 47 Eagle Scouts.

(information sources: John Alden, Ron Hagelin and Don Nolte)

DICK HUNTWORK, T-13, 1939-44

I joined Troop 13 about two weeks after the charter members, so technically I am not a charter member, but I took part in all the activities from the beginning.

Our first camping trip was to Backesto Park on 13th Street for an overnight. Our tents were still unbleached muslin (white) and had not been waterproofed (green) yet. We hiked from our meeting room in the basement of the First Congregational Church, at 3rd and San Antonio Streets, to the park and set up our camp. We were really tenderfeet and took a lot of razzing about our white tents....

(Scoutmaster) Ric Wells always had good things planned at the camps. In 1940 he was camp director at Camp Kidd, near Santa Rosa. What a good experience! During the third week of camp we took a canoe trip on the Russian River from Hopland to Jenner.

When WWII came along, Ric was really creative arranging transportation (with gas rationing, this was tough) and getting food (the powdered milk was really something). He arranged to use the school district's bus to take us to Yosemite along with Troop 10. We spent a week and hiked to the top of Yosemite Falls, to the top of Half Dome, and the ledge trail to Glacier Point—in addition to seeing all the attractions on the valley floor....

Rick usually took Suzy, the cocker spaniel with us, and very quickly she became our mascot. Occasionally Ric's wife, Betty, went along with us. She hiked with us to the top of the mountain in Big Basin. We were all tired, but she was still going strong.

Ric's artistic ability and our hard work kept all the equipment looking good. Everything was always painted green and yellow, and had a Black Cat or Ghost (patrol emblems) painted on it....

As a Scoutmaster, Ric was a disciplinarian, but we didn't suffer. I realize now, that was the best way to do it. We all worked or all played. When I went into the service in 1945, my Scout training was a big help to me in lots of ways.

RON HAGELIN, T-13, 1943-52; 1957-69

I found out about Troop 13 through my father, who was vice principal at Herbert Hoover Junior High School. Ric Wells was the art teacher at Hoover, and he and my Dad would carpool to save gas during WWII....

Troop meetings were spent in practicing and re-practicing Scouting activities such as signaling, knots, fire building with flint and steel (in the basement of the church on the wooden floor!), first aid, and sharpening and care of axes and knives. The Troop met once each week. The dues were always ten cents, or a can of food if we were going on a campout.

Details that stand out in my mind:

1. *The Seniority Ladder:* Each boy's name was attached with the most senior (by rank) at the top. Besides the position that came with being a Senior Scout, there were other advantages. If there was a choice to be made about special privileges, second servings on food, special treats that were limited in number, the call, "Seniority" could be heard.

2. *Prune Juice:* On most campouts, part of the breakfast ritual was for each boy to fill his canteen cup to the bottom rivet with prune juice. We all drank the juice at the same time, and the older boys checked to see that there was none remaining in any of the cups. We never suffered from any ill effects.

3. *Good Night and Good Morning:* Absolutely no talking allowed when it was time to go to bed. If Ric

heard someone talking early in the morning prior to our normal rising, he got the entire troop up at that time, and the talkers were identified. Group pressure prevented a repeat performance.

4. *Uniforms and Competition:* Every boy wore a full official uniform with shined shoes at every meeting. Patrol points were awarded for uniform completeness and neatness. Patrol awards were given periodically, based on those points.

(At Camp Hi-Sierra trips in the 1950s and 1960s) boys would have the opportunity to go backpacking in the Emigrant Basin Wilderness Area. Since I was one of the only troop members over 21, I often took the Troop on that trip. We fished, camped in the snow, and enjoyed the beauty of the area. Occasionally a bear would dig our fish out of the snowbank and we would lose our catch. Mosquitoes and storytelling around the campfire were a regular part of every hike.

PETER JORDAN DANIELS, T-13, 1947-58

I joined Troop 13 in the spring of 1947.... The first overnighter I went on was to Camp Stuart. The first summer camp was Camp Arroyo Sequoia, located north of Davenport on the coast. The camp had a swimming pool, tent platforms, and poison oak as high as your head. We did our own cooking. I returned home with a good case of poison oak, and tons of dirt. Ken Robison was the Camp Director....

I wonder if any of us will ever forget the many Hike-O-Rees held at the old Uvas Dam? The river water was always cold, which made the swimming events rather difficult. On one of these South District events both patrols felt they had done their very best and yet when the ribbons were awarded, both received red ribbons. I remember Ric saying to some of us, "Well, they finally got to me." He was referring to the judges.

We went to Tilden Park in the Berkeley hills for one of our overnight trips. Ric borrowed his in-laws' Model A flat bed truck, which had a new engine. The engine spun a rod bearing on the way. Some of the older Scouts dropped the oil pan, filed the bad rod cap, and had the engine running in time for us to return home on Sunday.

KEN BONE, T-13, 1950

I remember fondly the annual two week summer camps at Camp Hi-Sierra.... I will never forget the bad time Ric (Scoutmaster Ric Wells) gave me when I accidently put my hand in the cherry pie while reaching across the table one pitch black night after our campfire dinner! Troop 13 was one of the most positive activities of my life!

JOE MAFFEI, T-13

After storing eggs in the creek to keep them cool, a rock fight began on the opposite bank. We were trying to splash water on each other. We smashed almost all the eggs. Our breakfasts were not very large for the rest of the camp.

CARL WIGREN, T-13, 1973

While digging through an old rotten log looking for beetle grubs for Doug Calvin to eat, I broke Jerry Alden's ice axe. I asked Jerry if he had ever killed anyone, before I told him about the axe.

CHARLES LUNDY, Troop 13, San Jose,

("WE AIN'T SPOOFIN' THIS WAS HOOF-IN'" — A Second Class Scout Reports on His 14-Mile Hike)

Starting from King Road, I headed for the Lion's Den along Alum Rock Avenue. I was passed by a group of boys on bikes and they called me a "sucker." They don't know what fun it is to be a Scout.

A lady came along in a car and asked me if I would like a ride. I answered, "I sure would, thank you, but I'm taking my 14-mile Scout hike." I counted the paces between mail boxes, and it made the time and distance go faster.

A station wagon stopped and the driver asked if I would like a ride to the top. I told him no. Then he asked, "Are you sure?" "Yes sir!" was my reply.

At the entrance to the Park I took a little trail down and ate my lunch. After a rest I put my pack back on and hiked up the hill to the Den. There I met the rest of the fellows getting ready for a hike—just my luck. The Troop took a trail from the Lion's Den that led to a cliff where we had to go down by a cable. That night a few of us went on a walk to the top of a hill overlooking the Valley. We looked at the lights and the stars.

After a good night's sleep the Troop took another hike to the floor of the park to see and name birds. This hike was very interesting. I saw and learned the names of many birds I would never have known.

It was close to one-thirty before we started back to the Den. We took a shorter trail back. After lunch and when the place was spic-and-span, I started my hike home. Along the road back I watched to see how many birds I could name.

I knew quite a few now, which surprised me.

A woman asked where I was going and I told her. She said, "With all that on your back?" The pack wasn't heavy and it was easy going.

At King Road, my father came and picked me up. The hot bath and soft bed felt very good!

(Reprint: "Troop 13 Lucky Number" Newsletter 2/8/46)

(NEW ASSISTANT)

Corporal Bill Lundy of the U.S. Marines returned to his Scout "alma mater" when he signed up as Assistant Scoutmaster. Bill was one of the charter members of Troop 13 in 1939. He had 4 years of Scouting to his credit when he signed up with the "leathernecks." He is a Life Scout with 11 Merit Badges.

(Reprint: "Troop 13 Lucky Number" Newsletter 4/19/47)

SEA SCOUTS SECURE BUILDING FOR BASE

Council Commodore Marshall S. Hall has secured for the Council a building, 18' x 24', to be used as a Seascout base. The building was formerly used as Coast Guard Headquarters at Redwood City.

At present, negotiations are underway to secure a site at Palo Alto Harbor for the building.

(Reprint: "Troop 13 Lucky Number" Newsletter 2/8/46)

ALBERT HERSCHBACH, Troop 22, San Jose

Howard Hanson was the Scoutmaster when I went to Troop 22. We learned a lot in Scouting. We did not have camporees with other troops. We had field days at the Willow Glen school.

For a while I was in the Sea Scouts. They had a big boat at Alviso. We would have a cruise on Sunday. We would go out in the bay. One time we got stuck in the mud and had to stay overnight. We wore a uniform with a sailor hat.

Troops, 25 Years and Older

Troop 347, San Jose, 45 years of service

Troop 47 was chartered in March, 1944. Nine boys were registered of whom two were previously Cub Scouts. The Troop was described as an "Open Country Troop." Troop 347 holds its meetings every Tuesday at 7:00 P.M. at the We and Our Neighbors Club located at the corner of Union Avenue and Los Gatos-Almaden Road.

The first Scoutmaster was Art Downing and the first Committee Chairman was Kenneth Jessen. The original number 47 was changed when Pioneer District was formed and all its units were given a 300 digit number, making it number 347.

One of the troop's favorite activities is wilderness camping and pioneering at our private camp. This camp is on undeveloped private property in the Santa Cruz Mountains and has been loaned to the troop for almost twenty years.

The following Scoutmasters have encouraged the boys in the troop to plan and do the things they like to do but to do them safely and succesfully:

    1944-52 — Art Downing
    1952-53 — Harry Skold
    1953-54 — William Engel
    1954-56 — Art Downing
    1956-58 — Harlan Herbert
    1958-59 — James Lopez
    1959-63 — Dale Follas
    1963-65 — Charles Manley
    1965-66 — Jack Smith
    1966-67 — Thompson Mead
    1967-68 — Brinton Moore
    1969-69 — Stanley Manchester
    1969-72 — Lynn Powell
    1972-73 — Leo Coffman
    1973-75 — Howard Siggers
    1975-76 — Jerry Towner
    1976-   — John Boas (acting)
    1976-80 — John Newman
    1980-82 — Ian Morgan
    1982-85 — Ron Sloane
    1985-86 — Jeff Richter
    1986-87 — Paul Woods
    1987-   — John Newman

(information source: John Newman)

Troop 564, Los Gatos, 36 years of service

Troop 64 was chartered in May, 1954. Its sponsor was the First Presbyterian Church of Los Gatos. Church member, and Cubmaster of Pack 556, Paul Kraai was instrumental in the formation of the Troop.

The roster of Scoutmasters reads as follows: Bud Christensen, Paul Kraai, William Dougall, Harold Shuman, Dean Carl, Donald Youmans, Frederick Kirk, Walter Parle, Arthur Baldwin, William Resnick, Joe Mayer, James Lyon, Joseph Evers, and Tracy Scott. Two of these Scoutmasters received the Silver Beaver Award: Joseph Evers, 1973, and James Lyon, 1988.

Troop 64's meeting place in the beginning, was a construction shed on the church property. In those early days of the Troop, the thirty boys enjoyed hiking and camping at their favorite places, Camp Stuart and Camp Hi-Sierra.

A reorganization occurred in 1960 and the Troop was assigned the number 564. In 1980 the Troop became a part of the Pioneer District when their former Redwood District was eliminated.

In recent years, Troop 564 has continued to enjoy many of the same challenges and outdoor activities that their predecessors participated in, i.e. hikes that eventually build up to a yearly "50-miler" trek in the high country of the Sierra Nevada Mountains; the annual white water raft trip on the American River; and summer camp. A recent addition to their program is cave exploring.

The first Scout to earn the rank of Eagle Scout was William Maire in 1961. Since then Troop 564 has had 27 of its members become Eagle Scouts.

(information source: James L. Lyon)

Ready for a Hike

*Tasting the Stew
Scoutmaster Byron Favorite*

Troop 233, Willow Glen, San Jose, 35 years of service

Troop 33, now 233, was chartered November 1955. Its sponsor was the Willow Glen United Methodist Church. Recently they were given their own Scout room at the church.

Scoutmasters have been Mr. Mason, John George, Dr. Burt Morris, Byron Favorite, William Ross, Richard Roof, Robert Richardson, Harry Pottol, and Lawrence Summers.

Their troop has sponsored many and varied community service projects. One of these was the planting of poppy seeds at the opening of Santa Teresa County Park. They were planted at other beach parks, as well. The poppy planting was initiated by Scoutmaster Burt Morris. The symbol of the poppy was later adopted as our emblem now displayed on our neckerchiefs, jackets, shirts and sweatshirts.

They are known for their outdoor program which includes a campout or hike every month. These hikes prepare the Scouts for a "50 Miler" afoot or afloat in the summer. Some of the destinations have been Lake Berryessa, Yosemite, and Evolution Valley. The entire troop, under Byron Favorite, took a "100 Miler" in the Immigrant Basin.

This troop has had a program of regular advancement for Scouts. The first Scout to earn the rank of Eagle Scout was Wayne Doran in 1960. Since that time Troop 233 has averaged two a year for a total of 60 Eagle Scouts.

(information source: Barbara Wiley)

Patrol Sing Along, Troop 233, circa 1970

JOHN GEORGE, Troop 233, San Jose

Troop 25 and Troop 5 (of which I was a Charter Member) were full, so having to find a place for a group of former Cubs who had now reached the age of 11, and who were "gung ho" to become Boy Scouts—a bunch of dads decided to apply to charter a new troop, which we did.

We were faced with an entire platoon of 11-year olds (twenty, or more). With the help of Roger Vaggione, Eddie Pate, Conrad Anthenian, Bob Bye, et al, we took on this tribe of wild Indians.

We met at the Methodist Church at Minnesota and Washington.... Our goals were to run a tight ship, have one overnight a month, and work towards progress of individual accomplishments (ranks, merit badges, etc.). We did this! Although rain, hail, snow and sundry adverse experiences affected our pure and progressive trek onward.

Patience and durability were the watchwords, as in administration of anything. We, the leaders survived for four or five years, then relinquished the glory and honor to those who still had the heart and stamina.

In twenty years of Scouting my favorite and most touching moment occurred when I was asked to return to Troop 33 (233) and present the first Eagle Award to one of my 11-year olds. This made it all worth it. Men can cry, too. The recipient, a Mexican American boy, was one of our true Boy Scouts. His name was Wayne Doran.

Scouting is an admirable program for boys. I know, without Scouting, I could have experienced a very low spot in my life, but the men in charge salvaged what honesty and integrity that I have, such as it is....

ROBERT RICHARDSON, Troop 233, San Jose

... Troop 33 became Troop 233 and they met at the Willow Glen Methodist Church.... It was a crackerjack troop in those days. John George was Scoutmaster and also head of the committee. Then Dr. Burt Morris took over.... Byron Favorite followed as Scoutmaster and (served) for about ten years. Bill Ross, Dick Roof and Harry Pottel followed. Lawrence Summers, Favorite's nephew, is the present Scoutmaster. He received the Silver Beaver in 1990.

I came here in 1956. At that time I was asked to take Troop 33 out to Camp Hi-Sierra. I took Troop 233 on their first backpacking trip in 1960.

Troop 479, Cupertino, 34 years of service

Troop 79 was chartered in October, 1956. Its sponsors were the Cupertino Community Church from 1956 to 1968, and the Cupertino Rotary Club from 1968 to the present. They have met at the Community Church from 1956 to 1978, and St. Jude's Episcopal Church in Cupertino from 1978 to the present.

Their Scoutmasters were Burt Harde, Lee Marshall, Max Kernaghan, Joe Brown, John Cowley and Pete Goodell.

In the reorganization of 1960 they were assigned the new number of 479.

They are proud to have had about 25 of their boys become Eagle Scouts.

(information source: Howard Hill)

Troop 295, Willow Glen, San Jose, 33 years of service

Troop 95 was chartered in February, 1957. Its sponsor was the San Jose Teamster's Local 287. Jimmy Powers, the Teamster's presiding officer, helped found the Troop and offered strong personal and Teamster support for many years. The Troop has met weekly at Schallenberger School.

Scoutmaster Ed Sheldon served from 1957 to 1988. His knowledge of Scouting, his ability to teach, and his aptitude for handling young men has endeared him to hundreds of young men. Don Watts ran the "Knife and Fork" Patrol, a parent committee of several involved parents who assisted with troop needs.

In 1959, the Troop was assigned the new number, 295.

Troop 295 has participated in many activities, among them a snow trip to Lake Tahoe and a bicycle hike. It has built ten kayaks and used them, and won first place at the Spring District Camporee.

At least ten Eagle Scouts participated in our most recent Eagle Scout Court of Honor for Kevin Osler.

As can be seen, we have not slowed down with age. By building on our extensive experience, we look forward to even more exciting adventures to come.

(information source: Rod Rodler)

Troop 478, Sunnyvale, 33 years of service
"The Troop With the Band"

Troop 478 was chartered in 1957 in Cupertino. It was sponsored by the Cupertino Junior High School P.T.A.

When Walt Chronert became Scoutmaster in 1960, he moved the Troop to the Sunnyvale Presbyterian Church. One of Troop 478's outstanding contributions was the Troop Band, made up of 32 of the 55 boys. With Walt Chronert, as organizer, the Band functions were kept separate so that it would not interfere with the operation of the full troop. For example, while the Band performed at the Scout-O-Ramas for their music merit badge, the rest of the Troop was cooking meals to perfect their skills for the cooking merit badge. Frequently, the parents came early to listen to the Band and stayed to have the Scouts feed them dinner.

During the Santa Clara County Council's fiftieth anniversary celebration in 1970, the Band played from a stage set up to raise the speakers above the hundreds of Scouts assembled in a cleared area of the San Jose downtown redevelopment project.

The Band was an excellent public relations showcase for Scouting. It was in great demand from 1966 to 1974 for functions like the first DeAnza Day at DeAnza College in Cupertino, and the Wheel Chair Championships. The Troop 478 Band played for the Seals hockey games at the Oakland Coliseum. They played Christmas music on cable television and for many Eagle Scout Courts of Honor, and represented the Boy Scouts in many other spheres of community service.

Most of the musicians graduated from the Scout Band and played in high school; many of them continued their music through college.

(information source: Walter Chronert

Troop 407, Cupertino, 26 years of service

Troop 407 was chartered in November, 1964. It was sponsored by the West Valley Presbyterian Church. They met at the church.

The Troop 407 Scoutmasters: Ted Brown, Don Smith, Dave Fabec, Mr. Malcome, Joel Enns, Richard Lamy and Larry Grace.

The highlight of the Boy Scout program for Troop 407 has been the varied and exciting longterm summer camping experiences. The first was Hi-Sierra where they did their own cooking. They also went to Yosemite, a lake near Hetch-Hetchy, and Camp Lake. In the seventies they water skied at Lake Claire Engel in the Trinity Alps. During two of the years in the early seventies they ended up helping to fight forest fires. In the mid-seventies they made open kayaks and used them on Lake Shasta and the Sacramento River.

Summer camping in the eighties found the Scouts from Troop 407 at Camp Wente, Camp Chawanakee, and later at the 7,000 foot elevation at Camp Silverado.

Boy and adult leaders participated in four national Jamborees and two world Jamborees. They have taken numerous 50-milers on land and on water in the High

Sierras, the Trinity Alps and the Sacramento River.

The symbol of Troop 407 is the signal tower. Signal Tower is also the name of their monthly newsletter. At the Scout-O-Rama it has become a tradition for the troop to build a 20 foot tower "out of nothing but logs and rope." The Scoutmaster felt that creating a freestanding flag pole, assembling the patrol cooking table, and building various tripods for their campsite, were skills they had learned while building the signal tower.

Troop 407 has had 34 boys who attained the rank of Eagle Scout.

(information sources: Ted Brown and Larry Grace)

Troop 321, San Jose, 25 years of service

Troop 321 was chartered in May, 1965. It was sponsored by the San Jose 9th Ward, Church of Jesus Christ of Latter Day Saints which has remained its sponsor up to the present time. The church has been its meeting place.

Its first Scoutmaster was Richard Wase. Subsequent Scoutmasters were Sam Demonja, Newell Moulton, Milton Hatch, Sinclair Lewis, Peter Wolsey, Paul Plumb, Jack Hansen, Mike Bull and Dave Curtis.

A special event for Troop 321 is its annual canoe trip from Redding to Red Bluff on the Sacramento River.

An event that none of the Scouts will ever forget was a 50-mile hike in the high Sierras. One Scout had to be evacuated by helicopter due to acute appendicitis. Help was recruited by "fast, healthy, young Scouts in the troop."

Troop 321 has had 19 boys who reached the rank of Eagle Scout.

(information source: Kent South)

Camporee Cooking, 1966

Troops, 15 Years or Older

Troop 286, San Jose, 24 years of service

Troop 286 was chartered in February, 1966. Its first meeting place was Allen School as a self-sponsored troop. Over the years Troop 286 has met at several schools as it moved from Allen to Erickson Elementary to Gunderson High School to its present meeting place at Belden Elementary where, since 1982, the Troop has found it a supportive environment.

The first Scoutmaster of Troop 286 was Victor Borlang. Subsequent Scoutmasters have been Arthur O'Neil, Howard Warren, Dennis Jennings, Joe Perez, Bob Smearden, Gerald Cory, Mel Silveira, John Newlin and current Scoutmaster Ed Maisen.

The focus of the troop is backpacking and camping. They have travelled throughout the Bay Area and Central California from the Pacific to the Sierras. Outings have included Point Reyes National Seashore, Santa Cruz Mountains, and the Los Padres National Forest.

In 1984 the troop instituted its "Troop Backpacker Award." Any Scout or Staff who accumulates 20 miles of backpacking receives an embossed round leather patch. Since the "Troop Backpacker" has been instituted, several boys have logged close to 500 miles.

The troop has also gone on several special hikes, which include Philmont Scout Ranch in New Mexico in 1985 and 1989, and Mt. Whitney, California in 1988 and 1989.

Troop 286 attends summer camp annually at camps such as Hi-Sierra, Chawanakee, and Royaneh. They also have taken trips to points of interest such as Monterey Bay Aquarium, Hearst Castle and historical sites.

This troop has received numerous "Participant," "Standard" and "Proficient" awards at Camporees and Scout-O-Ramas, plus receiving the "Mayor's," "National President's" and "Honor Unit" awards many times in recent years.

The Scouts and Leaders of Troop 286 have accumulated over 2,000 hours of service to the community since 1984 in non-rank, non-award time. Troop participants at these events are given "service-hour" beads for the time they have contributed. Among their contributions to the community: traffic control, waiter duties, and helping on special events such as the "La Tour de Val" for the American Lung Association.

Since its founding, Troop 286 has produced 17 Eagle Scouts; the first, Gregory Wright, 1970; the latest Eugene Vicknair, 1988.

(information source: George Ruel)

Troop 266, San Jose, 23 years of service

Troop 266 was chartered in 1967. Its original sponsor and meeting place was Transfiguration Church on Glacier Drive. The church continued its sponsorship until 1974. In that year Troop 266 moved to Terrell School for its meetings, and the school P.T.A. offered its sponsorship from 1974 to 1989. In 1989 Elk's Lodge #522 of San Jose became the troop sponsor. The troop still meets at Terrell School.

Troop 266 got a good start with its first Scoutmaster, Erv Morgenthal, who stayed with them until 1975. Subsequent Scoutmasters were Ron Leedy, Sr., Mike Auran, Bill Berger, Jack Roe, Earl Nichols and the current Scoutmaster, Robert Ewen.

They are very proud of their troop's 17 Eagle Scouts.

(information source: Jack Roe)

Troop 434, San Jose, 23 years of service

Troop 434 was chartered in March, 1967 as an offshoot from Troop 440, sponsored by Joaquin Miller Junior High school. The P.T.A. at the school in West San Jose was the sponsor of Troop 434 until March, 1989, when the parents of the Scouts took on this role. Troop meetings were held in the multi-purpose room of the school. In mid-1988 the meetings were moved to Cupertino's Bethel Lutheran Church.

The original Scoutmaster was Jack Goodwin. Some of the subsequent Scoutmasters were Bob Hildebrand, Bob Carlson, Cliff Howser, Dave Dunn and Troy Lindsey. Ken Doty is now the troop's 11th Scoutmaster.

The original emphasis was on hiking and camping with activities organized around pioneering skills and water sports. Water sports included canoe building and constructing kayaks from troop-prepared kits. Pioneering skills included bridge building, rope lashing, and the use of hand tools. For over ten years a pair of lashed signal towers with a banner extended across the main concourse was a familiar sight welcoming Scouts and Scouters near the entrance of the Santa Clara County Fairgrounds at the Scout-O-Rama. The troop's annual 50-mile hike more recently has alternated with a 50–100 mile canoe trip.

In 1973 a tradition started for the boys to plan and run their own summer camp experience. All meals were planned and cooked by the boys. At the annual snow campout they pitch their tents in the snow and go sledding and skiing. Troop Scouts have gone to Philmont Scout Ranch in New Mexico, National Jamborees and even a World Jamboree in Australia in 1987.

The uniform of Troop 434 consisted of the short sleeve shirt without a collar, short pants, long green stockings with green tabs and web belt. Even though the styles of clothing have been modernized, the troop continues to wear the same basic uniform because it was felt that wearing shorts helped the boys display their ruggedness. The troop-provided neckerchief is a plain gold background with green border sporting a Smokey-the-Bear patch. The National Park Service authorized their use of the patch. When the Park Service stopped producing them, the troop was given permission to use the logo on their own patch with the T-434 numerals.

Troop 434 has had 33 Scouts attain the rank of Eagle. Among many others, some of the alumni include orthopedic surgeon Jeff Kneisl, and the Keswick boys, who all have Masters Degrees: Chris in Mechanical Engineering, Paul in Business Administration and Peter in Materials Science.

(information source: Art Keswick and Doris Livezey)

Troop 463, Sunnyvale, 22 years of service

Troop 463 was chartered by St. John's Lutheran Church in Sunnyvale in 1968. The church has sponsored them ever since.

The first Scoutmaster was Richard Anderson. Subsequent Scoutmasters were Chuck McRery, Max Bokelman, Roy McGill, Paul Williams, Albert Dalhuisen, Ed Fraser, Dudley McFadden, Gary Kersting and Don Prasek. The current Scoutmaster is Jim Holt.

Troop 463 goes on a 50-mile hike each year. In 1974 it was from the South Rim to the North Rim, and back to the South Rim of the Grand Canyon. In 1976 the hike was down the Shipwreck Trail in British Columbia, Canada. Another hike was a Trans-Sierra, starting in Sequoia National Park and ending with a climb of Mt. Whitney. Other hikes have taken place in the Sierras, Mt. Lassen area and the Trinity Alps.

Troop representatives have attended the 1979 World Jamboree in Sweden; others have attended the 1985 and 1989 National Jamborees in Virginia.

The troop's first Eagle Scout was John Bokelman in 1972. Twenty other boys have attained the Eagle Rank including the last two, Mark Chu Lin and Sharad Verma, in 1989. Troop 463 has earned the Honor/Quality Unit award each year since 1983, and the National Camping award each year since 1975.

(information source: Don Prasek)

Troop 508, Saratoga, 22 years of service

Troop 508 was chartered by the Redwood Junior High School P.T.A. in 1968. Meetings have been held continuously at the school up to, and including, the present.

Maurice Tripp, an outstanding Scouter, led the formation of the troop and served as the first Scoutmaster. Subsequent Scoutmasters were Lowell Cockel, Les Burns, George Gromeeko, Jim Runyeon, Jim Sweet, Gary Robillard, Brent Pingrey, David Bagby, Steve Carlson and John Christol.

Adventure oriented outings have been emphasized which include building snow caves and skiing in the Sierras, white water rafting the American River or canoeing the Russian River, sailing on San Francisco Bay, bicycling on outings, plus backpacking. Unusual adventures have included nine day canoe trips down the Trinity and Klamath Rivers, backpacking in Hawaii, sailing in the Florida Keys, and camping on Anacapa Island.

Troop members have regularly participated in World Jamborees from Idaho in 1969 to Australia in 1988, and National Jamborees at Fort A.P. Hill, Virginia. The troop continues its monthly service project of collecting newspapers for recycling at the Argonaut Shopping Center.

The troop has had a program of regular advancement including many projects for the community. The troop's first Eagle Scout was Dave Robertson, and the latest, Dean Tsai, with the troop awarding more than one Eagle per year on average.

(information source: Brent Pingrey)

Troop 294, Almaden Valley, San Jose, 20 years of service

Troop 294 was chartered by the Rotary Club of Almaden Valley in September, 1970. It has continued to be its sponsor to the present time. From 1970 to 1974 Troop 294 met at the following schools: Bret Harte Junior High, Los Alamitos Elementary, Greystone Elementary and Henderson Elementary. From 1974 to the present, Troop 294 met at Leland High School.

The troop's first Scoutmaster was Denton Wolfe. Subsequent Scoutmasters were James Staehs, Albert Wheeler and Andrew Cosby. The current Scoutmaster is David Worledge. Among the other dedicated leaders have been Rod Loehr, ten year veteran backpack leader, and Gerald Marks, chairman of the Council's chapter of the National Eagle Scout Association.

Troop 294 has attended the Stanford Area Council's Camp Oljato since 1979 and also has gone to Camp Hi-Sierra.

The troop has received the Honor Unit award and the Scout-O-Rama Blue Ribbon for the last ten years, along with numerous other awards ranging from the National Quality Unit award in 1985 to a first place in Camp Oljato's Aquacade in 1982. Among its contributions to service in the community, Troop 294 has conducted an annual Christmas food collection for the Women's Alliance (for battered women) and for the poor.

Over the troop's twenty years of existence, 28 Eagle Scouts have graduated from its ranks. The first was Mike Flake, 1973; the most recent was Andrew Penn, 1989.

In 1985 Troop 294 split into two groups and thus reactivated former Troop 211 in the Almaden Valley.

(information source: David Worledge)

Troop 577, Los Gatos, 15 years of service

Troop 577 was chartered in 1974. It was sponsored by the Los Gatos Christian Church which has remained their sponsor to the present. Meetings have been held at the church on Hicks Road in Los Gatos.

The founding leaders were Milton Davis, Alan Engel, Ward Gross, Joe McCurry and Ralph Martin. The majority of the Scoutmasters have served for three or more years, providing good continuity. Many of the leaders have been involved in church activities and leadership, some of them as pastors and deacons. The last Scoutmaster was Will Schligh. Kats Nishikawa is the present Scoutmaster.

From the initial registration of 11 boys, the number increased to 45 boys by the end of 1976. This number has remained fairly constant over the years. Troop 577 has been active in the Scout-O-Ramas and in-service projects affecting the church and community. Troop leaders have been involved in Leadership Training, some progressing to the highest level available.

The troop has had representatives who attended the 1989 National Jamboree in Virginia, and 14 boys and leaders travelled to the Philmont Scout Ranch in New Mexico. A large number attended Camp Hi-Sierra, while others went to White Stag leadership camp.

The first Eagle Scout awards were made to two boys in 1979. Since that time 13 additional Eagle awards have been presented.

(information source: Bob Wimmer)

Troop 227, San Jose, 15 years of service

Troop 227 was chartered in February, 1975 at the Santa Teresa Swim and Racquet Club in South San Jose. From its inception, Troop 227 has had strong parent participation on its committee that has provided leadership and fund raising. This has given the Troop the equipment and resources to have a strong camping program.

The troop's first Scoutmaster was Howard Tyler. Subsequent Scoutmasters were Jerry Harvey, John Metzler, Bob Yount, Gary Marshall and Joel Theriault. These leaders and great numbers of assistants have provided the leadership on monthly campouts over the last 15 years.

Troop 227 has attended a longterm summer camp every year, usually at Camp Hi-Sierra. Several years they offered an additional longterm high adventure outing for the older Scouts. These have included backpacking trips in the Sierras and 50-mile canoe trips to Lake Shasta. Those adventures were capped by a 50-miler to Philmont in 1984.

The troop has participated in many Scout-O-Ramas and Camporees. The Diamond Jubilee Jamboree at Ed Levin park in 1985 was a highlight.

This strong camping program, together with active weekly meetings, have produced over 15 Eagle Scouts, along with many other Scouts who have gone to some of the major universities in the United States. Troop 227's fine Scouts have served the Santa Clara County Council in many capacities. Each year they provide Scouts on staff to both Camp Hi-Sierra and Camp Stuart. Scouts from the troop have been active in the Order of the Arrow, and many of the Scouts have served, and are serving, in Order of the Arrow leadership positions.

(information source: Lyle White)

Troop 710, San Jose, 15 years of service

Troop 710 was chartered in September, 1975. It was sponsored by the Community Lutheran Church on Avenida Espana in San Jose, where it has been meeting since it was chartered.

The original Scoutmaster was Douglas Velberg. Subsequent Scoutmasters have been Marty Lyon, Gene Kelly, Jim Guinn, Roland Jackson, Joe Nalewajko, Ray Staiger, Bob Fitch, Bob Bradley and Bruce Harper. The current Scoutmaster is Rick Hobbs. Other troop leaders with outstanding service records have been Carl Woodall and Mel Woodall.

Troop 710 has participated in monthly campouts, the annual summer camp, and the 50-miler afoot and afloat. They have taken special interest in outdoor adventure activities, community service projects, and engaged in Clean Environment Projects at Henry Coe State Park and Pico Blanco in the Monterey Council area.

Troop 710 has had 5 Scouts who have attained Eagle rank.

(information source: Mel Woodall)

Special Scouts

CHARLES PEDERSON, T443

In July 1968 Second Class Scout Charles Pederson of T443, sponsored by the Cupertino Kiwanis Club, was awarded the Medal of Merit, one of the highest awards the National Court of Honor bestows on a Cub, Scout or Explorer.

He acted in a manner that reflected Scout teaching when he came upon an auto accident on one of our expressways and rendered first aid to a woman passenger who had sustained a massive cut. Her husband was unable to help because he was in a dazed condition.

The citation reads in part: "Scout Pederson acted to control bleeding until medical aid arrived. His prompt and proper action and assured manner bespeak Scout training and spirit in the best tradition of the movement."

General William Dean, USA (Retired), in making the presentation to Scout Pederson said that of the hundreds of medals that he had pinned on many brave men, none gave him as much pride as presenting this medal to this heroic Scout.

Since inception of the award in 1911, less than 200 of these Medals of Merit have been given. We can all take pride in this accomplishment of Scout Pederson.

(Reprint: Santa Clarion, 7/68)

SCOTT HECTOR, T520

Scout Scott Hector has been awarded Scouting's Hornaday Award for an outstanding long term conservation project. The award is presented by the Boy Scouts of America, with the cooperation of the New York Zoological Society, in honor of the late William T. Hornaday, a pioneer in the recognition of conservation and in inspiring others to work constructively for conservation.

"Since 1920 this award has been highly prized by those fortunate enough to receive it as recognition of exceptional and unusual service in a very important area of Scouting…. The Medal, in very unusual cases, (is awarded) by the National Council, upon recommendation by the local council."

Scott did his work in hybridizing pine trees for specific local problems, planted them and then maintained them until they were established. The project was started more than five years ago.

Only three of these rare awards have been earned in ten years in this Council. Our heartiest congratulations to Scott and his Advisor for this recognition.

(Reprint: Santa Clarion, 7/69)

SCOUT EARNS COVETED BICENTENNIAL COLONIAL PHILADELPHIA MERIT BADGE

RICK GALE, T-76

Rick Gale, a Life Scout and Assistant Senior Patrol Leader of Troop 76, received the Colonial Philadelphia merit badge at a recent Court of Honor. The Philadelphia Council, BSA, created the special merit badge for the Bicentennial. … Only a few hundred of these special merit badges will be presented.…

One of the first requirements for this merit badge is to visit Philadelphia either in 1975 or 1976. While there, you are to visit six historic shrines in Germantown or center city Philadelphia. You then have to make a map showing the locations of the sites visited, write a 200 word composition about the historical site. (You must) study the lives of ten famous Philadelphians, and the parts they played in colonial history, select six people, three of which were Philadelphia signers of the Declaration of Independence, and write an original composition of 50 words or more about each person. These are just a few of the requirements for this special merit badge that Rick completed.

A lot of time and effort went into the completion of the requirements for this badge. Congratulations, Rick, on a job well done!

(Reprint: Santa Clarion, July 1976)

HYATT DUNN, T-399

Hyatt E. Dunn, Jr. is an outstanding mentally handicapped Scout. He joined Troop 399 in 1971 and rose through the ranks to become, in 1977, the first handicapped Scout in the Santa Clara County Council to attain the Eagle Scout rank.

His Eagle Scout project, approved by the Council, was the reconstruction and improvement of the campfire area at Camp Stuart. He was presented his Eagle Scout badge at McKinnon School the same year he was 18.

(information source: Stephen Goodman)

OUR OWN EAGLE SCOUT JAY SALISBURY

JAY SALISBURY, T-144

"If it weren't for the other boys in the troop," says Jay Salisbury (signing through an interpreter), "I'd never have made it." He was talking as our council's first deaf boy to attain the Eagle Scout rank. Eagle Scout, Jay Salisbury, "reached for the stars" and went beyond when he received his award in 1973 as a member of Troop 144. Jay is an electronic technician at the San Jose IBM facility following specialized training at Goodwill Industries....

(Excerpt: Santa Clarion, 10/79)

PACKING FOR WEST POINT ACADEMY

ROBERT CRAIG & DAVID HAMM, T-363

Robert Craig and David Hamm, both of Los Gatos, started as Cub Scouts together in Cub Scout Pack 383, sponsored by the Alta Vista Home and School Club. As the two of them grew, they became the best of friends.

Both David and Robert joined Boy Scout Troop 363 where, in February of 1983, they received their Eagle Scout Awards "together." Rob and Dave have ... accomplished much together and soon, these two will accomplish even more "together."

Earlier this year it was announced by Congressman Norman Mineta that both boys had been appointed to West Point Military Academy! ... Best luck Robert Craig and David Hamm on being accepted to West Point!

(Reprint: Santa Clarion, July 1984)

MORGAN HILL SCOUT CREDITED WITH SAVING YOUTH

JOHN WELDER, T-711

... John Welder got to put his recently learned life-saving skills to the test Saturday (March 19) when he pulled two boys struggling in a rip tide off Sunset Beach (to safety). The 17-year-old Live Oak High School sophomore and Life Scout didn't think twice when he heard the boys yelling off shore, he recalls. He grabbed his boogie board and swam. Welder was on the beach during (a campout) of Boy Scout Troop 711 from Gilroy....

Welder earned a merit badge in life saving while working last summer at Camp Hi-Sierra, a Boy Scout camp near Pinecrest.... Assistant Scoutmaster Roy Westfall of Gilroy, ... witnessed the rescue. It's a story he thinks deserves mention in *Boys Life*, a scouting magazine. "This kid kept his cool," said Westfall. "I wouldn't have known what to do. He didn't make it look as important as it was."

(Excerpt: Gilroy Dispatch, March 1988)

THE SCOUT LAW

A Scout is Trustworthy

A Scout is Loyal

A Scout is Helpful

A Scout is Friendly

A Scout is Courteous

A Scout is Kind

A Scout is Obedient

A Scout is Cheerful

A Scout is Thrifty

A Scout is Brave

A Scout is Clean

A Scout is Reverent

Veteran Scout Troops, Santa Clara County Council

Troops, 50 years or older in 1990:

Troop 501	Los Gatos	Pioneer	71 years
Troop 539	Los Gatos	Pioneer	65 years
Troop 203	San Jose	Mene Oto	54 years
Troop 13	San Jose	Mt. Hamilton	50 years

Troops, 40 years or older in 1990:

Troop 41	San Jose	Mt. Hamilton	49 years
Troop 347	San Jose	Pioneer	46 years
Troop 549	Saratoga	Polaris	46 years
Troop 799	Morgan Hill	Gavilan	43 years
Troop 330	Campbell	Pioneer	41 years
Troop 488	Cupertino	Polaris	40 years

Troops, 30 years or older in 1990:

Troop 564	Los Gatos	Pioneer	36 years
Troop 260	San Jose	Mene Oto	35 years
Troop 563	Saratoga	Pioneer	35 years
Troop 233	San Jose	Mene Oto	34 years
Troop 371	Campbell	Pioneer	34 years
Troop 237	Morgan Hill	Gavilan	34 years
Troop 74	Santa Clara	Pioneer	34 years
Troop 470	Cupertino	Polaris	34 years
Troop 92	Milpitas	Mt. Hamilton	33 years
Troop 295	San Jose	Mene Oto	33 years
Troop 476	Cupertino	Polaris	33 years
Troop 409	San Jose	Polaris	33 years
Troop 325	San Jose	Pioneer	33 years
Troop 498	Sunnyvale	Polaris	32 years
Troop 139	Santa Clara	Mt. Hamilton	32 years
Troop 339	Campbell	Pioneer	32 years
Troop 363	Los Gatos	Pioneer	31 years
Troop 535	Saratoga	Polaris	31 years
Troop 373	San Jose	Pioneer	31 years
Troop 327	San Jose	Pioneer	31 years
Troop 318	San Jose	Pioneer	30 years
Troop 466	Sunnyvale	Polaris	30 years
Troop 395	San Jose	Pioneer	30 years
Troop 403	Sunnyvale	Polaris	30 years
Troop 48	Santa Clara	Pioneer	30 years
Troop 121	Santa Clara	Mt. Hamilton	30 years

Active Handicapped Units

The Santa Clara County Council has taken the leadership in the region and in the nation in encouraging the formation of Handicapped Scout Units. The Council formed the Sunrise Area Committee on Scouting for the Handicapped in 1976 and hired Scouting Professional Terrance Spooner as the Director of Handicapped Scouting. With excellent support in the form of grants for the program, and with the generous sponsorship of the business community of Santa Clara County, the program for handicapped boys has been very successful.

The key to the success, of course, was the commitment of the boys' parents and the volunteer Scouters who took their responsibility very seriously. James Wall, Walter Chronert, Lyman Hitch, Andy Bonfield, Ralph Storti, Harold Dunn, Ray Witherell, Robert Dodge, James Barber, Marjie Devitt and Peggy Pollack are just a few of the people involved in the program who say they have received more from "their boys" than they have ever given.

The following are the Handicapped Scout Units and their sponsors that were functioning in 1976:

Pack 398, San Jose
  serving the Deaf, South Bay Lions
Pack 399, San Jose
  Mentally Retarded, Lockheed Management Association
Pack 400, Cupertino
  Physically Handicapped, Cupertino Jaycees
Troop 228, San Jose
  Mentally Retarded, Foucar, Ray & Simon Trucking Co.
Troop 397, Cupertino
  Mentally Retarded, L.D.S. Church
Troop 398, San Jose
  serving the Deaf, South Bay Lions
Troop 399, San Jose
  Mentally Retarded, Lockheed Management Association
Troop 400, Cupertino
  Physically Handicapped, Cupertino Jaycees

Troop 798, Gilroy
  Mentally Retarded, South County Association
Post 399, San Jose
  Mentally Retarded, Lockheed Management Association
Post 776, San Jose
  Mentally Retarded, Binkley's Lapidary

Active Handicapped Units
Troops, 20 Years and Older

Troop 399, San Jose, 24 years of service

Troop 399 was formed December, 1966. It was sponsored by the Joseph McKinnon School P.T.A. and has always used the McKinnon School as its meeting place. Lockheed Management Association sponsored the troop from 1968 through 1974 when it was replaced as sponsor by the San Jose Royal Knights of the Roundtable in 1975. They have continued their support to the present.

The first Troop 399 Scoutmaster was Ralph Storti who served until Richard Gruver took over in 1973. James Wall was Scoutmaster from 1974 through 1979, and Ray Witherell, Jr. has held that position from 1980 to the present. Margie Dunn has served as Committee Chairman from 1982 to the present.

Scout troop membership has varied from a high of 28 in 1974 to a low of 5 in 1989. This has been a very active troop which has an enviable record of joint participation with other troops in the Scouting program.

(information source: Stephen Goodman)

Active Handicapped Units
Troops, Formed in the Eighties

Troop 88, Santa Clara, 3 years of service

Troop 88 was formed in October, 1987. The Santa Clara Rotary Club has been its sponsor both years and the troop has met at Buchser School in Santa Clara. Karen Bowman was its Scoutmaster for the years 1988-89. Troop 88 has been assisted by Andrew Inenaga, Committee Chairman, and George Delucchi, Sponsor Coordinator. There were 7 Boy Scouts in the troop both years.

Active Handicapped Units
Posts, 15 Years and Older

Post 776, San Jose, 15 years of service

Post 776 was formed August, 1975. It was sponsored by Binkleys Lapidary Supply. Dodge Construction Company sponsored it in 1978, Davis-Skaggs and Company from 1979 through 1984, and Barber and Barber sponsored it from 1985-87.

James Wall was the post's first Advisor. He was followed by William Smith from 1977 through 1979, Leo Powell in 1980, Hermo Peruit, 1981-82, Marj Devitt, 1983-85, Rose Reed, 1986-87. Robert Dodge has been Committee Chairman from 1983-87. James Barber has served as Sponsor Coordinator from 1979-87.

In 1976 Post 776 began with 5 Explorers and by 1987 it had grown to 21. The 1983 Advancement Report lists 18 Explorers who earned merit badges for the following skills: Building and Design, Coin Collecting, Cooking, Fishing and Wildlife, Home Repairs, Model Building, Painting, Plumbing, Rabbit Raising, Sculpture and Stamp Collecting.

(information source: Stephen Goodman)

Active Handicapped Units
Posts, Formed in the Eighties

Post 755, Santa Clara, 2 years of service

Post 755 was formed September 1980. Its continuous sponsor has been Agnews State Hospital, now called Agnews Development Center, and its meeting place was at Agnews. In 1981-82 Karen Healy was the Post Advisor.

Post 756, Agnews, 8 years of service
(soon to be reactivated)

Post 756 was formed September, 1981. It was sponsored by Agnews Developmental Center and its first Post Advisor was David Dotzler. He was followed in 1984 by Lenetta Thomas. During the years from 1981 to 1987 the membership averaged between 16 and 18 wheelchair-bound young people.

In 1987 James McCarthy became the Post Advisor, a position he held until transferred to another unit of the complex. He hopes to reactivate the Post in his new unit during 1990.

Cub Pack Histories

Introduction

As early as 1929 a pilot program for younger boys led to the first Pack Charters being issued in 1930. In 1949 the membership age was lowered to 8 for Cub Scouts. The Webelos Program, the last six months transition from Cub to Scout, was started in 1954. 1982 marked the beginning of the Tiger Cub Program for 7-year-old boys and their adult family members. Four years later the age requirement was changed for Cubs. Membership primarily based on grade in school started with Tiger Cubs in the first grade. These programs have helped instill Scouting values at a very early age, and have proven to increase the numbers of boys and their parents who contribute to the strength of Scouting in their home districts.

In the Santa Clara County Council brochure called "The Promise of Scouting," Cub Scouting was described as the beginning of a long adventure. It said, "The first step in Scouting is the Tigers. This gives 6-year-old boys in first grade a preview of what Scouting is all about. The program is fun with no formal uniforms or advancement requirements. Instead, Tiger Cubs and their parents, or guardians, attend informal meetings to share in Scouting experiences, activity leadership, and cooperation.

"At the end of the year, each Tiger is presented with a Cub Scout neckerchief and slide, to mark his transition into the next phase of Scouting.

"Cub Scouting is a home-centered program, as well. Boys 7–10-years-old work with their parents and friends in programs designed to open up the world for them. There are individual and team sports, science projects, craft activities, field trips and camping. The Cub Scout is encouraged to follow his interests and to explore the world around him.

"At age 10, the Cub Scout can become a Webelos who works at higher level skills to earn Activity Badges.... They continue forming habits and attitudes that prepare them for the responsibilities expected of a Boy Scout, such as independent thinking and self-reliance."

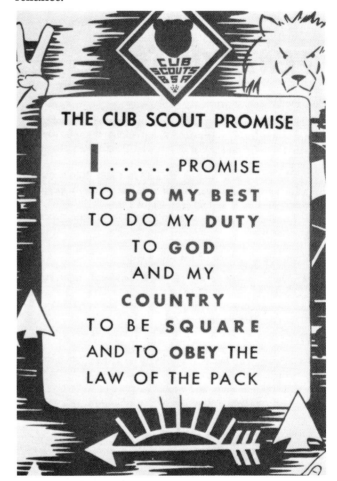

Packs, Twenty-five Years or Older

Cub Pack 349, San Jose, 29 years of service

Pack 349 was chartered in May, 1961. It was sponsored by the Home and School Club of George Payne Elementary School in west San Jose. The pack met for all meetings on the school grounds for many years. During the last five years a change occurred. Den meetings are now held in homes. Only monthly Pack meetings are held in the school cafeteria. The Home and School Club is still very supportive of the pack. The pack reciprocates by assisting with the school's spring festival and other activities.

The first Cubmaster of Pack 349 was Hursel Patterson, 1962-64. He was followed by Anthony Chiaravalle, 1965-67; Ronald Remmel, 1968-70; and Richard Lieberman, 1971-72. In March of 1972 James Duncan became Cubmaster and during the next twelve years Cubmasters were Sid Webb, Dick Narducci, Janice Freita, Jeffrey Stern, Gary Dirstine and David Drage. In 1985 both Sherry Roberts and Charles Barber took turns as Cubmaster. Cary Stover was Cubmaster for three years; Cubmaster Bob Dietz served most of 1989, helping to reactivate the pack. In the fall of 1989 Dietz followed our pack tradition and involved himself more deeply with the Webelos as Bruce Southwick assumed pack leadership as Cubmaster.

This very active Pack 349 has won the National Summer Time Pack Awards eight times; has won the National Presidents Unit Award, Commissioners Choice Award, and Mayors Award several years; and has been honored with Honor Unit Awards, the Jubilee Honor Unit Award at the Diamond Jubilee, and a Gold Medal at the 1984 Scout-O-Rama saluting the Olympics—among many other awards.

In April, 1989 Cub Pack 349 announced the formation of an affiliate Tiger Cub Group, "Tiger Cub 349."

(information source: Peggy Ann Southwick)

Pinewood Derby

Tiger Cubs BSA

WELCOME NEW TIGER FAMILIES!

Pack 349 would like to announce the formation on April 4, 1989 of our affiliate Tiger Cub 349....

The Tiger Cubs program is strictly family oriented and functions in parallel with the Cub Scout Pack. The first grade boys do not meet in a Den. Each Tiger Cub has an adult family member or neighbor as a partner. They meet together weekly for activities based upon a theme which is also the center of the monthly meeting held for all the families.

When all the families meet they are called a "Pride" of tigers. The pride will cover many fun subjects during the year but, always with the intent to Search, Discover and Share with each other. The leadership for the monthly meeting of the pride rotates among the different families who also have the option for choosing the theme.

Our Pack Tiger coordinator functions only during the formation of the pack and as an advisor to help with any difficulties.

The boys have an activity book with suggestions, a wall chart with stickers to keep track of the weekly meetings, and special iron-on paw prints for their shirts to keep track of the pride events. In the fall there will be a graduation for the boys and their families. They will receive a patch and certificate.

During the end of the summer they will have the theme "Cub Scouting, Here We Come." They will cover the basic Bobcat information. When they cross over and become Cub Scouts, they will be ready to receive their Bobcat badge.

The Tiger Cubs held their first monthly meeting.... The theme was "Getting to Know You." The Tiger Cubs will be our guests at many pack events, so, keep your eyes open for their distinctive Tiger shirts, and treat them with courtesy.

(Reprint: Cub Pack 349 "Cub Scout Courier"
Newsletter 4/20/89)

Cub Pack 492, Cupertino, 28 years of service

Cub Pack 492 was chartered in March, 1962. Its original sponsor was Regnart School P.T.A. in Cupertino. They met at the school for several years. More recently, the Den meetings were held at Regnart School or in Cubs' homes. Pack meetings are held in the Kennedy Junior High School Multi-Use Room, Mountain View High School Cafeteria or Lincoln School Auditorium.

The original Cubmaster of Pack 492 was Ted Evangel from March 1960 to February 1961. The first Cubmaster after a short lapse was Theodore Brown, in 1962. He was followed by Russell Beck, 1963; Frank Coen, 1964; Mike Cheshaek, 1965; and Norman Rosinsky, 1966–67. There is a gap in our records and the remainder of the information is for the past five years only. Cubmasters have been Carl Clemm, Chris Henry and Wes Harrison. Webelos Den Leaders have been Urban Cubbage, Ted Park and Wes Harrison.

Cub Pack 492 monthly Pack Meetings are on the following schedule: September — Kickoff; October — Pumpkin Carving; November — Father-Son Cake Bake and Auction; December — Christmas theme; January — Pinewood Derby; February — Blue and Gold Potluck Dinner; March and April — alternating, Scout Olympics, Basketball Tournament, Hike, Kite-Fly or Speaker; May — Scout-O-Rama and Camporee events; June — Potluck Picnic at a local park. The last two summers they had enough Pack events to qualify for the Summertime Pack Awards.

The Cub Pack has been fortunate this past five years to have had the helpful assistance of Scoutmaster Don Rosenbaum of Troop 494. Among his contributions: he donated the wooden Pinewood Derby track to the pack; his Troop 494 has coordinated their monthly newspaper drive with Pack 492, which has taken care of most of their financial needs; he has been the Auctioneer every year at their annual Cake Bake.

Cub Pack 492 proudly displays fifty ribbons on their Pack Flag.

(information source: Judy Harrison)

BILL CHIVERS, Troop 55, Los Gatos

When I grew up in Los Gatos I was a Boy Scout in Troop 55, sponsored by the American Legion. Our Scoutleader was Claude Smith and we met in the National Guard Armory.

This past year I was helping Mayor Jeanette Watson of Campbell do research on her Campbell History Book and I learned a couple of interesting things about the Campbell Boy Scouts. Troop 36 had Robert Herschbach as its leader and met in the Congregational Church. They raised money selling Christmas Trees. They took a couple of great trips, one to Yosemite and another to Canada. Herschbach's son, Dudley Herschbach, became an Eagle Scout who in the late eighties received a Nobel Prize for his work in Chemistry.

In Reverend Joseph Bennett's obituary in the Campbell Press of April 12, 1956, it was mentioned that Rev. Bennett had the first Cub Pack (maybe in the United States). It was organized in 1927, was called, "Experimental Den #1," and was modeled after the Cub Packs in England. The cubs were referred to as "Wolf Cubs." After two years the cub pack idea was adopted by the National Council of the Boy Scouts of America and the pack in Campbell was given official approval to continue under their charter system.

In a later paper (Campbell Press, 1969) Dick Morton, the first mayor of Campbell, was given credit for being a member of that first Cub Pack.

Cub Pack 419, Sunnyvale, 25 years of service

Cub Pack 419 was chartered in 1965. Written records of early den and pack activities have been lost, consequently information from more recent years must be used for this history of the Pack.

Pack meeting agendas reveal a regular cycle of pumpkin decorating contests, game nights, pizza feeds, Christmas parties and derbies. Pack meetings centered on Native American crafts, ceremonies and costumes have been educational and fun. One memorable pack meeting resulted from the purchase of party kazoos. Songs and rounds highlighted the evening. A rousing version of "For He's a Jolly Good Fellow" capped off the awards ceremonies, and a surprisingly sober "America" was played during the closing.

Cub Pack 419 has had 56 Cubs in 1989. In keeping with the 1989 Scout-O-Rama theme "Saluting Our Resources," this pack continues to help develop the most precious resource—their kids.

(information source: Cubmaster Carol Hellie)

Packs, Twelve Years or Older

Cub Pack 476, Cupertino, 12 years of service
since re-activation

Cub Pack 476 was re-chartered in November, 1978, after approximately two dormant years. The original sponsor was the St. Joseph of Cupertino Church. In 1989 the Holy Names Society of St. Joseph of Cupertino became the new sponsor. Monthly pack meetings are conducted at St. Joseph's school. After school den meetings and Webelos meetings have been held both at the school and at parents' homes.

The first Cubmaster was Howard Trudeau. He was followed by Dick Norby, Paul Schafer, Jack Custers and Jim Pierce. Tim McCullough is the current Cubmaster.

Traditional pack activities are the Pinewood Derby Race in January and the Blue and Gold potluck dinner in February. The Pack averages between twenty and thirty-five cubs.

Cub Scout Tom Egan went on to join Troop 476 and earned the rank of Eagle Scout.

(information source: Stephen Hill, Committee Chairman)

1951-53
ELINOR DIAS YERKOVICH,
Den Mother, Cub Pack 22

Being a part of Scouts was a very important part of my life. What I enjoyed and participated in for two years was marching in the parades downtown. Three times a year we would march and were very proud to do so.

The pack met weekly at my home, monthly at Jefferson Elementary School. We had several money making events. We had a Bazaar at the school. We had Pot Lucks. We had Cake Sales. We also had Donut Sales.

The ceremonies for awarding badges should be impressive. Someone should explain how the child earned his badges.

I would like to express my opinion and say that at least one of the meetings of the Scouts should be at a P.T.A. meeting so more parents could get involved and know more about Scouting and how good it is for their children.

Our committee included the following: Dr. Chan, Leon Beeman, Dave Tatsuno, Ethel Blumberg, Jean Caldwell, Jean Engles, Virginia Stratton, Martha Inman and Gayle Munser.

Veteran Cub Packs, Santa Clara County Council

Packs, 30 years or older in 1990:

Pack 502	Los Gatos	Pioneer	45 years
Pack 556	Los Gatos	Pioneer	38 years
Pack 54	Santa Clara	Pioneer	38 years
Pack 374	San Jose	Pioneer	36 years
Pack 377	Campbell	Pioneer	35 years
Pack 207	San Jose	Mene Oto	34 years
Pack 296	San Jose	Mene Oto	34 years
Pack 318	San Jose	Pioneer	34 years
Pack 105	Milpitas	Mt. Hamilton	33 years
Pack 394	San Jose	Pioneer	33 years
Pack 409	San Jose	Polaris	33 years
Pack 335	San Jose	Pioneer	32 years
Pack 122	Milpitas	Mt. Hamilton	32 years
Pack 563	Saratoga	Pioneer	32 years
Pack 61	Santa Clara	Pioneer	32 years
Pack 621	San Jose	Mt. Hamilton	31 years
Pack 214	Santa Clara	Mene Oto	30 years
Pack 325	San Jose	Pioneer	30 years

Varsity Scouting

Just as the Tiger Cub program was added to the Cub Scout program in order to fill a need, Varsity Scouting was introduced in response to a perceived need for boys who were not quite ready for the Explorer challenge.

Junior High Varsity Scouting is the newest outreach program of the Santa Clara County Council. It was initiated in 1984.

BOY SCOUTS UNVEIL NEW PROGRAM FOR MID-TEENS

Irving, Texas, January—A new program aimed specifically at mid-teen boys will be unveiled by the Boy Scouts of America next September.

To be known as "Varsity Scouting," it will offer heavy emphasis on "high adventure" activities and other programs which appeal to the older boy, according to Chief Scout Executive J.L. Tarr.

Tested for the past six years in 28 of the nation's 473 local Scout Councils, the program is the second new major thrust of the BSA in two years. Just over a year ago, Tiger Cubs, a program for 7-year-old boys, was introduced and to date has attracted some 142,000 youngsters.

Although membership in Scouting's youth programs has made substantial gains in recent years, officials acknowledged that the "greatest loss of boys in Scouting is during the 14 and 15 year age level."

Varsity Scouts will join a team, rather than a troop, under the direction of an adult coach (instead of a Scoutmaster), and will be led by a youth captain instead of a senior patrol leader.

In addition to high adventure activities, they will be encouraged to continue their advancement toward the Eagle rank, fulfill service projects, participate in special Scouting programs on council, regional and national levels, continue personal development in leadership, physical fitness, citizenship, in social and spiritual fields.

Specific participation in all five areas will be recognized with the awarding of VS (Varsity Scouting) jacket letters.

The Varsity program, which will be open to boys 14 through 17, will remain optional. Youths may continue in traditional Scout troops or may switch to co-education Explorer posts. (Exploring is the senior, career-oriented program of the BSA with some 605,000 members.) The key goal will be to reach many of the approximately 90% of American males, 14–17, who are not members of a Scouting program....

(Reprint: Santa Clarion, 1/85)

Explorer Post Histories

Introduction

Explorers were the latest of the three broad age group divisions of the Scouting Program introduced thoughout the United States by the National Council of the Boy Scouts of America. Boy Scouts were the first to be established in 1910, the Cub Scouts in 1930 and the Explorer Scouts in 1936. In 1949, Explorer age minimums were lowered to 14 for all boys. They could remain in a Scout Troop as members of an Explorer Crew, or join a separate post. Special-interest Exploring was started in 1958–59; ten years later girls were invited to join special-interest posts.

The programs for older boys, however, started much earlier than 1936. The oldest element dates from 1912 when the Sea Scout program was inaugurated. The local council had a Sea Scout committee as early as 1927. In 1931, 75 Sea Scouts were listed in 5 Sea Scout Ships and 1 Sea Scout Patrol. About the same number of Sea Scouts were active through the thirties.

In 1936 Explorer Troops and Rover Crews were mentioned in the Council Charter application but it did not list any youth members in either category. In 1938 the first two Explorer Troops were organized with the Santa Clara County Council.

By the first full year of our involvement in World War II, a Senior Scout in this council could be a member of a Scout Troop, a Sea Scout Ship, an Air Scout Squadron or an Explorer Troop. The first Air Squadron was formed in 1943, with two squadrons by 1945. In some areas of the country there was another option for older boys 18 and up called a Rover Crew; however, there is no record of a Rover Crew ever being established here in Santa Clara County.

Several of the Scouters in the council were actively involved with the Sea Scout program. Their enthusiasm carried the program from the late twenties up until the early sixties, when the emphasis of the program experienced a change of focus.

In 1958 all senior programs were integrated into the "New Exploring" program when the National Council made it a separate division of the Boy Scouts of America. About that time the titles, "Sea Exploring," "Air Exploring" and "Exploring" came into general use. The Explorers in a troop were members of a "Crew." To avoid confusion with the "troop" term long used by Boy Scouts, the "Explorer Troops" became known as "Explorer Posts."

The Explorer program offers young men and women, ages 14 to 20, opportunities for high adventure, personal growth, sports and athletic challenges and career development.

SCOUTING'S NEW MANAGEMENT CONCEPT

... The Council has had a study committee underway for several months. The committee's purpose has been to develop more equitable use of volunteer and professional manpower on the Council and District level. To this end, "service areas" have been set up which are designed to improve field service to Units and Unit Leaders.

A major step in this direction is the formation of an Exploring Division within the council, as requested by the National Council. All Explorer Posts of the council will be included in the division.

The Council Exploring Committee, under the chairmanship of Larry Hill, will be enlarged with additional volunteers from the Districts and will be responsible for organization, program and

---

service. A Professional Exploring Executive will work with the division....

These improvements, which have been approved by the National Council ... (will be) put into effect during the start of the program year in September and October.

(Excerpt: Santa Clarion, 9/72)

During the 1980s, career development has emerged as one of the most valuable aspects of the program. Explorers, with the help of educators and members of the business community, take a look at career options such as accounting, the law, high technology, communications, business and other fields.

The Explorer program matches a young person's interests and aptitudes with several facets of a specific career.

The Explorer Code

As an Explorer—

I believe that America's strength lies in her trust in God and in the courage and strength of her people.

I will, therefore, be faithful in my religious duties and will maintain a personal sense of honor in my own life.

I will treasure my American heritage and will do all I can to preserve and enrich it.

I will recognize the dignity and worth of my fellowmen and will use fair play and goodwill in dealing with them.

I will acquire the Exploring attitude that seeks the truth in all things and adventure on the frontiers of our changing world.

Posts, Twenty-five Years or Older

Explorer Post 121, San Jose, 31 years of service

Explorer Post 121, chartered in late 1961 is the oldest post in the council. It is still sponsored, as it was originally, by the San Jose 5th Ward of the Church of Jesus Christ of Latter-Day Saints (LDS). The first meeting place was in the LDS Chapel at the corner of Tenth and San Fernando Streets in San Jose. For most of its history it met at the LDS Chapel on the corner of White Road and Patt Avenue. Currently it is meeting at the LDS Stake Center on the corner of Cropley and Morrill Avenues.

The post has had at least ten different advisors over its nearly thirty years' existence. Some outstanding leaders were men such as Dale Pitman, who served three years and helped 5 boys complete Eagle. The boys remember him because of the water ski trips and snow trips he would take them on.

Jim Chidester is remembered for the canoe trips, and Larry Lloyd for the kayaks they made and used, and for the Washington, D.C. trip. Max Rasier, an early advisor, arranged an exchange trip through the Uintah Mountains of eastern Utah.

Bryan Hartley is their current advisor.

Over the years the post has helped at least a dozen or more boys on their way to become Eagle Scouts. One, Terry Hale, later became a Scoutmaster. Another, Robert Hartley, currently is an Assistant Scoutmaster.

Post alumni include several young men who have been active in the church; who have, for example, served as missionaries to Central and South America. A number have also served as Bishops.

Explorer Post 121 is proud to be an active part of Santa Clara County Council of the Boy Scouts of America.

(information source: Bryan Hartley)

Posts, Twelve Years or Older

Explorer Post 442, Sunnyvale, 12 years of service

In 1978 Santa Clara County Council established the first Explorer Post in the United States which has the career interest of being an officer in the military service. Members of this Explorer Post are referred to this post by their high school counselor in the local area.

Explorer Post 442 was started by Colonel Noburo Masuoka, USAF (Retired), who is a liaison officer for the United States Air Force (USAF) Academy. The Post's Associate Advisor is the liaison officer for West Point. Two other Air Force Academy Liaison Officers are also Associate Advisors.

As a result of this program, Explorer Post 442 members have received over 60 appointments to the USAF Academy, 3 to the Naval Academy and 1 to West Point. Numerous Explorer Scouts have received Reserve Office Training Corps (ROTC) scholarships to various universities such as Cornell and the University of California at Los Angeles.

Two female Explorer members were in the first graduating class of women from the Air Force Academy. Explorer Phung Le was one of the first Vietnamese refugees to graduate from the Academy. As of today there have been 6 Vietnamese Americans appointed to the Academy from Post 442.

Once a year during Christmas vacation, former post members at the various military academies, and ROTC Cadets, hold a reunion to talk about their experiences, and their future in the military service. Explorer Post 442 members have the opportunity of visiting many military bases since most bases have a Boy Scout coordinator.

(information source: Nobby Masuoka)

A Memorable Exploring Adventure

Father Bernard R. Hubbard, S.J., Santa Clara University's famed "Glacier Priest" led a group of 15 Explorer Scouts on a five-week expedition in Alaska during the summer of 1955. Twelve of the Explorer Scouts were from Bay Area Councils, three were from the Southeast Alaska Council.

Hubbard grew up in Santa Cruz. He attended Santa Clara University for two years before entering the Jesuit order. He returned to the University in 1923 as a professor of geology. Hubbard first went to Alaska in 1927.

His summer explorations became annual events. During the winters he made lecture tours, showing his films, with the proceeds going to support the Jesuits' missions for the Eskimos. In 1937 Literary Digest described him as the highest paid lecturer in the world.

Father Hubbard remained associated with Santa Clara University until his death in 1962.

(An account of this expedition appeared in *Boys Life Magazine*, May 1956.)

(information source: Bill Adams)

EXPLORER CANOE RACE

The annual Explorer Canoe Race held on Saturday, May 29, was judged a big success. A total of 24 teams started the race at Redding, California, with 17 teams finishing the race at Red Bluff, a total of 50 miles down the Sacramento River. There were over 80 cars loaded with a total of over 350 Explorers, leaders, families, and friends following the race all the way down the Sacramento River. This big event still continues to stimulate a lot of interest.

The winners of the race were: St. Mary's Post 793, first place, with a time of 5 hours, 50 minutes, and 43 seconds, a new course record; Morgan Hill Lions Club Post 791, second place with a time of 6 hours, 7 minutes, and 40 seconds; Los Gatos Christian Church Post 520, third place, with a time of 6 hours, 23 minutes and 40 seconds.

Congratulations to all Explorers who participated in this grand event. We extend a "Thank You" to Dave Osborn, Explorer Canoe Race Chairman, and his excellent staff, for conducting this outstanding Exploring Event.

(Reprint: Santa Clarion, 7/71)

OUR FIRST ALL GIRL POST

Post 332 is sponsored by the Lockheed Management Association and specializes in stewardess and related vocational areas. Some 40 girls attended the first meeting and Linda Robins is the advisor.

(Reprint: Santa Clarion, 8/73)

WELCOME NEW UNITS

    8 Medical, Kaiser Hospital
  104 General Interest, Milpitas
  180 Medical, San Jose Hospital
  181 Social Work, County Social Services
  308 General Interest, Pioneer District
  307 Medical, Good Samaritan Hospital
  318 Fire Science, Santa Clara Fire Department
  415 Dental, County Dental Association
  438 Merchandizing, Sear's Cupertino
  461 Social Work, S.V. Community Services
  572 Dental, County Dental Association
  777 Forestry, United States Fire Service,
       Morgan Hill

(Reprint: Santa Clarion, 12/73)

Explorer Crew at United Technology, circa 1965

EXPLORING

The 1972 Explorer Olympics are now in the advanced planning stage. Track and field events, car rally, chess tournament, canoe race, public speaking, basketball, golf, archery, table tennis, swimming and other events are all being considered as part of the Explorer Olympics. Co-educational in concept, events for our gals are a possibility. Winning post teams will go to Fort Collins next summer. National winners go to World Olympics in Munich, Germany, August of 1972.

Larry Hill, Council Exploring Chairman, proudly announces that 150% increase in Explorer membership has been achieved since a year ago. Exploring in the Pioneer and Polaris Districts has had the greatest increase. Larry predicts that because of the many new posts being organized that there will be an even greater increase. Most of the increase in new units and in membership is in posts sponsored by business, industry, associations, etc.....

Explorer Presidents Congress is set for April 12–16, 1972, in the nation's capitol. Cost, excluding transportation is $155.00, but as last year's attendees will tell you it is the best investment a post or sponsor can make....

A new Explorer Emergency Service Program, in cooperation with U.S. Office of Civil Defense, will be available after the first of the year. An action program, with four training sessions, with detailed helps in a 64 page book, will compliment any Post's program.

(Excerpts: Santa Clarion, 12/71)

POST 44
EXPLORER OLYMPICS WINNER

Dale Follas, Chairman of the Program Sub-Committee of the Council Exploring Committee, announced ... that Post 44 was the winner of the Council Explorer Olympics. The winning Post, all 19 members, will be traveling to Fort Collins, Colorado to compete in the National Explorer Olympics....

Paul Sharp, Advisor of Post 44, has given innovative leadership.... (Since) a total of $3,200 was necessary to take 19 members to Colorado, the post has raised $2,800 to date by assembling and selling 10 speed bikes, showing a movie, having a dinner with an organ concert, and manning a concession stand. Parents will assist by providing the remaining funds....

The post is sponsored by the Santa Clara Ward of the Church of Jesus Christ of Latter-Day Saints.

(Excerpts: Santa Clarion, 7/72)

COUNCIL EXPLORING EVENTS

Your Exploring Executive

Terry Tibor has worked for the past 4 years in the Polaris District as its executive. He will now serve as Exploring Executive and work directly with the Council's Exploring Committee and each District's Exploring Committee....

(Scout-O-Rama's) Explorer Hall:

This experience gives our explorers a chance to see what each post is doing, meet one another and show their expertise. At our Council Scout-O-Rama past displays have included: fashion show, airplanes, rock climbing, skindiving, archery, communications, electronics, automobiling, law enforcement, dentistry, veterinary medicine, and others.

Canoe Race: Our last race included over 250 young adults in twenty-five teams. They raced 51 miles down the Sacramento River from Redding to Red Bluff. Special trophies were awarded to the top three team members. The Award Campfire turned into a fun-time after a long day on the river.

Explorer Olympics: This spring, competition on a post basis was conducted to determine our Council's representation at the National Olympics in Colorado. Events included: basketball, swimming, track and field, chess, and other sports. Winners in Colorado were our official youth representatives to the World Olympics and lived in the U.S.A.'s Olympic Village in Germany.

Safety Road Rally: Last year's Explorer Rally covered 125 miles. 54 teams qualified, each with a driver and navigator. This is not a speed race but a test of timing and navigation. Rally plaques were provided for all participants.

U.S.A.F./Exploring: All U.S.A.F. facilities are open to Explorers and offer various programs, encampment and orientation flights. Lt. Robert Wisniewski is our liaison officer at Hamilton A.F.B. and he has published program outlines which are available at our Exploring Service Center.

(Reprint: Exploring Division Newsletter, 9/72)

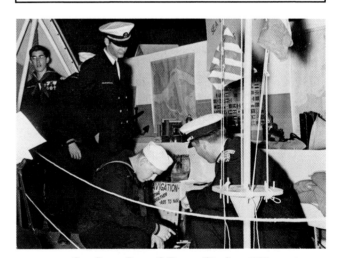

Sea Scout Scout-O-Rama Display, 1963

DORIS HAMBRICK
NEW EXPLORER EXECUTIVE
Elayne Roberts

"Enthusiastic about the Scouting program and very happy to be here" is how our newest employee, Doris Hambrick, describes herself. Doris, recently hired as Explorer Executive, is busy maintaining and expanding the Explorer program.

She describes the program as "exciting" because of the new High Adventure programs being planned, and the interest of companies in the area who have facilities that may help young people determine their careers.

Doris has worked for many years as a volunteer in youth programs, including both the Boy Scouts and Camp Fire Girls in Oakland and Alameda. She has also enthusiastically supported the foreign exchange program and has had students from England, France, Norway and Finland live with her.

A native of California and a graduate of University of California at Berkeley, she has two daughters and two sons.

Stop by and say hello to Doris and extend a welcome to our newest staff member.

(Reprint: Santa Clarion, 9/81)

VIETNAMESE EXPLORER POST 216 HISTORY
Hung Le, Advisor

A new Explorer post is organized in the Vietnamese community in Santa Clara County: Post 216. Originally, Post 216 had been organized in Dalat District, Vietnam (the number came from the day it was founded, the 22nd of November, 1966). It was baptized during the peak days of the war. A short period after its first anniversary, the members of the post had played an important role in response to the call of duty in burying the dead and clearing war-torn areas around the district, and in helping refugees on those first days of the Tet Offensive in 1968.

The post had taken responsibilities in running a makeshift refugee camp more than a month with no less than 500 refugees. It made various contributions of manpower on many occasions, such as a donation drive for flood victims, and distributing goods for war refugees in Hue....

After the communists took over the country in 1975, the post was disbanded and most of its leaders and members were lucky enough to get out of Vietnam. They, in turn, became refugees. Even so, imbued with Scouting spirits, these members worked with the Locator Service in Fort Chaffee ... to help distribute mail and locate relatives of refugees in the U.S. At night they also held occasional campfires for entertainment, and recalled Scout Oaths.

Beginning in 1976, the post was organized again in Minneapolis, Minnesota, to become one of the first Vietnamese Scout units in the U.S. ... the post had occasion to visit the West Coast two times, in 1978 and 1980, and to visit numerous National Parks....

In 1981, the post advisor and two other leaders had to move to San Jose. After a short transition period, he (the advisor) found that there are more than enough leaders to form another, 216 high-adventure Explorer Post. As of March 1982 the post has 17 strong, active members registered with BSA and has camped in the Los Angeles area and explored Pinnacles National Monument and Point Reyes National Seashore Park.

(Excerpts: Santa Clarion, 4/82)

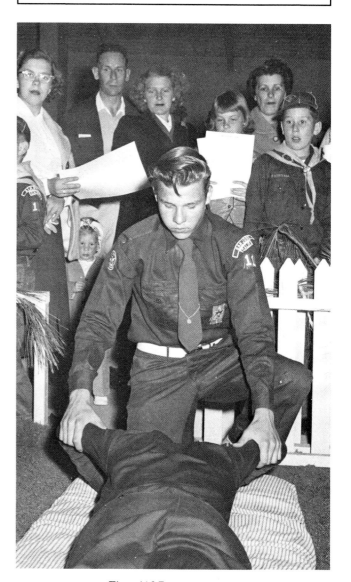

First Aid Demonstration

50 MILES DOWNSTREAM

The Exploring Division of the Santa Clara County Council will be sponsoring a 50 mile canoe race down the Sacramento River from Redding to Red Bluff. It will be held on the weekend of May 21 and 22. This event is for Explorers, Boy Scouts and Girl Scouts ages 14-20. All are encouraged to participate.

Teams of ten people are needed. Each pair of two will paddle a ten-mile segment of the race. There are four categories ranging from the novice to the pro. If you can't get your hands on your own canoe, we do have arrangements by which you can rent one. After spending a full, exhausting day on the warm and quite full Sacramento River, the evening will feature a barbecue and campfire.

The campgrounds are very accommodating with a pool, flush toilets and even showers—all for our use! After a good night's sleep we will all be rested and ready to participate in the Sunday water activities.

Sunday's activities will not be serious competition but more a way to have fun and meet new friends....

(Reprint: Santa Clarion, 5/83)

EXPLORING DIVISION TO HOST FIRST GALA BENEFIT AUCTION

The Exploring Division of the Santa Clara County Council will host the First Gala Benefit Auction. Enide Allison, Council Vice President/ Exploring, will serve as its chairperson. The auction is planned to assist the financing of the council's Exploring Division.

The Exploring Auction will be held ... May 11, 1984. The auction will begin at the (Marriott's) Pictorium with the 'showing of the film "Hail Columbia." The ... participants will then move to the California Ballroom of the Marriott Hotel where the silent auction will take place, along with dinner, followed by the live auction.

Enide reports that ... items secured include: two Super Bowl 1985 tickets, an earth satellite dish, two sets of sheepskin seat covers, a plane ride for four over Yosemite, golf for four at La Rinconada Country Club, one mobile telephone, a 19 foot sailboat, a Coleman Trailer, Membership in the Los Gatos Athletic Club ... plus much, much more!

Tickets for the evening will be $40 per person or $75 per couple....

(Reprint: Santa Clarion, 5/84)

Cross Country Skiing

Veteran Explorer Posts, Santa Clara County Council

Posts, 30 years or older in 1990:

Post 121	Santa Clara	Mt. Hamilton	29 years
Post 470	Cupertino	Pioneer	23 years
Post 221	San Jose	Mene Oto	23 years
Post 417	Sunnyvale	Exploring	20 years
Post 553	Saratoga	Exploring	20 years
Post 536	Saratoga	Pioneer	20 years

Troop 10 Christmas Toy Collection, 1943

III. Major Scouting Activities

Introduction

A number of council sponsored special activities have become traditional events that Scouts look forward to attending annually. Usually these have been focused on perennial council concerns, or on matters of regional or national signficance.

They may have been to commemorate an historic event such as our country's Bicentennial. Or they may simply have been to provide an opportunity to demonstrate Scouting achievements and/or skills, such as the Scout-O-Ramas. Sometimes, as in the case of the camporees, they were just a good way to have some fun and games, and engage in good-natured competition.

These major Scouting activities fall into two categories: those initiated outside the Santa Clara County Council, and those which originated with the Council. Frequently in the last seventy years the President of the United States has asked the Boy Scouts of America for help. In both World War I and World War II, Scouts were involved in war bond and scrap drives.

As recently as the early eighties Scouts helped combat the Med Fly infestation in Santa Clara County. Also county-wide, Scouts assisted in the "Get Out the Vote" campaigns, working on voter registration and urging citizens to participate in their government through the ballot box. Scouts were always encouraged to follow the Scout slogan to "Do a Good Turn Daily."

The Scouting Jamboree was a national encampment of Scouts and Scouters from every state in the union. Scheduled every four years, except for the war years, there have been twelve National Jamborees from 1937-1989. The Santa Clara County Council has usually sent a delegation; frequently their adult Scouters have been tapped for leadership posts at the Jamborees.

Representatives from the Council have also participated in international get-togethers, the World Jamborees. These are scheduled on a rotation that does not conflict with the national Jamborees. The earliest was held in England in 1920, the most recent, in Australia in 1987.

Good Turns

President Franklin D. Roosevelt requested the Boy Scouts of America to participate in a national program, the National Good Turn, in 1934. With people across the country suffering from the effects of the Great Depression, Boy Scouts collected 1.8 million articles of clothing, food and furnishings for the needy.

On the national level, Good Turns have been utilized for various causes. Scouts mobilized in 1912 for the first of a series of national civic Good Turns, including the promotion of a safe and sane Fourth of July.

Some more recent Good Turn projects were similar to the 1954 National Conservation Good Turn in which Boy Scouts undertook thousands of projects for conservation of soil and water, forests and wildlife. In 1958 for National Safety Good Turn, they distributed 50,000 posters and delivered 40 million Civil Defense emergency handbooks. In 1960 the Boy Scouts of America held their third get-out-the-vote Good Turn. In 1970 the good turn was amplified with the new acronym, SOAR (Save Our American Resources), and in 1977 energy conservation was emphasized in Project SOAR.

The community Good Turn in Santa Clara County usually came about in response to an emergency. For example, in 1968, the local Goodwill Industries, which provides rehabilitation and training programs for emotionally, mentally and physically handicapped people, had a devastating fire in their main warehouse. Since this warehouse held used furniture, clothing and household supplies that Goodwill recycled and sold to pay for their rehabilitation programs, those programs were in danger of being eliminated. Goodwill had their

Camporee, Grant Ranch, 1968

own annual Good Turn Day and on March 16, 1968, county Boy Scouts collected thousands of bags of clothing that helped replenish supplies lost in the fire. One of the services Goodwill Industries had provided for some time to the Santa Clara County Council, was the printing and folding of the Scouting newsletter, the Santa Clarion.

Santa Clara County Scouts continued to assist their handicapped and disadvantaged neighbors. In 1977, an annual Good Turn Day was scheduled on a November Saturday when Boy Scouts distributed Good Turn Bags for used clothing and collected them a week later, delivering the full bags to the Salvation Army. In 1988 and 1989 the Scouting for Food drives were initiated to help feed the homeless as well as the victims of the 1989 earthquake.

Troop Scout-O-Rama Display, circa 1970

CYCLETHON

The annual Diabetics Foundation Cyclethon will be May 16, with a cycling course from 20 to 100 miles in length. Scouts interested in helping others while working on cycling merit badge are encouraged to participate. Unit leaders will receive full information at Roundtables.

(Reprint: Santa Clarion, 3/76)

BOY SCOUTS JOIN MED FLY SWAT TEAM

The Santa Clara County Council BSA has been asked to enlist the help and support of all Cub Scouts, Boy Scouts and Explorers in the county to help combat the Medfly infestation. This special emergency action provides the opportunity for Scouts to do a major good turn for their community while accomplishing a much needed civic service project.

Our plan is two-fold:

1. We will distribute flyers to households within the territory of each pack, troop and post, urging all individuals to pick the fruit off the trees in volunteer compliance with the recommended action of the Medfly control authorities.

2. All Scouting families are encouraged to immediately pick their own fruit, especially citrus fruit, including oranges, limes, lemons, grapefruit and kumquats, as well as persimmons, avocados and other soft-skinned fruit. Picked fruit should be placed in sealed, plastic bags, weighing not more than 30 pounds and placed in standard garbage cans or consumed, canned or preserved at home. Do not transport any fresh fruit away from your home.

It is important that all Cub Scout packs, Boy Scout troops and Explorer posts comply and give the Medfly extermination program the utmost cooperation....

(Reprint: Santa Clarion, 1/81)

International Scouter, Charlie Orr, with friend Terry Bonfield, the last surviving member of the original Brownsea Island Troop, 1990

Camporees and Celebrations

Council camporees are held occasionally to commemorate special events of national or local significance. Some national events which have been recognized were the Jubilee Camporee of 1960, the Bicent-O-Ree of 1976, and the Diamond Jubilee Jamboree of 1975. Local Council events have been celebrated with the 50th Anniversary Rally of 1970, and the Scouting Extravaganza of 1980. The Council's 70th Anniversary Camporee will be held in the fall of 1990.

District camporees are part of the regular Scouting activities held annually in each district. These are weekend affairs often held at one of the state or county parks, which have more space for activities than is usually found in the council camps.

ROBERT RICHARDSON

Ted Rogers was a Field Executive and he and Bob Chapman asked me to be the Activities Chairman (when) Vint Matthews took over as District Chairman (of Mene Oto District). One of the first things we did as a District was to go to Coe Park. It had just been accepted as a State Park and was not officially open. We used it for a camporee. We had a group of handicapped kids, some in wheelchairs, up there. While they were wheeling around in their chairs the two Coe sisters came up to see the camporee. They saw the handicapped kids and said that this was just what they wanted. This was in the early '60s. After that I worked out a scheme and used the boys to run things at camporees.

JAMES STURROCK

The first Polaris District camporee that I attended was the one at Crite's Ranch up on Mt. Umunhum in 1958. That was the time we imposed the rule that everyone had to hike in. The troops were all in the habit of tailgating off of trucks and station wagons. Boy, did that generate a lot of complaints at Roundtable!

As part of the observation of the BSA's 50th Anniversary, we participated in the Council Jubilee Camporee held at Mt. Madonna State Park in July 1960. I served as District Campmaster.

In June '76 we celebrated the nation's bicentennial with a council-wide camporee called the "Bicent-O-Ree" held at Frank Bernard's ranch near Hollister. Andy Bonfield was the chairman and he did an excellent job of organizing and promoting the event. Unfortunately, he couldn't do anything about the record heat wave of 110+ degree temperature that we had to endure. Scoutmaster Jeff Crane, M.D., ran a field hospital that resembled a scene from a MASH movie as he tried to keep up with the heat prostration and food poisoning cases. We filled up all the hospitals for miles around.

A highlight was the two terrific campfire programs put on by Dr. Jack Cox and his shows staff. Another show was caused when a couple of wayward Scouts went off into the tinder dry woods to have a smoke and ignited a dandy brush fire which nearly destroyed the Mene Oto District Camp. Fortunately, the Forest Service Fire Crews were stationed at the Hollister Airport, and the Borate bombers where there within a few minutes to get the situation under control.

District Camporee, Troop 233, 1968

Eagle Scout Ed Fassett and Council President Robert Morris cut the 50th Anniversary Cake, Feb. 1970

50TH ANNIVERSARY UNDERWAY

The observance of the 50th Anniversary year of the Santa Clara County Council was kicked off February 10, with the Council dinner in honor of John D. Crummey, member of the Rotary Club committee which founded the Council in 1920. Some 350 Council Scouters and representative community citizens were in attendance....

W.J. Nicholson, past president of the Council, presented Mr. Crummey with a special award for over 70 years of service to his community ... the Silver Beaver Award for outstanding service to boyhood was given by Judge Marshall Hall and Austen Warburton, on behalf of the National Council.

President Bob Morris presented a special plaque to the San Jose Rotary Club for its role in organizing and financing the Council in its first year.

The Medal of Merit for Life Saving was presented to Sea Scout Richard B. Machado of SES 46. Cub Pack 132 under leadership of Cubmaster James Quiring conducted a special opening ceremony and Explorer Post 30, under leadership of Wayne Wright put on the closing ceremony.

The Order of the Arrow and members of the American Indians Traditions Club gave special dances; a tableau of the 50 years of Council program was given and Mr. Crummey spoke briefly on the early days of Scouting.

(Reprint: Santa Clarion, 3/70)

RALLY

Thousands upon thousands of boys, parents and friends of Scouting witnessed a spectacular opening "parade of flags," heard the booming of the salute cannon and visited the hundreds of displayed articles, the Jamboree-style Camporee, the demonstration of Cub activities at this climax event celebrating our 50 years of service to Boyhood.

Thomas Fletcher, City Manager of San Jose, headed a powerful committee that put on this tremendously successful activity. It will go down in history as one of the greatest spectacles in our colorful Scouting history. Its success can be measured by the fact that more than 5,000 50th Anniversary Patches were distributed and that additional thousands had to be placed on "back order" until we can have more made and shipped to us. Our congratulations and thanks for a job well done to all those who helped make it the "biggest show in town."

(Reprint: Santa Clarion, 11/70)

JOHN COX, M.D.

In the Nation's bicentennial year ... we had a big council camporee down at Frank Bernard's ranch near Hollister with about 4,000 boys. I was asked to do the campfire programs for the boys and the visitors, so I wrote and produced two programs. On Thursday night we did the story of Johnny Boy Scout, and then on Saturday night we put on a big historical extravaganza with a large stage under those beautiful oak trees. This was a pageant of the history of the country; it was a big spectacular. Then we put on a similar show again in 1980 for the Scouting Extravaganza held at Calero Reservoir.

BICENT-O-REE

It was truly a fantastic Scout camping experience! More than 2500 Scouts and Scouters were encamped at the Bernard ... (Ranch) for four days at the end of last month, participating in the Bicentennial Jamboree of the Santa Clara County Council. The countless hours of work that were spent by the steering and operating committees paid off in the truly quality program. It is impossible to recognize everyone that it took to make this encampment a success, however, a special thanks must be extended to General Chairman Mike Bernard, Vice Chairman Andrew J. Bonfield, Chief Campmaster Jim Staehs, Deputy Chief Campmaster Tony Ernat, Assistant Campmaster/Administration Jim Sturrock, Assistant Campmaster/Events Larry Herpel and Assistant Campmaster/Support Forces George Beekman. Every Scout and Webelos Scout will long remember his bicentennial camping experience—the campfire shows, the spectacular events, and the fun and fellowship of Scouting in the year 1976.

(Reprint: Santa Clarion, 7/76)

THE SAGA OF JOHNNY BOY SCOUT
John E. Cox, M.D.

The Bicent-O-Ree opening Campfire Show, at Bernard Ranch near Hollister, on Thursday night, June 24, (1976) was preceded by the Pledge of Allegiance, the Scout Oath and an invocation.

The show was "The Saga of Johnny Boy Scout," a story of the experiences of a new Scout with that unlikely name. He passes his tests in a grandiose manner. When asked what he knows about the history of the flag, he calls in a contingent of Marines to help show what he has learned. The detachment of U.S. Marines from Moffett Field produced a beautiful and thrilling pageant of the American flag....

Johnny experiences his Tenderfoot Investiture Ceremony, as the Scout song, "On My Honor," is sung (via recording) by the Air Force Academy Glee Club.

Johnny receives his Eagle badge in an appropriate ceremony.

The closing act was a campfire scene, with songs. As the Scoutmaster tells the Baden-Powell story, little vignettes of his life are visible at the rear of the stage. At bedtime, Johnny looks up at his Scoutmaster, and his admiration for Scout leaders is expressed. The sound of taps in the clear summer night closes the show.

The only dialogue heard came from a narrations booth, offstage. "Johnny Boy Scout" was wonderfully played by Ken Emanuel of Troop 535, who developed every bit of audience reaction possible. Johnny's voice was carried by Fred Hurt, also of Troop 535.

Dean Ladd, Commissioner of Redwood District, performed excellently as the Scoutmaster, while his lines were delightfully narrated by Robert Quincy, Scout Chairman of Mene Oto District.

The Saturday night closing campfire show had over 200 in the cast. It was an historical pageant of scenes from the west and east, starting with Indians and culminating with the Eagle module landing on the moon. The scenes were accompanied by projected slides, taped musical scores, and a narration most professionally done, by Tom Woods of radio station KLOK .... The Show Staff consists of: Director, John E. Cox, M.D.: Assistant Director, Dean Ladd; Production Manager, Ray Ryan; Stage Manager, Ray Ryan, Jr. (and many others)....

District Campsite, Bicent-O-Ree

EXPLORING

Bicent-O-Ree — It was exciting to see so many qualified and hard-working Explorers providing support services at the recent Council Bicent-O-Ree held in Hollister. George Beekman, Post 107, is to be commended for the outstanding job he did in organizing and supervising the over 60 Explorers and adults. Other involved in making the support services possible were: Kathy Shaw, First Aid; Marv Castle, Security; Steve Silva, Traffic; Greg Brown, Over-all Explorer Advisor, and Photography; Mike Flaherty, Communications; Fred Bailey, Fire Control ... fire engine, courtesy of the City of Campbell. Also, the Green Berets. Thanks again to all of you. You truly helped to make the event a success.

(Reprint: Santa Clarion, 9/76)

SCOUTING EXTRAVAGANZA

Come join in on the Scouting Anniversary Celebration of 1980 at the Scouting Extravaganza to be held at Calero Reservoir County Park on the weekend of May 30–June 1, 1980.

The Scouting Extravaganza is four events in one. The four events include the Cub Scout Rally ...; the Webelos Encampment ...; the Boy Scout Camporee ...; and the Explorer Adventure....

The fees for the Extravaganza are $2.50 for Cub Scouts; $3.50 for Webelos Scouts; $5.00 for Boy Scouts; and $3.00 for Explorers. Adult Leaders pay the same as the boys in their unit do. The fee includes such items as a patch, insurance and program materials. Note: the fee does not include food.

Units will receive iron-on decals for all boys and adults whose fees are paid in full on or before April 18, 1980....

The year 1980 will see the 50th Anniversary of Cub Scouting, 60th Anniversary of the Santa Clara County Council, and the 70th Anniversary of the Boy Scouts of America. The Scouting Extravaganza will add to these Scouting anniversaries....

(Excerpt: Santa Clarion, 3/80)

Ready for Camp

Scouting Extravaganza, 1980

DIAMOND JUBILEE JAMBOREE SCOUTS ON DISPLAY

If you were not at Ed Levin Park in Milpitas on October 13th you missed one of Scouting's greatest events. Over 4,000 Tiger Cubs, Cub Scouts, Webelos, Boy Scouts, Varsity Scouts, Explorers and Leaders celebrated Scouting's 75th Anniversary at the Diamond Jubilee Jamboree.

Scouts of all ages participated in morning activities, watched an aerobatic show, at noon they visited the midway merit badge demonstration and in the afternoon they were awed by the spectacular hang glider exhibition.

Three young men from Pack 191 won the Cub Scout Physical Fitness Championship held on Saturday morning. The winners were: Jered Daniels, Jason Daniels and Kevin Izu.

The day was drawn to a close by a spectacular arena show and over 7,000 watched this extravaganza to close the Diamond Jubilee Jamboree.

Scouting's family was on display to the general public and people of all ages saw that Scouting was alive and well.

(Reprint: Santa Clarion, 11/84)

District Gateway, Julibee Jamboree, 1984

75 EAGLE SCOUTS PARADE 75 FLAGS AT DIAMOND JUBILEE

The 5,000 Cub Scouts, Boy Scouts, Explorers and parents watching the Santa Clara County Council's Jubilee Jamboree show got the thrill of a lifetime when Eagle Scout Craig Porter, of Post 708, led 75 Eagle Scouts onto the Jubilee stage. Each Eagle was carrying a United States flag that had been flown over the Capitol Building in Washington, D.C.

The flags were sponsored by local businesses and individuals as a salute to the 75th Anniversary of the Boy Scouts of America. The color guard and flag sponsorship sales were organized by the Santa Clara County Council Chapter of the National Eagle Scout Association to further the spirit of Scouting in our Council. A portion of the net proceeds will be gifted to the Council and a portion will go to establish an annual scholarship fund. Beginning with the Eagle class of 1985, a college scholarship of ... $1,000 will be given....

(Reprint: Santa Clarion, 11/84)

JAMES STURROCK

These special camporees (i.e. the Bicent-O-Ree) became a tradition and we began to have them every 4th year. In June '80 we held the "Scouting Extravaganza" at Calero Reservoir County Park under the leadership of Bob Anderson, VP for Scouting. This was followed in October '84 with the "Diamond Jubilee Jamboree" held at Ed Levin County Park to celebrate the BSA's 75th Anniversary, again under Andy Bonfield's leadership. An event was being planned for '88, but a decision was made to postpone it until 1990 to coincide with the council's 70th Anniversary. The 70th Anniversary Celebration/Camporee has been scheduled to be held at Ed Levin County Park in October 1990 with Earl Burke as chairman.

1st National Jamboree, 1937 and
12th National Jamboree, 1989

National Jamborees

❦────────────────────────────❦

RAY SCHMIDT

(as told to interviewer) I attended the first National Jamboree (in Washington, D.C.). It was supposed to take place in 1935 but was cancelled because of a polio outbreak in Washington, and it was rescheduled for 1937.

The people who reviewed us were President Franklin Roosevelt, Secretary of the Interior Harold Ickes and Secretary of Labor Madam Frances Perkins. I had the honor of carrying the Texas flag in the parade. When I got to the end of the parade a man said to me, "'Do you know you are carrying the flag upside down?"

Our guide for our troop from South Texas was Lyndon Johnson. He was the secretary to the Congressman from Corpus Christi. He took us to see the Washington Senators baseball team, and to museums. We camped at Haines Point on the Potomac River for ten days.

After being in Washington, we went to Niagara Falls, West Point and New York City where we got to see Lou Gehrig. I still have my patches from the Jamboree and some newspaper clippings.

"The Brownsea Scouts"
National Jamboree, 1977

Most of our fathers worked for the railroad so we got passes. Otherwise we would not have been able to afford the trip, due to the still depressed economy of the nation. My trip expenses were underwritten by the local Rotary Club. Recently I saw one of the Scouts who was on the trip. He had become editor of Sports Illustrated.

Then came World War II, after which I worked for General Electric for 41 years. I have been a consulting engineer in San Jose since 1957. Here in the Santa Clara County Council I have been a Cubmaster at Booksin School. I have my Woodbadge training.

I have had two sons in the Scouts and have two grandsons in Scouts today.

(Doris Hambrick conducted this interview)

❦────────────────────────────❦

San Jose Troop 3 Gateway
National Jamboree, 1973

❦────────────────────────────❦

VINT MATTHEWS

I remember being chief physician for the Western Region at the 1957 Jamboree at Valley Forge, Pennsylvania. Japanese beetles in that area were an immense problem because they would crawl inside a human ear and cause chaos. The Army had assigned three otologists (ear specialists) to take care of the 300+ cases that developed in spite of the fact that all Scouts and Scouters had been warned to stuff their ears with cotton at bedtime.

The trip I went on to the 1960 Jamboree at Colorado Springs, Colorado, was interesting from a different standpoint. Those were the days when the delegates from the Western Region, a total of 1200 boys, occupied a whole train. As a member of the Santa Clara County Ferronologist Society, I had been able to obtain their private pullman coach which was hooked onto the end of the train for the use of the Scouters. Each night the train would stop at a pre-arranged spot and there would be some sort of activity for the 1200 restless boys that had been cooped up on the train all day.

They stopped at Winnemucca, Nevada and had a wonderful picnic in the town park. They had stopped in Portola, the railroad town, and in Salt Lake City, for a swim. It was a leisurely, enjoyable ride to Colorado Springs.

JAMBOREE

284 Scouts and their leaders are heading for the great National Jamboree being held at Farragut State Park in Idaho August 1 to 7th. Jamboree is different, exciting, challenging and relevant this year....

Staffing a Jamboree of 35,000 boys requires lots of adult volunteer help (in fact, over 8,000 men and older boys are already committed to staff positions). There are still a few positions open for campfire directors, staging personnel, lighting engineers, properties staff, competitive events supervisors, octathlon officials, obstacle course supervisors, Protestant and Catholic Chaplains, conservation and skill-o-rama personnel, boating, fishing and canoeing personnel, hiking, archery, riflery and lifeguards. Jamboree fees are $75. If you can serve at the Jamboree, please call the Scout Service Center for an application. It's a "once in a lifetime" opportunity.

(Reprint: Santa Clarion, 6/73)

*Sunnyvale Troop 478 Gateway
National Jamboree, 1973*

JAMES STURROCK

In July 1973 I attended the 8th National Jamboree at Farragut State Park, Idaho, and served as the Sub-Camp Commissioner of one of the 15 sub-camps. That year was the only time that a jamboree had been held at two different sites simultaneously. The other site was Moraine, Pennsylvania. The combined total made

Council Troop Gateway   National Jamboree, 1977

this the largest jamboree attendance (to date) of some 70,000. Also, this had been the only time when regular chartered troops, or patrols from troops, were allowed to attend. Santa Clara County Council sent the equivalent of ten full troops. I was in charge of the pre-jamboree training for this group and we held a Mini-Jamboree for this purpose at the County Fair Grounds.

In July 1977 I attended the 9th National Jamboree at Moraine, Pennsylvania where we had "More Rain" than we could handle. I served on the Regional staff involved with running activities and demonstrations. Santa Clara County Council had one troop in attendance.

In July '81 it was off to another jamboree, the 10th National Jamboree at Fort Andrew P. Hill, Virginia. This time I served as the Sub-Camp Commissioner for our Area 3 camp in the Western Region. Santa Clara County Council had two full troops at this jamboree.

In October '84 I was appointed chairman of the Council's '85 National Jamboree Committee and continued until after all jamboree affairs were completed. (And) we were off to the 11th National Jamboree in July '85. It was at Fort A.P. Hill again with two full troops. This time, however, I attended only part time as chairman of the council committee, and to observe our troops' operation.

JAMBOREE

Plans are currently underway for the 9th National Jamboree to be held at Moraine State Park, near Butler, Pennsylvania from August 3-9, 1977. The Santa Clara County Council will be allowed to send three provisional troops, or a total of 108 Scouts and 12 leaders. This will be a Leadership Development Jamboree, according to Andrew J. Bonfield, council Vice President for Special Events. For Scouts to qualify for participation they must be at least 12 years old and a First Class Scout by April 1, 1977. (They must) have earned the Hiking, Camping, First Aid, and Cooking Skill Awards, and have been active in (their) troop for at least six months....

The jamboree troop Scoutmaster must have served as Scoutmaster for at least one year during the three year period prior to April 1, 1977 and have been awarded the Scouter's Key or have completed the Wood Badge course prior to April 1, 1977....

The Jamboree will include a total of 40,000 participants from across the United States and representation from 109 Scout Associations from around the world.... The Jamboree fee has been set at $130 for the encampment, with the costs for transportation, equipment, uniforms, etc., not yet determined.

(Reprint: Santa Clarion, 6/76)

1981 NATIONAL SCOUT JAMBOREE

Thousands of Boy Scouts and Leaders will come together for a national encampment on July 29–August 4, 1981 at Fort A.P. Hill, Virginia, near Fredricksburg.

The contingent from the Santa Clara County Council will be made up of two troops. Each troop of 36 Boy Scouts will have four adult leaders who have been selected because of their experience and dedication to Scouting and its ideals. This group will travel to Virginia by air, leaving about July 20, 1981. The trip will probably include tours to Washington, D.C., Yorktown, Williamsburg, and possibly New York.

Activities at the Jamboree will include archery, orienteering, obstacle courses, physical fitness, conservation, marksmanship, swimming, boating, canoeing, handicapped awareness trail, competitive events, merit badge midway, and arts and science fair.

The Boy Scout ... (must) participate in a 3-day training experience; file a personal health and medical record prior to the pre-jamboree training; have been active in a troop for at least 6 months

prior to July 1, 1981; be approved by his Scoutmaster.

The total cost will be about $1,000 which includes the jamboree fee, transportation, troop equipment, pre-jamboree training, tours and insurance....

(Reprint: Santa Clarion, 4/80)

On the way at last!
To the 1985 National Jamboree

THE GREATEST SCOUTING ADVENTURE
Jim Horner, Scoutmaster, N.J. Troop 821

On July 15th at 11:30 P.M., sixty-five boys and eight adult leaders began one of our greatest Scouting adventures. We were on our way to the Eleventh National Jamboree at Fort A.P. Hill, Virginia.

Our first stop was in Philadelphia, Pennsylvania, where we saw the Liberty Bell and Independence Hall. The next day we went on to Baltimore, Maryland, and stopped to see Fort McHenry; then on to Annapolis and a tour of the Naval Academy. (That) evening we took a candlelight tour of Williamsburg....

The next day we were up at 7 A.M. and on our way for a ... cruise of the James River, ... then on to Washington, D.C. ... for a tour of all the memorials ... On Saturday morning ... we saw the White House, Capitol, Smithsonian Institute (Air and Space, American History, Natural History, etc.) as well as the National Archives and the Pentagon ... On Monday morning we went to the Capitol where we had the honor of meeting our Congressmen Norman Mineta and Don Edwards. We (had) held our

Scouts own service at Arlington National Cemetery on Sunday morning, and saw the changing of the guard at the tomb of the Unknown Soldiers…. After leaving the Capitol on Monday at noon, we were finally on our way to Fort A.P. Hill.

Once at the Jamboree site we had a lot to do; we spent the first day setting up camp and getting ready for the interesting weather. There was so much to do at the Jamboree, there wasn't enough time to do or see it all. There was the Merit Badge Midway, the Boy's Life Exhibit, Three Trading Posts and Program Areas, not to mention the storms. Many of the Scouts had the chance to meet Green Bar Bill at the Boy's Life booth and got him to sign their Scout Handbooks. Patch and pin trading was of major interest to most of the Scouts, and they made some good trades and good friends. The opening show featured the Beach Boys and the closing show featured the Oakridge Boys. Nancy Reagan spoke to the Scouts at the closing show, also.

Well, that about covers it in a small way. I think we all had a good time and learned a great deal about Scouting and ourselves.

Happy 75th Boy Scouts and many more.

(Reprint: Santa Clarion, 9/85)

Council Troop 821 Gateway National Jamboree, 1985

National Jamborees

0. 1935 — Washington, D.C. (cancelled due to infantile paralysis epidemic)
1. 1937 — Washington, D.C. (Invitation of President F.D. Roosevelt)
2. 1950 — Valley Forge, Pennsylvania
3. 1953 — Irvine Ranch, California
4. 1957 — Valley Forge, Pennsylvania
5. 1960 — Colorado Springs, Colorado
6. 1964 — Valley Forge, Pennsylvania
7. 1969 — Farragut State Park, Idaho
8. 1973 — Farragut State Park, Idaho & Moraine State Park Pennsylvania
9. 1977 — Moraine State Park, Pennsylvania
10. 1981 — Fort Andrew P. Hill, Virginia
11. 1985 — Fort Andrew P. Hill, Virginia
12. 1989 — Fort Andrew P. Hill, Virginia

World Jamborees

JAMBOREE

Mike Brady and Glen Fitzsimmons of San Jose and Ted Brown of Cupertino will lead a contingent of Boy Scouts to Canada next summer as part of a powerful show of international friendship, the XV World Scout Jamboree.

The Jamboree is expected to draw 15,000 Scouts from around the world to a picturesque campsite 50 miles west of Calgary in the foothills of the Canadian Rockies July 4-14, 1983. There, under the theme "The Spirit Lives On" Scouts from Argentina and Great Britain, from Israel and Egypt, from Zaire and Zimbabwe will break bread together, compete in events, trade tokens of friendship and learn more about each other.

Some 4,000 boys and leaders from the United States will attend, representing all 415 local councils associated with the Boy Scouts of

America. Mike Brady will serve as our council's contingent leader and Scoutmaster.

At the Jamboree, these Scouts will immerse themselves in action-packed activities such as river rafting, gold panning, archery, wilderness hiking, trap shooting, orienteering, lumberjack challenges and special contests. There will be competition in a dozen sports. And there will be a day at the famous Calgary Stampede, the granddaddy of rodeos.

World Jamborees are held once every four years. Next year's event will be the second held in Canada. That country hosted the 8th World Jamboree in 1955. The 12th World Jamboree was held in the United States in Idaho in 1967.

(Reprint: Santa Clarion, 12/82)

XVI. WORLD SCOUT JAMBOREE

The XVI. World Scout Jamboree will be held near Sydney, Australia. The site is Cataract Scout Park, which is 44 miles south of Sydney in the state of New South Wales. The park is a magnificent site of approximately 300 acres situated in scenic Australian bushland on a ridge overlooking the headwaters of the Georges River. It will be held from December 30, 1987 to January 10, 1988 (summertime in Australia) ....

Using the theme "Bringing the World Together," Scouts will test skills with fellow participants from many countries ... Activities include bush craft, commando course, cycle cross and trail bike riding, pioneering, and mud and water slides.... Off-site activities at nearby South Coast beaches and lakes include surfing ... sailing, water skiing, rafting and wind surfing.

MAURICE TRIPP, D.S.

I was Camp Director at the World Jamboree at Farragut, Idaho (1967). I attended the World Jamboree in Godollo, Hungary in 1933 and in Coldstream, England in 1957.

I had an interesting encounter with Lady Baden-Powell. She was my guest at the World Jamboree because I had escorted her son to the National Jamboree at Colorado Springs before he died. So when Lady Baden-Powell came over here she was our guest (both at our home and at the World Jamboree) and we had a lot of interesting experiences with Baden.... She was a charming lady and it was fun being her host.... I remember she couldn't drink out of a drinking fountain and would have to have a cup. I had a little collapsible plastic cup that folded up in my pocket. I carried it at all times so she could drink.

Lady Baden-Powell
World Jamboree, 1967

World Jamborees

1. 1920 — Olympia, London, England
2. 1924 — Copenhagen, Denmark
3. 1929 — Arrowe Park, Birkenhead, England
4. 1933 — Godollo, Hungary (former royal hunting preserve)
5. 1937 — Vogelenzand, Holland
6. 1947 — Moisson, France (between Paris and Rouen)
7. 1951 — Bad Ischl, Salzberg, Hungary
8. 1955 — Niagara-on-the-Lake Ontario, Canada
9. 1957 — Sutton Park, Birmingham, England
10. 1959 — Makiling Park, Philippines
11. 1963 — Marathon, Greece
12. 1967 — Farragut State Park, Idaho, U.S.A.
13. 1971 — Nippon, Japan
14. 1975 — Lillehammer, Norway
15. 1979 — (scheduled for Iran, but cancelled)
15. 1983 — Calgary, Canada
16. 1987 — Sydney, Australia

Fund Raising Events

Several times a year Scouters get together to raise funds to help finance the council operation.... The popular Scout-O-Ramas have been an annual event eagerly anticipated by all age groups. In the last few years successful events were planned that involved the Scouters such as the annual Golf Tournament and the Distinguished Citizens Dinner. Both functions have provided a clear view of the supporters of Scouting to the community at large.

Scout-O-Ramas are unique in that they are a major annual program activity as well as a fund raising source. Rallies, the Scout Circus and similar events have been held in most councils since the early years of Scouting. There is no record of the earliest such event in the Santa Clara County Council, but in the 1950s Scout Circuses and Scout-O-Ramas were held in alternate years at the San Jose State University Spartan Stadium. The last event at the stadium was the last Scout Circus in 1958.

Scout-O-Ramas were held at the Santa Clara County Fairgrounds continuously from 1959 through 1987. In 1988 the Scout-O-Rama event was moved to the newly opened San Jose Convention Center.

WILLIAM PURSELL

The first council event I went to here was a Scout Circus we held (in 1958) at San Jose State (University). It was in lieu of the Scout-O-Rama. At that time every other year we did a Scout Circus. We never went back to State after that. It (the Circus) was fantastic with Don Hines and his Cub Scouts. He was the butterfly collector and they were butterflies. Each kid made big butterfly wings (it was the simplest thing in the world), and he was running all over the field trying to catch them in an oversized net! It was a lot of fun. I don't think we ever did have a circus again.

Cub Scout Pack Scout-O-Rama Display 1961   Photo: Pat Reilley

Scout-O-Rama Ticket Sale

SCOUT-O-RAMA

If the Santa Clara Valley public wanted to know how extensive our environmental pollution problems were or to get some ideas on how Cubs, Scouts, Explorers and their families can help solve these many problems, then the 1971 Scout-O-Rama sure filled the bill.

Dom Cortese, Chairman of the Board of Supervisors and this year's Scout-O-Rama Chairman, waxed enthusiastic about the number of Units participating, the quality of the booths and the displays, and the thousands and thousands of people that poured into the Fairgrounds each and every hour.

The Scout-O-Rama Committee composed of Bill Heiss, Larry Hill, Sheriff Jim Geary, Judge John Racanelli, Dick Stark, Bob Dietz, and the more than 50 distinguished men who served as judges did one of the best jobs ever in the history of the Scout Council. Our sincere appreciation to this fine crew.

It was especially gratifying to have our good friends, Mr. and Mrs. R.R. Stuart, as honored guests at our Scout-O-Rama. They have maintained a keen interest in our Council program over the years. They are pleased with our multiuse Camp Stuart throughout the year and are happy to know of our plans to continue to increase the summer use of this fine camp in the years ahead.

(Reprint: Santa Clarion, 6/71)

SCOUT-O-RAMA

Our 1974 show was the biggest and best ever held. More Packs, Troops and Posts had booths and exhibits, more people came to see the show, and boys sold more tickets than ever before.

A Cub in a Morgan Hill pack won a 10 speed bike in the Mystery House contest and Victor Sale of Troop 240 in San Jose sold the most tickets winning a trip to Disneyland for him and his parents.

Dom Cortese, Chairman of the 1974 Scout-O-Rama, wished to convey his thanks to all those boys who did such a whale of a job selling those tickets, and to the Ticket Sales Chairman in the pack and troop for their efforts, and to the 17-man Scout-O-Rama Steering Committee that spent nearly 6 months preparing the Show. No participant was disappointed, and our visitors were impressed with the hundreds of fine exhibits.

(Reprint: Santa Clarion, 7/74)

Opening Ceremony, Scout-O-Rama 1963

SCOUT-O-RAMA '79

... This year's Scout-O-Rama will feature the new Arts and Crafts Fair, giving every registered Cub Scout, Boy Scout, Explorer and adult the opportunity to enter individual projects for display.... Ribbons will be awarded for participation, with one ribbon presented to each participant....

Categories:
* Photography — Photographs or slides you have taken....
* Art and Crafts — Any hand-crafted items— paintings, wood or leathercraft.
* Models — Model rockets, planes, cars, villages, etc. that have been built by the participant.
* Neckerchief slides — Carved, tooled, molded— handcrafted neckerchief slides made from any materials.
* Pinewood Derby Cars — anything goes in this category—antique cars, covered wagons, fire engines, banana cars, etc. so long as it would go down a Pinewood Derby track....

(Excerpt: Santa Clarion, 4/79)

SCOUT-O-RAMA

The Wonderful World of Scout-O-Rama is coming your way on May 6, 1978.... The General Chairman for this year's show is County Supervisor Rod Diridon ...
WHAT IS A SCOUT-O-RAMA?

- A one-day Scouting Extravaganza Show at the Fairgrounds featuring booth displays by all of the Packs, Troops and Posts in Santa Clara County Council, Boy Scouts of America.

- A chance for Packs, Troops and Posts to show each other just how great their own unit's program is.

- An opportunity for Cub Scouts and Scouts to earn valuable prizes through selling Scout-O-Rama tickets.

- An opportunity for Packs, Troops and Posts to add significantly to their treasury through the ticket sales revenue sharing plan.

- A powerful recruiting tool for new membership and leadership—an opportunity for ... interested Scout-age boys to come and see first-hand what Scouting is all about.

- An important source of revenue to help finance the Santa Clara County Council and continue to provide the Scouting Program to the youth in the Santa Clara County area.

(Excerpt: Santa Clarion, 3/78)

A SPECIAL BICENTENNIAL SCOUT SALUTE!

The Santa Clara County Council salutes the producers, directors, editors, cameramen, audio-visual technicians, projectionists, sound engineers, and all-around great Scouters who made the special bicentennial multi-media show "This is My Country—a Salute to Scouting and America" possible. The show was the highlight of both the Scout-O-Rama and the Scout-O-Rama luncheon this year, featuring 1500 slides, ten projectors, a 50 foot by 20 foot screen, and untold hours of hard work. Our special bicentennial Scout Salute goes to Council Vice President for Scouting Jim Staehs, Associate with McFarland Associates; Activities Committee Member Ken Curzon, Service Manager, Smythe European Mercedes-Benz; and Terry Spooner of the Council Staff. Thank you for a job well done.

(Reprint: Santa Clarion, 6/76)

Distinguished Citizen Honoree 1982
Enide Allison with Former President Gerald Ford

ENIDE ALLISON, HONOREE, DISTINGUISHED CITIZEN AWARD

Enide Allison, president of Allison Motors, will be honored as the 1982 recipient of the Santa Clara County Council's Distinguished Citizen's Award. The Scouting award will be presented ... November 23 at the banquet to be held at the Marriott Hotel in Santa Clara. Don Lucas, Council board member will serve as chairman.

Allison is the first woman to receive this award ... (She is) extremely active in community work and spent many years as an adult raising funds for cultural community, and other nonprofit organizations. After the death of her husband in 1978, Allison assumed the leadership role for the car dealerships, and in 1981 Oak Tree Mazda was named number one in combined car and truck sales in the nation.

Founder of Women in Business, a group of business women who meet monthly to exchange views and discuss the role of women in today's business world, she is also active in the field of drug abuse....

(Reprint: Santa Clarion, 10/82)

(Ed. note: Former President and Eagle Scout Gerald Ford was featured speaker.)

1988 DISTINGUISHED CITIZEN AWARD

Ray A. Silva, chairman of the Special Events Committee, is proud to announce the selection Kimball W. Small, of Kimball Small Properties, as the 16th recipient of the Santa Clara County Council's Distinguished Citizen Award. Mr. Small will be presented the .. award on ... November 22, 1988, at the San Jose Fairmont Imperial Ballroom. Tickets to the 14th annual black tie dinner will be $150 each....

Past recipients of the Distinguished Citizen Award include:

1975 — Dr. Frank S. Bernard
1976 — P. Anthony Ridder
1977 — William R. Hewlett
1978 — Glenn A. George
1979 — Stan Chinchin
1980 — Father Walter Schmidt
       Rabbi Joseph Gitin
       Reverend Philip Barrett
1981 — Halsey C. Burke
1982 — Enide Allison
1983 — Robert A. Fuhrman
1984 — Thomas T. Vais
1985 — Jan W. Passmore
1986 — Robert M. Hosfeldt
1987 — Donald L. Lucas

(Excerpt: Santa Clarion, 9/88)

(Ed. note: the 1988 Distinguished Citizen Award recipient was Kimball W. Small, the 1989 Distinguished Citizen Award recipient was Ray A. Silva.)

CHAMPIONSHIP GOLF EVENTS

"Swing a Club for Scouting" is the theme of the First Annual Boy Scout Pro-Am Golf Tournament to be held ... June 19, 1981 at the Saratoga Country Club. The tournament is designed to involve individuals and businesses in Scouting while having fun. Centered around playing with a "lady pro," the tournament will host a field of 60 amateurs and 15 professionals.

Entry fee for the event is $50 which includes a buffet lunch, tee prizes, golf cart and green fees. Other activities include hole-in-one, longest drive, and closest to the pin contests.

Businesses are involved by providing contest prizes as well as co-sponsorship or tee sponsorship. Tee sponsorships, which include one player spot is $200. Co-sponsorship is $1,000 which includes four player spots.

The 12:30 shot gun start will be preceded by a buffet lunch.

(Reprint: Santa Clarion, 5/81)

SCOUT MEMORABILIA AUCTION

Big collectors, small collectors, Woodbadgers, avid Scouters ... come one, come all to the Santa Clara County Boy Scout Memorabilia Auction, January 30, Agnews Auditorium.... Highlighting the event are patches, books, O.A. memorabilia, Knights of Dunamis paraphernalia, clothing and mementos from more than 66 contributors. Included is a personal, handwritten letter from Baden-Powell, and prize possessions from former Chief Scout Executive Alden Barber.

Chairing the fund raising event is Lester Steig, Council Executive Board member and active National Board member. Other Committee members include Ray Ewan, Bob Chapman, Bill Powell, Lyle Bull, Bill Adams, Glenn Helberg, Jim Daulton, Muffy Williams, Judy Griffin, Jim Sturrock, Jim Staehs, Maurice Tripp and Vinton Matthews.

More than 2,500 individual items have been identified and catalogued by the Women's Reserve for the auction. A sample of those items has been collated into a booklet available at the Council Service Center along with procedures for a mail or phone bid....

(Reprint: Santa Clarion, 1/82)

Order of the Arrow Ceremony, Camp Stuart

IV. Organizations and Special Programs

Introduction

From its earliest beginnings the Santa Clara County Council of the Boy Scouts of America has depended upon dedicated volunteer Scouters to orginate, develop and staff its many programs for the enrichment of the youth of the Santa Clara Valley. The following overview gives a brief history of the organizations and special programs encouraged and administered by this Council.

Boy Scout Memorial Foundation

The Boy Scout Memorial Foundation of the Santa Clara County Council was created on March 20, 1945 by a declaration of trust executed by the Council and the Trustees of the Foundation. The purpose of the Foundation was, "... to control, manage and administer, utilize, disburse and distribute all properties and funds accumulated to this Trust always in the best interest of the ... local Council...."

The founding Trustees who signed the Declaration of Trust were all community leaders of Santa Clara County. They were Chairman Charles Moore, and members, Robert Benson, John Crummey, Judge William James, Leland Madland, Fred Oehler and Senator Sanborn Young. Exactly a year later Articles of Incorporation were adopted in order to form a non-profit corporation.

The immediate goal of the Foundation was to raise a fund of $50,000 which was needed for the development of the San Lorenzo Scout Ranch and the John Brown Ranch, later called Camp Stuart. These camp properties had been deeded from the Council to the Foundation as provided by the Declaration of Trust.

Charles Moore was a very active chairman. In the early 1950s he spearheaded a drive to establish a Council Service Center. He raised funds, made contributions and generated enthusiasm for the project. On May 9, 1953 land for the service center was purchased from Kaiser Community Homes. The 4 lot parcel was located at the corner of Park and Newhall Avenues. Unfortunately, Chairman Moore died a week after ground breaking ceremonies took place in June.

The Council Service Center building was constructed mainly by volunteer labor and in-kind contributions from numerous building material companies. It was dedicated on February 7, 1954 and designated as the "Charles E. Moore Memorial Scout Building" by the Foundation Board. The founding chairman's outstanding leadership has never been forgotten.

Soon after the Foundation had been created, the San Lorenzo Scout Ranch property was sold in 1948. The Foundation continued the development of Camp Stuart, the 80 acre overnight camp in the Santa Cruz Mountain foothills above Saratoga, and Camp Hi-Sierra, the 100 acre summer camp near Yosemite in the Sierra Nevada Mountains between Longbarn and Pinecrest. In 1954, as these projects were being completed, two vacancies on the Board were filled by Fred Fletcher and Edmund Richmond.

When Santa Clara County Council Scout Executive Chester Bartlett retired in 1958, he continued to serve as Foundation secretary. His salary and expenses were paid by the Council which transferred the appropriate sum to the Foundation. The unused portion of this apportionment grew to $9,597 by 1975.

On the first of January, 1959, the Council began to pay the Foundation $125 per month rent for use of the Service Center. The Foundation then paid the real estate taxes, the insurance and building repairs, and completed the landscaping. The accrual from the rental payments took care of all those obligations—plus additional assessments on the Service Center, Camp Stuart and Camp Hi-Sierra.

Raymond Ewan, who succeeded Bartlett as the Council's Scout Executive, also succeeded him as Foundation secretary in 1961.

New tax laws decreed a fundamental change in the Memorial Foundation in May of 1966. It was necessary for the Council and the Foundation Trustees to create a Boy Scout Trust Fund to which all present and future Foundation funds would be transferred.

The current Trustees of the Foundation were to also serve as Trustees of the Trust Fund. At that time they included Dr. Frank Bernard, William Curtiss, Jr., Judge Marshall Hall, Edgar Jackson, Dr. Vinton Matthews, Robert Morris, Wilmot Nicholson, William Powell, Louis Ratzesberger, Jr., William Robertson and Austen Warburton. The Council was given the power to replace a trustee that "died, moved or refused to act."

By 1975 the Memorial Foundation had acquired $30,000 through bequests and gifts; had made a $7,000 grant to the Council to buy the Dose property addition to Camp Stuart; and had made a $5,000 grant to assist the Council to employ a Hispanic professional, in 1963, for special service to the Mexican-American youth of the valley.

In August 1973, Paul and Nessie Chesebrough donated 404 acres of forest land in the Santa Cruz Mountains north of Highway 9 and west of the summit. The property, soon named Camp Chesebrough, was the fourth parcel of land whose title was accepted by the Foundation. In 1983 the Chesebroughs generously donated an additional 140 acres to the Memorial Foundation.

In 1988 the Foundation Board carefully considered environmental, and other impacts on Camp Chese-brough, and then made the decision to upgrade the former logging property by selective thinning. Big Creek Lumber Company was contracted to harvest select Redwood and Douglas Fir trees that produced approximately a million board feet of lumber. The transaction resulted in an income of $109,000, the construction of year 'round roads and several new campsites on the property.

In recent years the Memorial Foundation has made interest bearing loans to the Council to offset deficits in its operating budget. Loans were repaid in a timely manner with leeway extended so that repayment would not adversely affect Scouting programs. At present the Foundation carries a $100,000 Council loan obligated in 1988. The Memorial Foundation has proven to be a great help to the efficient operation of the Santa Clara County Council. One long time contributor, for which they have been grateful, has been the Stella B. Gross Estate.

Other distinguished Scouters and community leaders, who have not yet been mentioned, have served as Trustees of the Foundation since 1979. They are Donald Allen, Jr., Andrew Bonfield, Jan Passmore, General Robert Huyser, Arthur Lund and John Lochner. They were joined by Trustees Nessie and Paul Chesebrough, Glenn George, Harry Goodfriend, Glen McLaughlin, Charles Munger, Jr., Albert Smith, and Eric Thorsen.

Alden G. Barber, retired Chief Scout Executive of the Boy Scouts of America, served as the Memorial Foundation Executive Director from 1979-84. He was succeeded by current Council Scout Executive Brian Allen. (A list of the Memorial Foundation members may be found in the Appendix.)

Camp Hi-Sierra, 1968

THE BOY SCOUT MEMORIAL FOUNDATION IN ACTION

In 1980 alone—Grants made possible:
- the cold storage of food at Camp Hi-Sierra;
- the replacement of a washed away camp fire amphitheater;
- Health Department-threatened sanitary facilities were replaced;
- excavation and repair of our small swimming and boating lake;
- platforms for tents for boys to sleep;
- and more.

Without this support this year and preceding years Boy Scouts literally would not have a summer camp.

• **Camp Stuart**—the greatest day camp in the world teetered on the brink of "No Water" and a grant from the Memorial Foundation provided for a well, pump and water storage.

• **Chesebrough Scout Reservation**—even unexplored wilderness needs potable water to allow for Scout use and a well and pump are under construction there—again because of the Memorial Foundation.

• At least 500 boys or more might have missed a chance to be a part of Scouting without the emergency financial support by the Founda-tion—filling an inflation-caused gap between expenses and the income that threatened the very existence of council service. Suppose one of those 500 had been your son....

(Excerpt: Santa Clarion, 12/80)

SME CAMPAIGN UNDERWAY

Under the direction of Council Sustaining Membership Enrollment (SME) Chairman Dell Boccignone, the 1988 campaign to raise $345,000 is underway. Our 1988 goal is a 9% increase over last year's goal, and the money raised will help provide a variety of services to the 32,000 youth expected to participate in Scouting in 1988.

The goal is divided into the following:
Family - $160,000;
Major Gift - $25,000;
Community - $70,000;
Challenge - $20,000;
Executive Board - $70,000.
Each division has its own leadership and organization responsible for attaining the totals.

The Family Campaign involves all the families of the youth that participate in Scouting. For a family contribution of $55. a boy will receive a discount on his summer camping program. The money in the Community, Board and Major Gifts Campaigns is contributed by businesses throughout Santa Clara County.... The timeline to reach our goal and celebrate our success is April 30 at the Scout-O-Rama....

(Excerpt: Santa Clarion, 1/88)

Sustaining Membership Enrollment

The Santa Clara County Council had been conducting successful sustaining membership campaigns for many years. However, in 1973, the National Council adopted a policy of encouraging local councils, on a nationwide basis, to offer an opportunity for the parents of the youth in Scouting to participate financially in sustaining the Boy Scout programs in their area.

It was to be the primary source of money needed to carry on the council's work with boys, units and leaders. In 1973 the Santa Clara County Council adopted the national plan and used the recommended four phases of the campaign which were council enrollment, district enrollment, community enrollment and family enrollment.

The following levels of giving were adopted: Benefactor-$5,000; Sponsor-$2,500; Guardian-$1,000; Patron-$500; Leadership-$250; Century-$100; Special and Family-$25.

Each year since 1973 approximately 75% of the Council's operating budget has come from its sustaining members. United Way of Santa Clara County has provided the other 25%.

Due to the success of the annual Sustaining Membership Enrollment campaigns the Council has been able to find new Scoutmasters, new Den Leaders in Cub Scout packs, merit badge counselors for vocational and hobby subjects, men and women who will organize new Scouting units, and to connect with members of other organizations who ask to use the Scouting programs for their own youth work.

COUNCIL FINANCE PROGRAMS MEET WITH WARM RECEPTION

How much is Scouting worth to you, your unit, your boys? "That's what the Family Sustaining Membership Enrollment (S.M.E.) Campaign is all about," states Ray Byrne, Council S.M.E. Chairman for 1981.

"Someone said, 'Nothing comes free.' As any other program this is true of Scouting. It costs our council to maintain our camps, provide District Executives, training materials, meeting notices, registration services, etc.," continues Ray.

The Family Campaign began February 1 and will be completed by March 15. Nearly 100% of the council Cub Scout packs, Boy Scout troops and Explorer posts are committed to reach each family in their unit and ask financial support for the council operations. A Family Sustaining Membership is $36 which entitles youth in that family to a reduced camp fee....

(Excerpt: Santa Clarion, 3/81)

Mene Oto District Camporee, 1966

PRESIDENT'S CLUB

BSA Executive/President's Club

The BSA Executive Club of the Santa Clara County Council was established in late 1967 to recognize individuals and firms that annually contributed more than $100 to the Council for its Boy Scout programs. Its originators were Council Executive Board members Patrick Peabody, Phillip Olson and Scout Executive Ray Ewan. They convinced William Adams, Jr., former Ponderosa District chairman, to assume responsibility for the new club's organization and promotion.

Chairman Adams scheduled a luncheon at the Sainte Claire Club in San Jose in May 1968. Past contributors and leaders of commerce, industry, education and government in the Santa Clara Valley were all invited. The informational luncheon filled the Sainte Claire Club to capacity and most of the attendees became charter members. Membership categories were: Benefactor-$5,000+; Sponsor-$2,500-$5,000; Guardian-$1,000; Patron-$500-$1,000; Leadership-$250-$500; Century-$100-$250.

The first project undertaken by the leadershp of the Executive Club in 1968 was in response to a Council-sponsored survey of ethnic minority boys in the Scouting program. The overall ratio of Boy Scouts to total number of available boys in the Council's service area was 1 in 4; in the East Side of the Council's service area it was 1 in 12!

By increasing the strength of the Executive Club to 131 members, the Club's funds and influence enabled it to hire two Spanish speaking Scouting professional staff members, plus adding two part-time para-professional staff. The end result by 1973 was a change in ratios. Scouting programs were now available to 1 in 5 of the youths in the Mexican-American community of San Jose's east side.

In 1970 the Council set up a new Explorer Division to improve provision of services to the growing number of young men and women aged 14 to 20 who were joining Explorer Posts. It seemed as if this might be another prime opportunity to help the Scouting program, so with the assistance of the Council's Scout Executive Ray Ewan, and his assistant Bob Chapman, the Executive Club prepared to launch a drive for funding the restructured Explorer Division. Under William Adams' able leadership the 1974 Executive Club had 212 members whose median contribution was $209 for a total of $44,344.

The Club assumed a low profile from 1975 to 1982 when it was re-activated by Council President Jan Passmore.

This seemed an ideal time to rename the club. The Council wanted to avoid the inference that a contributor to the Council had to be an executive. Thus the former BSA Executive Club became the new BSA President's Club. The idea of having the President's Club sponsor the annual Distinguished Citizen Dinner was enthusiastically endorsed by President Passmore, his Executive Board and the new Scout Executive, Brian Allen.

The eighth annual Distinguished Citizen Dinner in 1982, honoring Enide Allison, was the first to have the President's Club sponsorship. The event provided a showcase for marketing Scouting programs to prospective contributors and gave appropriate recognition to those who were contributors. The dinner program included all members of the President's Club by level of their contribution to the Council.

In 1987 in recognition of the effect of inflation on the value of money, the minimum level of contribution to the Council for membership in the President's Club was raised from $100 to $250. Two higher contributor levels were added: Pacesetter-$25,000+, and Distinguished-$10,000-$25,000. That year there were 5 Pacesetters, 3 Distinguished and 6 Benefactors. Total number of contributors was 592 with a median level of $948. Total contributions for 1987 were $561,250.

Past and present Council staff members that have been very supportive of the BSA Executive/President's Club include Assistant Scout Executive Robert Chapman, and Finance Directors Howard Robinson, Karen Weiseth and Jimmie Pickett, II.

(The BSA President's Club roster may be found in the Appendix.)

Scout Alumni Association

In late 1987 the Santa Clara County Council created the Scout Alumni Association for all former Boy Scouts and their parents, and adults who had, or were serving, in the local council or in another council as a Scouter. Annual dues are $25; the lifetime membership fee is $500. At the end of 1989 the Scout Alumni Association members were in the following categories: 50 annual, 5 lifetime, and 7 corporate members, plus 8 honorary members.

During 1988 the Alumni Association established a speakers bureau utilizing volunteers from the Bureau of Toastmasters International, District #4 who had been involved in Scouting. The speakers gave 21 service clubs a rundown on the Scouting programs of the Santa Clara County Council and advocated community support of these programs.

The Association is developing a membership application brochure and a Scout Alumni Survey. Its long range goal is two-fold: to provide the Council with a resource for Scouting positions, and to be a strong source of additional community support.

(The Scout Alumni Association roster as of December 31, 1989 may be found in the Appendix.)

Eagle Scout Association

In September, 1959, the Executive Board of the Santa Clara County Council authorized the formation of an Eagle Scout Association to be comprised of adult Eagle Scouts. The first official meeting of the Association was held October 27, 1959 when Richard Stark was elected President, James Sturrock, Vice President, Theodore Rogers, Secretary and Charles McNeil, Treasurer.

At this meeting committees were established to conduct Eagle Boards of Review, and to arrange the first annual Eagle Scout Recognition Dinner. At a prior organizational meeting it was decided that membership would be limited to persons over 21 who had earned the rank of Eagle Scout, or its equivalent; annual dues would be $2.00; and that the Eagle badge would be worn on a red, white and blue ribbon neck pendant.

The main purpose of the organization was to assist the Council in encouraging advancement of youths in Scouting to attain the rank of Eagle by
• providing Eagle Scout review teams;
• promoting recognition of Eagle Scouts by assisting in Courts of Honor;
• arranging the annual Eagle Scout Recognition Dinner;
• sponsoring the Knights of Dunamis, a fraternal organization for youth aged Eagle Scouts.

In 1957 a tradition was started whereby all Eagle Boards of Review were held at the Council level and all Eagle Scout candidates were reviewed by a board composed of adult Eagle Scouts only. The Association scheduled, staffed and conducted these reviews for the Council for almost ten years.

In 1967 the National Council delegated the Eagle Board of Review function to each Boy Scout troop committee. The association offered the services of its members to serve as "Guest Chairmen" to assist the troops in the transition period while learning to conduct Eagle Boards of Review.

The loss of one of the Association's main functions did not deter then President William Klee. He simply redirected the Association energies toward improving the Eagle Courts of Honor. The group also maintained a fund to give troops Eagle Badge presentation kits for their Courts of Honor.

An outstanding event sponsored by the Eagle Scout Association is the annual Eagle Scout Recognition Dinner. The first one was held at La Rinconada Country Club in Los Gatos in February, 1960 for 27 Eagle Scouts, class of 1959.

One of the most memorable dinners was in 1967 when Association President William Adams hosted more than 100 "new" Eagle Scouts and their sponsors. The featured speaker was former Olympian and Congressman Bob Mathias. Also memorable is the fact that former President Louis Bergna served as Master of Ceremonies at more than fifteen Recognition Dinners. Bergna, former Santa Clara County District Attorney, was the first recipient in the Santa Clara County Council, of the National Distinguished Eagle Scout Award.

The Eagle Scout Association suffered several setbacks starting in the mid-sixties. The first was an unsuccessful attempt to organize a chapter of the Knights of Dunamis, the National Order for young Eagle Scouts. In 1972 the National Eagle Scout Association started the decline of the local Eagle Scout Association (ESA) when it was unwilling to recognize already established council associations.

In 1975 the Council was issued a charter for a chapter of the National Eagle Scout Association, which effectively terminated the previous ESA chapter. Burton Corsen was elected the first chapter President. Corsen and several other members tried valiantly to continue activities that had been successful in the past, but somehow, its membership never regained the vitality of the former Association.

In November, 1979 the Council Chapter of the National Eagle Scout Association, and some former members of its predecessor, the Council Eagle Scout Association, celebrated the Chapter's 20th anniversary with a dinner meeting. During the dinner, Richard Stark, the Association's first President, recounted the illustrious history of the original Eagle Scout Association.

The following presidents of both groups were honored at the dinner:

E.S.A.: Richard Stark 1960
        John George 1961
        Paul Leedom 1962
        Samuel Miller 1963
        Kemp Allen 1964
        William Holms 1965
        Fred Logan 1966
        William Klee 1967
        Wm. J. Adams, Jr. 1968
        Henry Heckman 1969
        Louis Bergna 1970
        Harry Federico 1971
        Joseph Brown 1972
        Jerry Crosby 1973
        William Gallant 1974

N.E.S.A.: Burton Corsen 1975
          William Ritt 1976
          Richard DeVilbiss 1977
          Charles Orr 1978
          Donald Green 1979
                (last elected president)

Currently the annual Eagle Scout Recognition Dinner is arranged by a committee of adult Eagle Scouts appointed by the Scout Executive.

Order of the Arrow

HISTORY

In the early days of scouting some of the men who loved camping and the great outdoors joined together to promote camping within the Scouting organization. "The Order" was born in the summer of 1915 at the Philadelphia Council's new camp on Treasure Island in the Delaware River, north of Trenton, New Jersey. It became known as The Order of the Arrow, an honor society of campers that perpetuated Ernest Seaton's idealization of the American Indian.

As the organization has evolved, their main functions have been to honor the boys who have been chosen by their peers as the best campers, and to publish and distribute camping information.

The Miwok Lodge, No. 439, of the Order of the Arrow in Santa Clara County Council was chartered by the National Council of the Boy Scouts of America on June 15, 1950. Its totem was an eagle flying over a silver arrow. The Lodge was disbanded and its charter revoked by the National Council in October 1950. The apparent cause of the revocation was an injury of a Scout at one of the first Miwok Lodge events.

In 1963 the Executive Board of the Council authorized reactivation of the Order of the Arrow Lodge. The appointed organizing committee included Chairman Greg MacGregor, Fred Hilton and James Sturrock. They were assisted by Admiral Donald McKay, Lodge Advisor for the Oakland Area Council.

The National Council had issued a revised Order of the Arrow Handbook in 1960 and expected the newly appointed Lodge Advisor James Sturrock to establish and operate the new lodge "by the book."

The re-established Miwok Lodge of the Santa Clara County Council Order of the Arrow was assigned its former number 439 in March 1964. The Lodge adopted a Silver Fox as its new totem. The new Lodge immediately scheduled an election of Ordeal candidates by troops in the council. The first Miwok Lodge Ordeal for 88 Boy Scouts and 9 adult Scouters was held April 24-25, 1964, at Camp Stuart. Lodge officers were also elected.

The Macheck M'gult Lodge, No. 375, from the Oakland Area Council helped the fledgling Lodge by conducting the first Ordeal and the installation of lodge officers. Matt Follas, Post 347, was elected Lodge Chief; Marvin Bottom, Troop 425, Vice Chief; David Edgar, Troop 490, Secretary and Paul Hayes, Troop 484, Treasurer.

The Council Scout Executive Ray Ewan, who was also "Supreme Chief of the Fire" in the Order of the Arrow, appointed James Sturrock, Lodge Advisor, Jerry Collins, Assistant Lodge Advisor, and Don Gray, Staff Advisor.

Inductees into the Order, along with transfers from other lodges, brought the Lodge's total membership to 124 Arrowmen by the end of its first year.

Assistance was given by other lodges to help get Miwok Lodge off to a flying start. The Esselen Lodge, No. 531, of the Monterey Bay Area Council and the Royeneh Lodge, No. 282, of the San Francisco Area Council conducted consecutive investiture ceremonies for the first Brotherhood members and Vigil members.

During the first eight years the Miwok Lodge accomplished a great deal. Its Ordeal work parties constructed the ceremonial grounds and other sorely needed improvements at Camp Stuart. In recognition of this effort, and the many hours of service through camping promotions, and through the provision of staff for camporees and summer camps, Miwok Lodge received its first "Most Indian Lodge Award." It was given by Section W3A of the Order of the Arrow.

James Sturrock retired as Lodge Advisor in 1969 and was succeeded by Edward Gunion who served until 1977.

The 1970 Lodge Chief Frank Biehl spearheaded the building of a lodge hall at Camp Stuart and continued this effort for several years. The years of hard work by Lodge members and other Scouters culminated in the substantial building that stands on the hill above the ceremonial grounds. The Miwok Lodge Hall, a significant enhancement to Camp Stuart, was dedicated on August 23, 1976.

Another major project of the active 750 member Miwok Lodge was the 1973 production and distribution of over 1800 copies of a 107 page booklet called, "Where to go Camping." Evidently by 1974 the Lodge had proven its worth. It was honored by being called a National Standard Lodge. This designation has continued to the present.

The decade of the eighties witnessed extraordinary success of the Camping Promotion Committee, and although membership had declined, it was maintained at an acceptable level of 450 Arrowmen.

The Santa Clara County Council's Order of the Arrow Miwok Lodge, No. 439, has made an outstanding contribution of service to the youth of Santa Clara County in its first 25 years.

(Miwok Lodge Chiefs and Advisors roster may be found in the Appendix.)

MEMBERSHIP AND HONORS

Membership

After a Scout or Scouter has been elected as a candidate he must earn his entry into the lodge by undergoing an "ordeal." Then he is inducted during the Ordeal Ceremony as an Ordeal Member. After six months he may take a test to qualify him for induction into full lodge membership as a Brotherhood Member.

The Vigil Honor

The highest award in the Order of the Arrow, the Vigil Honor, cannot be earned. Nominees are selected by the Lodge Nominating Committee from those who have at least two years of membership and have demonstrated outstanding leadership and service. The award must be approved by the National Order of the Arrow Committee. The candidate then must complete his all night "vigil" and be inducted in the Vigil Ceremony.

Ordeal, Brotherhood and Vigil sashes are bestowed during impressive ceremonies, held separately for each award. Dr. E. Urner Goodman, founder of the Order of the Arrow, was the first recipient of the Vigil Honor.

(Miwok Lodge recipients of the Vigil Honor are listed in the Appendix.)

Wood Badge Training

"The pioneers of scouting realized that it was not enough that boys keenly desired to be Scouts, but also that leaders must be trained." That introduction began the book, *A History of Wood Badge in the United States,* published by the Boy Scouts of America in 1988.

Lord Robert Baden-Powell, the founder of Scouting, directed the first Wood Badge Course to train Scouting Leaders, in July 1919, at Gilwell Park in England. The park, on the edge of Epping Forest near London, offered an ideal setting for teaching the skills of Scouting. It was so successful that, through the years, thousands of Scouters from every Scouting nation of the world have made the pilgrimage to Gilwell Park for Wood Badge Training. The Course has also been exported to all countries that have a Scouting program for Wood Badge training.

In the thirties, James E. West, Chief Scout Executive of the Boy Scouts of America, escorted Lord Baden-Powell on a tour of the National Council's Schiff Scout Reservation in New Jersey. This tour led, in May of 1936, to the first Wood Badge courses conducted in the United States. However, the British orientation of the course was not popular here and the program was not repeated.

After World War II, Wood Badge Training was revived in the United States. The Wood Badge Course 1 was held in July 1948 at the Schiff Scout Reservation and was conducted by William "Green Bar Bill" Hillcourt, National Director of Scoutcraft. He also directed Course 2, held that October at the National Council's Philmont Scout Ranch in New Mexico, thus inaugurating successful Wood Badge Training in the United States.

The Scouting and Scoutcraft skills training was revised over the years. In 1967 the leadership skills concept was introduced; in 1979 Scoutcraft skills were re-emphasized.

In the mid-fifties the National Council permitted the training courses to be conducted by local councils. The first in the nation was given in 1953 by the Cincinnati Area Council. The first in Northern California was given in 1954 by the former San Francisco Area Council.

John Spencer, James Sturrock and William Sutcliff from Santa Clara County Council's Polaris District, attended regional Wood Badge Training course #114 held at Camp Chawanakee, Shaver Lake, California, in July 1959. In the late fifties and early sixties, many Council Scouters attended regional training courses. A roster of "Men of Gilwell," the name given to Scouters who had completed a Wood Badge course, included 56 Scouters from the Mene Oto, Pioneer, Polaris, Ponderosa and Redwood Districts of the Santa Clara County Council.

The interest of Scouters in this training resulted in the local Council conducting its first Wood Badge Course with Ted Rogers, Assistant Scout Executive, as director. Course #55-1 was held at Camp Hi-Sierra the week of August 25, 1966, with Jerry Collins as Senior Patrol Leader with four patrols of Scouter trainees. This has been followed by 24 Wood Badge Training Courses over the last 25 years involving Santa Clara County Council leadership.

The training courses have had the flexibility to adapt to changing needs of the Scout leaders and have always had top-notch leadership. Innovation has been attempted as in the 1973 cluster Wood Badge course, a joint venture of the Santa Clara County, Stanford Area, San Mateo and San Francisco Bay Area Councils. Course #W-9 given by the San Mateo County Council was held at its Cutter Scout Reservation. John Montgomery directed it, assisted by Anthony Ernat, Larry Herpel, Richard Kimrey and Frank Nixson from the Santa Clara County Council.

In 1976 women Scouters were invited to participate in the program. Marin County Council conducted the first Wood Badge Training Course in the Western Region to include women in May 1976. Santa Clara County Council's Course #WE3-55-18, held at Camp Stuart, was conducted in July and August with Larry Herpel, Director. While the course staff was largely from the Council, the trainees were from 7 different councils.

Records show that Karen Limes, from the Monterey Bay Area Council, was the first woman Scouter in the United States to have received her Wood Badge beads. She was followed by Santa Clara County Council's Judy Griffen and Carolyn Minker, who received theirs in February 1977. Bonnie Wilkinson was a Coach Counselor for a 1978 Wood Badge Course, thus becoming the first woman Scouter to staff a Santa Clara County Council course.

Most courses were conducted at Camp Hi-Sierra or Camp Stuart until the 1975 course held at the newly acquired Camp Chesebrough. This course was unique in that it was held totally in the wilderness of the Oil Creek Campsite. Since then most of the course have been given at the upper camp area of Chesebrough.

Due to the fact that Cub Scouting had become a viable part of the Scouting program by the mid-

WOOD BADGE

Why is it called 'Wood Badge'?

Wood Badge leadership training was originally presented by Baden-Powell for Scouting throughout the world. In recognizing the first learners, he awarded them each a wooden bead on a leather thong, from his African trophies, to be worn about the neck. Since then, it has been dubbed, "Wood Badge." Upon successful completion, a Scouter receives his certification and two beads, and becomes a member of Troop One, Gilwell, a group that numbers (in the) thousands in nations around the world....

What is Wood Badge?

Wood Badge is training in group leadership skills and operation. There are two parts to Wood Badge: the practical is an eight-day experience consisting of living with a group of Scouters in an outdoor/Scouting environment while being exposed to leadership and Scouting skills applicable in the development of both the individual and youth. Through this living/ working experience you develop a knowledge and understanding of leadership skills; what they are, how to use them, when each is appropriate, plus an intense personal motivation to apply these skills in the best way back home.

After the practical outdoor experience, a minimum of six months must elapse before your final certification. During this period you follow through on the commitment you made in the course of your practical experiences and are evaluated on your performance. Throughout this application phase you are assigned a counselor who acts as a resource man, as an evaluator and as your Scouting friend. He determines that you fully understand what you learned from the practical course and that you can apply it to the betterment of your Scouting position.

(Excerpt: Santa Clarion, 2/83)

seventies, Wood Badge Training for Cub Scouters was introduced as a separate program in 1977 by the National Council. In the Western Region the first course, #W-CS-1, was held at the Firestone Scout Reservation in Brea, California, in August 1977. Santa Clara County Council Scouter Glen Cantrell served as a Den Leader and remembers an intensive week-long staff indoctrination, followed by an exhaustive week-long course. Scouter Charles Bragga was there as a trainee.

The Cub Scout Wood Badge training courses are held only on the regional level. From 1977 through 1988 there were 21 Cub Scout Wood Badge training courses in the Western Region in which many trainees from the local council participated. Two Scouters, Loretta Shank and Elizabeth Sullivan, made history by traveling to Camp Pupukea, on the island of Oahu, Hawaii, to serve on a Cub Scout Wood Badge training course. Walt Stephenson was an instructor at regional Cub Wood Badge courses in 1989 and 1990.

Scouters who participated in these courses have returned with workable new ideas and valuable Scouting skills that have been a great asset to their own troops, packs and posts, and an overall benefit to the entire Santa Clara County Council.

(A list of the Council's 25 Wood Badge courses may be found in the Appendix.)

WOODBADGE '76—WOMEN SCOUTERS WELCOME!

The Santa Clara County Council will host a weekend Woodbadge Course to be held at Camp Stuart on the weekends of July 17 & 31 and August 14th. The course fee is $65.... Course Director Larry Herpel is assembling an outstanding staff. Training requirements are set for Scout Leaders, Committeemen, District Council Scouters.... A detailed flyer will be sent to all Scouters but clear your vacation schedule now.

(Reprint: Santa Clarion, 4/76)

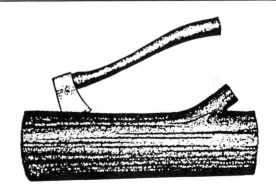

Women's Reserve

The Women's Reserve of the Santa Clara County Council, Boy Scouts of America, was formed in 1962 by six women, Eileen Brutsche, Carroll Favorite, Elaine Ho, Helen Hurt, Vi Schneider and Gertrude Wright. Each was either active in the Scout program herself, or was associated with a family member who was active.

The purpose of the Women's Reserve has been to provide a variety of services which would aid the Council office staff and District Executives. Women's Reserve members have met at the Council Service Center, generally on Tuesday mornings, to prepare large group mailings—folding, sorting, stuffing, addressing—and to help with general clerical work.

The Women's Reserve has also provided invaluable assistance at major Scouting functions of the Council including Scout-O-Ramas, Distinguished Citizen Dinners, Eagle Scout Recognition Dinners, Cub Scout Leaders Pow-Wows, and many other Council-sponsored functions.

Sample years when records of volunteer hours were reported: 1973 tallied 2,000+ hours; 1983 hours totaled 2,143. In recognition of this dedicated service the Women's Reserve has received many commendations. Beginning in 1972 the Santa Clara County Council noted the service of several of its long time members by bestowing upon them the Council's highest award for women, the Silver Fawn. Since 1975, the Silver Fawn has been replaced with the Silver Beaver Award.

Women's Reserve recipients of the Silver Fawn/ Silver Beaver Award:

Eileen Brutsche	Vickie Jones
Nessie Chesebrough	Helen Keyes
Vera Chronert	Jan Lewis
Glenna Corsen	Carolyn Minker
Beth Crane	Jane Reed
Carroll Favorite	Joan Reynolds
Jean Goodman	Vi Schneider
Judy Griffin	Diane Stalions
Alice Helberg	May Tindall
Elaine Ho	Muffy Williams
Helen Hurt	Donna Wood

Cub Scout Shelter Program Leaders
Star Baker, Mary Clarke, May Tindall, 1989

Eileen Brutsche, one of the founding members of the Woman's Reserve, was an inspiration to other volunteers for many years. Then she turned her energies toward assisting the program as a council staff member and registrar for 24 years before retiring in 1983. Another early member, Jan Lewis, had, as a volunteer since 1967, been focused on assisting with Scout-O-Rama. In 1978 Jan Lewis became the council receptionist and in 1984 she took on the job of office manager.

Diane Stalions, effective as a Sustaining Membership Enrollment chairman at both Mene Oto District and council levels, was Trading Post Manager for four years in the early 1980s.

Another Silver Beaver recipient, Beth Crane, moved out of traditional Woman's Reserve activities by organizing the successful Memorabilia Auctions in 1981 and 1982. She remains active in Polaris District training and communications responsibilities.

May Tindall, in the Mt. Hamilton District, was the catalyst for a Cub Scout Shelter Program for homeless children adapting the traditional training program to non-traditional needs in 1989. Mary Clarke, Pioneer District, and Star Baker, Mene Oto District, joined May in this innovative program.

The following have served as Chairmen of the Woman's Reserve:

Helen Hurt	Joan Reynolds
Dorothy Ittner	Jan Lewis
Vi Schneider	Jean Goodman
Brenda Jones	Carolyn Minker
Florence Jones	Judy Griffin
Carroll Favorite	Beth Crane
Gertrude Wright	Muffy Williams
Martha Gorman	Helen Keyes
Thelma Hinnard	Diane Patterson
	Glenna Corsen

There are many such women in the Woman's Reserve who are using their creative talents to make a difference. Members of the Woman's Reserve are registered as Scouters by the Santa Clara County Council. Through the last 28 years its roster has included hard-working, dedicated and outstanding women.

(The Women's Reserve roster may be found in the Appendix.)

Handicapped Scouting

Boy Scouting for handicapped boys in their own special troop, started in 1966 in the Santa Clara County Council with the formation of Troop 399 of Pioneer District.

The first sponsor of the Troop was the P.T.A. of the Joseph McKinnon School for the Mentally Retarded. The Troop met each Monday night at the school located on Moorpark Avenue in San Jose. It provided a modified Scouting program for 26 mentally handicapped Boy Scouts. The first Scoutmaster, Ralph Storti, was supported by Committee Chairman Henry Martus and Institutional Representative Harry Kelly.

Scoutmaster Storti started out with 12 boys, and almost as many parents, thinking that the parents could help the boys with their Scouting skills during the week. As time went by it was found that they could achieve better results by replacing the parents with interested Scouts from other Units.

Since its first year of organization, Troop 399 has offered six overnights and one week of extended camping at Santa Clara County Council's Hi-Sierra Summer Camp. Scoutmaster Storti believed that this was a meaningful experience for "his" boys because it gave them a chance to become involved with other Scouts—a very rewarding experience for both groups.

In 1970 Storti summed up his evaluation of handicapped Scouting by saying, "... the Scout uniform and the association our boys have with other Scouts helps to motivate them. Our boys feel a sense of belonging and of being brought into the normal everyday world. It is also our feeling that the rewarding and earning of badges will further motivate these boys to eventually learn to perform some type of work so they may help to support themselves.

"In the four years of our operation, only six boys passed Tenderfoot and three boys passed Second Class. These are the regular requirements that I refer to. We feel that rewarding the boys as they pass individual requirements will help to keep them in the program longer. Our boys are like all boys, they want to be recognized and rewarded for their achievements."

In May 1977 Ralph Storti received the first George Meany Award given by the Central Labor Council to a union member who had given outstanding service to youth as the Scoutmaster of Troop 399.

Troop 399 has been a consistent participant in general Scouting and Council activities. In 1972 the Troop was one of two handicapped troops in the nation to spend a week at the Philmont Scout Ranch in New Mexico. In June 1974, the troop, together with Pioneer District, hosted the 17th annual Jamborette with over 400 physically handicapped, mentally retarded and non-sighted Scouts and 100 adults. Participants from Los Angeles to Eureka, California, met on the grounds of Camden High School in San Jose. Following the traditional routine of being tested on Scouting skills, the Scouts had the opportunity to visit the Lockheed Missiles and Space Company Plant in Sunnyvale for a tour of the facilities. Another special event was a trip to Los Gatos for ride on the Billy Jones Wildcat Railroad at Oak Meadow Park.

After being observed by the National Council for some time, Troop 399 became a pilot unit for the development of a special Scouting program for the handicapped. On May 17, 1972, the Scouting Division of the National Council of the Boy Scouts of America adopted an "Incentive Program for Mentally Handicapped."

Bay Area Handicapped Camporee

The purpose of this program was to provide effective motivation for trainable mentally retarded boys in the Scouting program in order to learn simple skills and to achieve personal accomplishment.

The program consisted of standard skill requirements abbreviated for the mentally retarded. In recognition of his mastery of the skill, a Scout would be awarded segment patches that encircled his Scout badge as he successfully completed each requirement. Patch segments were also awarded for attaining additional abbreviated skills in proficiency areas such as citizenship, hiking, cooking, first aid and swimming.

In 1975 the formation of a council district for handicapped Scouting was considered but never implemented due to the absence of a sufficient number of handicapped Scouts and Units. However, in 1976 the Council leadership formed the Sunrise Committee on Scouting for the Handicapped and appointed Ralph Storti chairman. Scouting professional Terrance Spooner was hired in March in a dual role: as Director of Handicapped Scouting, and as the South Valley District Executive. The Handicapped Scouting directorship was initially funded by a grant from the Packard Foundation, secured by Walter Chronert.

The Sunrise Committee's purpose was to develop and utilize all resources in Santa Clara County in order to provide the most effective Scouting program for handicapped youth. The Director's purpose was to find young people who would benefit from the Scouting program through involvement in Cub Packs, Scout Troops and Explorer Posts. He was also charged with implementing programs which might achieve the partnership of handicapped units with other organizations.

Director Spooner was successful in developing a Council Advisory Committee of 33 members. He had also organized 7 new units serving 69 boys, and counted 25 handicapped boys who had been integrated into regular units. With five programs in the development stage, Spoooner had involved 197 handicapped youngsters in Scouting. That year's budget was financed 75% by grants from foundations, 21% by projects, 3% by individuals and 1% by service club contributions.

As a result of its meaningful program for handicapped Scouts, the Santa Clara County Council was given the honor of hosting the April 1977 Western Region Conference on Scoutiing for the Handicapped, and the May 1977 Handicapped Jamborette, with participants from Councils throughout California, Nevada and Oregon. County sheriff James Geary, chairman of the latter event, had been appointed

Chairman of Council's Advisory Committee on Scouting for the Handicapped in April 1977.

The Council hosted Camporees for the handicapped in June 1978 and 1982 when over 300 Scouts from troops throughout Northern California participated in a weekend of competition in Scout craft skills. In 1978, contributions from the McDonald's Corporation, Sambo's Restaurants, San Jose Knights of the Roundtable, and the Pacific Valley Bank made it possible to present the program free for all handicapped youngsters. Executive Board member and Mission College President Candy Rose chaired the 1982 event.

Two "Fun Days" were held at Independence High School. Both were jointly sponsored by the Council and the East San Jose Rotary Club. The first, in March 1979 for handicapped boys, was expanded a year later to include handicapped girls. The "Fun Days" were arranged by Council President Andy Bonfield and Rotary President Rocky Genovese.

Many fine leaders followed in these volunteers' footsteps along the trail blazed by Ralph Storti and Director Spooner. Professional Scouter Karen Weiseth served as the next Director until 1978. In January of 1979 James Wall, who had been an effective leader of several handicapped Scout units, was appointed the Council's first Assistant Council Commissioner for Handicapped Scouting. In August 1979, Walter Chronert was appointed Chairman of the Council's Committee for Handicapped Scouting. He was succeeded by Lyman Hitch in 1981. About the same time, Mary O'Niell was appointed Commissioner of Handicapped Scouting. Gradually, during the eighties, the Committee functions were assumed by the Council committees of Membership, Marketing and others.

Among the many strong supporters of the handicapped Scout program, Robert Dodge of Los Gatos deserves special mention. In addition to serving as a member of both the Troop 399 and Post 776 committees, for the past six years he has given Troop 399 a portion of the proceeds from the sale of Christmas trees from his ranch on Laurel Road. The Dodge ranch, in Santa Cruz County, has also hosted several overnight campouts by the Troop.

Present Scout units for the handicapped in the Santa Clara County Council include Troop 88, Troop 399, Post 756, Post 776. (Their troop histories may be found in Chapter II. Scouting Units.)

Development and Maintenance Committee

Camping privileges in Santa Clara County Council Scout camps are provided to their units free of charge, with only nominal fees to cover the cost of materials they use. In order to keep camp fees down, the Development and Maintenance Committee, inspires the contribution of volunteer labor and donated materials for the upkeep of Council properties.

This elite, but small group of men and women were referred to in the early '70s as the Camp Development Committee, then, a few years later, as the Building and Maintenance Committee. Since the spring of 1976 they have been affectionately known as the DAM (Development and Maintenance) Committee.

In 1976 approximately thirty Scouters worked as a close-knit unit under the chairmanship of Arthur Green, ably assisted by vice-chairman Dick DeVilbiss and Council Director of Properties, Glenn Helberg. These men have served in many different capacities in the last fifteen years working as volunteers improving the physical facilities for a quality program in all phases of Scouting. The composition of the committee has changed through the years, with some new workers pitching in to replace others, but many of the members have had real staying power and are still "hard at it."

These men and women have contributed their time, expertise and labor toward achieving these improvements over the past fourteen years:

Camp Stuart — Order of the Arrow Lodge: built A-frame kitchen wall; ladies rest room; deck; added wall tiling in kitchen, rest rooms and hallways, inside painting and floor tile. General: built pool showers, the next year, installed hot water heater for pool showers; added new siding and painting, pool area; added food storage room; built walk-in cooler and freezer; painted dining hall and refrigerators; built health lodge; and installed "building Jane's" John.

Camp Chesebrough — installed propane refrigerator for ranger facilities; installed 3,000 gallon water tank; built activity shelter.

Camp Hi-Sierra — enlarged lake; enlarged campfire site; enlarged archery range, replaced archery range cover; constructed new Par course; built foot bridge over river; refaced dam; dug new well and installed new water line; built waterworks pump house and winterized water pipes; remodeled scullery, added new cement floor; built walk-in cooler and freezer; installed new electrical panel in kitchen; built dining hall deck, and new porch for program building; remodeled health lodge; finished boathouse, started new shower building; painted cook's cabin, health lodge, kitchen staff restroom and latrines.

Service Center — remodeled equipment room and lounge in field staff office; installed suspended ceilings; painted kitchen, lunch room and accounting office; repainted buildings outside.

Twenty-five of the Scouters serving as members of the Development and Maintenance Committee have received the Council's highest award, the Silver Beaver, in recognition of their contributions toward improvement of the Council's facilities.

In addition to individual Scouter's contributions, many Santa Clara Valley companies generously contributed materials used by the DAM committee to improve the council's facilities.

The Development and Maintenance Committee estimates the market value of the materials contributed and work performed on improvement of the Council's Scouting facilities during the past fourteen years amounts to over $3,000,000.

(A listing of DAM Committee members and contributor companies may be found in the Appendix.)

Waterfront, Camp Hi-Sierra, circa 1970

The Santa Clarion

Throughout the past history of the Santa Clara County Council there had been a need for written communication between members of the Council leadership and between the Council and the Units. Several attempts at publishing a Council newsletter had been made with varying degrees of success. However, finally, in 1965, the Council put a winning combination together, even though it was destined to wait almost a year for a name.

In September 1965, the Santa Clara County Council published Volume 1, Number 1 of a newsletter with information focused on the Council and its six districts. It was mailed to all the Council's registered adult Scouters. Four issues of the unnamed periodical were published during 1965. Headlines and typewritten text were reproduced on both sides of 8½″ by 14″ yellow paper. The paper was folded into one-fourths for mailing. District Executive James Dumbolten was the editor, composition and printing was done at Council office, and the processing for mailing was done by the Women's Reserve.

The July 1966 issue bore the name "The Santa Clarion" for the first time. Monthly issues were published in 1966 and 1967; from 1967 through 1972 they remained in the original format with the simple addition of a short article under each District's heading.

A one-time-only special edition of The Santa Clarion was published for parents of all registered Cubs, Scouts and Explorers in February 1972. For the first time it was printed in newspaper style, with typeset and photographs on 22½″ by 14½″ newsprint, folded once to form 4 pages of text. The masthead gave credit for the special edition to the efforts of Sierra District Scouters, Louis Dixon, District Chairman, Stan Sibbert, Sibbert Typesetting Service, and Bob Selinger, Executive and Editor.

With the September 1975 issue, the format of the Santa Clarion changed to a newspaper style. And, for the first time it carried paid advertisements. That policy has continued to the present. Revenue from the ads have been helpful in paying a partial cost of the publication. By April 1978 the Santa Clarion had increased the number of photographs to 41, and the number of advertisers to 58.

Continuing the ongoing change in "the look" of the newsletter, the Council switched to the Suburban Press from 1976-79 for typesetting and printing, but continued to depend on the Women's Reserve to process the monthly issues for mailing. Starting in January 1979, the Meredith-Sun Publishing Company took over the printing job with typesetting by Prussia Graphics.

Nine issues each were published in 1981 and 1982, and then in 1983, the Santa Clarion became a bi-monthly periodical, which it remains today. The last "printer switch" was also made in 1983, this time to Independent Publications, Inc. which has continued to perform that function up to the present time.

In 1984 the Council began computer generation of its own mailing labels for registered adult Scouters. They also contracted with the Catholic Social Services for processing and mailing The Santa Clarion.

There have been several editors of the publication who have assumed that postion since Terrance Spooner was succeeded by Thomas Anderson in March 1976. Edward Fassett's tenure started in October 1977; Emile Mestressat started in January 1979; Elayne Roberts took over in February 1982, and she was succeeded by Paul Nakamoto that October.

Commencing with the May/June 1986 issue, Brent Nicolai became editor, followed by Scott Oldenburg with the May/June 1988 issue. Doris Hambrick started as editor of The Santa Clarion with the August 1989 edition, a responsibility which she continued into the spring of 1990.

With several false starts, that seemed to happen with regularity during the first 45 years of the Santa Clara County Council's existence, the last 25-year reliability of The Santa Clarion has set a record. A trustworthy communication link is extremely important in keeping a large Scouting membership informed and knowledgeable.

During its years of publication, articles concerning the Council in general have been written by the staff member responsible for the event covered by that article. District executives have covered district-related news and calendar of events. The long list of editors are to be commended for their ability to meet their deadlines—and still have it all make sense. The Women's Reserve has spent many of those twenty-five years "getting it all together." It seems entirely fitting that the fruit of all these labors have been enjoyed and appreciated by thousands of The Santa Clarion readers.

Order of the Arrow Vigil Honor Candidates, 1968
Mike Cooley, Leonard Favorite, Lynn Ferrin, David Pollock   Photo by Pat Reilley

V. Awards and Recognitions

Introduction

Awards that have been earned by Cub Scouts, Boy Scouts and Explorers in recognition for completion of difficult specific requirements for merit badges and ranks are the most important that Scouting has to offer. Working under the leadership of the Santa Clara County Council, innumerable adult volunteer Scouters have also earned awards in recognition for completion of structured training programs.

The earned awards are received after completing specific requirements. The honorary awards may be received for demonstrating dedication to the Scouting programs, its ideals and service to others.

Realizing the value of recognition for service, the National Council of the Boy Scouts of America has designated special awards for both heroism and leadership. Youth members of Scouting and adult Scouters, as well, may qualify for these.

Outstanding volunteer service is the other activity singled out for special recognition by the National Council and local councils for youth and adults working within the parameters of Scouting.

Several of these awards and recognitions have been established at different times throughout the eighty year history of the National Council. Others were established by the Santa Clara County Council since its first charter was granted in 1920. Each of these honors continue to be presented to deserving youth members and Scouters.

On occasion, other entities, ranging in a wide spectrum from governmental to special interest groups, bestow an award or recognition for exemplary service either to the Council as a whole, or to individual Scouts and/or Scouters, for work done within the Scouting program.

Youth Awards

Eagle Scout Badge

More than 25,000 American boys earn the Eagle Scout badge every year. In 1982 Alexander Holsinger of Normal, Illinois, became the one millionth Eagle Scout. Gerald Ford, in 1974, was the first Eagle to become President of the U.S.A. Due to the fact that a Scout must show unusual tenacity and dedication to improve his Scouting skills, his Eagle award places him in a very select group of Scouts. Statistics show that only 2% of all Boy Scouts attain the rank of Eagle.

Each troop conducts its own Court of Honor ceremony. It is usually held quarterly during the year for all ranks, including Eagle Scouts. An Eagle Court of Honor is a formal event when each of the achievers is presented his own well-earned Eagle Scout medal.

These Eagle Scouts received special attention:
1973 Jay Salisbury — Troop 144
    first Eagle with a handicap of deafness;
1976 Gary Hitch — Troop 148
    added third Silver Palm to Eagle
    (45 merit badges past Eagle required);
1977 Hyatt Dunn, Jr. — Troop 399
    first "special" Scout to attain Eagle rank
     in Troop 399;
1982 Bradley Jenkins — Troop 562
    grandson of an Eagle;
1988 Huan Cong Le — Troop 310
    first Vietnamese/American Eagle Scout.

Eagle Scout

Ever since the very beginning of Scouting, a boy had a long uphill climb before he could qualify to be called an Eagle Scout. Originally, a boy had to be 12 years old to join a troop and had to satisfy the requirements to become a Tenderfoot Scout. Today a boy must have completed the fifth grade, be at least 10 and 1/2 years old, and satisfy some preliminary requirements to become a "Scout" before qualifying as a Tenderfoot.

Advance continues through the ranks of Second Class and First Class with increasing emphasis on the basic Scouting skills, first aid, physical fitness, participation and citizenship.

For the higher ranks of Star, Life and Eagle, the emphasis changes to earning merit badges, some of which are required and some elective. There is also a focus on increasing levels of responsibility in troop leadership and service to the community.

To qualify for Eagle Scout rank a boy must have earned 21 merit badges, 11 of which were required, served six months as a Life Scout in a leadership position, developed and executed a service project, and participated in a personal growth agreement conference. By the time he has successfully completed those requirements, a Boy Scout has reached the top of the mountain and is able to soar like an Eagle the rest of the way. Meanwhile, with additional merit badges, he may qualify for his bronze, gold and silver palms to place on the ribbon of his Eagle Award.

(A list of Scouts who have earned the Eagle Scout award may be found in the Appendix.)

ALONG THE EAGLE TRAIL

AMERICA'S FIRST EAGLE

The National Eagle Scout Register lists 22 Boy Scouts who achieved Scouting's ... (highest) rank in 1912, the first year the awards were granted. Arthur R. Eldred of Oceanside, N.Y., has been acknowledged as the first Eagle Scout in America....

(Excerpt: Eagletter, Bulletin of the National Eagle Scout Ass'n., Summer 1989)

Dudley Herschbach, Eagle Scout, Troop 36, 1947
Dr. Herschbach, Nobel Prize in Chemistry, 1986

TRIPLE SILVER PALM AWARDED

Gary Hitch ... of Milpitas was recently awarded his third silver palm for his Eagle Badge at a Troop 148 Court of Honor. The third silver palm represents a total of 45 merit badges beyond those required for Eagle award....

(Excerpt: Santa Clarion, 5/76)

THIRD STAR/LIFE SEMINAR

Following two successful Star-Life Seminars held this summer and fall, the Council Scout Advancement committee is currently planning a third seminar designed to help Star and Life Scouts along the trail to Eagle. Featured sessions at the February 4–5 weekend at Camp Stuart will include Eagle Service Projects, review of required merit badges, Eagle paperwork, and other topics of direct importance to those Scouts who are approaching their Eagle Award....

(Excerpt: Santa Clarion, 11/76)

CALLING ALL EAGLES

A seventy-five member, all Eagle Scout, color guard will open the Santa Clara County Council's Jubilee Jamboree celebration on October 13th. Each of the Eagles will be carrying a United States flag that has been flown over the Capitol Building in Washington, D.C. If you are an Eagle Scout, of any age, or know of an Eagle Scout that would like to participate in the color guard, please contact Brian Vail....

(Excerpt: Santa Clarion, 7/84)

LETTERS TO THE EDITOR

Dear Editor:

My father, Max Jenkins, who is a past Silver Beaver recipient from Redwood District, is coming up from Arizona where he is active in the Phoenix Council. He is going to present the Eagle badge and Eagle charge to his grandson Bradley Clark Jenkins, at an Eagle court of honor on December 28, 1982 ... in Los Gatos.

He is hoping to see many of his old Scouting friends, and since we do not know the addresses of all those Scouters, would you include this announcement in the December issue of the Santa Clarion? ... The date is ... significant because it is the same date that Bradley's older brother John Philip Jenkins received his Eagle, December 28, 1976.

Bradley's Eagle service project was very unique and challenging, totaling over 944 hours with 33 people assisting him. He documented the tombstone inscriptions of Madronia Cemetery in Saratoga, California, and published a book titled: *Madronia Cemetery Tombstone Inscriptions, Saratoga,* ... The book has 170 pages and includes a history of the cemetery, and an invaluable alphabetical surname index listing....

Yours for better Scouting, Dr. Philip Jenkins

(Excerpt: Santa Clarion, 12/82)

NATURE TRAIL HELPS EARN HIGHEST RANK IN SCOUTING

Huan Cong Le is a trailblazer. Saturday, he became the first Vietnamese-born Eagle Scout from Santa Clara County.

But Le, 18 has blazed another trail—a nature trail through Hellyer Park that has been used by 2,000 schoolchildren since it was finished in March....

In 13 years in this country, Huan Cong Le has excelled in the classroom, in the community and in Scouting. He will enter the University of California, Berkeley, this year, after graduating with a 3.98 grade point average from Bellarmine College Preparatory.

Le, who recently moved to Morgan Hill from San Jose, also worked four years as a volunteer at Santa Teresa Hospital, wrote for the school newspaper and wrestled on Bellarmine's junior varsity team....

The trail Le cut is used by students from the Franklin-McKinley School District for nature hikes with (park) rangers. Before the trail, groups had to walk on the street.

Le designed the trail and directed a crew of 30 friends to clear the trail, 3 feet wide by a third of a mile.... Le and his crew cleared the path in one day without using power tools.

Speaking during the (presentation) ceremony ... Le recalled the feeling he had several years ago when he met his first Eagle Scout: "I thought, 'Gee, these guys must be really neat to have such a high rank.' Now, I kind of like the idea of little kids looking at me and saying, 'Gee, this guy must be really neat to have such a high rank.'"

(Excerpt: San Jose Mercury News, 7/10/88)

Order of the Arrow

The honor of becoming a member of the Order of the Arrow is one that cannot be earned by a Boy Scout on his own. This honor is bestowed on a Scout by members of his own troop. Since the Order of the Arrow is a national brotherhood of Scout campers, a Boy Scout must prove to his friends in the troop that he is an exceptionally good Scout and an unselfish camper.

Boys and adults are both eligible for membership in the Order of the Arrow, however, the lodge is run by the elected boy officers while the adults serve in non-voting, advisory capacities.

The Vigil is the highest honor the Order of the Arrow can bestow on a member. Recommendations are made by the Lodge Nominating Committee, and after approval by the National Order of the Arrow Committee, a candidate may be inducted as a Vigil Member.

(A list of the Miwok Lodge Vigil Honor recipients may be found in the Appendix.)

The Religious Award

RELIGIOUS AWARD PROGRAM

The religious awards programs offered by many faiths are in keeping with the religious principles of the Boy Scouts of America. The programs make every effort to strengthen a Scout in his religious obligations by encouraging him to enroll in the program of religious instructions, experiences and services which result in earning the religious award of his faith, and thus, causes the Scout to grow.

The pendants, or emblems, are awarded by the related religious groups. They are not a Scouting recognition. Each faith has its own requirements for earning its emblem. Most call for religious knowledge and service.

The Santa Clara County Council is fortunate to have religious relationships committees to give guidance, leadership and vitality to the spiritual phase of Scouting....

Since Scouting is non-sectarian, it espouses no creed and favors no faith over another. Instead, it provides programs and ideals that complement the aims of all religions. As a result, over 47% of all Scouting units are chartered to religious bodies.

One of the unique developments that has emerged from the partnership of Scouting with religious bodies is the religious emblem program....

(Excerpt: Santa Clarion, 7/88)

Major religious denominations have created special awards for First Class Scouts who perform outstanding service within their faiths. The following are a few examples of the Religious Emblems which can be earned by Scouts:

Ad Altare Dei	Roman Catholic;
Alpha Omega	Eastern Orthodox;
Ararat	Armenian;
Liahona (Compass)	Reorganized Church of Jesus Christ of Latter Day Saints;
Good Life	Zoroastrian;
In the Name of God	Islamic;
Religion in Life	Unitarian Universalist;
Light is Life	Eastern Rite Catholic;
Light of God	Ass'n of Unity Churches;
Living Faith	Lutheran;
On My Honor	Church of Jesus Christ of Latter Day Saints;
Ner Tamid	Jewish;
Pope Pius XII	Roman Catholic;
Sangha	Buddhist;
Unity of Mankind	Baha'i.

Several religious denominations have created God and Country award emblems. These may be earned, in most cases, by Boy Scouts and Explorers. Cub Scouts may earn a cloth religious emblem, a silver knot on purple background. God and Country Emblems are given by the following churches and non-sectarian agencies: Baptist, Christian, First Church of Christ Scientist, Episcopal, Methodist, Moravian, Polish National Catholic, Presbyterian, Protestant, and The Salvation Army.

Ad Altare Dei Awards, circa 1940
Scouts from Troop 41
St. Mary's Catholic Church, San Jose

CATHOLIC SCOUT SUNDAY

The observance of Catholic Scout Sunday this year was held at St. Raphael's Church in San Rafael. Santa Clara (County) Council had four boys and two adults (there) to receive emblems. There was a parade through San Rafael, led off by the 4th Degree Knights of Columbus Honor Guard....

The following boys of Santa Clara (County) Council were honored:

Ad Altare Dei Award:
Scott Helmes — Troop 556
Church of the Ascension, Saratoga
Brian Mauldwin — Troop 234
Saint Teresa's Church, San Jose
Mark Schreiber — Troop 633
Church of the Holy Spirit, San Jose

Pope Pius Award:
Michael Ohlis — Troop 535
Sacred Heart Church, Saratoga

The following adults of Santa Clara (County) Council were honored:

Saint George Award:
Diana Anderson — Troop 148
Saint Elizabeth's Church, Milpitas
Cheryl Sanchez — Pack 232
St. Francis Cabrini, San Jose....

(Excerpt: Santa Clarion, 4/79)

Records on file show the first religious award presented to a Cub Scout in Santa Clara County was the God and Family Award given, in 1978, to Webelos Mark Polland, Pack 466, Sunnyvale. Brothers Mark and Luke Watther, from Pack 367, Campbell, both won the Roman Catholic Award in 1979.

Honor Medal Recipient, 1977
Eagle Scout Paul M. Olsen and Mother

Present Honor Medal

National Court of Honor Awards for Heroism, Lifesaving and Meritorious Acts:
(presented to both Youth and Adult Members)

·Council records of the following awards were not available prior to 1968:

Honor Medal with Crossed Palms

The Honor Medal with Crossed Palms is given in cases where exceptional heroism and unusual skill has been demonstrated.

The Santa Clara County Council recipient of the Honor Medal with Crossed Palms is:
1989 — Scouter Richard Townsley: Eagle 1958, T-14, San Jose
On the job, in a building where fellow employees were trapped while seven workers were being killed by a gunman.

Honor Medal

The highest special award in Scouting is the gold Honor Medal established in 1922. It is awarded to Scouts and Scouters who save life, or attempt to save life, at risk of their own, showing heroism, resourcefulness and skill.

Santa Clara County Council recipients of the Honor Medal have been:
1977 — Eagle Scout Paul Olsen — T-443, Sunnyvale, lifesaving;
1979 — Explorer Christopher Batchlor — E-305, San Jose, lifesaving.

Heroism Award

The Heroism Award, which replaced the earlier "Certificate for Heroism," is awarded for demonstrated heroism in saving, or attempting to save, life at the risk of one's own life.

Santa Clara County Council recipients of the Heroism Award have been:

> 1988 — Eagle Scout John Arena — T-41, San Jose, lifesaving;
>
> 1988 — Life Scout Richard Gauthier — T-41, San Jose, lifesaving;
>
> 1989 — Life Scout John Welder — T-711, Gilroy, lifesaving.

Medal of Merit

The Medal of Merit is awarded by the National Court of Honor. It is given to youth and adult members who put into practice the skills and ideals of Scouting by doing some great act of service. This act does not have to involve the risk of life. A Medal of Merit recognizes heroic acts such as swimming and boating rescues, rendering first aid, and service in natural disasters like earthquakes, hurricanes and floods.

Santa Clara Council recipients of the Medal of Merit have been:

> 1968 — 2nd Class Scout Charles Pederson — T-443, Cupertino, lifesaving;
>
> 1970 — Sea Scout Richard Machado — SES-46, Santa Clara, lifesaving;
>
> 1978 — Star Scout Paul Legasa — T-363, Los Gatos, lifesaving.

Hornaday Medal

The William T. Hornaday Award

This national award for distinguished service in the field of conservation was established in 1914, and named for the first director of the New York Zoological Society, a pioneer in conservation. No specific guidelines must be met, however, the aggregate of work done must measure up to a meaningful body of work in the conservation field.

The Santa Clara County Council recipients of the Hornaday Award have been:

> 1959 — Scout Gary Gray, San Jose
>
> 1961 — Scout Peter Enright, San Jose
>
> 1964 — Scout Mark Enright, San Jose
>
> 1968 — Scout Scott Hector, Monte Sereno
>
> 1975 — Scout Stephen Barclay, Cupertino
>
> 1982 — Scout Jeff Ohlfs, Saratoga

HORNADAY AWARD GOES TO SCOTT HECTOR

Scout Scott Hector (T520) has been awarded Scouting's Hornaday Award for an outstanding long term conservation project. The award is presented by the Boy Scouts of America, with the cooperation of the New York Zoological Scoiety, in honor of the late William T. Hornaday, a pioneer in the recognition of conservation and in inspiring others to work constructively for conservation.

"Since 1920 this award has been highly prized (in the Santa Clara County Council) by those fortunate enough to receive it as recognition of exceptional and unusual service in a very important area of Scouting.... The Medal, in very unusual cases, (is awarded) by the National Council, upon recommendation by the local council."

Scott did his work in hybridizing pine trees for specific local problems, planted them and then maintained them until they were established. The project was started more than five years ago.

Only three of these rare awards have been earned in (the prior) ten years in this Council. Our heartiest congratulations to Scott and his Advisor for this recognition.

(Excerpt: Santa Clarion, 7/69)

Specified Age Group Awards and Scholarships:

Cub Scouts:

Arrow of Light Award

The Arrow of Light award is given to a Webelo Cub after completing Cub Scout requirements, as a symbol of graduating to the responsibilities of a Boy Scout.

SQUARE KNOT AVAILABLE FOR ARROW OF LIGHT

The Arrow of Light, Cub Scouting's highest award, is now represented by an embroidered square knot. The knot is formed by a red rope and a green rope appearing on a khaki background and bordered in yellow.

Boy Scouts, Explorers and adult leaders who earned the Arrow of Light Award as a Cub Scout, may wear the embroidered knot on the field uniform shirt immediately above the left pocket flap....

(Excerpt: Santa Clarion, 10/79)

Boy Scouts and Explorers

World Conservation Award

The award is made by the World Wildlife Fund of Washington, D.C. through the Boy Scouts of America. It recognizes achievement in environmental improvement, natural resource conservation and an understanding of world conservation problems.

LOCAL BOY SCOUTS EARN WORLD CONSERVATION AWARDS

Jeff Ohlfs, T-535, Saratoga, sponsored by the St. Andrews Episcopal Church of Saratoga; Ronald Murphy, Post 238 of San Jose, sponsored by the L.D.S. Church, 24th Ward, San Jose, and Phillip Wheeler, T-294 of San Jose, sponsored by the Rotary Club of Almaden, have earned the new World Conservation Award....

The purpose of the award is to point out to young people that countries of the world are closely inter-related through natural resources and that we in this country are interdependent with our world environment.

To win this award, Boy Scouts Jeff Ohlfs and Phillip Wheeler and Explorer Ronald Murphy earned Conservation and Environmental skill awards, merit badges in Environmental Science, Soil and Water Conservation, Fish and Wildlife Management, and Citizenship in the World.

(Excerpt: Santa Clarion, —

Explorers: Special Interest Awards and Scholarships

Young America Award

This award, first presented in 1968 by the Young America Foundation, is given to any young adult (Explorers and others) between the ages of 15 and 22, who have achieved excellence in the fields of science, religion, government, business, humanities, art or literature. They also must have been involved in service to their community and their country, and involved in improving the quality of life

National Exploration Award

This award program was developed in 1969. Since 1972 it has had annual financial and resource support from the international electronics firm, TRW. It gives recognition to Explorers who have demonstrated interest and competence in the natural and physical sciences; it will provide scientific training related to academic goals and possible careers. The three top-ranked winners receive college scholarships.

American Medical Association Recognition Plan

This Recognition Plan was first available in 1979. The plan is presented to Explorers and Explorer posts who have participated in projects in the fields of mental and physical health such as ecology, biology, humanics, chemistry, physics, psychology and others.

James S. Kemper Insurance Foundation Scholarship

Since its inception in 1942, this foundation has provided four-year scholarships to deserving young men and women who have demonstrated an interest in pursuing careers in insurance upon graduation. The scholarship provides tuition assistance at foundation-approved colleges and universities in traditional business curricula such as accounting, actuarial science, finance, insurance and risk management. The wide spectrum of approved study fields also includes communications, computer science, economics, chemical and mechanical engineering, industrial hygiene, and psychology.

National Eagle Scout Association Scholarship

This scholarship is available to members of the National Eagle Scout Association who are considering a military career. It consists of $1,000 yearly for a two-year program at New Mexico Military Institute in Roswell, New Mexico.

J. Edgar Hoover Foundation Scholarship

This scholarship was first presented in 1975 and is made available to Explorers who have demonstrated an interest in seeking a career in law enforcement. Each year, $500 tuition assistance scholarships, based upon merit, are presented to a worthy candidate in each of the Boy Scouts of America's six regions.

In 1981, Suzanne Schreiber was the recipient of the J. Edgar Hoover Award. That year Schreiber was the president of Explorer Search and Rescue Post 601, chartered by the Santa Clara County Sheriff's Department. She became the National Law Enforcement Explorer president for 1983-84. She was graduated from San Jose State University in 1987. Suzanne Schreiber is now a staff member of the National Organization for Victim Assistance (NOVA) in Washington, D.C.

Santa Clara County Council Eagle Scout Scholarships

Beginning with the class of 1986 a $1,000 scholarship has been awarded to a deserving Eagle Scout during ceremonies at the annual Eagle Scout Recognition Dinner. The recipients of these scholarships have been:
    1986 — Steven Von Dohlen
    1987 — Jason Covington
    1988 — Jack Eldredge
    1989 — Troy Bergstrom.

NESA SCHOLARSHIPS

The National Eagle Scout Association (NESA) distributed a total of $150,000 to 48 Eagle Scouts on June 1, 1988, to be used in support of their college educations. More than 1,500 applications were received. Selections were made by an 8-member national committee after screening some 70 regional selectees....

Grants are restricted to Eagle Scouts who will graduate from high school during the year of the grant, have an SAT score of at least 900 or an ACT score of 20, and have a need for financial assistance. They must be enrolled in an accredited college or university for the fall term.

(Excerpt: Santa Clarion, 9/88)

Adult Awards

National Council Awards:

Official Honors: National, Regional, Local

In 1926 the Boy Scouts of America created a category of awards which would honor American adults who, whether through the Scouts or independently, had provided noteworthy service to the youth of the nation. The Silver Buffalo, a national award, the Silver

Silver Antelope presented to Past President Bill Nicholson, Region XII Meeting, 1970

Ken Robison presents Silver Beaver to Charles Mitchell, 1957

Antelope, a regional award, and the Silver Beaver, a local award, have given recognition to some of the finest men and women in Scouting.

It is quite possible for one outstanding Scouter, who works most of his adult life for the betterment of youth in Scouting Programs, to end up being not only highly respected, but highly honored by his peers. This is the case of 70-year Veteran Scouter Lester Steig. In 1963-64 he was National President of Alpha Phi Omega, the Boy Scouts of America National Service Fraternity with 620 chapters. He was National President of Knights of Dunamis from 1970-72. He was awarded the Silver Beaver, 1964, Silver Antelope, 1974; Silver Buffalo, 1976, Distinguished Eagle Scout, 1970, and the Distinguished Service Award, 1976, in prior councils before continuing his service in the Santa Clara County Council.

The following Santa Clara County Council Awardees have received National Court of Honor recognition:

Silver Buffalo: (service at the national level)
　1976 — Lester Steig, PhD
Silver Antelope: (service at the regional level)
　1954 — Judge Marshall S. Hall
　1970 — Wilmot J. Nicholson
　1973 — Frank S. Bernard, PhD
　1978 — Dr. John E. Cox
　1987 — Earl S. Burke, Jr.
　1990 — Glen McLaughlin
Silver Beaver/Silver Fawn (service at the local level)

(This list, dating from 1934 to 1990, may be found in the Appendix.)

Silver Fawn:

This award was given to outstanding women Scouters in the Scouting program beginning in 1972, but the award was discontinued in 1975 and replaced with the standard Silver Beaver for both adult men and women.
　1972 — Eileen Brutsche, Carroll Favorite, Elaine Ho, Helen Hunt, Vi Schneider and Gertrude Wright, all charter members of the Women's Reserve; Vickie Jones, Janice Lewis, Women's Reserve members;
　1974 — Jane Reed, Joan Reynolds, Ann Warfield

BILL NICHOLSON

I was president for two terms ... (1960 through 1963 and again for 1968 and 1969). This came about when Larry Hill (Council President) and Ray Ewan (Scout Executive) came up into the hills in back of Los Gatos to see me one Saturday morning (at my home). After much sociability and coffee, they said they wanted me to be president (of the Council). This was out of the clear blue because I was no longer a (Scout) master, never on the board, really not doing much. They prevailed....

(When) I served again ... I was quite busy, one banquet giving out Silver Beaver Awards, finished up, and then Ellis Howard gave me one. It was totally unexpected and I ended up standing there, in tears. Later on I was given the Silver Antelope—at a Las Vegas convention. That was also a complete surprise, but no tears.

FIRST SILVER FAWNS AWARDED

A special highlight at the annual Scout-O-Rama judges luncheon, May 6, was the presentation of the first Silver Fawns (the equivalent of the Silver Beaver), to six charter members of the Women's Reserve of our Council. Since the awards are limited in number each year and were first authorized by the National Council in 1971, the six presented represented a two-year accumulation.

This two year accumulation was for the purpose of simultaneously recognizing the six ladies of Scouting ... who, in addition to several years of successful previous Den Mother experience, were also Charter members of the Women's Reserve when it was organized some ten years ago.

The ladies receiving this highest Council award for women had each tallied from 15 to 18 years of distinguished service to boyhood both on the community level and in Scouting. Our congratulations to: Eileen Brutsche, Carroll Favorite, Elane Ho, Helen Hurt, Vi Schneider and Gertrude Wright....

(Excerpt: Santa Clarion, 6/72)

Distinguished Eagle Scout Award

In 1969 the Distinguished Eagle Scout Award was established in order to recognize men who attained the rank of Eagle Scout as a youth and have gone on to render distinguished service to their community and their profession as an adult. Santa Clara County Council Awardees are

    1976 — Louis P. Bergna
    1982 — Albert B. Smith
    1986 — Michael H. Antonacci
    1988 — Dr. Vinton S. Matthews.

Louis Bergna, 1st Distinguished Eagle Scout

AT THE PINNACLE OF SCOUTING

Santa Clara County District Attorney Louis P. Bergna joined an elite group of 300 Scouters Wednesday when he was presented the Distinguished Eagle Scout Award at a luncheon in San Jose. The plaque and solid-gold medallion are awarded only to ... Eagle Scouts who subsequently distinguished themselves in their careers. It was the first time the honor has been bestowed in Santa Clara County....

(Excerpt: San Jose Mercury, 4/29/76)

ALBERT SMITH EAGLE IN PROFILE

Al Smith earned his Eagle Scout Award in Troop 39, now Troop 539, of Los Gatos in 1940. In 1982 Al Smith was the recipient of the Distinguished Eagle Scout Award at a barbecue in Los Gatos, hosted by the Los Gatos Rotary, Lions and Kiwanis Clubs.... (This) Award is very special. Less than 500 outstanding Americans have been so honored.

During Al Smith's life, he has been very active in community and business affairs. Once the Mayor for the town of Los Gatos, Al is the retired Chairman of Orchard Supply Hardware. Al currently serves as a member of the Executive Board of the Santa Clara County Council, Boy Scouts of America.

Al was very instrumental in the acquisition and operation of the Billy Jones Railroad at Oak Meadow Park in Los Gatos. He also was one of the founders of Camp Hi Sierra....

(Excerpt: Santa Clarion, 10/84)

(Editor's note: Smith is the current chairman of the Council's Memorial Foundation.)

Veteran Recognition

As the years have passed since the Boy Scouts of America was established, many Scouters have continued to be active over a long period of time. In recognition of this serivce, veteran pins are awarded in five year increments starting with the 5th year of service and ending with the diamond 75-year Veteran Pin.

Explorer Spurgeon Award

William H. Spurgeon, III, a California businessman and National Committee Exploring member organized the first special-interest posts in California in 1956. With Spurgeon as prime advocate, businesses, industry, labor unions, hospitals, trade associations, and other non-traditional sponsors started to back career-interest posts. This award is named for him and is given to outstanding Explorer post leaders.

At the 1990 Council Recognition Dinner Colonel Noboru Masuoka received the Explorer Spurgeon Award. Masuoka had created an Explorer post that enables young men and women to qualify for appointments to U.S. military academies.

National Council Scouter Training Recognition:

In 1928 the Volunteer Training Service inaugurated a "Five Year Progressive Training Program" leading to a training award called the "Scoutmaster's Key." This was later reduced to a three year program and the award became the "Scouter's Key," a green ribbon with broad white stripe, and pendant.

For service in other adult positions it is also possible to qualify for the Scouter's Training Award, a green ribbon with narrow white stripe, and pendant, and the Scoutmaster Award of Merit.

Exploring leaders may earn the Exploring Training Award. A trained Explorer advisor, or service team member, is entitled to wear the Exploring Key.

The Webelos Den Leader Award of cloth is given for completing training on the Den Leader level. It can also be a pendant worn suspended from a gold ribbon around the neck.

Other awards can be worn suspended from a ribbon around the neck: the Cubmaster Award, a gold ribbon with two blue stripes with Cub Scouter pendant; the Den Leader Award, a blue ribbon with gold stripe with Cub Scouter pendant; the Den Leader Coach Award, a blue ribbon with Cub Scouter pendant; the Cub Scouter Award, a gold ribbon with blue stripe with Cub Scouter pendant.

National Awards, Specialized Area:

Order of the Arrow, Vigil Honor

This is one of the few awards for which both Boy Scouts and Scouters are eligible. The National Council first chartered the Miwok Lodge No. 439 in the Santa Clara County Council in 1950, and re-chartered it in 1963. Since that time many Boy Scouts and Scouters have been presented the Vigil Award.

(A list of the Vigil Honor recipients may be found in the Appendix.)

SKIP BRELAND RECEIVES AWARD

(Professional Scouter) Skip Breland, A Vigil member in the Miwok Lodge of the Order of the Arrow, was honored by receiving the Distinguished Service Award of the Order of the Arrow. The award is given at the National Order of the Arrow Conference biennially, this year (the conference) being held in Fort Collins, Colorado.

The Order of the Arrow is the Honor Camper brotherhood of the Boy Scouts of America.... The Distinguished Service Award (is presented) to those Arrowmen who have rendered outstanding service to the Order....

(Excerpt: Santa Clarion, 10/79)

Whitney M. Young, Jr., Service Award

This award may be granted to an individual, or to an organization, who has made an outstanding contribution through Scouting to low-income urban/rural youth. The lapel pin award may only be worn by Scouters who have received the award as an individual.

National Awards from Other Organizations:

The Religious Award

Several religious denominations have created special emblems for Scouters who perform outstanding service within their faiths. The Religious Emblems which can be given to Scouters are:

Allaho Akber	Islamic Council;
Distinguished Youth Service	Ass'n of Unity Churches;
God and Service	Methodist/Presbyterian;
Good Shepherd	Baptist;
International Youth Service	Reorganized Church of Jesus Christ of Latter Day Saints;
Shofar	Jewish;
Lamb	Lutheran;
On My Honor	Church of Jesus Christ of Latter Day Saints;
Prophet Elias	Eastern Orthodox;
Religion and Youth	Unitarian/Universalist;
Saint George	Roman Catholic and Eastern Rite Catholic;
Salvation Army Scouter's Award	The Salvation Army.

George Meany Award

The George Meany Award, approved by the AFL-CIO Executive Council, is a national recognition for an adult union member who has made a significant contribution to the youth of their community through Scouting. The ribbon with pendant award is available to only one member of each City Central Labor Body annually.

In May 1977 Ralph Storti, Scoutmaster for seven years, of Troop 399 for handicapped Scouts, received the first George Meany Award given by the Central Labor Council in Santa Clara County.

In January 1990 former Scoutmaster William Wegner, Order of the Arrow Advisor for eight years, also received the award, only the second presentation by the Central Labor Council in this county. Wegner is Associate Advisor of the Order of the Arrow, Section W3A.

Green Seal Conservation Award

The Green Seal Conservation Award is given by the U.S. Department of Agriculture to the Scout Council with the best conservation program of all the councils in the Region.

COUNCIL WINS NATIONAL AWARD

We have just been notified by the National Council, that our Council has been selected as the winner for Region 12 of the United States Department of Agriculture Green Seal Conservation Award for 1969.

Included in the work done in this Council which won us this award were our continuing conservation projects at both Camp Hi-Sierra and Camp Stuart, and also for providing a qualified conservation man on the camp staff.

The earning of some 237 conservation merit badges and the participation of some 1900 Scouts and leaders in the Castle Rock, Big Basin-Ano Nuevo State Park trail-o-ree in 1969 were other achievements which qualified the Council for this outstanding conservation award....

This achievement definitely points out another long-time activity of the Boy Scouts of America which is still quite "relevant" in today's world!

(Reprint: Santa Clarion, 4/70)

Howard Taylor, Camp Director, 1932

Gold Seal Conservation Award

This is the United States Department of Agriculture's award given to the Scout Council with the best conservation program of any Council in the nation.

In 1973 Agriculture Secretary Earl Butz sent the Santa Clara County Council a congratulatory letter which accompanied the Gold Seal Award for 1972 presented at the Region 12 meeting. It stated in part, "Through participation in such programs, Scouts can gain a better understanding of resource protection and use. At the same time, they begin to develop a sense of individual responsibility toward proper management of the natural resources on which America's strength and welfare rest."

The award was based on the efforts of the boys and their leaders who supported the Council's SOAR Program, Trail Days, Camp Hi-Sierra and Camp Stuart conservation projects, Eco-mile, Keep America Beautiful, and numerous individual unit projects on behalf of their area's environment.

Santa Clara County Council Awards:

Benefactor Award

In January 1974, two awards were presented at the annual business meeting. They were in recognition of Scouters who had given generously of themselves, and of their resources.

As outgoing Council President, Frank Bernard was given a Benefactor Member Plaque. A special presentation of the Council Benefactor Award was made to Paul and Nessie Chesebrough for their generous gift of the Camp Chesebrough property in the Santa Cruz Mountains.

RESOLUTION

By Action of the Executive Board of the Santa Clara County Council, Boy Scouts of America, meeting on December 10, 1981, we record again our deep respect for the interest, support and generosity of Mrs. Winifred Handley Stuart, who on the death of her husband, Reginald Stuart, perpetuated and enhanced his gift of their home and arboretum on the historic John Brown tract in Saratoga, California, for the benefit of generations of Scout families. We decree that this Resolution, together with the action made for her award of the Silver Beaver by this Council before her passing was known, be sent to the descendents of the Stuarts together with our deepest sympathy.

(Note: Mrs. Stuart passed away on October 22, 1981)

(signed) Jan W. Passmore, President
Robert N. Allexsaht,
Scout Executive Secretary

(Reprint: Santa Clarion, 2/82)

Distinguished Citizen Award

The Santa Clara County Council had long felt the need to recognize community leaders who had given service above and beyond the call of duty to their communities, for the causes they believed in. In that spirit the Distinguished Citizen Award was created and sponsored by the Council to honor community leaders with exceptional qualities of leadership and altruism.

In November 1976 a dinner was held at the San Jose Hyatt House to honor Dr. Frank Bernard with the first award. Since that time an annual dinner has been given in honor of a selected recipient, who may,

or may not, have been active in the Scouting Program in Santa Clara County.

In 1982, the President's Club organization of the Council assumed responsibility for the sponsorship of the Distinguished Citizen Award Dinner.

The esteemed recipients of this annual Santa Clara County Council Award have been,

1975 — Dr. Frank S. Bernard
1976 — P. Anthony Ridder
1977 — William R. Hewlett
1978 — Glenn A. George
1979 — Stan Chinchin
1980 — Father Walter Schmidt
        Rabbi Joseph Gitin
        Reverend Philip Barrett
1981 — Halsey C. Burke
1982 — Enide Allison
1983 — Robert A. Fuhrman
1984 — Thomas T. Vais
1985 — Jan W. Passmore
1986 — Robert M. Hosfeldt
1987 — Donald L. Lucas
1988 — Kimball W. Small
1989 — Ray A. Silva

DISTINGUISHED CITIZEN AWARD

Halsey C. Burke, President and Chairman of the Board, Burke Industries, Inc. is the 1981 recipient of the Distinguished Citizen's Award....

Extremely active in community affairs, Halsey has served as Rotary District Governor, Rotary Club of San Jose President, San Jose State University President's Council member, San Jose Chamber of Commerce Advisory Board, San Jose Water Works Director, (and in other capacities)....

(Excerpt: Santa Clarion, 10/81)

Good Scout Award

Learning that Council's all over the country were giving this award to distinguished Scouters who were also community benefactors, the Santa Clara County Council began, in 1974, to honor these generous people.

A special event was held in their honor and proceeds from that event were used to further Scouting programs in the county area.

Santa Clara County Council recipients of the Good Scout Award are:

    1974 — Dr. Frank S. Bernard
    1979 — Robert C. Wilson
    1987 — Andrew J. Bonfield
    1988 — Judge Edward A. Panelli

GOOD SCOUT AWARD DINNER HONORS DR. BERNARD

On Tuesday evening, December 10, the Council's first "Good Scout Award" dinner will be held to honor our council's greatest benefactor, Dr. Frank S. Bernard....

Dr. Bernard's contributions of his time, talent and financial means to this Council over the past 16 years have been outstanding. For consistency of concern that the Council would be able to meet the very difficult years of rapid growth with no let-down of its services, past president Frank Bernard has given service on a Council level that is without parallel. His exceptional service has also extended to a Regional and National level....

The causes he has helped include the Institute for Medical Research, O'Connor Hospital, National Conference of Christians and Jews, University of Santa Clara, the United Fund,

foreign food relief, and (others)....

With Dr. Bernard's permission, the proceeds of the "Good Scout Award" will be used to help defray an unexpected deficit facing the Council which is due to increased inflationary costs and decreased contributions from SME and other income sources....

(Excerpt: Santa Clarion, 11/74)

1988 SCOUTER'S REUNION BRUNCH

The Third Annual Scouter's Reunion Brunch will be held Sunday, August 14 at the Italian Gardens ... the award ceremony (will) commence at 1:00 P.M. Chairman Murphy Sabatino is pleased to announce that California Supreme Court Justice Edward A. Panelli will receive the Santa Clara County Council's ... Good Scout Award.

(Excerpt: Santa Clarion, 7/88)

Eagle Scout Class Recognition

At the annual Eagle Scout Recognition Dinner, all Scouts who have earned the Eagle Scout rank during the previous calendar year are recognized as members of the Class of that year. In recent years, a prominent Scouter, generally an Eagle Scout himself, is recognized by having a particular Eagle Scout Class named in his honor. Those who have been honored in Santa Clara County Council are:

    1985 — General Robert E. Huyser
    1986 — Michael H. Antonacci
    1987 — Dr. Vinton S. Matthews
    1988 — Glen McLaughlin
    1989 — L. William Krause.

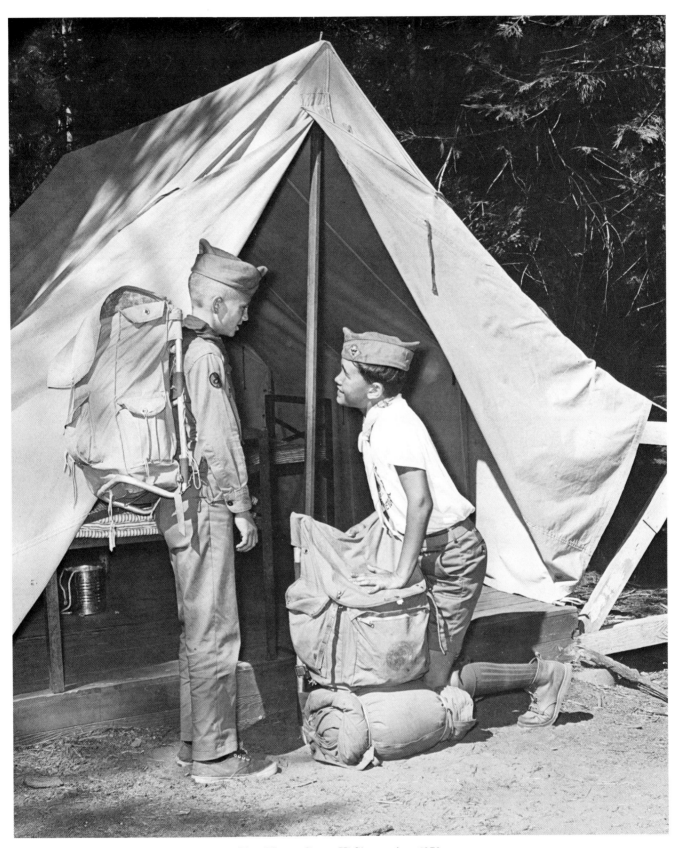

Tent Mates, Camp Hi-Sierra, circa 1970

Camp Arroyo Sequoia Cook House and Dining Hall
Built 1931 and destroyed by flood, 1940   Courtesy of Al Smith

VI. Council Properties

Introduction

When the council was first organized in 1920 its headquarters were in donated space at the San Jose Chamber of Commerce offices, in the Growers Bank Building on First Street in San Jose.

With the growth of the council it was necessary in 1925 to move to its headquarters to 515 Growers Bank Building in San Jose. The office rent was $12.50 per month for 396 square feet. In that year their annual budget included an expenditure of $3200 for "Camp Property," but the item was not explained.

Sometime in 1930 or 1931 the council headquarters was moved to 213 Bank of America Building at the corner of Santa Clara and First Streets in San Jose.

In 1941 the Council moved to 315 Security Building on First Street in San Jose. It remained in rented office space until February 1954 when the Council was able to move into a newly built office of their own on Park Avenue at Newhall Street in San Jose. It was formally dedicated as "The Charles E. Moore Memorial Boy Scout Building," and informally called the Scout Service Center.

Camping and other activities are essential to Scouting and adequate facilities have always been needed for these programs. Several campsites were leased, or used temporarily, by the council in the twenties and early thirties, among them Alum Rock Park, Big Basin, Camp Swanton and Yosemite. In 1931 the council had a little more money, and more boys to accommodate, so it purchased the Camp Arroyo Sequoia property with the idea that this investment would become a long term campsite.

In 1944, the council was given an 80 acre parcel three miles south of Saratoga, which was named Camp Stuart in memory of the son of the donor. In 1949, the council acquired a site in the Sierra Nevada range called Camp Hi-Sierra. In 1973, the council was given a 404 acre parcel in the Santa Cruz Mountains which was named Camp Chesebrough in honor of donors, Paul and Nessie Chesebrough. In 1983 they donated an adjacent parcel of 140 acres.

In 1945, a separate entity called the Boy Scout Memorial Foundation was created whose purpose was to administer the properties and to insure their protection. In 1946 Articles of Incorporation were adopted to form a non-profit corporation in order to manage these properties in the most efficient way.

The Council Executive Board continued to believe that camping was an essential part of its present and future Scouting programs. Each succeeding administration pursued an extensive camp development, maintenance and replacement plan, upgrading facilities as funds and manpower became available.

IN SEARCH OF HIGH ADVENTURE

Boys join Scouting for fun, excitement and adventure. Everything a boy hears about the Scouting program before he joins as a Cub Scout, Scout or Explorer deals with the excitement of exploring the unknown—the challenge of new frontiers. The opening pages of the Wolf Book and the Scout Handbook promises adventure unknown to any other 8 or 11 year old.

We have an obligation to these new members in our great program—and the committee's new members to come, in addition to those now a part of the Scouting program. We must fulfill this promise of High Adventure!

What is High Adventure? How do we keep it in our Scouting program?

High Adventure for a boy is anything he hasn't done before. It is an experience, a new horizon to explore.

Cub Scouts can find High Adventure in a field trip to a zoo or the local hamburger stand, or a week at day camp. Scouts seek High Adventure in the outdoor program and at summer camp, or exploring new interests in the Merit Badge program. Explorers can find High Adventure in discovering new career opportunities, or with older Scouts at Philmont or other other National High Adventure bases.

Every week and at every meeting and activity, we must all strive to add High Adventure experiences to our program to fulfill our promises to the youth of America.

(Reprint: Santa Clarion, 3/78)

"The Charles E. Moore Memorial Boy Scout Building"
The Council Service Center

Council Service Center

The land at 2095 Park Avenue was purchased on May 9, 1953 from Tract 262 of Kaiser Community Homes by the Boy Scout Memorial Foundation.

Plans for the headquarters building were drawn by Sobey and Green, Architects, and dated May 26, 1953. The Architectural Commmittee was composed of David Slipher, Paul Frechette and J.J. Reiter.

After the building was completed, the Council was able to buy a small adjoining parcel in June, 1954, bordered by Park Avenue and Highway 17. It was purchased from the State of California when the Highway Department decided it wasn't needed for widening the highway.

The Santa Clara County Council had survived for almost 35 years in rented space, and its staff and volunteers were more than ready to have a place of their own. A committee of enthusiastic businessmen, headed by Charles Moore, the president of Joshua Hendy Iron Works in Sunnyvale, went to work to solve the problem of putting up a building—without any cash!

The cost of the completed building was estimated to be $42,000. It was built through the support and financial efforts of the businessmen of Santa Clara County, and by the generous donation of time, material

and services by the Scouting volunteers and their friends.

Ground was broken on June 14, 1953. Unfortunately, Charles Moore, the man who had spearheaded the building drive, died unexpectedly a week later at the age of 59.

Although Moore was sorely missed, his friends rallied to complete the project. The construction of the building was undertaken by Cliff Swenson, who served as general contractor. He was assisted by Bill Ondrasek, also of Carl N. Swenson, Inc. Their foreman, Al Stevens, took over as job superintendent.

The financial contributions that Moore and his committee had solicited came rolling in as promised. Cliff Swenson was also heavily involved in requesting and coordinating the contributions of time, material and money from approximately 175 business firms, individuals and labor organizations. These, and other "in-kind" contributions ensured completion of construction in time for the February 7, 1954 dedication. The new Scout Headquarters was named "The Charles E. Moore Memorial Boy Scout Building."

In 1965 floor space on the property was increased through the generosity of the Westminister Presbyterian Church of San Jose. Frank Brown, a City of San Jose building inspector, knew that the building on the church grounds was no longer needed. He was instrumental in getting it moved to the back of the

Council property. Again, with the aid of volunteer Scouters, the building was refurbished; it served as the Council Field Office until 1982.

(A list of building contributors may be found in the Appendix.)

⚜ ——————————————————————— ⚜

AUSTEN WARBURTON

... It was thought we needed space, and we also felt it would be wise to have our own building instead of renting.... We were able (to) because monies were made available again, I think, through the Foundation. Moore (Charles), the industrialist, who had been very interested in the program early, William F. James, who was a superior court judge and juvenile judge for many years, and a friend of Moore's, and some of these people had helped ... with the financial end of the Foundation deal. Marshall Hall had been an associate of Judge James and was very close.

The Judge was a strong supporter of the Scouting program, and those two were big advocates of having our own headquarters, our own building. They, in their earlier terms on the Foundation, were helpful. (They) decided we should buy and fund the property which was at the tag end, the Park Avenue end, of the Kaiser Tract, a residential development that extends off to the west from there.

They were able to get it, I don't know what finagling they may have done in terms of getting a good price.... I think they got it from the Kaiser people.

Then, of course, the building was built and it was thought that it would be big enough to serve us for centuries to come, or at least, quite some time.... But it didn't take too long for the program to be so well received that we began outgrowing ourselves. For the last number of years, as you know, one of the concerns, both of the Foundation and Council, is to either expand the facility there so as to provide more office and working space, or perhaps sell it and find another spot.

⚜ ——————————————————————— ⚜

Charles E. Moore

⚜ ——————————————————————— ⚜

BILL PURSELL

It seems to me that when I started (1956), the back office was the Council Executive's office. That was Ray Ewan's office and before that it was Bartlett's. The office adjoining that was Alice Saint John's, she was the Council secretary for years and years. It seems to me that there was an access into the overhead over Ray's office where the Council records used to be stored. They have moved a lot of partitions around since then, and the room with the fireplace was the conference room, but it is full of offices nowadays.

⚜ ——————————————————————— ⚜

**SCOUT SERVICE CENTER
RENOVATION**
Dedicated December 15, 1975

The story of the Santa Clara County Council office redecoration and renovation is the story of volunteers and staff working together to accomplish a real objective that all of us are proud of.

It started with Glenn and Alice Helberg who dreamed of what could be done. With a dream and great sales pitch they bargained, cajoled and even scrounged as much as they could to make this dream a reality. Then they added personal commitment, George Wise and sixty hour weeks

---

to this dream. Their enthusiasm caught on and a Council Vice President, Jerry Crosby, and his troop became involved. They, with our professional volunteer painter, Jim Masterenko, painted the outside of the building. Art Green, our Chairman of Building and Maintenance, his side-kick, Dick DeVilbiss, Big Red, Gene and Eunice Ellsworth also got into the act. John and Carolyn Minker took care of the plumbing, stocking and moving. Betty Iapello and Sherry Straley worked countless hours on stocking shelves and painting here and there. Reed Graham and his crew of volunteers did the parking lot, the vocational educational classes took care of the carpet and linoleum. Ray Witherell, Jr. provided and laid the carpet in the receptionist's office in the Field Center. The professional staff have painted, moved, and laid carpet, and the office staff have cleaned and scrubbed. The Order of the Arrow, Paul Crompton, Ed Gunion, Bob Richardson, Pete Poillon and others, scraped, sanded and taped. Bob and Pauline Baird took care of the electrical work, and of course, Bill Powell and Paul Etheridge took care of the office furniture.

Are there others like Gary Hitch, Steve Gracie, Richard Kohl, Jim Bryson (his beautiful display and the signs he engraved for us) Lisa and Kathy Kohl, Phillip Straley, Allen Minker...? Yes, lots of others, many for an hour or a day like Willis Hanna who painted the kitchen, or the Women's Reserve who have always been there and who hosted our open house. Yes, many who didn't give their names....

To all we say that this has been a work of real dedication and the only dedication of this service center can be to you who have made it happen. $47,000. WORTH OF IMPROVEMENTS ... FOR A TOTAL ACTUAL COST OF $3,500....

(Reprint: Santa Clarion, 2/76)

TED ROGERS

I got the extra building behind the main building by maneuvering from a church, bought it and set it up in there. The building used to be the "Staff Room." (It was) purchased from a local church for a couple of hundred bucks, and it cost more to have it moved and installed than the building cost.... It was after I had been there (at the Council office) for seven or eight years.

Council Camps

Alum Rock Park

One of the earliest written records of Boy Scout camps has been found in Eugene Sawyer's 1922 *History of Santa Clara County*. He reported that, "Fifteen acres in Alum Rock Park were set aside for the exclusive use and jurisdiction of the local Scouts, and were first used in 1921."

Alum Rock Park had been created in 1872 by Mayor Adolph Pfister and the San Jose City Council. The 400 acre park was in a canyon located in the eastern foothills of San Jose. The canyon contained mineral springs that were thought to contain medicinal qualities. The name Alum Rock Park came from an alum-impregnated formation on the north side of the creek near the junction of Penitencia Road and Alum Rock Avenue.

By 1901 the city had added a bath house, outdoor swimming pool, visitors' cottages, a tea room, playground apparatus and a central fountain to which several kinds of mineral waters were piped from the mineral springs. In 1915 the Native Sons and Native Daughters of the Golden West added a log cabin filled with relics of pioneer days.

By 1921 the park included approximately 1,000 acres. During the years the Boy Scouts were using their fifteen acres, the park was a popular destination for all Santa Clara County residents for picnics, hiking, and horseback riding along its beautifully wooded trails.

Although there is no formal record of how frequently, or for what period of time the Boy Scouts took advantage of this camp facility, many of the early Scouters in Santa Clara County remember this camp experience as one of the best.

MARSHALL HALL

The first place I camped was in Alum Rock Canyon at a site which was offered to the Scouts. They had built wooden floors for the tents. I remember the area was full of poison oak. We went to Santa Cruz and camped the second year.

KEN ROBISON

Some of the troops went up there (Alum Rock Park). They had that terrible smelling swimming pool called the Natatorium and the kids couldn't pronounce it. That was before my time, but I know it was used some.

Camp Swanton

In 1924 the Council leased the old University of California engineering camp. (There were a large number of stakes driven all over the property.) It was located 16 miles north of Santa Cruz on the Coast Highway at Little Creek near the old community of Swanton.

The town of Swanton was named for Fred Swanton, the well-known early day promoter. Swanton, in the late 1890s, had laid out and promoted the plans for a casino and boardwalk for the beach at Santa Cruz, which was patterned after Coney Island in New York. He was also responsible for building the first hydroelectric plant in the area. The town of Swanton was quite small, but it boasted a hotel, fish hatchery, post office, and a railroad.

When the railroad was abandoned in 1922-23 it became too difficult to get to the camp, so the university discontinued the camp's use as a summer training location. Several buildings had been built for the engineering students such as a sheet metal mess hall, a cook shack, tent platforms and a caretaker's cabin. It was very convenient to have those buildings in place when the Council started to bring in their first campers. Some time later Little Creek was dammed for a place to swim.

Camp Swanton was used for summer camping from 1924 to 1930 by the Boy Scouts of the Santa Clara, San Benito, Monterey, Santa Cruz Counties Council.

*Camp Swanton Mess Hall —
Now Al Smith's train storage shed*

The sheet metal mess hall has withstood the ravages of time and is still in use by Scouter Al Smith who, sometime later, purchased the property. The campers used to line up outside for their turn to be served in the mess hall. Dating back as far as 1924, the boys, while they were waiting in line, autographed the side walls of the sheet metal building. Many of those signatures are still legible in 1990.

In 1931 the Council decided to stop leasing and to purchase some land as a campsite. They decided on a parcel of approximately 370 acres about 3/4 of a mile north of Camp Swanton, east of the Coast Highway, at the confluence of Little and Scott Creeks. The boys had frequently hiked there in the past. It was to be called Camp Arroyo Sequoia.

AL HERSCHBACH

We had a camp over by Davenport.... There was an old narrow gage railroad track up there; it used to run all the way to San Francisco. We would hike to the beach. I took a big old wood stove up there and that is what we cooked on. I took a siren up there and when we wanted the boys to come in we would crank it up. That was Camp Swanton.

JIM STURROCK (1989)

We left Al Smith's new house to visit the camp sites. First we drove a short distance down the hill and then a 100 yard jog to the right on the old highway to the Camp Swanton site. Some of the buildings here date to the time we used it as a camp. One building that was used as a store and a mess hall has corrugated iron siding which is still covered with the signatures of Scouts who were campers there during the twenties. This is where they stood in line while waiting to buy candy at the camp store.

Prior to its use as a Scout camp the site was used by the University of California as a civil engineering training camp. Ken (Robison) says that surveying stakes were all over the hills in those days. Today it is used by Cal Poly as a forestry training center, and Al has left it for this purpose in his will....

Camp Swanton Mess Hall Signatures

Camp Arroyo Sequoia

Camp Arroyo Sequoia is located about 3/4 miles up the old railroad bed from Camp Swanton at the confluence of Little and Scott Creeks, on the east side of the Coast Highway. The Council purchased this former logging camp property of approximately 370 acres and used it for summer camping from 1931 to 1940.

In 1931 the San Jose Rotary Club assumed, as that year's community project, the building of a mess hall/assembly room at a cost of $2,250. The San Benito, Monterey and Santa Cruz Counties supported the joint camping facilities costs until they formed the Monterey Bay Area Council in 1932–33.

In 1933–34 the Council, and then president Ernest Abbott, were recipients of business community help in getting a swimming pool at the camp. Earl Heple of the San Jose Construction firm used his large equipment to dig the hole and the Santa Cruz division of Portland Cement Company donated the aggregate. Al Smith's father Stanley Smith, was Camping Chairman at that time. When the swimming pool was completed in 1934 they couldn't use it the first year due to a polio epidemic.

During the first several years Duncan McKinley, the Scout Executive, built a small ranger's cabin from surplus lumber. Herman Biel, who liked the quiet life, stayed at camp year round as caretaker. A health cottage and a small "Lincoln Log" cabin for summer resident clergy were also constructed on the property.

The land was so steep in the canyon (arroyo) there wasn't enough flat space for large numbers of campers to use, so several camping areas were developed for troops with different levels of camping skills. The camp for 14-year-olds up on the side of the hill was called Pioneer Camp.

The terrain between the two creeks became a disaster area on February 29, 1940 when a devastating flood destroyed the mess hall and the adjoining cook shack. Unfortunately, what didn't wash out in the 1940 flood

Camp Arroyo Sequoia Swimming Pool   Courtesy of Al Smith

on Little Creek, washed out two years later with a flood on Scott Creek.

Although a volunteer work party, during Easter week, temporarily restored the camp for use in the summer of 1940, the second flood sealed its fate. The Council decided to sell Camp Arroyo Sequoia in 1944.

Scouter Al Smith recalls that the Council leased the property from him for summer camp use in 1948 for the sum of $1.00, but has not used Arroyo Sequoia since that time.

KEN ROBISON

(In regard to public support) … when we wanted a swimming pool over at … Arroyo Sequoia, the Santa Cruz Davenport cement factory … said they would donate the cement. And somebody went down to the Granite Construction Company at Chittinden Pass and they said they would haul up the concrete. Bud Heple, came over and supervised the building of the pool. (Later he got killed up here at Lexington Dam.) I think the big pool cost them three thousand dollars in actual outlay. It was colder than a bugger because it had no heat. The creek water just ran in and ran out. The kids ran in and out, too.

AL SMITH

The camp (up Little Creek) had a name, Arroyo Sequoia, which was a combination of Spanish and Latin, I believe, and there even was a song about it, "Arroyo Sequoia, where Scouts were made." There were four or five (camping areas). They had little group camps depending upon the Scouts' maturity. (The one for 14-year-olds was called Pioneer.) The thing I remember about Pioneer, it started out as Woodcraft Camp but Pioneer was a more exciting name.

We used to walk up the creek and then they decided to build a direct trail up the side of the hill.

One work party of Scouts started down the hill and one work party started up the hill. The group going down the hill said to the others, "You better come up the hill a little more or you are going to miss us." The guys coming up the hill said, "You better go down a little more or you are going to miss us." When they came together they had to build an eight foot ladder to join the two trails.

One night the regional executive came to visit a special campfire up at the Pioneer Camp and when they started down one of the party walked off the ladder. The next day we started a connecting trail so they met exactly.

In 1940 there was a flood … (the last camp) we ran here was in 1940. Later it was decided that with weather like this Camp Arroyo Sequoia was not an ideal place. Then the Council bought the land in Felton, and the 1941 camp was in Felton.

ROTARY'S GIFT TO SCOUTING

The Rotary Club of San Jose is assuming, as its Community Project for the current year, the building of a mess hall and assembly room for the Boy Scouts of America in the area comprising Santa Clara, Santa Cruz, Monterey, and San Benito Counties. This building will be erected at the permanent Boy Scout camp near Swanton, California, at a cost of $2,250.

In fostering this project, the San Jose Rotary Club expresses its complete confidence in the program of the BSA, and in the administration of this program in this area. It is our feeling that no type of work can prove more beneficial to the health, morals and civic growth of our boys than this program which has already proven itself to be proficient in every way.

Particularly are we interested in the summer camps, where the boys are placed under competent Scout executives; where they can live out of doors, study nature at its source, and receive the benefits of rigorous and systematic exercise. Under these conditions, boys learn to cooperate cheerfully, recognize constituted authority, and follow needful regulations obediently. The development of these characteristics will prove of untold value to these boys in later life.

It is our hope that the building which we are erecting will add comfort and pleasure to the leisure time of the boys while in camp.

R.B. Leland, President, San Jose Rotary Club
(circa 1931)

KEN ROBISON

I spent too many years over here, summers, and a lot of other time, too. (Robison was Camp Director for several years.) Of course, along came the war, and a different executive, and the executive board was getting old. They had all kinds of reasons for selling out. They would come over for one day in the summertime and invariably it would be a nice cool day. Up there (in the Santa Clara valley) it would be summer, but down here it would be cool and misty. But I never heard one of the kids object to the weather at all.

The Board decided it had everything against it, and 45 miles from San Jose looked pretty far, so they bought that dumb piece of land in Felton. It turned out financially all right, I guess.

JIM STURROCK (1989)

(When the History Task Force visited Al Smith's place at Swanton) ... we drove on a dirt road along the banks of Little Creek to the site of Camp Arroyo Sequoia. This was a former railroad grade used by the logging companies. A small level site at the confluence of Little and Scott Creeks was once a logging camp. This is where the camp mess hall was built in 1931 and was washed away by the flood of 1940. It seems that the flood brought a large tree down the creek which went through the cook shack and pushed the cast iron cook stove right through the mess hall and out the other side. The remains of the old stove are still visible there today, but the cook shack and the mess hall are long gone.

MICHAEL ANTONACCI

I recall once a Scout Executive named White (Harrison White, SE 1923-30). He had a camp at Swanton up the coast. I think that Mr. Smith (Al Smith) who had become quite a Scout leader, now owns the land. But White asked me to go there and evaluate it because he was developing the place. He got a little provoked with me when I told him he should stop developing it for several reasons. First, it didn't have any flat area; it was on stumps of Redwood trees that had been forested which were eight to ten feet in diameter and you couldn't build anything on top of them. And then, it was a little too remote. I had learned that the parents wanted the camp where it was not too far and where it was easily accessible. So I discouraged him from developing it.

AL SMITH

... I knew this place (Camp Arroyo Sequoia) was up for sale and Ken (Robison) and I bought it (1944) through Cooper Chow Realty. Then Ken got another interest and I bought out his share. The first people I brought over here said, "What did you buy this goat ranch for?" I had been accused of buying it from the Boy Scouts on an insider deal, but we bought it through the realty company.

I looked in the tax records and there was an adjoining 220 acres for sale, it was a tax deal. My dad advised me, "Don't buy it. If nobody paid the taxes, it isn't worth anything."

Then in 1948 a hard-nosed guy by the name of Marshall Hall, wrote a lease and they came back here and had a camp for one more summer. I argued long and loud that they should leave the water lines that they put in here as part of the property, but they said, "No way." I was to get one dollar which I don't think was ever paid.

Camp Bonnie Brier

Following the decsion that Camp Arroyo Sequoia was not going to be their longterm camp site, the Council began a search for other camping accommodations for their Boy Scouts. Their inquiries led them to the Boulder Creek area and they found a spot they thought had good potential.

In the 1920s Mr. and Mrs. Stanley Hiller, Sr. had purchased a 160 acre plot of land, some of which fronted Bear Creek Road, and other portions of it ran along Bear Creek. They acquired it as a summer retreat because of its proximity to the creek and its heavily wooded terrain. Mrs. Hiller called the retreat "Bonnie Brier."

It was located just a mile from the town of Boulder Creek. The family constructed a road and a small bridge over the creek in order to get to the ridge where they built their home.

In the early forties, Hiller was made aware of the Santa Clara County Council search for a camp site to replace Camp Arroyo Sequoia. Hiller offered the use of a portion of their retreat for a summer camp. However, the Boy Scouts only camped there two or three summers.

World War II continued to drag on, with its gas shortages and other constraints, and it became unfeasable to return to Camp Bonnie Brier.

There is no written record of how Camp Bonnie Brier was used. It may have been used for summer camping in addition to the San Lorenzo Scout Ranch in the early forties, or it may have been used for weekend camping only.

A footnote to the Bonnie Brier story: following his father's death, Stanley Hiller, Jr., former president of Hiller Helicopters, inherited the portion that the family had always referred to as, "the Boy Scout end of the property." In December, 1977, Stanley, Jr. deeded a portion of his parcel (which was adjacent to the property where Boy Scouts had camped in the forties) to the Stanford Area Council, BSA. Their newly acquired property was developed in the late seventies, as a campsite, by our neighboring Council. They call it the Boulder Creek Scout Reservation.

(information source: Stanley Hiller, Jr.)

LARRY HILL

We had a camp up at Boulder Creek called Bonnie Blair (Brier). It was really a very primitive camp. It was outside Boulder Creek. It was really a nice spot, a beautiful spot, but it was really primitive. I remember Marshall Hall ... drove the truck and he was really involved in it.... It wasn't along the river, it was kind of away from the river ... We had tent platforms.

San Lorenzo Scout Ranch — a.k.a. Felton Scout Ranch

This camp has been known both as San Lorenzo Scout Ranch and Felton Scout Ranch.

Ken Robison, Camp Director, remembers that the Council purchased 40 acres of land along the San Lorenzo River near Felton (one property north of where the Safeway Store is located today). The Lay family, former owners of the Santa Cruz Lumber Company, owned the land. They had cattle on adjoining acreage, which had to be fenced off by the Council. Only one building, a 19' x 16' cookhouse, was built on the property that was used just a few years and then sold.

Scouter Al Smith was hired by Robison as a camp assistant at the Scout Ranch in 1941. One of his favorite duties was driving the camp truck into Felton for supplies.

Scouter Glenn George remembers camping there with his patrol in 1942. George was a brand new patrol leader that year. Scouter Joel Gambord has a triangular pocket patch dated 1945 with the name San Lorenzo Scout Ranch. Gambord camped there with Troop 13 in 1946 as well.

No written records have been found of the transactions but from these Scouters' reports it is assumed that the San Lorenzo Scout Ranch was purchased about 1941, used until 1947, and sold sometime in 1947 or 1948.

Al Smith leased (for $1.00) the property at Camp Arroyo Sequoia to the Santa Clara County Council in order that it could be used for Scout camp the summer of 1948 before it transfered camping activities to Camp Hi-Sierra in 1949.

KEN ROBISON

(Duncan) McKinley came in 1941, and he was the (Scout) Executive that said the camp (Arroyo Sequoia) was too far away.... So they closed that camp down and still held the property. And then they bought a little piece of property outside of Felton, which was

not suitable for a camp at all. It was too close to town and kids were sneaking out of camp at night to go over to the stores in town to buy candy and anything else. It was too civilized, but during the war (WWII) transportation and all the rest of it was a problem.

AL SMITH

My dad was on the board (executive). In fact, he was the camping chairman who decided to buy the place in Felton.... I don't know what they called that camp (San Lorenzo Scout Ranch). The kids could walk into town and get hamburgers and milk shakes. It (the camp) was across the bridge about half a mile towards Ben Lomand, then turn right and cross a rickety bridge over to the far side. We had about 135 acres, or something like that.

Cook Shack, San Lorenzo Scout Ranch
W.G. Adams, Cook, circa 1945

GLENN GEORGE

In the summer of 1942 I went to my first Boy Scout Camp in Felton. I had just become a patrol leader of the Panther Patrol in Troop 37 that met in the basement of the Calvary Methodist Church on the corner of Naglee and Morse....

Well, you might remember that on December 7th of 1941 a little war broke out. It was called W.W.II. Many things happened here in our country, but what affected me the most was food rationing and gas. Here we are trying to plan our trip to summer camp, (and) none of the fathers had enough gas to get us over the hill. And what were we going to do for food?

We got all the mothers together and they looked at all of their red and blue stamps to see how many of these little babies they could give to their sons for Scout summer camp. Since we weren't going to be home anyway, what was the big deal on giving us stamps? What we didn't know was these stamps were for all staples, sugar, meat and so on. Since I was the patrol leader I had all of these red and blue things, but I knew what to do with them.

We start out in somebody's station wagon, all of the patrol, with gear—hot day, and we get into Felton before noon and go right to the Felton general store. I had a list of goodies to buy, pancake mix, syrup, beans, milk and so forth. I send my buddies to get this stuff and I go to the meat department. Well, I see the biggest piece of meat I have ever seen. This one piece will serve everyone. So I asked the clerk how many red stamps for this piece? I don't really remember the exact amount but it was over 1,000. That just took care of all my problems. No more stamps. let's get out of here and go to camp.

We set up camp and built a beautiful "refer" or cooler, which we hung from a tree. Burlap sacks and ends of orange crates looked good. This gorgeous piece of meat went in there, after we doused it with water. Every hour, or so, we would sprinkle water on our cooler and look at our steak. It got better looking each time.

Next day, repeated this watering, and now it's dinner time. The fire was glowing and now to take the steak out of the cooler. It was blue not red. So what did that mean? I didn't know and neither did my fellow Scouts.

I don't know why I smelled it, but I did. Let me tell you something. Blue steak smells different than red steak. I got a hold of a camp leader and he told me, "Don't eat that meat." We all stood around the fire and wondered, what are we going to have for dinner? A good buddy of mine, I thought, was the patrol leader next to our camp. so I asked him for some food, anything at this point. He said to me, "How many stamps do you have.?" I said, "None." He said, "Too Bad!"

Well, after a few choice words, he gave me one can of beans. That's what the Panther Patrol had for dinner. I think that's where the term, "lean and mean" came from.

That's not all I remember about World War 2, but at the moment, that was the most important.

Camp Stuart

On August 24, 1944 Reginald Ray Stuart and Grace Dell Stuart gave 80 acres of their ranch property to the Santa Clara County Council for use as a Boy Scout camp. This property is located at 16191 Bohlman Road at an elevation of 2200 feet three miles southwest of Saratoga, California. Mr. and Mrs. Stuart donated the property in memory of their son "Red."

The property has a long history. For many years it was erroneously called, "The John Brown Place." John Brown, a Civil War abolitionist of Harper's Ferry fame, had been dead and buried long before his widow, Mary Ann Day Brown, came west to the Saratoga area. She, and other members of the family, settled on the property in 1881 where she lived until her death in 1884. The property went through several hands and was purchased by the Reginald Stuarts in 1921.

The Stuarts were interested in conservation and the environment. They enthusiastically went into a tree planting program over a period of years which successfully introduced many species of native and exotic trees, shrubs and plants to their property.

A later transaction, May 18, 1959, with Freda and William Dose added 60 acres of an adjoining piece of land to the Camp Stuart lands. (Today the camp property consists of 170 acres.)

Because of its close proximity to town it is an ideal spot for weekend camping. There are no fees charged for the year-round camping programs. The Troop camping area provides individual campsites for up to seven troops at the same time. These campsites include tables, fireplaces, water and latrine facilities.

The Camp Stuart hiking trails provide an opportunity for hikes from one to ten miles, in and around the camp. A special Trail Camping Area has been set aside which will accommodate two Troops. All equipment, food and water must be backpacked to the camping area.

Swimming is available at the camp pool during the summer season. Swimmers pay a 25¢ service charge to help defray its maintenance costs.

COLUMBIA 3947

SANTA CLARA COUNTY COUNCIL

BOY SCOUTS OF AMERICA

315 Security Building   84 South First Street

SAN JOSE 16, CALIFORNIA

November 7, 1944

Mr. and Mrs. R. R. Stuart
1120 Glen Drive
San Leandro, California

Dear Mr. and Mrs. Stuart:

We had our first regular Executive Board Meeting following the vacation period, last week, at which time the Board Members were informed of your very gracious gift to this organization. While, of course, everyone was familiar with the fact that we had received such a gift and knew something of the donors from the newspaper stories, this was the first opportunity we have had to really tell the whole story.

You will be interested to know that Mr. Charles E. Moore, President of the Joshua Hendy Iron Works of Sunnyvale, who is our Camping Chairman, was particularly enthusiastic and proposed that we, as soon as possible, proceed to raise a sum of $50,000.00 to be devoted to the development of the Stuart Scout Training Reservation and our Scout Ranch at Felton. Preliminary plans are underway. We contemplate, among other things, the construction of a 30' x 75' swimming pool at both camps.

The Board asked that I extend to you an invitation to be our guests of honor on January 18, the occasion of our Annual Meeting, at which time we shall try to express our gratitude in a rather concrete manner.

The caretakers have departed, as you may already know, and as yet we have been unable to find anyone whom we have considered satisfactory.

I will tell you again how sorry Mrs. Mathews and I are that we could not accept your invitation for "breakfast" on the 11th, but that's just one of the holidays that isn't a holiday for me, but I do hope that we may have a "rain check" for another date.

With all good wishes, I am

Sincerely yours,

O. B. MATHEWS
Scout Executive

OBM:dr

Reginald Ray Stuart

Reginald Ross "Red" Stuart
For whom the camp was dedicated

Camp Stuart, also known as the "Stuart Training Reservation," is used extensively for Boy Scout training and leadership development courses. Its dining hall doubles as an indoor learning center for up to 75 people. Permanent three-sided, roofed shelters, called the "Adirondacks," can house 75 participants.

In addition to the facilities available for Boy Scouts, a special Webelos Camping area can be used by any Cub Scout Pack's Webelos Den for overnight camping.

A special Cub Scout Day Use area is reserved for the exclusive use of Cub Scout Packs for day outings and picnics. During the summer months, in recent years, Camp Stuart's main use has been as the site for the Cub Scout Day Camp.

Adult and youth members of The Order of the Arrow, the Boy Scout honorary camping organization, worked for several years to construct a lodge at Camp Stuart. The Miwok Lodge Hall was erected on the hill above the ceremonial grounds and has proven to be a well used addition to the camp. Scouting volunteers started the building in 1970; it was completed in 1976.

Camp Stuart has a resident Ranger to assist campers in making the best possible use of the camping facilities. Claude (Smitty) Smith was among the Camp Rangers with the longest tenure. He was on duty from 1955 until retirement in 1965. Glenn Helberg followed Smitty as Camp Ranger from 1966 to 1985. The current ranger is Michael Hannah.

KEN ROBISON

There is a trail from Overlook Road in Los Gatos that goes right over to Camp Stuart, which was always known in those days as the John Brown Ranch. Mary Brown, an old gal here in Campbell was a daughter, or granddaughter of Mary Brown.... Anyway, this is "John Brown's body lies a moldering...," you know. It was known as that before the Stuart's had the thing.... But anyway, she (Mary Brown) is buried in the cemetery over there. She had quite a bad time.

We camped up there lots, because it was an interesting place and was easy hiking distance out of Los Gatos, and we used it for overnight (camping). So our troop got well acquainted with the Stuarts, and "Red" Stuart, ... he was a little bit older than I. Then "Red" was killed in the war (WWII) and so they decided that they would give the place to the Boy Scouts in his memory. In fact, on the lower side of the road up there, there is a concrete bench that has a bronze plaque. It's a thing which nobody in the Council seems to know anything about. (The plaque is now mounted on a post in the upper level training area.)

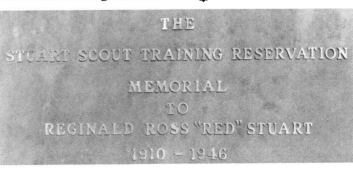

THE
STUART SCOUT TRAINING RESERVATION
MEMORIAL
TO
REGINALD ROSS "RED" STUART
1910 – 1946

I think their son's name was Reginald, same as his dad's, but everyone called him "Red" because of his hair. Anyway, we camped there a lot, so the Stuarts decided they would give eighty acres out of the one hundred sixty acres they had there.

Stuart, himself, had gone to the University of California and had been very interested in forestry, and his son "Red" followed along with that same interest. Both of them had classes from Dr. Metcalf. "Woody" Metcalf by that time was, I guess, Forester Emeritus of the university, and so they planted up there a tremendous number of trees, and called it the Washington Arboretum.

Dr. Metcalf was, of course, kind of a fairy godfather to anyone interested in the woods. He was the author of many books on forestry and trees and the coast and all.... But, he told us that was the (most) famous arboretum between the one at Davis and the one at Santa Barbara. I just used to have fits to see what they were doing with those trees up there, cutting them out. Those trees were all individually marked with a metal plaque on each one of them as to (their species). Dr. Metcalf said it had the finest variety of conifers, that was what they specialized in, of any place on the coast.

Property Research by R.R. Stuart
(Obtained by Doris Hambrick at
the University of the Pacific Library, Stockton)

"Believed by the Padres to belong to the Mission Santa Clara, tho (sic.) declared later by the courts to be a part of the Public Domain, the Stuart Camp site was purchased in 1881 for a home by Mary Anne Brown, widow of the abolitionist. A sketch of the cabin occupied by Mrs. Brown, her two daughters, and son-in-law, James Fablinger, appeared in 1888 in the Santa

Clara Valley section of Picturesque California. A description of life at the Brown home may be found in the October, 1885 Overland Monthly.

"In 1884 the Browns sold the property to Ludvig Lundblad and Louis Nissen. The new buyers divided the land lengthwise, Lundblad taking the eastern half and Nissen the remainder. The former set out a prune orchard and the later some grapes.

"At the turn of the century, J.W. Northrup bought both properties and spent considerable money in altering the old house. After several transfers the Lundblad property came into the hands of Father Nolan of East Oakland and the other piece was purchased by Dr. Small who built the upper house.

"During February, 1921, we contracted to buy both of these tracts. At that time there was a small grove of Monterey cypress and Douglas firs on the Northrup place and a single eucalyptus tree near the house on the Small property.

"That first spring of 1921 we had the caretaker transplant a dozen native Douglas firs, but they had all died before the end of the first summer. The next spring we planted a lot of Monterey cypress at the upper place for a wind-break. We also planted a row of eucalyptus trees. During one week rabbits or rats nipped off every one of the latter trees. The cypress grew. The following year we put in more cypress, both at the upper place and along the road at the lower house.

"About this time, Woodbridge Metcalf of the University of California advised us that the Monterey cypress would prove a short-lived tree in this locality— a fact which we soon discovered. Thru (sic.) his assistance, we began the planting of other varieties: a few redwoods, Port Orford cedars, and Coulter, Japanese, and Monterey pines. Once he brought us a small Western Yellow pine and three Sequoia gigantias. We set them out at various places about the ranch and they are still growing.

The Stuart Tree
Where Reginald and Winifred were married

"A tangle of brush and poison oak covered the entire side hill between the two houses. During a winter of the middle 1920s, the caretaker grubbed out and burned tons of this brush. The next spring we planted most of this side hill and ran pipe lines all over the area so that the trees could be watered easily during the dry season. As a protection against animals, we put small loops of woven wire fencing about each tree.

"In 1930–31 we started setting out trees on the bare hill across the road from the lower house. On much of this hill the soil had been entirely washed away, so we dug holes in the rocky surface and pushed up hundreds of loads of top soil in a wheelbarrow. Since this year was the tri-centennial (bi-centennial) of Washington's birth, this grove was called the Washington Arboretum.

"In the winter of 1932 we traded an old tractor for day labor in planting redwoods on the entire side hill northeast of the upper house. Our last planting was just below the concrete reservoir.

"The trees were purchased from many local nurseries, the University of California, and the Pacific Lumber Company. Thousands of tiny redwoods and Port Orford cedars were set out in the nursery located in the ravine between the two houses. The Redwood Camp is now located there.

"One day in the early '20s, we met James Fablinger walking up the hill on which he had made his home almost fifty years earlier. The late Senator Phelan was a frequent visitor, climbing up the steep trail from his beautiful Montalvo. Once he drove Gertrude Atherton to the ranch. In the early '30s, Ralph Edwards was our guest and later wrote a short play for one of our fiestas. During one summer the son-in-law of Jack London was our caretaker.

"Thru (sic.) the years many events—weddings, christenings, picnics and countless week-end trips, wove unforgettable memories for us about the old ranch. In August, 1944, Mrs. Stuart and I gave the property to the Santa Clara Council of the Boy Scouts of America. We hoped it might be an aid in training boys to become resourceful, independent citizens. We have been more than satisfied...."

Claude E. "Smitty" Smith, 1963
Naturalist and Camp Ranger, 1955-1965

MAURY TRIPP

Smitty (Claude Smith, longtime camp ranger) lived in the building that was just beside John Brown's widow's family's residence. And, you can still see some of the old orchard trees, the pears and prunes that were planted by the widow Brown's family. They are growing in among the fir trees, and so forth, in several spots up there. The last time I actually hiked out there, several years ago, they were still there. I am sure some of the prune trees are still there, because they almost live forever....

I guess some of the things involving interesting and significant historical events at Camp Stuart involve President Hoover and some of his people. I wasn't present at the time, but it was related to me, I think, by Mr. Stuart, or his wife. And probably (verified) by the old camp ranger (Smitty) up at Stuart that moved to Portland.... Well, Hoover (and his wife) planted a lot of trees up there on the area from the road toward the Cub Scout area, especially. They came up there frequently. Hoover was a friend of Stuart.

A lot of the trees were planted by the University of California Forestry Department as experimental efforts to see if they would grow in this area.

AUSTEN WARBURTON

We (our troop) has been up to Stuart and had some great experiences at Stuart. (The camp) was a gift from the Stuart family to the Scouts, and was the old place developed ... by the John Brown family. According to the rumor ... his widow came out and wanted to be as close to her husband in Heaven as she thought she could get on earth. (She) landed on the top of the mountain at the end of Bohlman Road.

The Stuarts took over and developed it into practically an arboretum there with a lot of exotic and fine trees.... We were concerned with some of the ramifications at Stuart over rights-of-way, water rights, and various things of this sort ... because of potential encroachment by the developing neighborhood below us, our need for water and their need for water, and the compromises that were worked out on that. We also wanted to acquire some additional property to add to Stuart, to enlarge our camp facility.

Glenn Helberg, Camp Ranger, 1966–1985

Cub Day Camp Ceremony, 1980
In Smitty's Circle

SCOUTS TRAINING IS PUT TO USE AT CAMP STUART
Clover Cummings

A bugle blows—uncertainly at times. The pitch isn't perfect. But the notes are recognizable. To a young boy's mind they spell "Assembly." Tents empty hurriedly; a line forms—of eager, if sleepy faces. So begins a day at a Boy Scout camp.

This summer, in 22 camps of the nine Bay Area councils of the Boy Scouts, 35,000 youngsters are spending a week or more. Supervising them are almost 4,000 adults—all on a volunteer basis. The 22 camps cover 5,700 acres with hundreds of miles of hiking trails and campsites. For the boys' recreation and education there are swimming pools, lakes, boats of all kinds, archery ranges, horses, burros, rifle ranges and ski tows. But of all the facilities of Scouting probably most important are those provided by Nature herself.

In this respect, Camp Stuart is a fine example. Its 140 acres atop a mountain, four miles up a narrow, winding road from Saratoga, contain great trees, shrubs, wildflowers and grasses of endless variety. There is a minimum of man-made structures, but the natural environment has been developed to allow the utmost opportunity for learning while roughing it. There, Scouts are able to apply to outdoor situations what they have learned at home in year-around training programs.

A visit with San Jose Troop 233 at Camp Stuart provided a look at a typical day in camp. The troop had packed in the night before. They hiked to their campsite in the rain, and it rained most of the night. But a Scout's tent is weathertight; so there was a minimum of discomfort.

The "A" Frame

Training Area

Reveille at 8 o'clock found the morning fairly clear, but cold.... Building fires, cooking breakfast and policing the camp preceded the day's main activities.... Under the direction of Scoutmaster Byron Favorite, leaders in the troop were placed in charge of the instruction of each group.... Favorite was assisted by Albert Herschback, a veteran of over 30 years in Scouting.

Dispersing to various areas of the camp, each group began its project. At the campsite, one eager group raced against time to build an observation tower out of rope and eucalyptus limbs. In other areas, the Scouts learned the use of rope and knot tying; how to use an axe; identification of animal spores; identification of trees, shrubs and grasses; lessons in soil conservation. The nature study classes were under the direction of Claude Smith, camp ranger and another veteran with over 40 years in Scouting.

Lunch break was followed by a similar afternoon schedule with time out for occasional refreshment at the camp trading post....

After dinner cleanup came the Scout's greatest delight—the evening sing around a campfire. Scouts know an unusual number of songs, and deliver them with good harmony as well as unbounded enthusiasm.

Before breaking camp, the troop attended chapel service Sunday morning....

(Excerpt: San Jose Mercury News, 7/28/63)

BILL NICHOLSON

During all the years (1959-63), things went along pretty much as usual, boy long, cash sort, people short, yet all very rewarding.

We did have one flap. Some property (44 acres) adjacent to Camp Stuart came up for sale, as I think I remember, for $44,000. The Foundation (Memorial Foundation) did not want to buy this, so we, the Council, went ahead on our own and bought it. Things finally evened out.

JACK COX

(John Brown's widow) died here and is buried in the Saratoga Madronia Cemetery. R.R. Stuart and his wife were lovely people who had taken over that property and later donated it to the Santa Clara County Council for a camp site, and it has been such ever since.

We had troop camp sites there, but it has been used primarily for training. I have spent many hours up there taking or giving training. Also, we have the Order of the Arrow lodge building and ceremonial grounds at Stuart.

Mr. Stuart wrote a poem called "Blossom Day from John Brown Mountain" in 1928. Blossom day was anytime in the spring when all the blossoms in the valley were in bloom. You could look out over the valley and it looked like a blanket of snow, the white prune blossoms were so apparent. When I was sitting with him at some Scouting dinner one evening, I said, "You should bring that poem up to date." "Oh," he said, "It's beyond me now. I don't think I could do it." I said, "You could say something like...." He said, "You could do it. You do it for me and send me a copy." So, I wrote a continuation in 1970 called "From John Brown Mountain."

Order of the Arrow Lodge Hall

Camp Stuart then and now

Around 1928, R. R. Stuart, while at his home, which is now our own Camp Stuart, wrote down his thoughts while looking down upon Santa Clara Valley from his mountain in a poem, "Blossom Day from John Brown Mountain."

Forty years later, Dr. Jack Cox, Santa Clara County Council Commissioner, reflecting on Mr. Stuart's work, and with Mr. Stuart's consent, prepared a second poem, reflecting the changes in John Brown's Mountain:

Blossom Day from John Brown Mountain

by R. R. Stuart
Circa 1928

Upon a saddle near the Mountain top
Two thousand feet above the blossom's drifted snow,
Amid huge evergreens, I stand and watch
The changing epochs in the plain below.

*   *   *

I saw the valley ere the White Man came,
A verdant sward of multi-colored flowers.
The simple native moves across the scene,
And in the distance bleak Diablo towers.

I saw the padres with their cavalcade
March through the Valley in that ancient day
To plant the missions for the Red Men's souls,
And leave the first faint markings of the King's Highway.

I saw the ranchos with their teeming herds,
Vast domains of the oak strewn plain.
The dons and donnas and the peons poor
And all the trappings of the Spanish reign.

I saw the soldiers raise the Stars and Stripes
And make the capital at San Jose.
I saw the miners and the others come
Searching each canyon for its hidden pay.

And later, on Alviso's swampy shores
Huge wharves and bins to store the golden wheat.
For harvest fields spread out from brim to brim
Changing to grain the Valley's gift of meat.

Today I see the orchard's myriad blooms,
Ten thousand acres as a garden plot,
Thus Magic hides Utility's stern brow
Makes poetry of prune and apricot.

*   *   *

A golden cycle and a thousand years,
Man's struggle upward from the soil to God,
Is typified in every mystic bloom
Which bursts the bonds that bind it to the sod.

Oh, Santa Clara, with your wealth undreamed
And joy and happiness and gifts untold,
Give thought to those whose vision blazed the trail,
Their faith was boundless and their spirits bold.

From John Brown Mountain

By John E. Cox, M.D.
Circa 1970
As R. R. Stuart might see the Valley at this time

Now time has passed — another 40 years.
Again I stand upon the Mountain side.
(No longer does the land belong to me,
I gave it free that camping Scouts could bide.)

Again I view the distant changing plain,
The blossoms now have scattered and are few.
A million others found my garden spot
And came to build and start their lives anew.

I see the factories on the valley floor
To serve man's needs and his ability
To push aside the bonds of time and space
To reach the moon or yet defend his peace and liberty.

So "progress" came to smite the vale below
With crowded roads and heavy, smoky skies.
But man awakes and shall his earth reclaim
With God-given will and his own enterprise.

I saw the change from oaks to cattle land
And then from grain to blossomed orchard trees.
I trust the crop of children we will grow
Shall prove their lives to be worth more than these.

For this I gave my valued mountain-top
That boys who would could climb its slopes to me,
And pledge with me to those who blazed the trail
That "in our time we'll keep our faith with thee."

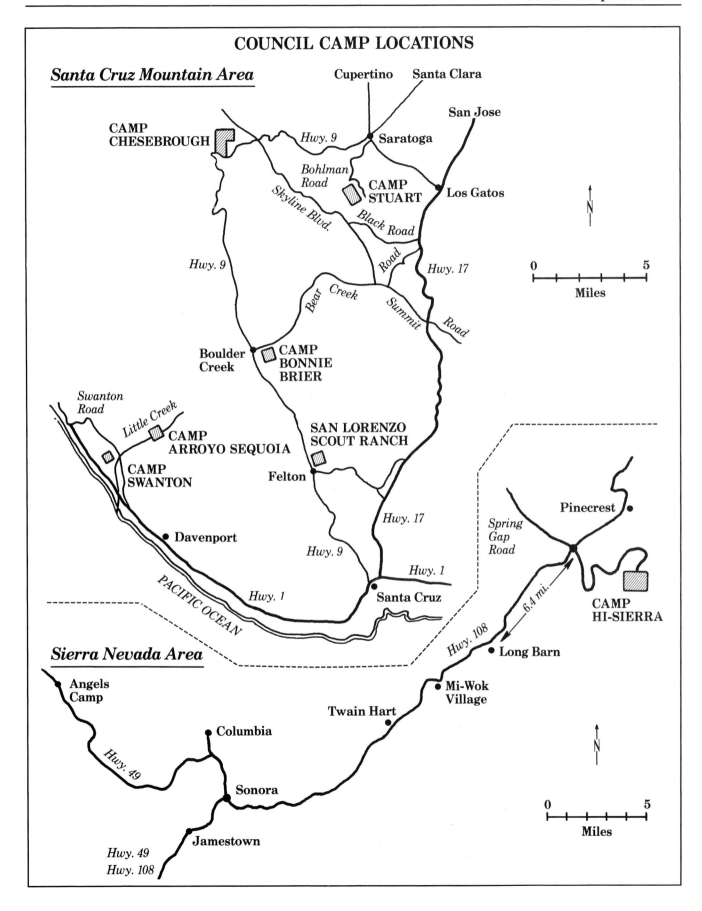

COUNCIL CAMP LOCATIONS

Santa Cruz Mountain Area

Cupertino   Santa Clara

San Jose

CAMP CHESEBROUGH

Hwy. 9   Saratoga

Bohlman Road   CAMP STUART   Los Gatos

Skyline Blvd.

Black Road

Hwy. 9   *Road*   *Hwy. 17*

Bear Creek   *Summit Road*

Boulder Creek   CAMP BONNIE BRIER

Swanton Road

Little Creek   CAMP ARROYO SEQUOIA

CAMP SWANTON

SAN LORENZO SCOUT RANCH

Felton

Davenport

Hwy. 17

Hwy. 9

Hwy. 1

Hwy. 1   Santa Cruz

PACIFIC OCEAN

0   5
Miles

N

Spring Gap Road   Pinecrest

6.4 mi.   CAMP HI-SIERRA

Hwy. 108   Long Barn

Sierra Nevada Area

Angels Camp

Mi-Wok Village

Twain Hart

Columbia

Hwy. 49

Sonora

N

Jamestown

Hwy. 49
Hwy. 108

0   5
Miles

Camp Hi-Sierra

In 1949 the Council purchased 100 acres of land in the Sierra Nevada Mountains for the sum of $10. The bargain price really represented a donation of that land to the Boy Scouts. The Council called the property Camp Hi-Sierra. It has an elevation of 5,000 feet and is bisected by the north fork of the Tuolomne River. The campsite is 160 miles from San Jose off Sonora Pass Highway 108 between Longbarn and Pinecrest.

Scouters Ken Robison and Bob Kirkwood found the site which was owned by Ed Jenness. Jenness had homesteaded the land in 1879. From 1903 to 1912 it was leased to the Sonora Logging Company, which conducted the largest lumber operation in the area. More than 600 men were employed by the company, all of whom lived in the immediate area. Scouter Eric Thorsen assisted Scout Executive Chester Bartlett in facilitating the arrangements for the purchase.

The Council first used the land as a camp in 1948. In May, 1949, Edward Jenness, "for the sum of $10," signed over 100 acres of his property to the Santa Clara County Council for the use of the Boy Scouts. The first two or three years there was only a cook shack with everyone eating outdoors.

Once again, the Scouting volunteers pitched in and constructed the mess hall, tent platforms, the Health Lodge, latrines and showers, and developed the water system. They even devised a dam that was convertible so that when the camping season was over, the Tuolomne River could return to its natural flow. The dam was needed for aquatic sports during the seven-week summer camping session.

Camp Hi-Sierra has a well-trained staff of Scouting professionals, volunteer Scouters and junior staff. The Council is proud that all the equipment, facilities and staff necessary to assist campers to work on and complete advancement requirements are available at Camp Hi-Sierra. The programs include Nature Conservation-Ecology, Aquatics, Field Sports and Handicrafts.

There is also high adventure, backcountry and outpost camping. The camp provides a special opportunity for Senior Patrol Leaders to 'sharpen their leadership skills, as well.

The parents of the campers like the fact that there is a doctor on call full time at the Health Lodge. The boys who have come to camp for adventure often end up mentioning how nice it is to have a Trading Post where concession and convenience items can be obtained at a reasonable cost.

The current camp ranger is Alan Buscaglia.

Dining Hall

ERIC THORSEN

At one time I was involved with Camp Hi-Sierra and went up on the inspections and things like that. Under Bartlett (Scout Executive) they were talking about purchasing a Sierra camp site.... They mentioned Tuolumne County. My father had a mill at Tuolumne above Sonora. I knew the area and some of the people. I had worked in the woods under a civil engineer who lived up in that area most of his life. And I also (knew) one of the department heads in the mill was on the Board of Supervisors (of Tuolumne County).

I passed the word on to the group that was going to look over the Brown Mill site up there. The group got in touch with both of them and they were quite helpful on the thing; it gave them a little "in" on the county. The Brown Mill site is where Camp Hi-Sierra is now.

Dining Hall Construction, circa 1950

KEN ROBISON

Bob Kirkwood was the Assemblyman.... He was our chairman of our camping committee, and when I came back from Philmont, the national camp, he said (that) our biggest job is to find a camp site. So in the fall of 1946, and on into 1947, we visited (properties). I remember Kirkwood saying, "Well, we have to make up our mind pretty soon." We visited forty-three different pieces of property looking for land. Everybody was scouting out property to go to visit, and we visited that one up there (near Sonora).

Bob Kirkwood was a real good man, good thinker, good organizer. His camping and activities committee was very active.... That was my assignment, to help to find some land. So we finally settled on Hi-Sierra. We bought it from Ed Jenness. We bought one hundred acres of it. Ed offered us more land, but they (the Council) felt that one hundred acres was plenty.

Me and my wife, we became very friendly with the Jenness', and he said, "Why don't you buy that 300 acres adjoining the camp?" I said, "Gee, Ed, I would sure love to, it is great and fine country with water on it and everything else, but I can't afford that." He said, "Buy it and pay for it when you can."

Then, when we got into Hi-Sierra they decided to build a mess hall up there. Cliff Swenson was active in the Council then, and was very much involved in building the place, doing as much pre-fab as we could down here, cutting stuff. Cliff had somebody in Sunnyvale who knew snow loads and that kind of stuff, but everyone thought it was crazy to build the thing like we did with the steep pitch and all the rest.

CLIFF SWENSON

In the 1950s, together with my company and other volunteers, we built the first dam and the dining hall at Camp Hi-Sierra.

BILL NICHOLSON

In the middle 1950s I became interested in Camp Hi-Sierra and used to bring work parties (8-10) from the Company (Nicholson Construction Company) to open and close camp and do construction. My construction superintendents would go up on Friday evenings in pickups with work tools and materials. We built latrines, latrines and latrines, plus the doctor's cottage, additions to the mess hall and so on. We worked from 'can see' to 'can't see' on Saturday and again on Sunday morning, winding up with a big barbecue before heading back.

(Scout Executive) Chet Bartlett used to give us a bad time, so one time we worked up an invoice for a weekend's work. We included all the payroll at double time, travel time and mileage, equipment rental, materials, overhead—the works. It came to about $3800! We typed it all up and sent it in. It took quite a while before we would admit that we didn't mean it.

Dam with Removable Spillway Section

AUSTEN WARBURTON

A lot of people were participating, helping to build, and getting the layout. We had the mess hall that was constructed, and it had an upstairs entryway in case we wanted to use it in the wintertime. And, for that matter it had not been used in the wintertime until my outfit (Explorer Post 77) decided we wanted to go in.

We made our own snowshoes. The kids found some material on how to make snowshoes and we made, what they called then, burp shoes. (They were) sort of rounded, (and) rather difficult to walk on, because you are apt to step on one shoe or the other.

Waterfront, circa 1980

We had a few problems in persuading Scout headquarters that it was safe and proper for us to go up and use the facility. Ken was encouraging but the administration had reservations as to the capacity of the group, I suppose, to safely undertake that challenge. But, we did it. We got permission, and as I say, we made most of the gear, which was a good experience for the young fellows.

We went down into camp, we were down there a couple of winters and found that we were able to go up to the top of the (south) ridge over the snow faster in the winter on our snow shoes than we could in the summertime through the manzanita brush.

(The first couple of years, soon after the mess hall was built) we went in with substantial questioning by the administration. But, we did it successfully and I think that ultimately led to a greater use of the facility by other Scout units. It was exciting for the kids to come in, having been there in the summer program, and then come back and find the snow up to the roof line and have to go in through the snow door, drop down inside. Then carve your way out so that you could get through the regular doorway. It was a true and meaningful experience they had as well as, of course, the experience of preparing these things.

AUSTEN WARBURTON

We were in on some of the development of the early days of Camp Hi-Sierra with Ken (Robison), Chet Bartlett (Scout Executive), and the committee. Eric Thorsen, on the Council committee, was tremendously interested and involved in that situation....

Ken was in the Explorer program and he also, usually, had charge of Hi-Sierra camp. Ken was a great outdoorsman.... He was familiar with nature study, he could identify the trees, plants and animals, and he thoroughly reveled in the outdoor life.... Most of my involvement with Ken in those years related to the youngsters we had in the Explorer program and with references to the programs at the Hi-Sierra Camp. We, for example, were encouraged on the trips in the wintertime by Ken. We were encouraged to take ... longer pack trips.... Ken was very vital in that kind of programming for the Scouting organization.

He also had a charisma about him, as far as the young people were concerned. (For example) with young Bill Wilson, they became fast friends. It wasn't just a Scout executive working with kids, but, he became a real friend to share experiences and encourage boys in these things they were doing. He did a fine job, and as we were concerned about the acquisition of the camp and how it was going to be handled, we got into some interesting discussions because that was a venture that we had not gotten into before.

(In relation to the history of Camp Hi-Sierra) I met Ed Jenness through Ken. He was a fascinating person.... He came into the area as a boy of about sixteen and grew up there at a time when it was somewhat a wild country.... He lived down toward Sonora.... He came into the area with nothing and (became) a major landholder. That included, not only our area, but an area he later sold, I think, to a Baptist

church, so I think we still have a church camp group adjacent to ours. His stories were fascinating, and some of the other stories we picked up concerning the area were fascinating.... One that you might be interested in related to Wood's Creek.

There are several Wood's Lakes, Wood's Creek and so forth, and I got this story from him (Jenness). As I remember it, Wood was going through, along some trail and wearing a red flannel shirt that he had just bought, and to him, of course, that was a lovely, wonderful thing. All of a sudden an Indian coming up the trail sees him and pulls a gun on him and tells him to take off his shirt. He wanted his shirt, and obviously, the gun being on Wood, he decided he had better comply. So, he took off his shirt and handed it over to the Indian. The Indian put the gun down to put on the shirt, and as he was putting on the shirt, Wood grabbed the gun and shot the Indian—but it made a hole in his shirt.

VINTON S. MATTHEWS LODGE DEDICATION

The "Dr. Vinton S. Matthews Health Lodge" is the new name of the health lodge at Camp Hi-Sierra. The special presentation was made July 21 at the camp by past Council President Andy Bonfield.

This honor was given to Dr. Matthews for his outstanding contributions to Scouting and his community service work. For 20 years, he and his wife Grace, have recruited doctors to serve as medical officers at Camp Hi-Sierra, as well as providing vital medical care themselves. As a result, Camp Hi-Sierra, has enjoyed a record of medical health and safety unexcelled in the Western Region.

(Reprint: Santa Clarion, 8/82)

VINTON MATTHEWS

I became Camp Doctor at Camp Hi-Sierra in 1955. My office nurse, Grace, started going to camp every summer later for the full eight weeks of summer camp. To date, I have 35 years in as Camp Doctor and Grace has 28 years as Camp Nurse.

Although the most common problems were exhaustion and sore throats from yelling, these are some of the interesting medical sidelights of Camp Hi-Sierra I remember:

- *Only one case with a "Hot appendix";*
- *One Scoutmaster who lost an eye chopping wood;*
- *One Boy Scout who was running a 105 degree fever. We kept him overnight in the Health Lodge upper bunk, and that night, in a delirious state, he burst through the window and fell onto the porch and stairway. In the commotion he was finally found, covered with blood and mud in Blackfoot Camp after he had waded the creek. I had him sent down to the Sonora Hospital;*
- *The time it rained for five days and nights, and most of the kids got hypothermia, with temperatures ranging from 92 to 97 degrees. After rotating the Scouts twenty at a time through the Health Lodge, I told Camp Director John Burney I was giving him eight hours for the sun to come out and dry out the Scouts. Otherwise I was going to pull my rank as Vice President of the Council and Brigadier General of the National Guard and call out the Guard to take 250 kids to Sonora. John made the sun come out!*

Camp Chesebrough

On August 21, 1973, the Memorial Foundation of the Santa Clara County Council received a donation of 404 acres of prime forest land in the Santa Cruz Mountains from Paul and Nessie Chesebrough. It is in Santa Cruz County on Highway 9 two miles west of Skyline Boulevard.

The property was originally owned by the Hubbard and Carmichael Logging Company which built and operated a lumber mill at the Oil and Mill Creek junction. William and Edith Van Antwerp purchased the land in 1928.

Upon the death of Mrs. William C. Van Antwerp in 1949, Paul Chesebrough inherited the property from his aunt, Edith. After several years of trying to decide the best use for the property which might keep it in its natural state, the Chesebroughs decided to give the land to the Boy Scouts so they could use and enjoy it as a wilderness camping experience.

In 1983 an additional 140 acres, adjacent to the original 404 acre property, was given by the Chesebroughs to the Santa Clara County Council. In 1988 the Council contracted with a lumbering firm to selectively cut down some of the trees in order to

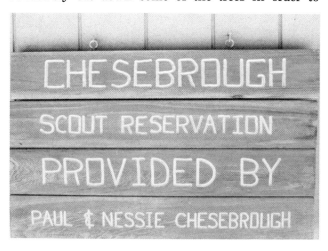

enhance the health and productivity of the remaining trees. This was part of an improvement program which upgraded the roads and hiking trails on the property.

Camp Chesebrough, under the management of the Memorial Foundation, has become a year-round camp in the beautiful redwoods of the Santa Cruz Mountains offering a primitive wilderness camping area to hundreds of boys and their leaders. The "Big Basin to the Sea" trail, which runs along one of the Chesebrough property lines, provides access to an unlimited network of hiking trails. The entire 544 acre reservation has a capacity or approximately 300 campers and backpackers.

Plans for the future call for each campsite to be equipped with a latrine, water, a flagpole, a campfire circle, and possibly tables and stoves.

Nessie and Paul Chesebrough, 1989

Camp Chesebrough, also called the Chesebrough Scout Reservation, is just fifteen minutes drive south of the city of Saratoga. It has campsites for weekend camping each of which can accommodate 30 campers. Campers are required to pack in their equipment, food and water. No vehicles, horses or pets are permitted. All troops must check in and out with the Resident Ranger.

Camp Chesebrough furnishes the ideal setting for a troop to camp with its own equipment, under its own leadership, with its own program, in a Boy Scout camp with only the barest essentials provided.

The camp has developed into an important Council training center where the annual weeklong junior leader's training courses are conducted along with other special weekend training events. It is also the site for council sponsored Wood Badge courses.

The current camp ranger is Bob Berkhardt.

WOOD BADGE TRAINING

The first weekend Wood Badge course, sponsored ... by the Santa Clara County Council, was brought to an exciting and meaningful conclusion in July at Camp Chesebrough. Among the highlights of the course was the dedication of the camp and the new pole barn at the closing dinner, with Nessie and Paul Chesebrough in attendance. Another feature was the building of a unique interconnecting pioneering project which used leadership skills, scoutcraft skills, teamwork and fun.

Wood Badge is a unique advanced training experience for Boy Scout adult leaders. Men and women learn together how Scouting works in the life of a boy. Our Scouting community will benefit from the training received by the 32 participants....

The staff headed by Course Director Earl Burke, included Roy Adams, Howard Davis, Dick DeVilbiss, Judy Griffin, Glenn Helberg, Jack Mortensen, Bob Porter, Pete Presta, Pat Reilley, Don Simpson, Carl Stalions, Bill Winter, Carl Woodland and Bob Yount....

(Excerpt: Santa Clarion, 9/84)

Wood Badge Activities at Camp Chesebrough, 1987

Willis Hannah, Red Livingston, and Ron Nance.

Besides the activity shelter at Chesebrough Scout Reservation, these men have been hard at work at Camp Hi-Sierra finishing the new Maintenance Building. Through the procurement of Jim McDonough, a plumber spent one week finishing the plumbing portion of the building at Camp Hi-Sierra.

Daily, the DAMC are looking for building materials.

(Reprint: Santa Clarion, 9/84)

HEROES OF DAMC

The ongoing heroes of the Development and Maintenance Committee (DAMC) have been donating their time, money and efforts to further our council's facilities. In case you have wondered where the new 20 X 60 foot activity shelter at Chesebrough Scout Reservation came from, we wish to thank the efforts of: Bill Wegner, Dick DeVilbiss, Jim McDonough, Jack Currie, Art Green, Richard Baas, Don Boisseranc, Jim Brent, Mark Brent, Carl Stalions, Tony Ferranti, Melvin Hill, Abe Hendricks, Mike Riddle, Mike Hance,

The Activity Shelter and Chesebrough Building

SANTA CLARA COUNTY COUNCIL

Boy Scouts of America

2095 PARK AVENUE   —   SAN JOSE, CALIFORNIA 95126   —   Telephone 243-5335

September 4, 1973

Mr. & Mrs. Paul Chesebrough
2909 Franciscan Court
San Carlos, CA 94070

Dear Mr. & Mrs. Chesebrough:

This is to acknowledge your recent letter regarding the deed
to the land and to let you know we have received it.

At a meeting of our Executive Committee yesterday, it was
unanimously moved that I express to you both on behalf of the
Executive Board their sincere appreciation for your most generous contribution to the program of Scouting in Santa Clara
County. To this I add my own personal gratitude for giving
us the wonderful opportunity of making this beautiful area
available for our youth in the years ahead.

We will be planning on our Camp Committee visiting the property within the next two or three weeks and then follow this up
with a request to our National Camp Engineering Service to send
a field man to help us with the long range planning and good
environmental use.

We will be looking forward to having you both as our guests at
a future meeting of our Council Board so they may give you their
personal appreciation and also make public acknowledgement of your
gift of Camp Chesebrough to us.

I will keep in touch with you on this and trust it will be possible for you to be with us.

Sincerely yours,

Raymond J. Ewan
Scout Executive

RJE/dj

SERVING OVER 23,000 BOYS IN CUBBING, SCOUTING AND EXPLORING

Up it goes!

VII. Biographies

Founders and Benefactors

Council Founders

The men who are listed as Council Founders in the histories of Santa Clara County are John Crummey, Edmund Richmond and Robert I. Bentley, Jr. Bentley and several other men who attended the organizational meeting on August 20, 1920 were elected to the first Executive Board. These men, Archer Bowden, J. Derrol Chace, Dr. J.L. Pritchard, Charles Snyder and A.B. Post, also served in other board capacities through the twenties.

Bentley and Bowden both served as Council President. Chase was the first Council Secretary, Snyder was Vice President and Treasurer, and Richmond and Pritchard were Council Commissioners.

The following biographies are of two committee members who played key roles in founding the council, but did not go on to become Council Presidents.

John D. Crummey

John Crummey (1878–1976) is one of the important leaders who established the Council here in Santa Clara County in the fall of 1920.

John Crummey's father, D.C. Crummey, was the son-in-law of John Bean who had invented an important orchard spray pump in the 1880s. The pump was very successful in eradicating a fruit fly that was extremely harmful to the fruit crop. The pump was the anchor of an industrial company that became a leading producer of farm equipment and machinery which was later known as Food Machinery Corporation of San Jose.

D.C. Crummey ran the plant, and when son John grew up he became the general manager of the operation. John was a civic minded person and was quite involved in many of the organizations that tried to improve the quality of life in the valley. During World War I he served on the Liberty Bond sale committee and at war's end he was active on the Armenian and Serbian Relief committee. In 1919 he was Vice President of the San Jose Chamber of Commerce, founding president of the Civic Welfare Club, and on the board of the Young Mens Christian Association.

John D. Crummey
Founder

As one of the influential members of the Rotary Club, he joined Robert I. Bentley, Jr. and Archer Bowden on a committee to organize a Boy Scout Council in San Jose. They convened a meeting of interested businessmen on August 20, 1920, elected officers, and completed and signed an application for a charter for a local Scout Council. It is believed that John Crummey, together with the San Jose Rotary Club, underwrote the cost of the fledgling council for the first year of operation.

In March 1970 during the observance of the 50th anniversary year of the Santa Clara County Council, a dinner was held in honor of John Crummey. Over 350 Scouters and other friends were in attendance. Mr. Crummey received a citation for outstanding achievement in community service from the United Fund and an award of appreciation from Goodwill Industries. Council President Wilmot Nicholson presented him with a special award for over 70 years of service to this community. Former Council President Judge Marshall Hall and attorney Austen Warburton presented John Crummey the Silver Beaver Award on behalf of the National Council, BSA, for outstanding service to boyhood.

John Derrol Chace
Founder

John Derrol Chace

John Derrol Chace (1894–1954) holds a very special place in the early history of Scouting in Santa Clara County. He attended the organizational meeting and was the first elected secretary of the newly organized committee. The committee applied for a charter from the National Scout Office for a Boy Scout Council in San Jose that same day, August 20, 1920.

As a new officer, he signed the application form as "J.D. Chace, Secy. of Local Council" in the space designated for "Secretary of Local Council, Scout Executive or Scout Commissioner." He then served for two months as nominal Scout Executive until the first Council employee, Julius Rainwater, could come from Chicago to assume the Scout Executive's duties.

John Derrol Chase was born in Santa Cruz and moved to San Jose with his family at an early age. He graduated from Stanford University in 1916. He was regarded as one of the best quarter mile runners ever to race for Stanford.

During World War I, a Council of Defense was appointed by Governor William Stephens to coordinate local patriotic effort. John Derrol Chace was its secretary. Historian Eugene Sawyer stated in his *1922 History of Santa Clara County,* that Derrol Chace made a very patriotic Secretary, "giving not only of his entire time, but the use of his automobile, to the Defense Council."

One of the Defense Council's tasks in 1917 was to increase food production. About this time the 100 Boy Scouts of the First Methodist Church, under the leadership of Rev. Frank McLain, each pledged himself to "feed a soldier." The Rotarians financed the effort, and before long, the Boy Scouts, together with other high school and Normal School (now San Jose State University) students, were producing "student-raised" crops on over 200 vacant lots, to assist the war effort.

Before the end of WWI he became a Lieutenant commanding a company of the 8th Infantry in France.

Chace, past President of the Rotarians and the San Jose Country Club, was a member of the Sainte Claire Club of San Jose, and the Bohemian and Olympic Clubs of San Francisco. He was an avid flyer and golfer.

When Derrol Chace's father, John R. Chace, was agent for the Associated Oil Company, Derrol was his assistant and succeeded his father upon his death. J. Derrol Chace was Postmaster from September, 1931, until his resignation in January 1937.

A Council Benefactor's Profile

While benefactors come in many different forms, the benefactors in this listing have all contributed to the landholdings of the Santa Clara County Council.

One person, an industrialist, gave of his time, talent and resources to develop the council's service center building. Another person wanted to make a meaningful contribution to an organization that was dedicated to helping young people. He gave 100 acres of prime mountain property to the Boy Scouts at the token sale price of ten dollars. The other benefactors are couples who have given large parcels of land for youth camping. As couples they have a great deal in common.

The husband was successful in his chosen career. The wife was intelligent, supportive and shared her husband's interests. As a couple one of their main pleasures was in nature, and the couple was vitally interested in conserving California's natural resources. The couple was firmly convinced of the value of the Scouting program to the youth of our nation.

These benefactors were generous in their gifts of land to the Boy Scouts, ensuring that the land would be preserved in its primitive and natural state for the future, and used as a training and learning experience by young people of the present.

Council Benefactors

Edward Jeness

Edward Jeness, a rugged individualist, was one of our California pioneers. In the early 1870s he came to the High Sierras, as a young man, and homesteaded several hundred acres of forest land that surrounded the Tuolumne River in Tuolumne County.

The Jeness family called their homestead, "Saint's Rest," and in those early days they grew a fine potato crop for the markets at Sonora, Long Barn, Pinecrest, Cold Springs and the Strawberry Hotel.

In the years from 1903 to 1912 one hundred acres of his land was used by the Sonora Logging Company, the largest lumber operation in the area. More than 600 men were employed by the Sonora company and all made their homes in the immediate area.

On May 21, 1949, Edward Jeness deeded one hundred acres to the Boy Scout Memorial Foundation of the Santa Clara County Council "... in consideration of the sum of Ten dollars."

The property transfer came about as the result of a Council decision to come to grips with a problem that had not yet been solved. After years of what has been described as "inadequate" outdoor camping facilities in the Santa Cruz Mountains, in 1948-49 the Council sent out several teams of volunteers in search of property which would better suit the needs of the Boy Scouts of Santa Clara county.

Camping and Activities Chairman Robert Kirkwood and Professional Staffmember Ken Robison, with the help of Eric Thorsen and others, found this prime camping property. It was bisected by the North Fork of the Tuolumne River, its level area made an ideal campsite, and the mountain forest provided the perfect terrain for hiking and exploring.

A few years later, Ed Jeness offered the Council additional acreage but at the time the Council declined to accept it. Benefactor Jeness gave the additional acres to a church youth group from Sonora prior to his death in his mid-nineties.

Reginald Ray Stuart, Grace Stuart, Winifred Stuart

Reginald Stuart (1882-1975) was born in Iowa and went through school in Dows, getting his teaching credential at Iowa State Normal School in 1904. With a short stopover in Vancouver, Washington, he arrived in San Jose, California, in 1910 and taught at San Jose High School. He moved to Oakland in 1914, where he taught for 33 years. He married Grace Dell Harris in 1934.

In August 1944 Reginald and Grace transferred, to the Santa Clara County Council, the title for 80 acres known as the "John Brown place." The land, with buildings and an arboretum, was off Bohlman Road in the foothills of the Santa Cruz Mountains, three miles southeast of Saratoga. The Stuarts donated the scenic property in memory of their son "Red" who had loved the natural beauty of the setting, and had enjoyed the occasional visit with Scoutmaster Ken Robison and his troop when they hiked across the hills from Los Gatos. The Council named the acreage Camp Stuart.

Stuart retired in 1947 to a life of writing and travel. He wrote more than eight books, then came out of retirement in 1956 to become the Director of the California History Foundation. The job included the responsibility for the Western History Collections at the University of the Pacific in Stockton, California. While there he established the Jedediah Smith Society and began the publication of *The Pacific Historian.*

Reginald and Grace Stuart consolidated the Western History materials of the library and contributed their own lifetime collections. They were honored upon the termination of their work there by having the Stuart Library named for Stuart, and they both received the prestigious Order of the Pacific from the University in 1965.

Grace Stuart, a native of Kansas, had been a schoolteacher for forty years. Following their years with the university, she and Reginald moved to Pleasanton, California, where she was active in the historical activities of Livermore and Amador Valleys. She died January 30, 1966.

Reginald remarried and he, and the former Winifred Handley (Stuart), spent the remainder of their days at the family home called Lynnewood in Pleasanton.

Reginald Stuart received the Silver Beaver Award in 1961 and Winifred received the Silver Beaver Award in 1981, shortly before her death.

Charles E. Moore

Charles (Charlie) Moore (1894-1953) lived on an 1100 acre estate on Overlook Road in Los Gatos. Moore was president of three companies: Moore Machinery, Moore Industrial Company and Industrial Assets.

He acquired the 33-year-old Joshua Hendy Iron Works at Sunnyvale in 1940 and transformed it from a 60-employee plant to the largest marine engine firm in the country. During World War II the plant was one of the nation's chief defense production firms. Moore sold the business in 1945 to California Shipbuilding Corporation. Westinghouse Electric Corporation took it over later.

Charles Moore traveled widely as a technical advisor to the federal government on tool machinery. In 1941 he went to Europe for the office of production management to advise tool manufacturing plants in the United Kingdom. Following the war he was an industry consultant in Greece for the State Department. He went to Italy in 1947–49 as a Marshall Plan consultant.

On returning to California, Moore became involved in the Santa Clara County Council, BSA. He was a vice president of the council and chairman of the Boy Scout Memorial Foundation Board.

Moore endeared himself to all future Scouters when, in 1952, he became interested in finding a permanent headquarters building for the Council operations. When a piece of the Kaiser Community Homes surplus property became available, he urged the Foundation to purchase it. Together with the help of Judge William James and others, the Boy Scout Memorial Foundation Board secured the property, eventually adding another piece obtained when State Highway 17 surplus property was for sale.

Moore worked on all aspects of developing the property for the Scout's use. He solicited contributions, monetary and in-kind, and persuaded the business/labor communities to donate building supplies and labor.

Groundbreaking ceremonies at the corner of Park and Newhall Avenues were held June 14, 1953, for the new Scout headquarters.

Moore died suddenly of a heart attack one week later.

When the building was dedicated February 4, 1954 it was called "The Charles E. Moore Memorial Boy Scout Building."

Paul M. and Nessie E. Chesebrough

Paul Chesebrough (1902–1989) was born in Jersey City, New Jersey. His parents were both native Californians. His father was working in New York City at that time. After Paul's sister, Ruth, was born, the family returned to San Francisco. In a few years they moved to Wilmington, California. Paul was a Boy Scout there for only a short time before his Scoutmaster was called to serve in World War I and the troop disbanded. The family returned to San Francisco in 1918 when Paul entered high school.

Paul spent any spare time he had at the Marina Green and Crissy Field where airplanes became a part of his life. He worked at a flying school in Petaluma from 1924–26. He returned to San Francisco where he was employed by Pacific Air Transport until 1927. Mills Field (now the San Francisco airport) was just getting started. He and two friends opened an airplane repair shop in San Bruno. This venture lasted until the middle of 1929. During the Depression years there was not much work, and less money.

Paul made the decision to return to school. For his first classes he rode the electric train to San Mateo Junior College. Later he took a ferry across the bay to complete his engineering studies at the University of California, Berkeley. He went to work part time at United Air Lines (UAL) in Oakland and attended Boeing School of Aeronautics.

As a meteorologist with United Air Lines he was domiciled in Chicago, then Denver. There he met Nessie Harpole and was married in 1942. Upon the close of World War II, United Air Lines opened Pacific Operations and they came to San Francisco in 1945. They have resided in San Carlos since 1947 where their daughters, Elaine and Meryl, were raised. Paul retired from UAL in 1960.

Paul Chesebrough died on November 30, 1989, just one month short of his 87th birthday. Before his death, he was a member of the OX5 Pioneers, an organization of men who worked on the OX5 airplane engine; the American Aviation Historical Association; Sempervirens; Save-the-Redwoods League and the Golden Gate Chapter of the American Red Cross.

Nessie Chesebrough was born in Van Houten, New Mexico, in 1917, and spent her school years in Raton. She attended Stephens College in Columbia, Missouri. In 1940 she moved to Denver where she was employed by Continental Oil Company until her marriage to Paul Chesebrough.

Paul Chesebrough inherited a large property southwest of Saratoga in the foothills of the Santa Cruz Mountains. The land had been owned by the Hubbard and Carmichael Logging Company and was purchased in 1928 by Mr. and Mrs. William Antwerp. In 1949 it was bequeathed to the Chesebroughs by Paul's aunt, Edith Van Antwerp.

Paul and Nessie were dedicated to the idea that this beautiful undeveloped property would remain unspoiled so that it could be enjoyed by the people of California as open space. They gifted large parcels to the Mid-Peninsula Open Space District and the Sempervirens Fund. Some property was also sold to the Sempervirens Fund.

They discussed the disposition of a portion of the property, which later became Camp Chesebrough, with Scout Executive Ray Ewan. He was enthusiastic about the possibility of the donation of the property to the Santa Clara County Council for use by the Boy Scouts as a camp. The Chesebroughs were pleased with the idea that the property could be kept in its natural state if used by the Scouts for learning about the great outdoors. The transaction was consumated in late 1973.

By 1977 the 404 acres of primitive trails and forest land were available to Scout troops for training sessions and weekend camping. Six years later, they donated an adjoining parcel of 140 acres to the Santa Clara County Council.

In 1988 the Chesebroughs received a memorable Christmas gift from Scout Executive Brian Allen, Don Boissaranc and Pat Reilley. The men had collaborated on a video tape recording of the property which graphically demonstrated the effects of an approved logging operation in 1988. The tape showed the many areas that had been opened up for camp sites, and the improvements of the access roads.

Nessie Chesebrough shared her husband's interest in working as a volunteer for the Red Cross. Both Paul and Nessie Chesebrough have served on the Santa Clara County Council's Executive Board for several years. They were also active members of the Boy Scout Memorial Foundation Board. Nessie continues to serve in these capacities, as well as being a contributing member of the History Task Force.

Paul and Nessie Chesebrough received the Benefactor Member Award in 1974 and each received the Silver Beaver Award in 1981.

Council Presidents

A Council President's Profile

The Council membership, from its earliest days, has drawn community leaders who were active, not only in their business or professional careers, but who were dedicated to making this valley the best place in the world to live and raise a family.

The twenty-nine Council Presidents, whose terms of office have spanned the first seventy years, have been comprised of three state legislators, four mayors, three Superior Court judges, two superintendents of large school districts, one four-star general, and one

lieutenant commander in the Navy. These men, in addition to a doctor, a dentist, a Ph.D., bank presidents, company presidents and business owners have all contributed their expertise and leadership in providing the best program possible for our youth.

Many of these men were elected for more than one term as Council President. Former Santa Clara Councilman Wilmot Nicholson holds the record for the longest tenure, six years in office. Andrew Mortensen and Judge William James each served five terms. Three presidents served four years each: Mayor Marcus Vertin, Senator Clark Bradley and William Powell. Four presidents served three years each: Judge Marshall Hall, Superintendent Laurence Hill, Dr. Frank Bernard and General Robert Huyser. Thirteen presidents served two years each and six were in office for one year.

This dedication has made for continuity and has given several presidents the opportunity to successfully complete longterm projects they had started. Remarkably, these Presidents were all carrying on their daily work load, and contributing their services to other community organizations, at the same time they were keeping the Santa Clara County Council, BSA, headed onward and upward.

The profile of a Council President that emerges is a man of vitality—outgoing, diplomatic and articulate. He is usually close to, or at retirement age, and has achieved an enviable reputation in his chosen field. He is fiscally conservative, yet can be flexible. He is goal-oriented, while being sensitive to the shades of differences in the goals of his Board.

Most assuredly, this man cares deeply about the welfare and training of the future generation. Therefore, he willingly commits his time, energy and brain power to insure that each future leader has the opportunity to develop his, or her, young mind and body to its highest potential.

Due to the fact that some years term of office began in January and other years began in July, it has been difficult in many cases to ascertain the exact term. Based on council annual charter applications, it appears probable that terms of office for the years 1931 through 1973 began on July 1 of the previous year and continued through June 30 of the elected year. Starting in 1974 the terms began on January 1 of the elected year. In four cases it is known that a president was not able to complete his elected term of office. In each of these cases the next elected president has stepped in to complete that term and then has continued on to serve his elected term.

(information source: James Sturrock)

Robert Irving Bentley, Jr.:
1920

"R.I." Bentley (1888-1968) was one of the key people in bringing the Scouting program to Santa Clara County. He was the grandson of a Methodist minister and son of the well known cannery owner, R.I. Bentley, Sr., who headed California Packing Company in San Jose and was a founder of the San Francisco Opera House. The Bentley family lived at 1410 The Alameda.

In 1914, Bentley, and the late George Muirson, pooled their resources to establish a company for the manufacture of canning labels. In the early days their business name was the Muirson Label and Carton Company.

The firm grew rapidly and covered most of the block at 435 Stockton Avenue in San Jose by the time its stock was purchased by International Paper Company in 1960. Muirson Label also owned manufacturing facilities in Peoria, Illinois, and Meriden, Connecticut. Bentley remained as chairman of the board until his retirement. He was also a director of the First National Bank.

R.I. Bentley will always be remembered, however, as one of the "founding fathers" of the San Jose Council of the Boy Scouts of America. He, together with fellow Rotarians John Crummey and Archer Bowden, initiated the organizational meeting on August 20, 1920, where Bentley was elected the first President of the Council. As its President, he officially signed the original application for the Council Charter.

Bentley served as the Council representative to the National Council of the Boy Scouts of America from 1920-22.

Archer Bowden:
1921 & 1926

Archer (Archie) Bowden (1885-1953) was assistant district attorney in San Jose before leaving to serve in World War I. When he returned after the war he was appointed City Attorney for San Jose, a position he held until he resigned in 1943.

Bowden was active in the San Jose community which had a population in the early twenties of 42,000. He was president of the Members Forum of the San Jose Chamber of Commerce, and in 1922, was president of the American Legion which had been founded in 1919.

Bowden was present at the organizational meeting of the San Jose Council of the Boy Scouts of America and agreed to be the fledgling organization's first Vice President at the historic meeting of August 20, 1920. Then he continued on the Council as its second President. He was elected for a second term in 1926.

Walter L. Bachrodt:
1922 & 1925

Walter (Walt) Bachrodt (1890-1945) was appointed San Jose Superintendent of Schools in 1921. He remained in that post until his retirement in 1945. He had received his teaching credential at San Jose Normal School in 1909 and served in World War I. Following the war he entered Stanford University and was graduated with both bachelor and master degrees. While there he was a member of the Phi Beta Kappa Honorary Fraternity.

Besides his presidency of the Santa Clara-San Benito Counties' Council, he was a past president of the San Jose Community Chest, the Santa Clara County Tuberculosis Association, the California Association of Public School Superintendents and the California Teachers Association, Bay Section.

During his first term as Council President, in 1922, a charter revision permitted the San Jose Council jurisdiction over the entire Santa Clara County. President Bachrodt was the Council representative to the National Council in 1924.

Walter Bachrodt was very supportive of the Boy Scout Program because he believed it was of great benefit to all boys, particularly the less fortunate ones. Throughout his 23-year tenure as Superintendent he continued to assist the Scout Program in many ways, for example, on several occasions he was able to provide unused school space where local troops could meet.

Wendell C. Thomas:
1923, 1924

Wendell Thomas was the manager for the International-Mack Corporation. In 1925 he lived in Los Gatos at a home he called "Wenedmar." He later became a realtor/insurance agent with an office on The Alameda in San Jose.

In 1923 the Santa Clara County Council incorporated. Late in 1923, the National Council, BSA, assigned San Benito County to be part of the jurisdiction being serviced from the Santa Clara County Council headquartered in San Jose. The council's new name was the Santa Clara, San Benito Counties Council.

Thomas was the Council representative to the National Council for 1923 and 1925.

Wendell Thomas died January 16, 1941.

Andrew M. Mortensen:
1927, 1928, 1929, 1931 & 1932

Andrew (Andy) Mortensen (1875-1951) was a distributor of General Petroleum products during the years he served as Council President. In 1931 he resigned as manager of General Petroleum Corporation to head his own company which manufactured air compressors for service stations and garages.

Mortensen, a native of Westfield, Wisconsin, came to San Jose in 1922 to manage the California Prune and Apricot Growers Association. He later headed the San Jose Chamber of Commerce, and after five years as president of the Santa Clara, San Benito and Monterey Bay Area Council, BSA, Mortensen was president of the San Jose Rotary Club in 1931-32.

It was during his first term in office, in April 1927, that Monterey and Santa Cruz Counties were added to the charter jurisdiction approved by the National Council.

During Mortensen's succeeding terms as President, his Vice Presidents represented the outlying geographical areas of Santa Cruz, Watsonville, Monterey, Pacific Grove, San Juan Bautista, Los Altos and Palo Alto.

In 1934 Andrew Mortensen was the first local council Scouter honored by the presentation of the Silver Beaver Award.

Judge Harry Clifford Lucas:
1930

Harry Lucas (1879-1952) was born on Plymouth Street in Santa Cruz in the same house in which he died. His father was city treasurer of that city for many years after he arrived in 1849. Harry attended Stanford University and received his law degree there in 1902.

Harry Lucas was state assemblyman from Santa Cruz 1906-10. He then served as inheritance tax appraiser for Alameda County 1910-14. From 1914-24 he was counsel for the inheritance tax department for the state of California.

Judge Lucas officiated as a Superior Court judge in Santa Cruz from 1924-31. He resigned from the bench to become general counsel, and a vice president, of the Pacific Greyhound Lines.

H.C. Lucas served on the Santa Clara, San Benito and Monterey Bay Area Council starting in 1928 as a Vice President under President Andrew Mortensen. In 1929 he and his friend, Dr. Henry Watters of Watsonville, were both Vice Presidents of the Council. Watters went on, in May, 1933, to be the first President of the newly chartered Monterey Bay Area Council from 1933-38

Henry Gustav Watters, M.D.:
1933 (through April 1933)

Henry G. Watters (1885-1964) was a physician practicing in Watsonville. He had graduated from Watsonville High School in 1903, then left the area to graduate from medical school. In 1911 he came back to Watsonville to join his father, Dr. P.K. Watters, in running the Watsonville Hospital and Training School for Nurses.

He was very active in support of youth, their education and recreation. In 1930, he was presented the first copy of the *Manzanita*, the Watsonville High School annual. The copy was autographed by every member of the graduating class and a page in the book was dedicated to Dr. Watters. The page chronicled his loyal support for high school affairs, which included the securing of the high school athletic field.

Dr. H.G. Watters represented the Counties of Monterey and San Benito County as a Council Vice President from Watsonville in 1927, 1928 and 1929.

Henry G. Watters had the distinction of being the only Council President who began his term serving in Santa Clara County, and completed that year serving as the first president of the newly formed Monterey Bay Area Council. He functioned in that capacity from May 1933 to 1938.

Almon Edward Roth:
(May) 1933, 1934

Almon (Dutch) Roth (1887-1964) was born in the Midwest and came to Mendocino County, California, with his parents, as a youngster. Roth was graduated from Stanford in 1909 and received his law degree in 1911. He attained the Stanford Hall of Fame for his track and rugby accomplishments. He married Mildred Hayes, daughter of J.O. Hayes, publisher of the San Jose Mercury newspaper.

Almon Roth was Stanford University's first controller, holding the position from 1909 to 1937. He became president of the San Francisco Employers Council in 1939, and went on to play a major role as peacemaker in the San Francisco waterfront labor/management confrontations in the forties.

Early in 1933 the counties of Monterey, San Benito and Santa Cruz separated from the Santa Clara County Council to form their own Council on May 1, 1933. When Dr. Henry Watters resigned to be first president of the new council, Almon Roth assumed the presidency for the remainder of 1933 and was elected to a full term of office in 1934.

During Roth's presidency the Council's Constitution and By-Laws were reviewed and amended. They were approved by the Council January 15, 1934, and submitted to the National Council.

Hamon Hercynius Hallin:
1935, 1936

Hamon (Hal) Hallin (1904-69) was born in Cambridge, Minnesota, and came to Santa Clara County in 1924. He immediately went into partnership in the insurance firm of Hallin and Bookwalter, with offices on Lincoln Avenue in San Jose. Hallin was treasurer of the Augustana Lutheran Church from 1927 to 1940. He also joined the Willow Glen American Legion Post 318 and the San Jose Kiwanis Club.

A veteran of two world wars, Hallin commanded the San Jose Naval Reserve Fifth Fleet Division from 1925-1938. During most of those years he was very active in the local council's Sea Scout program. He was officially listed as "Portmaster" in 1927 and 1928.

Hallin's son, Harold, (Cub Pack 9, Troop 50, Willow Glen) remembers that his father convinced the U.S. Navy to donate surplus whale boats to the Sea Scouts. One memorable weekend, Hallin, son Harold, and their friends, sailed up the bay to Mare Island to collect the empty whale boats, and towed them back to Alviso. Harold also recalled some great trips his father took the boys on, one of them to Arizona's Grand Canyon and Utah's Bryce Canyon.

In 1935, during Hallin's presidency, the Santa Clara County Council adopted the revised Constitution and By-Laws. The Cub Scout program was initiated in 1936 with the forming of six packs.

Hal Hallin received the Silver Beaver Award in 1948.

Theo M. Wright:
1937, 1938

Theo (T.M.) Wright (1876-1946) was a 70 year resident of San Jose who represented the former Twentieth District as an Assemblyman from 1914-16 and from 1918-32. For eight years he was chairman of the State Ways and Means Committee. He had authored the Wright Act, the former prohibition act for the state of California, and was equally well known for being the "Watchdog of the State Treasury."

Other measures he introduced, or sponsored, included water conservation, veteran's welfare, the establishment of a farm at Agnew State Hospital, and the building program for the State College System.

In 1940 he headed the San Jose committee for China Relief.

After retiring from public life, Theo Wright was president of the Wright-Eley Printing Company on Second Street in San Jose from the early 1930s to the late 1940s.

Ernest A. Abbott, D.D.S.:
1939, 1940

Ernest (Ernie) Abbott came to Santa Clara County in 1904 and attended Campbell High School. He was graduated from the University of Pennsylvania, returned to San Jose in 1914 and practiced dentistry for 48 years. He maintained an office at 57 East Santa Clara Street from the early 1930s until his retirement in the mid-1950s.

Dr. Abbott was very supportive of the camping program at Arroyo Sequoia on the coast near Davenport. He was proud to have three sons who were Eagle Scouts.

Ernest Abbott was the ninth Scouter to receive the Santa Clara County Council Silver Beaver Award (1940).

Judge Marshall S. Hall:
1941, 1942, 1943

Retired Superior Court Judge Marshall Hall earned his undergraduate and law degrees at Stanford University and started practice in 1933. He was president of the County Bar Association in 1946-47 and served as a judge from 1958 to 1978.

His first camping experience with the Scouts was in Alum Rock Canyon east of San Jose. He camped at Santa Cruz the next year. Hall helped form Troop 15 and was Senior Patrol Leader, which he felt gave him the leadership experience that led to becoming an officer in the Coast Guard Reserve. At one time he served the Council as "Sea Scout Commodore."

As Council President he was concerned with getting proper water and sewer facilities for the Scout camps. He continued to work on Scout projects as a past president. In addition to serving in many other capacities, he was an active organizer of the Memorial Foundation in 1945.

Judge Marshall Hall was one of Santa Clara valley's earliest Scouts, with continuous service since 1920. He received the Silver Beaver Award in 1943; the Silver Antelope Award in 1954. He was an active member of the Executive Board and the Memorial Foundation until his death on September 13, 1990.

Judge William F. James:
1944, 1945, 1946, 1947, 1948

William (Billy) James (1875-1966), San Jose attorney, and later Superior Court Judge, had an active interest in problems of juveniles, and the William F. James Boys' Ranch was named in his honor.

James helped raise money for Camp Stuart and the Scout Service Center Building. He was one of the original trustees of the Memorial Foundation, and was one of the signatories of the Declaration of Trust in 1945.

Judge William F. James was believed to be California's oldest practicing judge when he retired in 1963. He was still a consulting attorney when he died in 1966, just before his 91st birthday.

Judge James received the Silver Beaver Award in 1947.

Marcus J. Vertin:
1949, 1950, 1951, 1952

Marcus (Marc) Vertin (1896–1959), Mayor of Los Gatos from 1932-1940, was also a cashier at the Bank of Los Gatos in the twenties, and an accountant/realtor/insurance agent from the early 1930s to the early 1950s. He was a Town of Los Gatos Planning Commissioner from 1950-59.

Vertin moved to Los Gatos in 1915 and was Scoutmaster of Troop 2 of Los Gatos from 1925-32. Well-known playwrights, Ruth Comfort Mitchell and Wilbur Hall wrote a Scout play in 1925 which was given to the National Council as a gift from Troop 2. In 1927 his troop was very active in a program to prevent railroad accidents.

Marc Vertin received the Silver Beaver Award in 1939.

Clark L. Bradley:
1953, 1954, 1955, 1956

Clark Bradley, a San Jose attorney, was Mayor of San Jose from 1950-1952. He was elected in 1954 to the 20th Assembly District, and served from 1962-1974 as State Senator from the 18th District.

Senator Bradley was president of the Downtown San Jose Kiwanis Club.

He actively supported and monitored the construction of the Charles E. Moore Memorial Scout Building.

Clark Bradley received the Silver Beaver Award in 1955. He died December 11, 1983.

Laurence J. Hill:
1957, 1958, 1959

Laurence (Larry) Hill (1908–89) earned a BA in Education at San Jose State University and an MA at Stanford University.

As a Boy Scout, Hill reached the rank of Star Scout. As an adult, in the early thirties while teaching at Willow Glen High School, he became Scoutmaster of a troop in East San Jose. Later, as Superintendent of Campbell Union High School District (1946-69), he fostered the organization of troops in the high school district. During his tenure the district grew from 527 to 16,000 students.

Hill helped build a Youth Center behind Willow Glen High School which was used by many youths, including a Scout Troop. He also helped set up Camp Stuart. Hill later served as Scout District Chairman.

Hill felt one of his biggest contributions was in recruiting both Bill Nicholson and Dr. Frank Bernard into Scouting. Both became Council Presidents.

Larry Hill received the Silver Beaver Award in 1955.

Wilmot J. Nicholson:
1960, 1961, 1962, 1963 and 1968, 1969

Wilmot (Bill) Nicholson was a graduate of Santa Clara University with a degree in Civil Engineering. He served as a City of Santa Clara Councilman from 1952-58 and was also Mayor. Nicholson is a past president of the Santa Clara Chamber of Commerce.

He began his involvement in Scouting as a Cubmaster in the late forties.

Nicholson owned a construction firm specializing in industrial and commercial buildings. He supervised volunteers at Camp Hi-Sierra building tent platforms, the Health Lodge, latrines and showers.

During Nicholson's administration, adult Eagle Scouts formed the Eagle Scout Association in 1959.

In July 1969, following his presidency, Nicholson became chairman of the Council long-range development program. His last long term involvement was as president of the Memorial Foundation for ten years.

Bill Nicholson has the longest tenure of any council president, having served six years. He received the Silver Beaver Award in 1962, and the Silver Antelope Award in 1970.

William S. Powell:
1964, 1965, 1966, 1967

William (Bill) Powell owned a book, stationery and office supply store at 81 South First Street, San Jose during the 1940s and 1950s. He is active in the San Jose Rotary, and is a Paul Harris Fellow.

During Powell's busy term of office the Order of the Arrow Lodge was reactivated in 1964.

In September 1964, the Westminister Presbyterian Church in San Jose gave a surplus building to the

Council. Powell learned about the potential gift, made the decision to accept it, and moved it to the rear of the Scout property all within a three day period. The problem was the fact that the building was scheduled for demolition on Tuesday following the Labor Day holiday. Powell was able to obtain volunteer help to get the building moved over that weekend to the Council property at Park Avenue and Newhall Street. Later that fall it was converted into the new Council Field Office.

Following his council presidency Powell was a National Council Representative. He continues to serve as a member of the Memorial Foundation Board.

Bill Powell received the Silver Beaver Award in 1956.

Robert B. Morris, Jr.:
1970, 1971

Robert (Bob) Morris worked for International Business Machines (IBM) in their Real Estate Division in San Jose. He retired in May 1988 as Director of Environmental Program at IBM.

Morris was active in Scouting since 1936 starting as a Boy Scout in Troop 6 at Tarrytown, N.Y. He became an Eagle Scout in 1940 and was a member of the BSA national service fraternity, Alpha Phi Omega, while attending Michigan State College.

As an adult, Bob Morris was a Scoutmaster. He was also a member of the executive committee for the Boy Scout Councils in Minnesota, Vermont and New York. He has served on the National Properties Committee and has been involved in long-range planning activities for the Fairfield County Council, Connecticut. Currently, Morris is "straw boss" for the construction of two large log cabins and three pavillions, at various Scout camps in that state.

Before Morris was Council President in Santa Clara County, he led the Council troops to the 1969 National Jamboree.

During Morris' presidency the Council celebrated the 50th Anniversary of Scouting in Santa Clara County. In February 1970, a dinner was held with one of the Council founders, John Crummey, as honored guest. Crummey was given a Silver Beaver Award. Morris also presented a plaque to the San Jose Rotary Club for financing the Council for their first year.

Morris is the only Scouter to have served as both Council President and Council Commissioner, and the first Eagle Scout to have filled either position. Robert Morris has a Scouters Key and received the Silver Beaver Award in 1967.

Dr. Frank S. Bernard:
1972, 1973 (through December)

Frank Bernard (1903-1985) founded Bernard Food Industries in 1950 and owned it until his death. He was a former chairman of the National Conference of Christians and Jews, Santa Clara County chapter. He was also on the board of directors of the former Community Bank of San Jose, as well as being a board member of several cultural and educational institutions.

During Bernard's presidency, Council meetings were held either on the third floor of the Sainte Claire Club or the wine cellar of Paolo's Restaurant at 16th and Santa Clara Streets in San Jose.

Bernard became involved with the Scout program in Santa Clara County through his company. He had developed an innovative method for dehydrating foods and his excellent products were frequently used by Scouts on hikes and camping trips.

Bernard owned a ranch near Hollister which he offered as the site of the 1976 Bicent-O-Ree. Bernard was also instrumental in expanding the local council's Explorer program. He served on the regional board and national council of the Boy Scouts of America.

Frank Bernard was awarded the Silver Beaver in 1963 and the Silver Antelope in 1973. He was presented with the first Good Scout Award as well as the Benefactor Member Plaque in 1974. He was the honoree at the first Distinguished Citizen Dinner in 1975.

Charles N. Munger:
1974, 1975

Charles (Charlie) Munger was a native born San Jose Scouter who had been a Boy Scout in Scoutmaster Hoppe's Troop 21 at the First Presbyterian Church.

As an adult he was appointed the Sustaining Membership Enrollment Chairman in the Sacramento Council, BSA. When his company, Pacific Telephone, transferred him back to the San Jose area, his friend Bill Powell conscripted him as a member of the Santa Clara County Council Executive Board.

Among the responsibilities of his Council presidency were: the building of a surplus in the treasury of $6500 at the end of 1974; the appointment of Randy Kohl as new Scout Execuitve when Ray Ewan retired in 1975; the monitoring of a large volunteer effort to renovate the Scout Service Center; the transfer of all camp properties from the Council to the Memorial Foundation; and the establishment of the Distinguished Citizen Dinner in 1975.

Charles Munger received the Silver Beaver Award in 1972.

Blair R. Egli:
1976 (through August)

Blair Egli was Vice President of the Bank of America, Park Center Plaza Branch.

In the January 1976 edition of the "Santa Clarion," he shared his objectives for the year as being: 1) to enchance the image of Scouting in the community; 2) to work in partnership with the churches, schools, civic organizations, business, trades, industry and the professions; and 3) to instill the fundamental purposes of the BSA motto, "Duty to God, Country and Family" in order to develop young men and women of good character.

Blair Egli served until he was promoted to the Bank of America's Oakland Branch as manager. Vice President for Administration, C. Donald Allen, Jr., was elected to succeed him as Council President in September 1976.

C. Donald Allen, Jr.:
September 1976, 1977, 1978 (through June)

C. Donald (Don) Allen, at the time of his election as Council president, was a Vice President and Manager of the Central Bank in San Jose, and active in the United Way, Rotary Club and Los Altos Chamber of Commerce. He is now President of the Cupertino National Bank.

In 1944 Allen started as a Cub Scout with Pack 12 in Oakland, California. As an adult he became involved in helping raise funds for the Polaris District in the 1960s, and was chairman of that district 1972-74. In 1975 he served as Sustaining Membership Enrollment Chairman and Council Vice President for Cub Scouting. Allen was elected Council President in September 1976 when President Blair Egli was unexpectedly transferred.

Allen resigned as president before completing his second term due to his increased responsibilities as chairman of the 1978 Grand Jury. He currently serves as Treasurer of the Memorial Foundation Board.

Don Allen received the Silver Beaver Award in 1973.

Andrew J. Bonfield:
July 1978, 1979, 1980

Andrew (Andy) Bonfield was a Tax Practitioner/ Enrolled Agent with offices in Los Gatos. He was past president of Rotary, past chairman of the Los Gatos Taxpayers Association, and on the Santa Clara County Parks and Recreation Commission, County Property Assessment Appeals Board, and Property Tax Review Board. He retired to Hawaii in 1986.

Bonfield is a naturalized U.S. citizen who was born in England. Besides his Scouting experience as a boy, he has served in leadership positions on pack and troop level, and at district and council level. He chaired the 1976 Bicent-O-Ree and the 1984 Diamond Jubilee Jamboree.

He completed Don Allen's term as Council President when Allen resigned.

Andrew Bonfield was presented the Order of the Arrow, Vigil Honor, in 1973, the Silver Beaver in 1975, and the Good Scout Award in 1982.

Jan W. Passmore:
1981, 1982

Jan Passmore was the president of Corroon & Black, an international insurance broker firm in San Jose. He has been an active community volunteer in Goodwill Industries, Hope Rehabilitation Services, Alexian Brothers Hospital, and the United Way.

He became a Life Scout in Union City, Indiana, and is a Brotherhood member of the Order of the Arrow.

As an adult he was Vice President for Finance and a capable fund raiser for the Santa Clara County Council.

During his presidency he stabilized the direction of Scouting, assisted in building an active Board, reactivated the President's Club, and helped select Brian Allen as Scout Executive. He also appointed a Council Hispanic Advisory Committee.

Jan Passmore received the Silver Beaver Award in 1982 and was the recipient of the Distinguished Citizens Award in 1985.

General Robert E. Huyser, U.S.A.F., Retired,
1983, 1984, 1985

Robert (Dutch) Huyser was born in Colorado in 1924. Following high school graduation in 1943, he was drafted into the Army as a private. Huyser entered the aviation cadet program and has been flying ever since. It is estimated that Huyser logged over 10,000 hours of flying time which included combat missions in three wars.

Among the other responsibilities he was assigned, he was Chief of Combat Operations for the Far East Bomber Command. As a four-star General, Huyser was Deputy Commander-in-Chief of the U.S. European Command under General Alexander Haig, headquartered in Stuttgart, Germany.

After retiring from active service, Dutch Huyser came to the San Jose area. He recalled the following

about his involvement with the Scouting program: "...
In an effort to try and do my bit I decided to contribute
as much time as I could to youth programs. After
considerable research it was apparent the youth
organization in the local area that needed the most
help and had the potential for producing the most for
the nation was the Boy Scouts. I had never had the
opportunity to be a Scout as I was reared in a rural
remote area ....

"I was asked to serve on the board and was elected
President in December, 1982.... At the beginning of
my tenure we had 9800 scouts and when I turned the
Council over to my successor we had 25,000 scouts;
the cost per year per scout was $93. We lowered that
to $49. The income was about one/half million dollars
a year; our indebtedness was $260,000 and we reduced
that to zero. The camps were run down and we did
about $250,000 improvements. We established in-school
scouting and instituted the Tiger Scout program in
Santa Clara County...."

During his presidency the first Gala Explorer
Auction was held, and a gigantic Diamond Jubilee
Jamboree celebrated Scouting's 75th Anniversary.

General Robert Huyser received the Silver Beaver
Award in 1985.

Glen McLaughlin:
1986, 1987

Glen McLaughlin is the Chairman of Venture
Leasing Associates, and the chairman of the board
of Cupertino National Bank and two international
firms.

His early Scouting began with Troop 9 in Shawnee,
Oklahoma, where he achieved the rank of Eagle Scout
(3 Palms), received the Explorer Silver Award, and the
God and Country Award, and became Lodge Chief
of the Order of the Arrow. He attended the second
National Jamboree at Valley Forge, Pennsylvania, in
1950.

McLaughlin was able to attend a World Jamboree
in Bad Ischl, Austria, in 1951, and he felt that
experience gave him an international outlook that was
responsible for his venture into international business.
He is also convinced that Scouting helps build
confidence and self-reliance and that it helped him to
become a pilot for the United States Air Force as a
young man.

As an adult he became active with Troop 508,
Saratoga, and has been on the Council since 1982, the
Foundation Board since 1986, and has served as
President for Area III, Western Region, BSA, since
1988.

During his presidency of the Santa Clara County
Council McLaughlin 1) concentrated on fiscal stability
and finished his term with the largest cash balance
in the decade; 2) had all Service Center operations
computerized; 3) initiated two new programs, Junior
High Varsity Scout on the East Side and the Olympic
Sports Explorer Post in Los Gatos. He also appointed
a History Task Force to document the Council's seventy
year progress.

Glen McLaughlin received the Silver Beaver Award
in 1985, the Silver Antelope Award in 1990, was made
a Baden-Powell World Fellow in 1986, and was honored
by the Council when it named the Eagle Class of 1988
the "Glen McLaughlin Eagle Class."

John B. Lochner:
1988, 1989

John Lochner came to California in 1954 and started
a cabinet and countertop business in 1959 in Los Gatos.
He served on the Los Gatos Town Council from 1972
to 1980, and was Mayor twice during that time.

He has been president of the Los Gatos Chamber
of Commerce and the Lions Club, and has chaired
many fundraising committees for his church and
countywide charitable organizations. He is well-known
in Los Gatos as a church choirmember and song leader
for community events.

Lochner was a Boy Scout in Webster, New York,
in 1940. In Los Gatos he organized the Explorer
Olympic Development Post 813 in 1972. He was the
Institutional Representative from the Los Gatos Lions
Club to BSA Troop 539 for eleven years. He served
as Council Vice President for Finance in 1986–87.

As Council President, his goal for 1989 was to raise
$1.5 million for Scouting activities. He and his board
surpassed his goal by raising the finances for a
$1,700,000 budget.

John Lochner received the Silver Beaver Award in
1987.

Carl E. Cookson:
1990

Carl Cookson was born in San Jose and graduated
with a B.S. Degree in Business Administration from
San Jose State University. From 1957 to 1976 he was
consecutively a vice president of Valley Title Company,
and First American Title Insurance Company. In 1976
he became owner and Chairman of the Board of the
Santa Clara Land Title Company, a position he has
retained to the present.

Cookson is a community leader who is active in a
variety of non-profit, political and artistic organiza-

tions. In the recent past he has been a member of the board of the San Jose Chamber of Commerce and its political action committee, the National Conference of Christians and Jews, the Mexican American Community Service Association, the San Jose Hospital Foundation, the San Jose Symphony, and the Arts Council of Santa Clara County. Carl Cookson has received commendations from San Jose mayors Hayes and McEnery for his community service.

Carl Cookson has served on the Santa Clara Council Executive Board since 1986.

Professional Scouters

A Council Scout Executive's Profile

The Scout Executive of the Boy Scouts of America has full responsibility for implementing the policies of his Council, and must manage the financial commitments of carrying out the Boy Scout program for maximum impact. He must be experienced in Boy Scout procedures and be a man of integrity. He must establish high standards for the organization and represent the agency in the community.

The nine executives that were hired from 1920–1982 to handle the day-to-day conduct of the Council's affairs fit the Scout Executive's profile of a man in his forties who had held several executive positions as a professional Scouter before coming to Santa Clara County, including that of Scout Executive; he was a dedicated worker, and a forward-looking leader, doing a commendable job in handling the council budget, and being an exemplary manager for the staff members who served under his leadership.

The three Scout Executives who served the longest were Ray Ewan, 16 years, Chester Bartlett, 13 years, and Duncan McKinley, 10 years.

ON MY HONOR I WILL DO MY BEST:

Scout Executives

Julius H. Rainwater:
November 1920 - December 1923

J.H. Rainwater had been a Field Executive in Chicago from October 1918 until 1920. He was hired as the San Jose Council's first Scout Executive at an annual salary of $3,000.

Totaling numbers for the first few months of council operation, Rainwater estimated that there were 279 Boy Scouts in ten troops registered by December 31, 1920; 480 Boy Scouts in eighteen troops by the end of 1921; and 536 Boy Scouts in twenty-seven troops by the end of 1922. When he left the council to take a job as Executive Director of the Community Chest in San Jose, he reported 826 Boy Scouts in thirty-six troops at the end of 1923. He resigned from the profession in February, 1924.

Former Council President Larry Hill remembered Rainwater as the Scout Executive with a group of Scouts camping at Boulder Creek when they ran short of money and had to hike home.

Harrison E. White:
January 1924 - December 1930

Harrison (Harry) White (1892-1963) was 32 when he became Scout Executive for the Santa Clara and San Benito Counties Council, BSA.

He was proud of completing the organization of six District Committees during that year. It was also the first year the Council had to pay rent for office space, and that an automobile was listed as an expense.

In 1925 his salary was raised to $4,200. "Camp Property" was listed as a capital expenditure of $3,193. Since land near Davenport on the Pacific Ocean was leased from the University of California about that time, the money was presumably for the development of that property.

In 1926 a newspaper called "The Scout Bugle" was first published. It referred to a Camp To-to-ka-no. This campsite was renamed Camp Swanton, for a very small town of that name nearby.

Elmo Stevenson was promoted from Field Executive to Assistant Scout Executive in 1927, and Alvin Rhodes continued as Field Executive. In 1928 Lester H. Quinley became a Field Executive, and Elmo Stevenson was no longer on the staff. In 1929 Egbert Rozeboom, from Palo Alto, became a Field Executive.

Harrison White left the Council in January, 1931, to become Scout Executive in Santa Ana, Orange County, California.

Duncan E. McKinley:
January 1931 - August 1941

Duncan (Dunc) McKinley (1887-1966) was Field Executive in Oakland and Huntington Park, California before coming to San Jose as Scout Executive at the age of 44.

He was a former Army Colonel in World War I who like to do things "strictly by the book."

In 1931 McKinley's annual salary was $4,000; his assistant, Lester Quinley made $3,000. During his administration, he and Quinley helped train Scoutmasters in a six-week course, with one field training weekend at Big Basin or other campsite. He also organized the start-up of Camp Arroyo Sequoia.

During McKinley's tenure Santa Cruz, Monterey and San Benito Counties formed their own Monterey Bay Area Council (May 1933), and northern Santa Clara County separated to form Stanford Area Council (January 1940).

Duncan McKinley was transferred to Los Angeles as Assistant Executive in August, 1941. He returned to Army duty from 1942-46, and retired from Scouting in January, 1948.

Oscar B. Matthews:
August 1941 - August 1945

Oscar (Matt) Matthews (1887-1945) had been a Scout Executive in Huntington, California and a Field Executive in Los Angeles before transferring to San Jose at age 54, where he served the Council during the difficult years of World War II. The Council office consisted of three rooms on the second floor of the Bank of America building on First Street.

The Camp Stuart property in the Santa Cruz Mountain foothills southwest of Saratoga was donated to the Council in 1944 by Grace and Reginald Stuart. Also, the Boy Scout Memorial Foundation was established during his administration.

Oscar Matthews died in office, at the age of 58, on August 26, 1945.

Chester D. Bartlett:
January 1946 - April 1958

Chester (Chet) Bartlett (1897-1966) came to the San Jose Council at age 60 after having been a Scout Executive since 1923 serving in Arizona at Douglas, and in California at Marysville and Bakersfield. Bartlett's assistant was Harold Alexander.

During the important post-war years, two projects demanded Barlett's administrative skills. The first was the Council's purchase of Camp Hi-Sierra, where Past President Bill Nicholson and other volunteers built tent platforms, the Health Lodge, latrines and showers. Bartlett pitched in with the digging of ditches and other heavy construction projects.

Another milestone project was the completion, in 1954, of the Charles E. Moore Memorial Boy Scout Building which functions as the Council Service Center at 2095 Park Avenue in San Jose.

During his tenure Boy Scout membership grew from 1631 to 7582.

Chester Bartlett became Scout Executive Emeritus on April 15, 1958 and functioned in that capacity until January 1960. He retired in August 1961 after 38 years of service to Scouting. Chester Bartlett died November 3, 1966.

Raymond J. Ewan:
April 1958 - December 1974

Raymond (Ray) Ewan (1909-85), a native of Philadelphia, began his professional Scout career as a Field Executive in Chico in 1943. He went on to become the Scout Executive for Auburn, and later, Petaluma. Ewan then arrived in San Jose, at the age of 49, to start the longest administration of any Santa Clara County Council Scout Executive up until that time. Over the span of sixteen years he had three capable assistants: Harold Alexander, former Field Director Ted Rogers, and Bob Chapman.

During the Ewan "years," Nessie and Paul Chesebrough gave a wilderness area in the Santa Cruz Mountains to the Council which was named Camp Chesebrough; The Order of the Arrow Lodge was reactivated; and the BSA Executive Club, later renamed the President's Club, was established. Ewan took the leadership in straightening boundary lines and renaming districts, as well.

Ewan was the first Scout Executive to retain a public relations firm to handle publicity for major events such as the Scout-O-Rama. He also hired the first urban outreach worker, and the first woman Exploring Executive, Karen Thuener.

Ray Ewan was respected for being able to motivate volunteers "in a low key, persuasive manner" to take on responsible jobs. His emphasis on program techniques accounted for much of the major Council growth during his administration. He retired from professional Scouting December 1, 1974.

Raymond Ewan was the first Eagle Scout to serve the Santa Clara County Council as Scout Executive. He received the Silver Beaver Award in 1981. Raymond Ewan died August 31, 1985.

Randolf B. Kohl:
December 1974 to February 1977

Randolf (Randy) Kohl had served as District Executive and Scout Executive in New York state before being promoted to Director of Exploring on the National Council staff. After being hired by the San Jose Council, he brought in E. Earl (Sonny) Hays as his assistant. Later he hired the first woman, Letitia Maldonado, to work in a district.

Kohl brought to the Santa Clara County Council some of the concepts of management that were being instituted at that time nationally, such as the new "Recommended Plan for Council and District Organization" to replace the "Traditional Plan."

Two successful fundraising programs initiated during Kohl's administration were the Golf Tournament and the Distinguished Citizens Dinner. Randolf Kohl left the Council in February 1977 to become the Director of Field Service in the Chief Seattle Council.

Robert N. Allexsaht:
January 1978 - March 1982

Robert (Bob) Allexsaht, an Eagle Scout himself, came into the program as a Field Executive in Buffalo, New York in 1950. He progressed through the ranks and then became Scout Executive in Utica, New York in 1960, and in Kansas City, Kansas in 1972. Prior to coming to the San Jose Council he was the Director of Finance for the Western Region. The Council felt he had the right qualifications to put them on a solid financial footing.

Allexsaht was the first Scout Executive to be sensitive to instituting an outreach program to interest Vietnamese in the benefits of Scouting for their youth, and he hired a part-time worker to recruit them.

Tom Anderson became Assistant Scout Executive until he left to become Scout Executive in Yakima, Washington. Ed Weiseth also assisted in the administration of the Scout Office, later leaving to become the Scout Executive for the Crater Lake Council.

Robert Allexsaht left the Council in mid-March 1982 and retired from Scouting June 1, 1982. As an avid outdoorsman, he was accomplished in wilderness survival and backpacking. After leaving the Scouting Program he assisted former Council President Frank Bernard in the dehydrated food industry.

Brian L. Allen:
June 1982 to present

Brian Allen arrived in San Jose June 1, 1982, after serving as Scout Executive in Morris, Illinois, from 1975-1982. He had held District Executive and Director of Field Services positions since 1962 in Wisconsin, Indiana and Illinois prior to coming to San Jose.

Allen was President of the national BSA service fraternity, Alpha Phi Omega, at Wisconsin State University, and was a member of the Varsity Club there. He is an Eagle Scout, is a member of the Order of the Arrow Lodge and has been Section Chief.

Brian Allen has developed new outreach programs to attract low income, minority youth such as the In-School Scouting, Varsity and Career Awareness Programs. These programs include additional training in science and athletics, and provide valuable career information.

During the years of his administration, with efficient Assistant Scout Executives Ken Allen and Jay Lowden, plus the District Executives, Brian Allen assisted the Council in increasing Scout membership from 12,000 to 32,000, and maintained a cost per youth of $55 per year.

A Professional Staff Member's Profile

The term "Professional Scouter" applies to a person who has been trained by the National Council in Scouting procedures, management and programs. The person starts as a District Scout Executive, and after gaining experience, he, or she, goes on to serve in various management positions. Frequently a Professional Scouter becomes a Scout Executive in a local Council.

The Professional Scouter is a man, or woman, who has decided to follow a professional career in the field of Scouting. He, or she, likes camping, backpacking and outdoor sports. The Santa Clara County Council has had many fine Professional Scouters who have made the program stronger and more meaningful for the council adult volunteers as well as the youth members. A representative group of these Professional Scouters reflect the character of these dedicated men and women.

Professional Staff Members

Kenneth Robison:
1940 - 1953

Kenneth (Ken) Robison joined the Los Gatos Boy Scout Troop 3 in 1923 at age 12. He was Assistant Scoutmaster at 18 in the Kiwanis Club-sponsored Troop 39, Los Gatos, under Scoutmaster Sewall Brown.

In 1926-27 he was employed to accompany Assistant Scout Executives Alvin Rhodes or Elmo Stevenson down to King City, the farthest "outpost" of the Santa Clara, San Benito, Monterey Bay Area Council, BSA. He also drove Scout Executive Harrison White over to the coast on occasion to check on Camp Swanton.

In 1931 he was made Camp Director of Camp Swanton and later was the first director at Camp Arroyo Sequoia. During the thirties Robison served the Council as a Commissioner. In 1939 he went to National Training School to become a professional Scouter.

Robison had his first job as a member of the professional staff in 1940 when he was given the assignment of Field Director for the council. Following the war years, he worked for the National Council in New Mexico serving as Camp Director for Philmont Scout Ranch, 1946-47. He came back to the Santa Clara Council in 1948. As Assistant Scout Executive, he was assigned the task of assisting the Council committee with their camp property search. Robison was sent, with Assemblyman Bob Kirkwood, chairman of the Camping Committee, to check out 43 different properties. They finally settled on a one-hundred-acre parcel on the Tuolumne River for which owner Ed Jeness charged them $10!

Robison was involved in the building of the facilities for the site they named Camp Hi-Sierra, with Council member Cliff Swenson, who donated the engineering, labor and supervision. Robison remembers they used as much pre-fab material as possible. The largest building, the mess hall, had a steeply pitched roof so that it could take the heavy snows of winter.

In 1953 Robison left the profession to take a position as Recreation Director with the Campbell Union High School District.

1956 Ken Robison received the Silver Beaver Award. In 1990, at age 79, after 67 years as a Scouter, Ken is still listed as an Assistant Scoutmaster of the same Troop 3 he joined in 1923, later called Troop 39 and today called Troop 539.

Claude E. Smith:
1955 - 1965

"Smitty" was one of the first Boy Scouts in Santa Clara County. He joined Scoutmaster Ray D. Hartman's Boy Scout Troop 1, Los Gatos and was a member from 1916-20. He was a Scoutmaster in Oakland and then returned to Los Gatos. With the sponsorship of American Legion Post 158, Smith started Troop 55. He was their Scoutmaster from 1927-34.

He then became District Commissioner, and later Leadership and Advancement Chairman for the Council.

In 1955 Smith began a new scouting career as Program Ranger at Camp Stuart. R.R. Stuart had given the Council 80 acres that was originally the property of Mary Brown, widow of John Brown of Harper's Ferry fame during the Civil War. It was located in the foothills south of Saratoga and needed a permit from the Division of Forestry to operate on a yearly basis.

Camp Stuart was also known as Stuart Scout Training Reservation. There Smith conducted classes on nature and conservation for Boy Scouts and their leaders. Smith was a director of the Santa Clara Valley Audubon Society and instructed Girl Scouts and Camp Fire Girls on the Audubon Society's trail at Montalvo Arboretum.

During his tenure as Ranger, Smith lived in the last building left from the occupancy of Mary Brown. He retired in 1965 to move to Washington. In December 1965 he was honored by having a new camp fire circle at Camp Stuart named in his honor.

Claude Smith holds a 40 year Scouter veteran card. He is the recipient of the Scoutmaster's Key and received the Silver Beaver Award in 1940. In 1990 at the venerable age of 88, "Smitty" still resides in Tacoma, Washington.

Theodore Rogers:
1956 - 1970

Theodore (Ted) Rogers started as a professional Scouter in Tacoma, Washington, in 1949. From there he went to Phoenix in 1952. He remained in Arizona until 1956 when he came to the Santa Clara County Council, BSA.

Rogers worked a year and a half with Scout Executive Chester Bartlett prior to his retirement. He worked twelve years under Scout Executive Ray Ewan.

Rogers remembers a significant conversation with Assistant Scout Executive Harold Alexander when Rogers first arrived in San Jose. Alexander maintained that the San Jose area had reached its peak growth. Rogers felt that, "San Jose would be like Los Angeles one of these days." Rogers was told he was crazy. However, the great growth in population, and incidentally, Boy Scout membership, did occur during the period he was here with the council.

During his stay he became Assistant Scout Executive, a position he held until 1970 when he moved to Glendale as Scout Executive. Ted Rogers retired from the profession in 1976.

William Pursell:
November 1956 - 1963

William (Bill) Pursell started out in Troop 28 at Garfield Junior High School in Berkeley, and achieved Eagle rank in 1942. His father was Scoutmaster and, later, chairman of the troop committee. His brother was also an Eagle Scout.

After college Pursell ran into an old friend who had gone into the Scouting profession. He suggested that Bill might do that, too. A year or so later, Pursell was interviewed at a regional meeting, signed on with Scout Executive Chester Bartlett, and was sent to National Training School at Schiff Reservation.

He returned in March, 1957, and went to work with Ted Rogers in the West Valley District. Pursell was under Chet Bartlett for a year before Ray Ewan took over as Scout Executive in April, 1958. District Executives at that time were: South District, Ralph Libby, Los Gatos/Saratoga, Don Gray; North District, Doug Walton; Campbell, Frank Woodland.

One of Ewan's first priorities was to straighten boundary lines and rename the districts. Ted Rogers became the Field Director and Pursell took the job of District Executive in the newly-defined Polaris District. He and Scoutmaster Bill Sutcliff, a former professional, worked together to organize new units in the Cupertino area. Polaris District went from 28 to 109 units, with over 4500 youths, during his eight years there.

Bill Pursell left the Santa Clara County Council for a job in the Phoenix (Arizona) Council in 1963. He returned to California for employment with the Stanford Area Council from 1965–69, then worked in Sacramento two years before he left the profession in 1971.

Karen Theuner Weiseth:
1974 - 1978

Karen Theuner became a Scout professional in 1971. She was hired by the Santa Clara County Council as an Explorer Executive in 1974. In four years she became Exploring Director and led the Exploring Division to the top of the Western Region.

She was promoted in February of 1978 to Director of Scouting for the Handicapped for Western Region, Area 5. Her responsibilities included coordination of Scouting for the handicapped in the six Bay Area Councils.

Karen Theuner married Council Field Director Ed Weiseth in the late seventies. She was named Finance Director for the Santa Clara County Council in 1980. In 1982 Karen T. Weiseth became a Consultant to the Council and left Scouting a short time later.

Karen Weiseth is now a Special Education Teacher in Medford, Oregon where husband Ed is the Scout Executive for the Medford BSA council.

Letitia Maldonado:
September 1975 - 1980

In 1975 Leticia Maldonado was the second female Scouter on the Council staff. She had the title of Community Aide and was listed in the Mene Oto Section of the Santa Clarion newsletters as a paraprofessional. However, she worked in the position of an Assistant District Executive for two years.

Maldonado was born in Fresno and was graduated from San Jose State University. In 1977 she was a graduate of the National Executive Institute of the BSA.

Her enthusiasm and interest in the Cub and Scout programs made her a favorite with both the youth members and the Scouters in the Mene Oto District. In October 1977 she assumed the position of District Executive, Gavilan District. she became District Executive of the council's largest district, Mene Oto, in the spring of 1979.

A short time later Letitia Maldonado accepted a new challenge with the San Francisco Bay Area Council as Field Director working in the Oakland area. She left the profession in 1989.

Outstanding Scouters

An Outstanding Scouter's Profile

The profile of an outstanding Scouter is very similar to that of a Council President's profile. In fact, many one of these outstanding Scouters could have served the Council well as its president.

The outstanding Scouter who has worked with the Council is a man with enough energy to spend many volunteer hours in a field of his interest in Scouting. He comes from the ranks of business, industry and the professions. He is realistic about his commitment to the organization, and, he may prefer digging camp trenches in muddy denims, or he may prefer hosting recognition dinners or golf tournaments. However, as an adult Scouter he is sincerely dedicated to providing opportunities for youth to attain their goals.

William J. Adams, Jr.

William (Bill) Adams became a Boy Scout in Santa Cruz Troop 69 in 1928, which at that time was a part of the Santa Clara County Council. His troop was sponsored by the American Legion Post. His Scoutmaster, Al Huntsman, was a Legionnaire, a great outdoorsman, and incidentally, the foreman of the Portland Cement quarry at Davenport. Adams became an Eagle Scout in Santa Cruz.

Adams graduated from Santa Clara University magna cum laude with a B.S. degree in Mechanical Engineering in 1937. He worked for General Electric in Schenectady, N.Y. and developed remote controlled gun turrets for the B-29 and other high altitude bombers during World War II. In 1946 he joined Food Machinery Corporation (FMC) and was employed on the east coast, mid-west and west coast.

Adams had two sons in San Jose Troop 6 and he was on the troop committee in those years. From 1962–68 he was Chairman of the Ponderosa District, which encompassed San Jose north of Santa Clara Street and Alum Rock Road, and included all of Santa Clara and Milpitas.

In 1968 Adams chaired the founding of the BSA Executive Club as a vehicle to recognize present investors in Scouting and to encourage new investors through major monetary gifts. He also urged the change in the name to the BSA President's Club as the sponsor of the Distinguished Citizens Annual Dinner.

Adams was a member of the Eagle Scout Association for several years before serving as president in 1968. A highlight of his presidency was the 1968 Eagle Recognition Dinner honoring over 100 new Eagle Scouts at La Rinconada Country Club, with a stirring address by Olympic Decathlon Champion Bob Mathias.

In 1980 Bill Adams was named Coordinator of the Community and Family Sustaining Membership Enrollment (Friends of Scouting) Program. He has been on the Council Executive Board from 1962 to the present. Bill Adams received the Silver Beaver Award in 1969.

Michael H. Antonacci

Michael (Mike) Antonacci was born in New York in 1903. He remembers the year of 1910 when his uncles were involved with YMCA programs, and that the YMCA took a leadership role in New York City in the fledgling Boy Scout Movement.

Antonacci was a Tenderfoot in 1914. By 1916 he successfully climbed the ladder from Star to Life to Eagle Scout. In 1916 he moved to Los Angeles, where he was in a compulsory ROTC unit in high school and had no more time for Scouting.

The busy schedule Antonacci had in the 1930s seems to be part of the profile of many of the other outstanding Scouters. In his own words, "... in the thirties I had become the City Planning Engineer, now called Director of Planning, for the City of San Jose. I had a city council meeting on Monday nights, a planning commission meeting on Tuesday nights, an orchestra rehearsal on Wednesday (I was the first chair 'cello). Then on Friday I played in the string quartet. This quartet was started by our first violinist, and was named the Mendelsohn Quartet in his honor. This was the same Dr. Mendelsohn that Dr. Jack Cox went into practice with in Saratoga—so this left me with only Thursday night free."

Of course, Thursday night was soon "taken" for a couple of years when Antonacci became Scoutmaster of Westminister Presbyterian Church Troop 3.

Antonacci was appointed to the Executive Baord in 1933 when Almon Roth was president.

Michael Antonacci was awarded the Silver Beaver in 1977, and the Distinguished Eagle in 1986.

Louis P. Bergna

Louis (Lou) Bergna was raised in San Jose and joined Troop 19, sponsored by the Willow Glen American Legion Post, and later joined Troop 25, sponsored by the Willow Glen Methodist Church. He earned his Eagle under Scoutmaster Forest Owen in 1938.

He graduated from Santa Clara University with a B.S. degree in 1944 and a J.D. law degree in 1948. In 1957 he was elected District Attorney of Santa Clara County and served for 25 years, retiring in 1982.

As a Scouter, Bergna was Chairman of the Redwood District in the early 1960s, president of the Eagle Scout Association in 1970, Master of Ceremonies of the Eagle Scout Recognition Dinners for 15 years, and a sponsor of the Knights of Dunamis, a boys' honorary Eagle Scout organization.

Louis Bergna was presented the plaque and solid-gold medallion which signify the Distinguished Eagle Award in 1976. It was the first such award given to any person in the Santa Clara County Council.

Walter D. Chronert

Walter (Walt) Chronert didn't have the opportunity to be a Scout as a boy. However, as a young man in World War II, he was impressed by former Scouts who served with him in the Army.

As soon as his oldest son Bill became 8 years old, the whole family joined the Boy Scouts. Vera Chronert became the Den leader; Walt worked with the Webelos. That launched a family career in 1955 that the Chronert family still pursues today.

In that year Chronert had been a Postal Inspector in Gary, Indiana when he was transferred to Los Altos. He joined Troop 478 in Cupertino as Assistant Scoutmaster and later he became Scoutmaster.

In 1960 Troop 478 moved to Sunnyvale Presbyterian Church. That became the site of intensive Scouting activity in the next 14 years. Two additional troops were formed and it served as the location of most of the Polaris District functions. During that time the troop cut down the prune orchard at the corner of Fremont and Hollenbeck Road so that a large sanctuary and parking lot could be constructed.

One of Chronert's outstanding contributions was the organization of a troop band, made up of 32 of the 55 boys. The band performed at parades and Scout events for seven years and has the distinction of being the only troop band during the seventy-year history of the Santa Clara Council.

Resigning as Scoutmaster in 1974 to become the Chairman of the Polaris District, Chronert also went on the Council executive board. He was Vice President for membership 1983-86, and worked ten years under County Supervisor Rod Diridon on the Scout-O-Rama steering committee.

One of his most satisfying assignments was as Chairman of the program for handicapped Scouts. The highlight of that program was the combined Bay Area Council Handicapped Camp-o-ree. This was held in conjunction with the Council's "Extravaganza" at Calero Reservoir County Park in June 1980. Over 125 handicapped Scouts and Explorer Scouts attended the event, many camped overnight for the first time in their lives.

Walter Chronert has his Woodbadge training and holds the Order of the Arrow, Vigil Honor. He was given the Award of Merit in Polaris District and the God and Country Award by the Sunnyvale Presbyterian Church. The Silver Beaver Award was presented to him in 1971. His wife, Elvera Chronert, received the Silver Beaver Award in 1981. Their son Gary is an Eagle Scout.

John E. Cox, M.D.

John (Jack) Cox became a Scout in Richland Park, New Jersey when he joined Troop 3 in 1923. He spent some of his teen years as an orderly in a veteran's hospital in New Mexico and was transferred to the veteran's hospital in Palo Alto, California.

Cox became Scoutmaster of Troop 40 in Mayfield, a suburb of Palo Alto, from 1931-35. He has had an ongoing involvement with Scouting as an adult as demonstrated by these highlights of some of his contributions:

- Field Commissioner, Stanford Area Council 1940-41;
- Scoutmaster, Troop 49, Saratoga, 1946-47;
- Council Executive Board, 1946-79;
- Troop Committee Chairman, Troop 40, Saratoga Lions Club, 1949-55;
- Hi-Sierra Camp Doctor, 1953-62;
- Council Roundtable Training Commissioner, 1958-60;
- Post Committee Chairman, Post 40, 1960;
- Council Commissioner, 1971-74 and 1976-79;
- Council Vice President, 1975;
- Area III, Vice President, 1976-77;
- Area III, Commissioner, 1978;
- Council Advisory, 1980 to the present.

Somehow, in between all his Scouting commitments, Jack Cox found time to get a medical degree from Stanford University, and spent his medical career in General Practice in Saratoga.

He has been recognized for his dedication to the Scouting Program in the following ways:
- Order of the Arrow: Ordeal, 1941; Brotherhood, 1972; Vigil, 1974;
- Scoutmaster's Key, 1949;
- Silver Beaver Award, 1960;
- Woodbadge, Camp Hi-Sierra, 1966; Update, Camp Stuart, 1973;
- Silver Antelope Award, 1978.

Jack Cox has an unusual profile in that not only has he been a Boy Scout and has served innumerable hours as a volunteer Scouter, he has also been a "paid professional" as a Field Commissioner in the Stanford Area Council while attending Stanford University.

In 1990 Jack Cox received his 50-year Veteran Award.

Glenn George

Glenn George is a San Jose native who earned the rank of Life Scout in Troop 37 which met in the basement of the Calvary Methodist Church at Naglee and Morse Streets in San Jose. He became the Patrol Leader of the Panther Patrol in 1942.

George, Chairman of the Board of Joseph George Distributors in Santa Clara, has been very active in community affairs as is demonstrated by his leadership role in many organizations in the area. He has been president of the San Jose Rotary Club and president of the Camp Fire Council of Santa Clara/San Benito Counties. George has served on the Boards of San Jose Hospital, San Jose Chamber of Commerce, the Red Cross, and the United Fund, and has been a Director for the American Cancer Society, Goodwill Industries and the Spartan Foundation.

His support of the Scouting program has been as a San Jose Rotary Club troop committee member, and his membership on the President's Advisory Committee and the Memorial Foundation. He has been a leader in Council fund raising efforts directed toward expanding the program to reach more of this country's youth.

Glenn George is a recipient of the San Jose State University School of Business Award and the 1978 Distinguished Citizen Award of the Santa Clara County Council, BSA. He received the Silver Beaver Award in 1983.

Scout-O-Rama, 1969   Photo, Pat Peabody

Edward H. Goddard

Edward (Ed) Goddard was a Mechanical Engineer for Lockheed. He later ran his own backpacking equipment company.

He became involved as an adult in the Scouting program in 1957 when Fred Yule recruited him to be a Neighborhood Commissioner in the Polaris District. Soon he became a Round Table Commissioner. In five years, the Round Table Training Program went from 14 troops to 44 troops. He was also Woodbadge trained.

Goddard was always interested in getting the boys out and hiking, and he stimulated competition between the troops to go on "fifty milers." After three years, Goddard estimated that close to 75% of the troops in the Polaris District were doing fifty milers and enjoying the "true wilderness experience." It appeared to have increased the boys' interest in camping which he felt made a difference in the attendance at Camp Hi-Sierra. Goddard was also a Woodbadge Instructor at Camp Hi-Sierra in 1970, and he was given a World Scouting emblem by Course Director Tom Smith.

Edward Goddard received the Order of the Arrow Vigil Honor in 1967 and the Silver Beaver Award in 1981.

Stephen H. Goodman

Stephen (Steve) Goodman, a civil engineer, prior to his retirement in the early eighties, was manager of the Santa Clara County Sanitation District No. 4, with offices in Campbell. He has been a registered Scouter in the Santa Clara County Council for 33 years.

He became an active participant in the Scouting Program in 1956 when he was appointed Finance Chairman for Pioneer District by then Council President Larry Hill.

In 1962 he became troop committee chairman for two years. Goodman then became Scoutmaster of Troop 318 from 1966–69. In 1970–74 he was Chairman of the Pioneer District. Steve began a stint on the Executive Baord in 1970 and has been a member ever since, functioning from 1975–79 as Vice President for District Operations.

Goodman has conducted conferences at Camp Stuart and has taken a training course at Philmont National Training Center in New Mexico. He has chaired judging committees at Scout-O-Ramas, as well as the 1976 Bicent-O-Ree.

Stephen Goodman received the Order of the Arrow Vigil Honor in 1976, the Scouter's Award in 1970, and the Silver Beaver Award in 1969. His wife, Jean, was President of the Woman's Reserve and received the Silver Beaver in 1978.

Arthur K. Lund

Arthur (Art) Lund was a Cub Scout for three years and went on to become a Life Scout.

Lund received a BA degree Cum Laude with Departmental Honors in Business Administration from San Jose State University. During his undergraduate years he was student body president and cadet commander of the R.O.T.C. He received his J.D. at U.C. Berkeley's Boalt Hall of Law and began his law practice in San Jose in 1961. Soon thereafter he became associated with the law firm of Rankin, Oneal.

Art Lund is chairman of the board of San Jose National Bank and of the O'Connor Hospital Foundation. He is a director of the San Jose Convention and Business Visitors Bureau and a member of the advisory board of San Jose State University, as well as serving on many other boards and agencies in the county.

When this prominent San Jose lawyer has leisure time he likes to fly and to hunt and fish.

Arthur Lund is currently serving on the President's Advisory Committee and the Memorial Foundation for the Santa Clara County Council, BSA.

Karl Mann

Karl Mann (1886–1983) was born on a farm in Iowa and received his Civil Engineering degree at the Iowa State College. He spent the early 1950s in Idaho where he was president of the Kiwanis Club, and on the Executive Board of the Council and Scoutmaster of Troop 325. From 1956–58 he was Assistant Scoutmaster of Troop 58 in Cimarron, New Mexico.

Mann came to Santa Clara County in 1958 and served in many capacities including Commissioner for Pack 24, Roundtable Staff, Training Staff, and the staffs of Camp Stuart and Camp Hi-Sierra. In the mid-sixties he utilized his carpentry skills by building all the cabinets, drawers, film trays and other interior features when the Scout Service Center on Park Avenue in San Jose was undergoing a complete renovation.

In 1981 Karl was honored in his 91st year with a feature article in the Santa Clarion describing his long and distinguished career as a Scouter. He was quoted as saying, "I remember best working with the boys ... when I was 2 years old, I remember running to my mother, her picking me up and cuddling me. I felt such warmth and so good that I just wanted to pass on that good feeling through helping boys."

He received the Silver Beaver Award in his previous council before coming to Santa Clara County Council. He received the Order of the Arrow Vigil Honor here in 1968.

Vinton S. Matthews, M.D.

Vinton (Vint) Matthews joined the Scouts in 1932 in Grand Rapids, Michigan, where he earned his Eagle Scout Award. He moved to San Jose and the award was presented to him when he joined Troop 11 in 1935 when Irvin Copple was their Scoutmaster.

Matthews was a Boy Scout delegate enroute to the First National Jamboree in Washington, D.C., in July 1935, when it was cancelled by order of President Franklin D. Roosevelt because of an infantile paralysis (polio) epidemic. Matthews was in New York City with 10,000 other Boy Scouts from all over the country. Mayor LaGuardia and Jimmy Durante put on a show for them all at Central Park. While in New York, 15-year old Vinton, dressed in his Scout shorts, visited the National Council headquarters and had a memorable 15-minute chat with the first Chief Scout Executive, James E. West.

Matthews graduated from U.C. Berkeley, a cadet major in the ROTC Coast Artillery, and served in the Army Artillery during World War II, seeing action in the invasion of France. When the war was over he returned in 1946, and graduated from Stanford Medical School in 1951. Dr. Matthews was in General Practice in San Jose from 1952–1989. In 1947 he had joined the California National Guard and retired as a Brigadier General in 1972.

Matthews became Camp Doctor at Camp Hi-Sierra in 1955 serving a week each year under the Chairmanship of Dr. Fred Schilla. He has dedicated time during the summer to this service for nearly 35 years. His wife, Grace, has been Summer Camp Nurse there for a week or more since 1962. In 1988 and 1989 the couple covered the full eight weeks of summer camp at Hi-Sierra.

In addition to being the physician "on call," Matthews has been a member of the Council Executive Board since 1956, a Vice President for 25 years. He was Mene Oto District Chairman for nine years, has served on numerous Eagle Boards of Review, and conducted many Courts of Honor. Dr. Matthews has been the presentor of the Silver Beaver Awards at the annual Recognition Dinners for many years. He has followed in the Scouting tradition of his father, Vinton H. Matthews, who was one of the most active and hard working supporters of building the Council Service Center before his untimely death.

Dr. Vinton Matthews was honored in 1985 when the health lodge at Camp Hi-Sierra was dedicated in his name as "The Dr. Vinton S. Matthews Health Lodge." He received the Silver Beaver Award in 1957, the Distinguished Eagle Scout Award in 1988.

Charles S. Orr

Charles (Charlie) Orr joined Cub Scouts in the Covered Wagon Council in Omaha, Nebraska, in 1935. He achieved the Eagle rank in 1938.

Orr is a graduate of the University of Nebraska with a master's degree from Omaha University. He served as a principal in the San Jose Unified School District from 1960 to 1986 in the Jefferson, Allen and Schallenberger elementary schools.

As a Scouter, Orr became an Assistant Scoutmaster in Troop 233 in 1965, the same year he was made District Commissioner for Mene Oto District. He has remained interested in Troop 233 since that time, taking the boys to Scout camp several years and on fifteen "fifty miler" backpack trips. He was president of the Eagle Scout Association in 1978.

He has been to Philmont Scout Ranch three times and taught International Scouting at one session there. Orr has taught Woodbadge courses at Gilwell Park in England since 1977. He is presently the International Representative for the Santa Clara County Council and corresponds with over forty Scouters in all parts of England, Japan, India and France. Terry Bonfield, the last surviving member of Baden-Powell's first Scout camp on Brownsea Island in 1907, became one of Charles's best friends.

Charlie Orr has served on the Council Advisory Committee and Finance Committee, and worked on fundraising, Scout-O-Ramas and many other Scouting projects. However, he believes his greatest satisfaciton in Scouting came when three of the Scouts he had taken on backpack trips grew up to be the leaders of "fifty milers" themselves.

Charles Orr earned his Woodbadge beads in 1969. He was the recipient of the Silver Beaver in 1968, and the Award of Merit in 1971.

Robert W. Richardson

Robert (Bob) Richardson is a Chemistry Professor at San Jose State University. Richardson's father had worked for Robert Bentley, Jr., who was the first Council President in 1920.

In 1956 Richardson took Troop 33 (now 233) to Camp Hi-Sierra because their Scoutmaster had resigned. The troop met at the Willow Glen Methodist Church. Richardson took Troop 233 to camp for several years. In 1966 he took the troop on its first backpacking trip.

Working with District Chairman Vint Matthews, Richardson became Activities Chairman and helped select the district name. They decided on an Indian name, "Mene Oto" meaning "many waters." Richardson served on the Junior Leader Training staff for several years, and presided over many Eagle Courts of Honor. He was a member of the Council's Eagle Scout Association.

One of Richardson's most outstanding contributions was to successfully work handicapped youngsters into the Scouting program.

Robert Richardson received the Order of the Arrow Vigil Honor in 1970, the Silver Beaver Award in 1964.

Milton P. Ryder

Milton (Milt) Ryder (1899–1976) was a purchasing agent and supervisor of construction for the Richmond Chase Canning Company for 37 years. Born in Maine, Ryder came to California in 1910. In 1923 he and his wife moved to San Jose. He was a charter member of American Legion Post No. 399 having served in the Navy in World War I.

Ryder was Council Commissioner for the Santa Clara County Council from 1940–61, the longest service of any Council Commissioner.

His civic activities received well-deserved recognition when he was presented the San Jose "Distinguished Citizen Award" in 1955.

Milton Ryder was given his 40-year service pin in 1975. He had received the Silver Beaver Award in 1945.

Albert B. Smith

Albert (Al) Smith was raised near Los Gatos. He earned a bachelor's degree in crop science in 1944 and a master's degree in agriculture in 1956 from Cal Poly. He taught agriculture classes in Manteca and returned to the valley to teach 17 years in the Campbell High School District.

As a youngster he was a member of Troop 39 (now 539) in Los Gatos where he became an Eagle Scout. He was an Assistant Scoutmaster for 40 years and was also an active Explorer advisor.

In later years Al became president of the family company, Orchard Supply Hardware, and was an elected Councilman and Mayor in the Town of Los Gatos.

Smith grew up near Vasona Junction and developed a life-long fascination with trains as they traveled past his home on a daily basis. A few years after the Council decided not to pursue the development of the Arroyo Sequoia campsite on Little Creek, Smith purchased this property as well as the Camp Swanton Property on the Pacific Coast near Davenport. Through the years he has assembled a collection of old locomotives and rail cars there.

These locomotives were originally used in 1915 to pull sightseeing cars on the grounds of the Pan-Pacific Exposition in San Francisco. Two locomotives have been restored and are housed in a miniature round-house. His caboose sits on a siding where the Camp Swanton latrine once stood. Smith has frequently hosted the Council, and boys from many different troops, at outings on his property. They have a great time riding the "Swanton Pacific Railroad."

Albert Smith is a member of the Council Executive Board, and President of the Boy Scout Memorial Foundation. He was awarded the Silver Beaver in 1980 and the Distinguished Eagle in 1982.

Lester R. Steig, Ph.D.

Lester (Les) Steig was an educator and retired as the Assistant Superintendent of Schools in San Francisco.

Steig's involvement in the Scout program has been different than most of the other outstanding Scouters in the Santa Clara County Council. Steig served as Scoutmaster in North Dakota for different troops from 1925–30, and in Montana from 1930–35. After coming to California, he served on the Executive Board of the Stanford Area Council from 1946–55, and on the San Francisco Council from 1956–75. He joined the Santa Clara County Council Executive Board in 1975 and is still serving on the Board.

Les Steig has been a member of the BSA National Council since 1966, National Eagle Scout Association Executive Board since 1970, and National Explorer Committee since 1964. He has also participated on the Uniform and Insignia Committee. From 1962–64 he was the National President of Alpha Phi Omega, the BSA National Service Fraternity that has 620 university chapters. From 1970–72 he was President Emeritus of the Knights of Dunamis.

Lester Steig is a 70-year veteran having been continuously registered in Scouting since 1916. He was awarded the Silver Beaver in 1954, the Silver Antelope in 1974 and the Silver Buffalo in 1976 while serving previously in other councils. In 1970 he received the National Distinguished Service Award. Steig is the only Scouter now serving in the Santa Clara County Council to have received the Silver Buffalo Award and the Distinguished Service Award, two high national awards.

James P. Sturrock

James (Jim) Sturrock graduated from Georgia Tech with an MS in Aeronautical Engineering.

Sturrock's heritage is firmly rooted in the Scouting tradition. In 1908 his father, a native of Scotland, at the age of 15, had helped to organize a Scout Troop in the city of Lanark. That was just one year after Lord Baden-Powell had run the experimental Brownsea Island camp across the border in England. The senior Sturrock became a leader of that early troop in Scotland, before he emigrated to Florida.

In 1932, following his father's footsteps, Jim joined Troop 3 in West Palm Beach, Florida. By 1933 Sturrock was a Patrol Leader and a Life Scout. In Troop 13, in 1938, he was the first Scout to get his Eagle, and he later earned the Bronze, Gold and Silver Palms. His two brothers also became Eagle Scouts in Troop 13. He went on to be Assistant Scoutmaster of Troop 3 in Atlanta, Georgia, during the four years he attended Georgia Tech. While there, he helped organize the Alpha Phi Omega (APO) chapter and was its president. He also was involved in organizing several other APO chapters in the Southeastern states.

During World War II Sturrock became a Captain in the Army Air Corps stationed at Wright Field, Dayton, Ohio. Since the call to duty had interrupted his education, he took his family back to Atlanta in order to complete his Engineering degree.

Throughout his career he was involved in five different Councils. Besides the Gulf Stream Council, West Palm Beach, Florida and the Atlanta Area Council in Georgia, he was an Assistant Scoutmaster and Scoutmaster in the East Texas Area Council, Longview (1948-51); Neighborhood Commissioner, Tecumseh Council, Springfield, Ohio (1951-52); Assistant District Commissioner in the Los Angeles Area Council (1953-57).

In the Santa Clara County Council from 1958 to the present, Sturrock has served as Roundtable Commissioner, District Commissioner in the Polaris District (1957-64); and as Order of the Arrow Lodge Advisor, Assistant Council Commissioner, Council Vice President and Council Commissioner (1964-82), and a member of the President's Advisory Committee (1983 to the present). He was chairman of the Council's National Jamboree Committee in 1985, and has served as chairman of the History Task Force since 1987.

James Sturrock earned his Woodbadge beads in 1960. He received the Silver Beaver Award in 1964, the Order of the Arrow Vigil Honor in 1966, and became a Fifty-five Year Veteran in 1987.

Clifford W. Swenson

Clifford (Cliff) Swenson was raised in San Jose, one of four sons of Carl N. Swenson, president of the construction company he founded. In 1957 Cliff took over as president of the company.

Cliff was a Boy Scout in Troop 16, San Jose, and earned the rank of Life Scout with ten merit badges, under Scoutmaster Harry Harder.

In 1953, he served as general contractor for the construction of the Charles E. Moore Boy Scout Building on Park Avenue at Newhall Street in San Jose. His firm furnished the Job Superintendent Louis Stevens, the labor and much of the material. Swenson also solicited and coordinated the contributions of time, material and money from over 17 businesses, labor organizations and individuals.

In 1949 Swenson had also donated time, talent, material and labor for the construction of the first dam and the dining hall at Camp Hi-Sierra.

Clifford Swenson was a member of the Santa Clara County Council Executive Board for several years beginning in 1948. He has been serving on the President's Advisory Committee since 1965.

J. Eric Thorsen

Eric Thorsen lived in Berkeley as a child. He was sent to the Santa Cruz Mountains south of Los Gatos to a progressive private school called Montezuma School for Boys for some of his education. After his father bought a ranch in Santa Clara County in 1918, Thorsen frequently visited the area. In 1928 his father put him in charge of one of his ranches here.

Eric Thorsen joined the Santa Clara Rotary Club in 1942 and the Rotarians soon conscripted him to be a Scoutmaster. He was Scoutmaster of Troop 49 from 1943-1956. In the late forties he assisted Scout Executive Chester Bartlett in securing the property near Sonora for Camp Hi-Sierra.

Following those years of service to Scouting, Eric Thorsen became a member of the Executive Board. He has been a member of the Memorial Foundation since 1982.

Eric Thorsen received a Silver Beaver Award in 1960.

R. Maurice Tripp

Maurice (Maury) Tripp received his M.S. degree in Geophysical Engineering at the Colorado School of Mines, and his D.S. degree at Massachusetts Institute of Technology. His company is headquartered in the city of Santa Clara, where innovative engineering principles are applied to the field of medical pathology to develop surgical instruments.

Tripp joined Troop 28 in Sheboygan, Wisconsin in 1928, and reached the rank of Eagle Scout. In 1936 he became a Scoutmaster in Golden, Colorado. Through the years he has held the posts of Cubmaster, Explorer Advisor and Chairman, Camping Chairman, Volunteer Training Chairman, Roundtable Commissioner and District Commissioner at the local level.

On the national level, he has been a member of the National Council, Philmont Committee, U.S. Representative to the World Jamboree in 1933, Camp Chief at the World Jamboree, 1967, and U.S. Representative, Western Hemisphere Conference, 1968.

Maurice Tripp has been a registered Scout for 61 years. He has received his Woodbadge beads, the Order of the Arrow Vigil Honor in 1973, and the Silver Beaver Award in 1976.

Austen D. Warburton

Austen Warburton was born and raised in the city of Santa Clara. He was graduated from the University of Santa Clara and has practiced law in San Jose since 1941. World War II years 1942–1946 were spent in the service.

His first involvement with the Boy Scouts was as an Assistant Scoutmaster for Troop 77, sponsored by the Methodist Church in Santa Clara. Later he was an Advisor to Explorer Post 77.

Warburton was an early leader of several Explorer backpacking groups that hiked the Pacific Crest trail, and winter snowshoeing groups that packed into and through Camp Hi-Sierra.

Warburton has been a member of the Santa Clara County Council Executive Board. He is currently on the President's Advisory Committee and is a member of the Boy Scout Memorial Foundation. He has been Legal Advisor to the Council since the 1950s, helping to resolve problems such as the suit for right-of-way through the Camp Stuart property in Saratoga by an adjacent property owner.

Austen Warburton received the Silver Beaver Award in 1959.

Scout-O-Rama, 1969   Photo, Pat Peabody

Prominent Scouters

A Prominent Scouter's Profile

A prominent Scouter is a person who has a national/international, statewide or regional reputation in his own field and who has been in the Scouting program. Among former Scouts who have received the Nobel Prize are Dr. Ernest Lawrence who developed the cyclotron and Dr. Ralph Bunche, who was awarded the peace prize. Dudley Herschbach, an Eagle Scout from Campbell Troop 36, shared the Nobel Prize in chemistry in 1986.

Theodore Roosevelt was the first Honorary President of the Boy Scouts of America. John F. Kennedy, former member of Troop 2, Bronxville, New York, was the first U.S. President ever to have been a Scout. Gerald Ford was the first U.S. President to have been an Eagle Scout.

Santa Clara County Council has prominent Scouters who have been excellent elected representatives on the national, state and regional level. Each has been a Boy Scout in Santa Clara County; each has been a popular and revered lawmaker; each has been personally involved in the Council's programs for youth.

The following are a few of the prominent Scouters we are proud to have in Santa Clara County.

The Honorable Norman Y. Mineta

Norman Mineta, U.S. Congressman representing the 13th District since 1974, joined Cub Scout Pack 611 in San Jose when he was 9 years old in 1940.

When he was ten, along with 120,000 Americans of Japanese ancestry, Mineta and his family were interned by the U.S. Government as a "security risk" during World War II. On the day he left San Jose, May 29, 1942, Mineta wore his Cub Scout uniform and was permitted to act as a messenger between cars on the train.

In late 1942, the Mineta family were moved from Santa Anita Racetrack in California to an internment camp at Heart Mountain, Wyoming, where he continued his activity in the Boy Scouts. On one weekend in the summer of 1943, Mineta's troop invited the Boy Scouts from the Scout Council surrounding Heart Mountain into the camp for a jamboree. Mineta was buddied with Alan Simpson, who now serves as a Member of the United States Senate. He and Norman Mineta have been friends for 46 years.

The internment was the focus of the Civil Liberties Act of 1988, in which the United States formally apologized for the denial of Constitutional rights and offered compensation to an estimated 60,000 surviving former internees.

Norman Mineta and his family returned to San Jose following the war and he went into the insurance business. He was elected Mayor of San Jose in 1972.

Congressman Mineta served on the Santa Clara County Council Executive Board from 1967-74, and has continued to serve on the President's Advisory Committee since 1975.

The Hon. Dominic Cortese

Dominic Cortese, Assemblyman for the 24th District, has long been a supporter of Scouting in the Santa Clara Valley. Born in San Jose, Cortese was a Boy Scout in Troop 14.

During his years as a county supervisor and Assemblyman Cortese was active in the Council's ongoing activities. From 1969 to 1974 he was the chairman of the countywide Scout-O-Ramas and in 1976 he accepted the responsibility of the chairmanship of the Long Range Planning Committee. It included preparing a ten year plan for the Council covering the areas of membership, finance, program, properties and manpower.

Prior to being elected to the Assembly in 1980, Cortese had been an effective member of the Board of Supervisors of Santa Clara County for twelve years. Assemblyman Cortese currently chairs the Water, Parks and Wildlife Committee and the Select Committee on California Wine Production and Economy. He is a member of the Assembly Committees on Agriculture, Economic Development, and the Select Committee on Small Business, among many other committees.

Dominic Cortese is a longtime member of the Santa Clara County Council's President's Advisory Committee.

The Hon. Rod Diridon

Rod Diridon, a Life Member of the Scout Alumni Association, represents the Fourth District on the County of Santa Clara Board of Supervisors. He joined the Cub Scouts in 1947 and later became a member of Boy Scout Troop 26 in Dunsmuir, California.

As a Scouter Diridon has contributed a great deal of time and energy to the Scout-O-Rama program. He served as General Chairman from 1975 to 1985 for the Scout-O-Ramas held at the County Fairgrounds and was presented with a special award of merit for that service. Andy Bonfield, then Vice President and treasurer of the Santa Clara County Council, presented Rod Diridon with a plaque in appreciation of his dedication to the Scouting program at Diridon's annual testimonial dinner.

In addition to holding the full-time job of County Supervisor, Diridon is chairman of the San Francisco Bay Area Metropolitan Transportation Commission. He has chaired the County Board of Supervisors four times and is currently in his fourth term as chair of the Transit District Board in Santa Clara County.

He has been either president or founding chair of over fifty organizations and agencies, i.e.: San Jose Y.M.C.A., San Jose State University Dean's Council, the San Jose Jaycees and the San Jose Trolley Corporation.

Rod Diridon has been Chairman of the Special Olympics Board and has long been a member of the Santa Clara County Council, BSA, Executive Board.

Appendix

1. Bibliography

General History

Arbuckle, Clyde, *History of San Jose,* Smith & McKay Printing Co., Inc., San Jose, CA, 1985

Bruntz, George G., *History of Los Gatos,* Valley Publishers, Fresno, CA, 1971

Caughey, John W., *California,* Prentice-Hall, Inc., Englewood Cliffs, N.J., 1970

Sawyer, Eugene T., *History of Santa Clara County,* Historic Record, Los Angeles, CA, 1922

Scouting History

Murray, William D., *The History of the Boy Scouts of America,* Boy Scouts of America, 1937

Bezucha, R.D., *The Golden Anniversary Book of Scouting,* Golden Press, N.Y., 1959

Jameson, A.A.; Pratt, George D.; Murray, William: Editorial Board, BSA, *Handbook for Boys,* Boy Scouts of America, New Brunswick, N.J., 1st edition, 1911 (Editorial Board re-issue 1976)

Peterson, Robert W., *The Boy Scouts,* (American Heritage) Houghton Mifflin Co., Boston, 1984

Scouting Guides

Function Program: *Advancement Guidelines,* BSA, New Brunswick, N.J., 1977

Insignia Guide, BSA, New Brunswick, N.J., 1989

A History of Wood Badge in the United States, BSA, New Brunswick, N.J., 1988

Camp Leader's Manual, Chesebrough Scout Reservation, Santa Clara County Council, San Jose, CA

Camp Leader's Manual, Camp Stuart and Stuart Training Reservation, S.C.C.C., San Jose, CA

Camp Leader's Manual, Camp Hi-Sierra, Santa Clara County Council, San Jose, CA, 1979

Newspapers and Periodicals

Los Gatos Times Observer, Los Gatos, California

San Jose Mercury News, San Jose, California

Santa Clarion, The, Santa Clara County Council Newsletter, 10/65 to 3/90

2. Glossary of Scouting Terms

Advisor, Explorer — A man or woman (21 or older) who is the leader of an Explorer post.

Akela — A term of respect in Cub Scouting; it may refer to a Cub Scout leader, parent, teacher, etc. The term comes from Rudyard Kipling's *Jungle Book.*

Alpha Phi Omega (APO) — A college service organization made up of former and current members of BSA.

Baden-Powell, Robert S.S. — The founder of the worldwide Scouting movement.

Boy Scout — A registered youth member of a Boy Scout troop. He must have completed the fifth grade and be at least 10 and 1/2 years old and not yet have reached his 18th birthday. "Scout" is a synonymous term.

Boy Scouts of America — The legal name of the Scouting organization in the U.S.A. Its abbreviation is BSA.

Boys' Life — The monthly magazine of the Boy Scouts of America.

Camporee — A District or council camping event with organized competition.

Chartered organization — A religious, civic, fraternal, community, education, or other entity chartered by the BSA to operate a pack, troop, post, or ship.

Chief Scout Executive — The top professional officer of the BSA.

Commissioner — A volunteer Scouter who is commissioned to serve chartered organizations in the operation of the scouting program.

Cub Scout — A registered youth member of a Cub Scout pack. He must have completed second grade and be from 7 to 10 years old.

Cubmaster — An adult volunteer, 21 or older, who leads a Cub Scout pack.

Den — A subdivision of a Cub Scout pack, usually composed of 6 to 10 boys.

Den chief — A Scout or Explorer who assists a Cub Scout den leader.

District executive — A professional Scouter responsible for a district within a local council.

Eagle Award — The highest rank a Scout can achieve.

Explorer — A registered youth member of a post. He or she must have completed the eighth grade and be at least 14-years-old or may be 15 or older and be in any grade; membership may continue up to age 21.

Exploring Executive — A professional Scouter who works with Explorers.

Exploring Journal — The quarterly magazine for all registered Explorers.

Good Turn — A service to others by an individual or a Scouting unit.

Jamboree — A national or international camping event.

Local council — An administrative body responsible for Scouting within a designated territory.

Lone Scout — A boy who follows the Boy Scout program as an individual without membership in a troop. There are also Lone Cub Scouts.

Merit badge — An award to a Scout for completing requirements in one of more than 100 career and hobby fields.

National Council — The corporate entity of the BSA. It is made up of local council representatives, members at large and honorary members.

National Court of Honor — A committee of the Boy Scouts of America which is responsible for administering lifesaving and meritorious conduct awards and other recognitions.

Order of the Arrow — Scouting's national brotherhood of honor campers which promotes Scouting's outdoor programs.

Pack — The unit that conducts the Cub Scout program for the chartered organization.

Patrol — A subdivision of a Boy Scout troop, usually with 5 to 10 members.

Patrol leader — The elected youth leader of a patrol.

Post — The unit that conducts the Explorer program for the chartered organization.

Pow wow — A one-day training conference for Cub Scout leaders.

President, Explorer post — The elected leader of a post.

Rank — In Scouting, the position or degree earned by passing certain tests. The six ranks are Tenderfoot, Second Class, First Class, Star, Life and Eagle.

Region — One of six geographical administrative units of the BSA: Northeast, Southeast, East Central, North Central, South Central and Western.

Roundtable — A program-planning and morale-building meeting of adult leaders, usually held monthly.

Scout Executive — The professional staff leader of a local council.

Scouter — Any registered adult member of the BSA.

Scouting **magazine** — This publication for Scouters has six editions annually.

Scoutmaster — The registered adult (at least 21) leader of a Boy Scout troop.

Sea Explorer — A registered member of a Sea Explorer ship.

Senior patrol leader — The key elected boy leader, who helps the Scoutmaster administer a troop.

Ship — The unit that conducts the Sea Explorer program for the chartered organization.

Skipper — The adult leader (Advisor) of a Sea Explorer ship.

Tiger Cub — A boy who is in the second grade, is 7 years old, and who, with an adult member of his family, participates in the activities of his group and pack.

Troop — The unit that conducts the Boy Scout program for the chartered organization.

Unit committee — A group of men and women appointed by the chartered organization to administer the affairs of its pack, troop, post or ship.

Varsity Scout — A registered youth member of a Varsity Scout team. He is between 14 and 17 years old.

Webelos Scout — A Cub Scout who is 10 years old and is preparing to become a Boy Scout. His den is led by an adult male.

3. Santa Clara County Council Membership

(Reference Chapter I)

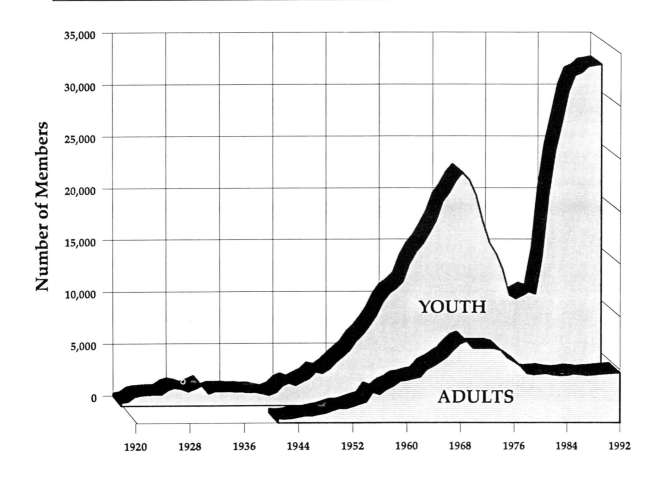

Total Membership, Santa Clara County Council, BSA

YEAR	YOUTH	ADULTS	YEAR	YOUTH	ADULTS
1920	279		1956	6,755	2,653
1921	387		1957	7,582	3,148
1922	837		1958	8,533	3,438
1923	971		1959	9,846	3,895
1924	1,016		1960	10,745	3,999
1925	1,063		1961	11,191	4,157
1926	1,062		1962	11,839	4,294
1927	1,482		1963	13,537	5,042
1928	1,688		1964	14,695	5,363
1929	1,582		1965	15,464	5,768
1930	1,364		1966	16,580	6,171
1931	not available		1967	17,777	6,877
1932	1,906		1968	19,581	7,446
1933	1,139		1969	20,420	7,666
1934	1,345		1970	21,551	not available
1935	1,344		1971	22,316	not available
1936	1,343		1972	21,665	not available
1937	1,289		1973	20,156	not available
1938	1,289		1974	17,645	6,845
1939	1,237		1975	15,592	6,144
1940	1,256		1976	14,519	5,765
1941	1,126	380	1977	13,005	5,330
1942	991	344	1978	10,581	4,607
1943	1,218	402	1979	10,207	4,502
1944	1,857	550	1980	10,501	4,567
1945	2,116	648	1981	10,836	4,592
1946	1,902	655	1982	10,633	4,458
1947	2,257	789	1983	14,130	4,427
1948	2,556	905	1984	20,179	4,444
1949	3,186	1,121	1985	24,304	4,557
1950	3,051	1,326	1986	27,120	4,507
1951	3,475	1,326	1987	30,045	4,439
1952	4,110	1,523	1988	31,624	4,490
1953	4,644	1,742	1989	31,917	4,550
1954	5,233	1,944	1990	32,500 (Est.)	4,600 (Est.)
1955	6,158	2,847			

4. Boy Scout Memorial Foundation Members (1989)

(Reference Chapter IV, Page 84)

Albert B. Smith, President
C. Donald Allen, Jr. Treasurer
Nessie Chesebrough
Glenn A. George
Honorable Marshall S. Hall
General Robert E. Huyser
John B. Lochner

Arthur K. Lund
Glen McLaughlin
Wilmot J. Nicholson
William S. Powell
J. Eric Thorsen
Austen D. Warburton
Brian L. Allen, Executive Director

5. BSA Presidents Club Members (1989)

(Reference Chapter IV, Page 86)

PACESETTER MEMBERS
Knight Foundation
Stuart Foundations
United Way of Santa Clara County

DISTINGUISHED MEMBERS
A Tool Shed, Inc.
Heritage Cablevision
URSA Institute

BENEFACTOR MEMBERS
Alum Rock Communications Center, Inc.
Paul & Nessie Chesebrough
Citti's Florist
Lee H. Brandenburg
Lockheed Missiles & Space Company
Lockheed MSC Employees
   'Bucks of the Month Club"
The Lucas Dealership Group
Mr. & Mrs. Glen McLaughlin Olivetti
Advanced Technology Ctr.
Ray Silva Insurance Associates, Inc.
Stella B. Gross Charitable Trust
Mr. & Mrs. J. Eric Thorsen

GUARDIAN MEMBERS
Apple Computer, Inc.
Alum Rock Union Elementary
   School District
Florence Nelson Foundation
FMC Corporation
Mr. & Mrs. Glenn A. George
Harman Management Corporation
E.A. Hathaway & Company
Mr. & Mrs. Robert M. Hosfeldt
Joseph George Charitable Trust
Pacific Western Bank
Tyler Peak/Jack Peak Travel
Price Waterhouse
Prussia Graphics, Inc.
Santa Clara Land Title Company
Syva Company
United Way of the Bay Area

SPONSOR MEMBERS
Ainsley Development Company
Alexander & Alexander of California
Allied Travel
American Airlines
Emerson Arends
Bank of America
Bank of the West
Miles H. Barber/Allied Management
   Services, Inc.
Bay Area Lincoln Mercury Dealers
Buchalter, Nemer, Fields and Younger
Collishaw Corporation
Consolidated Freightways, Inc.
Mrs. Caroline Crummey
Cupertino Electric, Inc.
Cupertino National Bank
Dr. Yvette del Prado

Deloitte, Haskins & Sells
Rod Diridon
Embassy Suites, Santa Clara
Ernst & Young
ESL Incorporated
Excelan/Novell Corporation
Ferrari, Alvarez, Olsen & Ottoboni
Fireman's Fund Insurance Companies
General Electric Company
Hopkins & Carley
Intel Corporation
KPMG Peat Marwick
L & L Maintenance Inc.
Mr. & Mrs. John B. Lochner
M.E. Fox & Company, Inc.
Millbrook Elementary School
Miller, Morton, Caillat & Nevis
Montgomery Elementary School
Oak Tree Mazda & Allison B.M.W.
O'Connor Foundation
O'Connor Health Services
Olimpia, Whalen and Lively
Jan W. Passmore
Peter L. Pavlina/Pavlina Realty
Pettit & Martin
PG & E Company
PRX, Inc.
Ben Reichmuth
Robert W. Richardson
Rotary Club of Almaden Valley
San Jose Medical Center
San Jose Mercury News
San Jose National Bank
San Jose State University,
   Department of Intercollegiate Athletics
San Jose State University,
   President Gail Fullerton
San Jose State University,
   School of Engineering
Albert B. Smith
Ervie Smith & Associates
Peter Coe Verbica
Viking Electric, Inc.
Villa Felice
Westinghouse Electric Corporation
Mr. & Mrs. Christopher P. Whittell
The William Lyon Company
Donald D. Young/Citation Insurance
   Company

PATRON MEMBERS
Aetna Life & Casualty
Air Systems, Inc.
All California Title Company
Brian & Jan Allen
B.P.O.E. S.J. Lodge, #522
Bank of Santa Clara
Berg & Berg Developers
Michael J. Bonasera, Jr.
Brandenburg, Staedler & Moore

Dr. Joseph Brown/Cupertino Animal
   Hospital
Kenneth L. Brown
Mr. & Mrs. Earl Burke
Cal Emblem
Chevron U.S.A. Inc.
Mrs. Beth Chinchen
Mr. & Mrs. Burton Corsen
Mrs. Faith Davies
Diana Fruit Preserving Co.
Diversifed Loan Services
Robert Dominguez, D.D.S., Inc.
Jeff L. Fischer/Darling-Fischer, Inc.
Jerry H. Glass, D.D.S., Inc.
Hon. Marshall S. Hall
Mr. & Mrs. Thomas L. Hall
Charles Hebel
Hewlett Packard
Housing Authority of the County of
   Santa Clara
Kemper Insurance Group
Kiwanis Club of San Jose
Kiwanis Club of South San Jose
Dr. & Mrs. Harold Klepfer
Mr. & Mrs. Thomas Lackovic
Taylor La Croix
Sam C. Lazarakis/Arthur Young & Co.
Robert Leonard
James R. Livingstone,
   CPA/Livingstone & Company
Arthur K. Lund
Mr. & Mrs. Gerald Marks
Jerome Millon
New York Life Foundaton
Wilmot J. Nicholson
Plaza Bank of Commerce
Reed & Graham, Inc.
Reeds Sport Shop
Mr. & Mrs. Jim Renwick
Robinson & Wood, Inc.
Terrance J. Rose, Inc.
Lanny Ross
Rotary Club of Los Gatos
Rotary Club of Morgan Hill
Rotary Club of San Jose East
Rudolph & Sletten Inc.
Jose Salame
Phillip Sanfilippo
Santee School
Security Pacific Foundation
Schlumberger Technolgies
Reed Sparks/State Farm Insurance
Shapell Industries of Northern California
Mr. & Mrs. Donald Simpson
Smythe European
Storage Dimensions, Inc.
Toeniskoetter & Breeding Dev.
Universal Sweeping Services
West Engineering Sales, Inc.
Mr. & Mrs. Jerry Williams

LEADERSHIP MEMBERS

Paulette Abt
Mr. & Mrs. Leroy T. Adams
Mr. & Mrs. William Adams, Jr.
Don Ainge/MGIS
Alexander & Bohn

American Savings Bank
Robert Anderson
Arcadia Development Company
Armanino Foods
Ashford Development

Bank of America, Sunnyvale
W.F. Batton
Bay Area Interconnect
BFI Waste Systems
Dr. Steve Bo, D.D.S.

The President's Club of Santa Clara County Council, Boy Scouts of America is composed of individuals, families, organizations, corporations, and foundations who have contributed $250 or more in cash, services or goods to Scouting this year.

Mr. & Mrs. Dell Boccignone
David Broquard
Mr. & Mrs. Raymond Bryne
Mr. & Mrs. Edward A. Burke, Jr.
William Busch
Caesar's Palace
California Land Title Company
Campbell North American
Hugh Campbell/Merry Mart
Stephen H. Caplan/KBM Office Furniture
Carson Valley Inn, Minden
Carter & Sabes
Dr. Joseph Casey, M.D.
Children's Shelter
Stanley & Diane Chinchen
Mr. & Mrs. Walter Chronert
Mr. & Mrs. Larry Clark
Clark's Coin Laundry Service, Inc.
Mike & Mary Clarke
Coastal Dealer Services
Mr. & Mrs. Rich W. Cole
Leo J. Coleman
Roger Conant
Country Club Villa Properties
The Cove
Dr. & Mrs. Jeffrey Crane
Cumming-Henderson, Inc.
Cupertino Community Recycling Center
William Curtis/CRI Properties
Leon Davis, Jr.
Davidson, Kavanagh & Brezzo
Gregory S. Davies
Mr. & Mrs. James O. Daulton
Mr. & Mrs. Ray Davilla
De Anza Properties
Bill Deane Inc.
Deaton, Michaels & Hall, CPA's
David Delozier/Petersen's Insurance Company
Kevin & Anita Del Grande
Della Maggiore Tile, Inc
Delucchi, Robinson, Streit & Company
Devcon Constuction
Richard DeVilbiss
William R. Drve
Jerome L. Dvorak, CPA
Mr. & Mrs. Charles Erickson
Ehrlich-Rominger Architects
Environmental Systems, Inc.
Erdman—Lee
Everton & Oliff
Fairmont Hotel, San Jose

Financial Guardian Insurance Brokers, Inc.
First Interstate Bank
Fischer Middle School
Brad Frederickson/Shearson Lehman Hutton
Frontier Ford
William Foulk
Founders
Grand Escapes
Gilroy Elks Lodge #1567
Gilroy Foods, Inc.
Goldsmith Seeds, Inc.
Mr. & Mrs. Stephen H. Goodman
Larry W. Grace
E.M. Greenawalt
Grubb & Ellis
Harry Hall
Doris Hambrick
Hastings Plumbing, Inc.
Dave Haugh
Bryan Hausle
Health Dimensions
Larry Hecht
Richard Herington
High Sierra Casino/Hotel, Tahoe
Mr. & Mrs. Lyman Hitch
Hollander-Smith
Dave Horton
Matthew Hurley/Prestige Properties
General & Mrs. Robert E. Huyser USAF (Retired)
Independence High School
JC Paper Company
Mr. & Mrs. Darrel D. Jensen
Jenssen Scales
Carl Karcher Enterprises
Michael J. Kearns
Mr. & Mrs. Wayne Keyes
KICU TV 36
Kiwanis Club of Los Altos
Claton J. Klein, CLU/Corroon & Black
KNTV Channel 11
Kwik Kopy Printing
LDS Church Los Gatos 1st Ward
Mr. & Mrs. Gordon F. Levy
Bob Lewis Volkswagen—Puegeot
Live Oak High School
Los Gatos Athletic Club
Mr. & Mrs T.J. Lowden
Lowery & Little, Inc.
Lusamerica Foods, Inc.
Markovits & Fox, Inc.
Randy & Ildiko Merten

Michaels Restaurant
Midway Sign Company
William C. Miller
Milpitas High School
Pete Molitor
Jack Moore
Mr. & Mrs. Jack Mortenson
Moyer Chemical
The Mozart Develop. Company
Charles Munger
Paul T. Nakamoto
Mr. & Mrs. Frank Napier
Emeka Nchekwube MD, Inc.
Lee Norman/Allied Pacific Insurance Services
North American Title Co.
Northern CAL Fertilizer
Oakridge Golf Course
Scott Oldenburg
Buffy Osti/Buffy's Bail Bonds
PACCAR Financial Corporation
Pacific Motors
Pioneer High School
Poppy Hills, Monterey
Pyramid Painting Inc.
R.C. Smith Engineers, Inc.
Realprop Development Company
Renco Properties
R.G. Speno, Inc.
Donald B. Richardson, Jr./Wool, Richardson & Graff
The Ritz-Carlton, Laguna Niguel
Riverside Associates
Kenneth Rodrigues & Associates
Dr. John S. Rollins, MD.
Rotary Club of Cupertino
Rotary Club of Gilroy
Rotary Club of West Santa Clara
Ruzzo, Scholl & Murphy
San Jose Blueprinting Service & Supply Company
San Jose Country Club
San Jose Hospital Foundation
San Jose Water Company
Saratoga Lions Club
Mr. & Mrs. David Schrader
Michael Schmit
Mr. & Mrs. Marion Sellers
Shared Resources, Inc.
Shea Homes
Ed Sheldon
Sierra Meat Company
Alson Silva

Mr. & Mrs. Alan B. Simpkins
Specialty Truck Parts, Inc.
Sprangler Elementary School
St. Paul Fire & Marine Insurance Company
Ed Stahl/Travel Advisors of Los Gatos
Carl & Diane Stalions
Alex Stepovich DDS, Inc.
Mr. & Mrs. Daniel Stuart
Mr. & Mrs. James P. Sturrock
Taco Bell, #3682

Therma Inc.
May Tindall
Barrett Tomlinson
Doug Turner/Century 21
Universal Maintenance
University Construction Company, Inc.
Waste Management of Santa Clara County
Mr. & Mrs. Frank E. Weingart
Western Financial Savings Bank
Western States Oil Company

Dave Wheeler
Art Wilson Golf Shop
Winchester Insurance
Mr. & Mrs. William Winter
YMCA of Santa Clara Valley
Mr. & Mrs. Bob Yount
Joseph Zertuche/Rayo Financial
(as of press time)

PRESIDENT'S CLUB

DISTINGUISHED MEMBERS
Glen & Ellen Mclaughlin

BENEFACTOR MEMBERS
Glenn & Bobbe George
Mr. & Mrs. Robert M. Hosfeldt
Santa Clara Land Title Company

GUARDIAN MEMBERS
Bank of America
Citation Insurance Company
Coast Counties Truck & Equipment Co.
Corroon & Black
Insurance Brokerage of San Jose
M.E. Fox & Company, Inc.
Terrance J. Rose, Inc.
San Jose Mercury News
San Jose State University

SPONSOR MEMBERS
Mr. & Mrs. Stanley Chinchen
Cornish & Carey
Guardian Life Insurance
Goodwill Industries
IBM Corporation
Kimball Small Properties
L & B West Associates
Pyramid Homes, Inc.
Terrance J. Rose, Inc.
Wells Fargo Bank

PATRON MEMBERS
Mr. & Mrs. Leroy T. Adams
Kevan & Anita Del Grande
Devcon Construction Inc.
Mr. & Mrs. A. Carl English
Gilroy Foods, Inc.
Hollander-Smith Construction Co.
Johanson & Yau
Raisch Products
Reed Jonas & Lee
Ruth & Going, Inc.
Touche Ross & Co.
Dr. Martin Trieb, M.D.
Winchester Mystery House
YMCA of Santa Clara Valley

LEADERSHIP MEMBERS
Almaden Golf Center
American Bank & Trust
Harry F. Aumack, Jr.
Berger Lewis Accountancy Corp.
Robert T. Bettencourt
Dave Blessing
Ralph N. Borelli/Borelli Investment Co.
Clayton Bruntz/Compro Insurance Services
Jeff Bumb/The Flea Market, Inc.
California Business Bank
Peter S. Carter
Mr. & Mrs. Delmar Dewhitt
Denco Controls

LEADERSHIP cont'd
Goldrich & Kest Construction, Inc.
Good Samaritan Hospital Foundation
Maurice G. Hahn Physical Therapy
Hansen Brothers Construction
Mr. & Mrs. Earl Hayes
Jack Healey Insurance
Ron Helstrup/Alphagraphics
Lee Howard/Howard Motors
Independent Pension Services, Inc.
Mr. & Mrs. Richard Jones
Robert S. Kieve
Lee Meyers Company
Walter & Karen Loewenstern
Orchard Supply Hardware
Peterbilt Motors Company
George L. Quinn, Jr./Geomax
Mr. & Mrs. Verne Rettig
Len Rohde/Burger King
Dr. & Mrs. K.G. Romine
San Jose British Motors
San Jose Medical Center
Theodore E. Schenk/New England Mutual
Sequoia Institute
Mr. & Mrs. Gary Schwing
Carl N. Swenson Co. Inc.
The Steinberg Group

(This listing represents additional sponsors and donors since the printing of the program.)

6. *Scout Alumni Association Members (1989)*
(Reference Chapter IV, Page 87)

Corporate Members

Burke Industries
California State University, San Jose
Citti's Company
Coakley Heagerty Companies
Lucas Dealership Group
Pacific Western Bank
San Jose Mercury News

Lifetime Members

Paul Chesebrough
Nessie Chesebrough
Rod Diridon
Mary Ann Diridon
Wilmot J. Nicholson

Annual Members

Leroy T. Adams
William Adams
William J. Adams, Jr.
C. Donald Allen
Michael Anderson
Michael H. Antonacci
Louis P. Bergna
Bruce Bonfield
Dell Boccignone
George Bunonocore
Walter D. Chronert
Richard Cole
John E. Cox, MD
Andrew J. Cummings
William Curtiss
James O. Daulton
John Davis

Stephen D. Dempsey
L. Brent Dickson
Dominic Fanelli
John F. Foley
Malcom R. Gaddis
Bert George
Glenn George
Stephen H. Goodman
Creaghe H. Gordon
Marshall S. Hall
Wayne P. Keyes
Harold H. Klepfer
Thomas Lackovich
Thomas L. Legan
John Lochner
Arthur K. Lund
John Maltbie

Gerald W. Marks
Vinton S. Matthews
Glen McLaughlin
Randy Merten
G. Jeffrey Moore
Peter Pavlina
Larry Pedersen
Chuck Robel
John Satterstrom
Ray A. Silva
Albert B. Smith
James P. Sturrock
Richard Tanaka
J. Eric Thorsen
Robert E. Winter
John Yearwood

Honorary Members

Tom Adams
Brian Allen
Larry Clark
Doris Hambrick
Richard Harrington
Ben Love
Jay Lowden
Richard Parker

7. *Order of the Arrow Lodge Chiefs and Advisors*
(Reference Chapter IV, Page 89)

Term Served	Lodge Chief	Lodge Advisor
1964*	Matt Follas	Jim Sturrock
1965	Paul Hayes	Jim Sturrock
1966	Marv Bottum	Jim Sturrock
1967	Ken Brunges/Mike McClusky	Jim Sturrock
1968	Jeff Haugaard	Jim Sturrock
1969	Gary Gabriel	Ed Gunion
1970	Frank Biehl	Ed Gunion
1971	Frank Biehl/Ed Fassett	Ed Gunion
1972	Ed Fassett	Ed Gunion
1973	Mike Murphy	Ed Gunion
1974	Scott O'Dell	Ed Gunion
1975	Paul Crompton	Ed Gunion
1976	Brian Cronquist	Ed Gunion
1977	Eric Parnell	Ron Irvin
1978	Jonathan Fung	Ron Irvin
1979	Bob Stillwagon	George Martin
1980	Mike Betz	George Martin
1981	Mat Weingart	Bill Wegner
1982	David Low	Bill Wegner
1983	Tom Lackovic	Bill Wegner
1984	Jim Moncrieff	Bill Wegner
1985	Ken Bower	Bill Wegner
1986	Jim Metzler/Ed Hannum	Bill Wegner
1987	Mike Jolley	Bill Wegner
1988	Doug Cortney	Bill Wegner
1989†	Doug Cortney	Paul Nakamoto
1990	Steve Griefer	Jim Holt

*Term of office for Lodge Officers began in January
†Term of office for Lodge Officers began in mid-year

8. Order of the Arrow Vigil Honor Recipients

(Reference Chapter IV, Page 89 and Chapter V, Page 101)

The names for 1966 through 1981 have been verified from National Council data. Names for 1982 through 1989 have been reconstructed from records provided by Bill Sheldon and Bill Wegner.

A = Adult. All others were youth members when inducted.

Name		Year	Name		Year
Douglas Bertholdt		1966	John E. Cox	A	1973
Marvin Bottom		1966	Don Iapello	A	1973
Jerry Colins	A	1966	Maurice R. Tripp	A	1973
James Sturrock	A	1966	Ted Vanover		1973
Paul Balleck		1967	Bob Welenofsky		1973
Kenneth Brunges		1967	Steve Gum		1974
Bert Carmody		1967	John Hopson	A	1974
Leanord Favorite		1967	Raymond J. Ryan	A	1974
Edward Goddard	A	1967	Doug Wardian		1974
Mike McClosky		1967	James H. Anderson	A	1975
Robert Stillwagon		1967	Paul Crompton		1975
Gary Bertholdt		1968	Robert Howell		1975
Mike Cooley		1968	Michael Murphy		1975
James Ernest		1968	Scott Odell		1975
Don Fallas		1968	John Pugmire		1975
Lynn Ferrin		1968	Raymond J. Ryan, Jr.		1975
Ted Hall	A	1968	Brian Chronquist		1976
Jim Horner	A	1968	Jonathan Fung		1976
Karl Mann	A	1968	Ronald Irvin	A	1976
David Pollock		1968	John Minker	A	1976
Norman Spaulding		1968	Robert Quincy	A	1976
Daniel Brady		1969	Craig Rouse		1976
Jeff Hauggard		1969	Ronald Workman	A	1976
George Lozito		1969	Dick Berry		1977
Michael Lozito		1969	Dennis Fitts		1977
Frank Biehl		1970	Michael Howell		1977
Gary Gabriel		1970	Dick Lange		1977
Edward Gunion	A	1970	Eric Parnell		1977
Peter Poillon	A	1970	Joseph I. Ungaro	A	1977
Robert Richardson	A	1970	Emile Mestressat		1978
Bruce Bonfield		1971/72	Walter Chronert	A	1979
Herb Davis, Jr.		1971/72	Lance Fung		1979
Jim Dumbolton	A	1971/72	Vernon Kuhn	A	1979
Jim Enslen	A	1971/72	Robert Stillwagon, II		1979
Ed Fassett		1971/72	Michael Betz		1980
Denis Hatch		1971/72	Don Fulk		1980
Glenn Helberg	A	1971/72	Gerard Hilgart		1980
Kenneth Melin		1971/72	Paul Nakamoto		1980
Roger Wright		1971/72	Edwin A. Weiseth	A	1980
Dan Andreen		1973	David Dunn	A	1981
Doug Andreen		1973	Michael Koop		1981
Bob Bergman		1973	Brian Mauldwin		1981
Andrew J. Bonfield	A	1973	Matthew Weingart		1981

Name		Year	Name		Year
Earl Burke	A	1982	Mike Jolly		1986
David Low		1982	Gary Marshall	A	1986
Bill Murphy		1982	Michael Pesta		1986
John Stephenson		1982	Richard Robinson	A	1986
			Ken Schott		1986
Tom Lackovic		1983			
Boyd Pett		1983	Rich Kolowitz	A	1987
William Wegner	A	1983	Kenny Rogers		1987
			Rufus Rogers	A	1987
Larry Clark	A	1984	Paul Stringer		1987
Erick Johnson		1984	Steve von Dohlen		1987
Jim Metzler		1984			
John Phillips	A	1984	Don Andrews		1988
			Doug Cortney		1988
Ken Bower		1985	Bryan Havsle	A	1988
Scott Brown	A	1985	Chris Kearns		1988
Wayne Conley		1985	Wayne Keys	A	1988
Justin Horner		1985	Lynn Sheldon	A	1988
Scott Jackson		1985			
Devin Lindsey		1985	Troy Bergstrom		1989
James Moncrieff		1985	Arthur S. Green	A	1989
Ivan Orup		1985	Steve Griefer		1989
			Bill Sheldon	A	1989
Ted Brown	A	1986			

9. Wood Badge Courses

(Reference Chapter IV, Page 91)

Year	Course No.	Host Council	Location	Course Director
1966	55-1	Santa Clara	Hi-Sierra	Ted Rogers
1970	55-2	Santa Clara	Hi-Sierra	Monty Groves
1973	Update	Santa Clara	Stuart	Dick Kimrey
1973	W-9	San Mateo	Cutter	John Montgomery
1974	W-19	Stanford	Boulder Creek	Roy Eckert
1974	WE3-55	Santa Clara	Stuart	John Montgomery
1975	WE3-55-19	Santa Clara	Chesebrough	Dick Kimrey
1975	WE3-55-9	Santa Clara	Stuart	Tony Ernat
1976	WE3-31-1	Stanford	Boulder Creek	Ted Reed
1976	WE3-55-18	Santa Clara	Stuart	Larry Herpel
1977	WE3-25-8	Monterey Bay	Boulder Creek	Bob Moger
1978	WE3-55-3	Santa Clara	Stuart	Frank Nixson
1979	WE3-31-12	Stanford	Boulder Creek	Ivan Gendzel
1980	WE3-20-80	San Mateo	Cutter	Warren Olson
1981	WE3-25-81	Monterey Bay	Boulder Creek	Bill Dumas
1982	WE3-55-82	Santa Clara	Boulder Creek	Dick DeVilbiss
1982	WE3-23-82	Mt. Diablo	Lindblad	Dick Du Val
1983	WE3-31-83	Stanford	Boulder Creek	Bob Rutherford
1984	WE3-20-84	San Mateo	Cutter	Steve Lindley
1984	WE3-55-84	Santa Clara	Chesebrough	Earl Burke
1985	WE3-25-85	Monterey Bay	Pico Blanco	Gary Crawford
1986	WE3-55-86	Santa Clara	Chesebrough	Don Simpson
1987	WE3-55-87	Santa Clara	Chesebrough	Burt Corsen
1988	WE3-25-88	Monterey Bay	Pico Blanco	Rich LaValley
1989	WE3-55-89	Santa Clara	Chesebrough	Tom Smith

10. Women's Reserve Members

(Reference Chapter IV, Page 93)

Charter Members

Janilee Allen	Glenna Corsen	Helen Hurt #	Margaret Rowell
Sharon Badal	Glenda Couch	Dorothy Ittner	Vi Schneider #
Star Baker	Beth Crane	Brenda Jones	Jane Semdahl
Shirley Beall	Faye Christensen	Florence Jones	Jean Sigman
Carol Beasworrick	Eunice Ellsworth	Vickie Jones	Jan Slafter
Dianna Beekman	Carroll Favorite #	Helen Keyes	Diane Stalions
Lorraine Bergtholdt	Ruth Furlow	Jan Lewis	Sherry Straley
Margret Bernardino	Jean Goodman	Marie Lewis	Jane Tennant
Inger Boklund	Martha Gorman	Ruth Marshall	May Tindall
Agnes Booles	Shari Graves	Carolyn Minker	Plina Thompson
Barbara Brink	Judy Griffin	Alice Mounts	Alma Van Cleave
Eileen Brutsche #	Enid Hanna	Liz Moscato	Pat Wall
Dorothy Cavarello	Shirley Hannah	Suellyn Murphy	Betty Whitney
Barbara Carolan	Alice Helberg	Diane Patterson	Muffy Williams
Nessie Chesebrough	Thelma Henard	Clara Porter	Bernice Witherell
Vera Chronert	Doris Herschbach	Minne Quincy	Mary Witschard
Jean Cole	Marguerite Hines	Jane Reed	Donna Wood
Kay Cook	Verna Hitt	Joan Reynolds	Gertrude Wright #
Doris Cooley	Elaine Ho #	Margaret Ritchie	Alta Young

11. Development and Maintenance Committee Members and Contributors

(Reference Chapter IV, Page 96)

Members

Articles in the Santa Clarion list the following Scouters as prominent contributors of time and skill to the Development and Maintenance Committee:

Richard Alarez	Paul Crummey	James Headley	John Minker
Richard Baas	Stuart Dando	Kenneth Heckman	Jerry Murphy
Fred Beall	James Devine	Alice Helburg	Sue Ellen Murphy
William Beck	Richard J. DeVilbiss	Glenn Helberg	Paul Nakamoto
Donald Boisseranc	Raymond R. Doying	Paul Helberg	Ronald Nance
Frank Biehl	Eunice Ellsworth	Joseph A. Hendrix	Micheal Riddle
Earl S. Burke	Gene Ellsworth	Pat Hendrix	Teddy Rose
Shirl Burton	John Eshbough	Arlene Henry	Cirtis Sanders
Skip Breland	Mark Eshbough	Ken Henry	Frederick Southard
Hope Breland	Tony Ferranti	Gerard Hilgart	Carleton Stallion
James D. Brent	Don Fulk	Melvin Hill	Sherry Straley
Mark Brent	Joan Fulk	Al Hurt	Marvin Strand
Wes Briggs	Reed Graham	Robert Johnson	Mike Troiano
Sam E. Case	Arthur S. Green	Ronald Jungles	James Wall
Vic Collard	Pat Green	Robert Lacey	William L. Wegner
Jack M. Currie	Willis C. Hannah	C.F. Livingston	George Wise
Jackie Currie	Micheal Hans	James McDonough	Walter Wolfenden
Elezibeth M. Crane			

Contributors

The following companies are among those who have contributed materials used by the Development and Maintenance Committee to improve the Council's facilities:

Bard-Parker	Floorcraft	Royal Glass
Beaver Lumber	Ford Motor	Tollner Paint
Bernard Foods	Glidden Paint	Viking Materials
Buckles-Smith	International Business Machine	West Valley Ford
Campbell Lumber	Kaiser Aluminum	Winchester Plumbing
Eastside Paint Center	Kaiser Cement and Gypsum	Zellerback Paper
Fiberglas		

The Development and Maintenance Committee estimates the market value of the materials contributed and work performed on improvement of the Council's Scouting facilities during the past fourteen years amounts to over $3,000,000.

12. Eagle Scout Award Recipients

(Reference Chapter V, Page 100)

The awards made in territory now served by the Monterey Bay Area Council, No. 25, are listed prior to May 1, 1933.

The awards made in territory now served by the Stanford Area Council, No. 31, are listed prior to January 1, 1940.

Equivalent awards listed: Air Scout/Explorer Ace Award = (A), Explorer Silver Award = (S). There are no known Sea Scout/Sea Explorer Quartermaster Awards.

1921			Allen Lucy	T	1		Harry Stark	T	35	
Maurice Powell	T	2	McFeeley	T	2		Ralph Towle	T	35	
Charley Stein	T	1	Eason Monroe	T	1		Ralph Weymouth	T	1	
			James Nute	T	1					
1922			Clifford Vertress	T	12		**1929**			
Roy W. Guerin	T	15	Francis G. Winner	T	1		Robert Batterson	T	12	
Albert Schwaldt	T	2					Thomas Beall	T	1	
Philip Snyder	T	2	**1926**				Bert Beede	T	9	
Elms Stevenson	T	6	Glenn Burleson	T	12		Fred Haslund	T	22	
			Joseph George	T	1		Harry Hoenes	T	9	
1923			Ernest Graf	T	2		Fred Howard	T	1	
Warren M. Goodrich	T	1	John Graf	T	2		Robert Loehr	T	21	
Andrew Janson			John Hansen	T	22		Douglas Rogers	T	90	
Warren Lopez	T	7	Eugene Knight	T	1		George Shore	T	35	
Carroll W. McMurrey	T	5	Hollis Snell	T	1		Harrison M. Terry	T	75	
Clyde Schoen	T	2					John Wither	T	80	
			1927							
1924			William Burke	T	12		**1930**			
David W. Dresbach	T	1	Peter Hansen	T	22		Billy Chisholm	T	66	
Wilbur Fair	T	22	Clarence Hoehn	T	1		George Dorward	T	86	
Lyndon Farwell	T	2	Dick Lean	T	22		Alger Fast	T	66	
William C. Hansen	T	22	Harold Main	T	2		Bryon E. Lanphear	T	50	
Jack Hensell	T	22	Stewart Norris	T	66		Gordon C. Leland	T	21	
Rudolph Israel	T	1	Raymond Scott	T	2		Frances Lind	T	54	
Milton L. Jenkins	T	1	Ronald Scribner	T	1					
Leland Johnson	T	22	Elwood Swane	T	1		**1931**			
Wilbur Karnes	T	22	Wendel Viall	T	1		Angelo DaVico	T	71	
Grant Peters	T	7	Melvin Whiteman	T	2		Walter Hanna	T	32	
Raymond Rhodes	T	21	Yancy Williams	T	18		Harry McDonald	T	90	
Paul J. Walker	T	1					William Tatum	T	62	
			1928				Lawrence Wellisch	T	18	
1925			Bobby Arthur	T	35		William Winter	T	61	
Wallace Biddle	T	1	Robert Bias	T	66					
Georgen S. Buchanan	T	1	Leeighton Brownton	T	18		**1932**			
Perry Field	T	12	Gilbert Byrne	T	66		Hiram N. Bishop	T	54	
John J. Fleutsch	T	2	Fredrick Clapp	T	74		Leonard Clark	T	36	
Bruce P. Griswold	T	12	Anthony Dinos	T	40		Roy S. Devoe	T	36	
Charles L. Holton	T	1	Karl Kratsenstein	T	66		Howard Fitzsimmons	T	90	
Sanford Jones	T	21	Edw Schneider	T	3		Don Fyfe	T	69	

1932 cont.

James M. Gibb	T	2
Charles Klotz	T	36
Everest Lanini	T	36
Fred Lanini	T	36
Roy Lanini	T	36
R J. Larson	T	36
Daniel G. Lockwood	T	86
Lymann Lowe	T	90
Arthur Michielseen	T	98
Thomas Miller	T	36
Frank Moore	T	36
Fred T. Rixey	T	90
Barney Shaw	T	36
Marvin Tudder	T	75

1933

William Adams	T	69
Harry Bloom	T	26
Frank Bravo	T	33
James Breen	T	33
James Craig	T	45
Frank Fillmore	T	33
Bill Halley	T	26
Harry H. Harter	T	18
Preston Hatch	T	36
Thomas Hawkins	T	33
Charles Homewood	T	47
Waverly Jarvis	T	33
Walter Mazzone	T	18
George R. Miller	T	63
Arthur Pack	T	33
Willis Pack	T	33
Paul Palmer	T	29
Curtis F. Pullen	T	2
Charles Schulz	T	35
Charles Schulze	T	33
Darrell Sedgwick	T	29
Elmer Spencer	T	33
Eddie Stark	T	33
Noel Voge	T	26

1934

Armand Donatello	T	25

1935

Wayne Bonham	T	25
William E. Cooper	T	5
John George	T	5
Warren Miller	T	25
F. A. Owens	T	25
Robert W. Pullen	T	2
Leonard W. Scott	T	60
Lowell W. Scott	T	5

1936

R. Lee Bales	T	101

1937

Victory Bond	T	5
Robert Jones	T	39
Pat Taylor	T	3

1938

Robert J. Arthur	T	7
Louise Bergna	T	8
Riley Brittan	T	10
Robert McArthur	T	39
Raymond Stewart	T	10
James B. Thomas	T	3
Bob Williams	T	11

1939

Vernon Appleby	T	126
Lynn Brittan	T	10
Roy Frazer	T	21
Lynn Hunwick	T	25

Henry Jacoby	T	12
Alfred Shepperd	T	7

1940

Burch Calkins	T	21
Paul Farnham	T	34
Harry Frederico	T	10
Bruce McGrady	T	39
Albert B. Smith	T	39
Richard Smith	E	1
Bob Williams	E	1

1941

Robert Bernal	T	25
Al Bolton	T	8
Jack Bolton	T	7
Harlan Heath	T	11
Robert Irons	T	25
Robert Sheppard	T	7
Paull Tevis	T	59
Richard W. Welde	T	7

1942

Douglas Wagner	T	25

1944

Ted Bohlander	T	7
Robert Casella	T	37
Edward Weeden	T	19

1945

Harold Fonda	T	15
Raymond Sommer	T	25
Clement Stechelin	T	10
Gene Worthington	T	11

1946

Charles R. Buck	T	62
John Cassedy	T	41
Jack Danforth	T	82
Ronald Hagelin	T	13
Johnny Polson	T	55
Clement Stechelin	T	10

1947

Louis Bonsi	T	41
John Burton	T	55
William T. Ellis	T	12
Leonard Gibson	T	55
Bob Olson	T	55
Bernard J. Spera	T	11

1948

Glenn A. Butler	T	1
Ray Clark	T	21
Robert Fox	T	13
Donald R. Ryan	T	16
William Shepherd	T	2
Richard Sisemore	T	2
Warren Stannard	T	25

1949

Roy Beach	S	9
Maurice Bessiere	T	41
Fred Boehma	T	55
Louis Bonsi	T	41
Gene Broderick	T	25
Herbert Bryant	T	55
Charles Buck	T	62
John Burton	T	55
Jeremy Carlson	T	13
Jack Cassedy	T	41
Ray Clark	T	21
Jack Danforth	S	6
Donald Deming	T	13
Arlan Deutsch	T	14
Jerry Dodd	T	13

George Dulas	T	49
Bill Ellis	T	21
Richard Ellis	T	51
Barksdale Fortson	T	2
Robert Fox	T	13
Edwin Gehrhardt	T	5
Leonard Gibson	T	55
Ronald Haeglin	T	13
Thomas Halverson	T	17
Dudley Herschbach	T	36
Charles Hiatt	T	49
Donald Higgins	S	86
Harvey Hudnall	T	41
Rolland Langley	T	49
Teddy Leavenworth	T	41
Robert Leslie	T	62
Charles Lundy	T	13
Richard Lundy	T	55
William McCollan	T	16
Sidney McIntyre	T	49
James McKay	S	40
Don McSuistion	S	40
Bob Meyer	T	14
Paul Meyer	T	34
John Moeller	T	13
Ralph Morroco	T	41
Edwin Mosher	T	13
Anthony Oliver	S	40
John Palmieri	T	41
Harry Pankoski	T	2
John Polson	T	55
John Price	S	86
Oliver Price	T	34
Frank Rose	T	41
Edward Rosenborough	E	2
Donald Ryan	T	16
Michael Saso	S	40
William Schulz	T	7
Frank Shepherd	T	2
William Shepherd	E	2
Richard Sisemore	E	2
Edward Smith	T	13
Raymond Sommer	T	25
Bernard Spera	T	11
Warren Stannard	T	25
Clement Stechelin	T	10
Dennis Tedford	T	49
Hubert Vargus	T	31
Noel Whaley	T	31
Owen Winston	T	49
Terry Worden	T	49
Joek Wuesthoff	T	41

1950

Bill Angwin	T	39
Junior Ball	T	2
Charles Bock	T	41
Karl Schwarz	T	55

1951

Bob Cassell	T	13
Robert Lees	T	13
Larry Liden	T	57
Tommy Mason	T	2
Robert Mitchell	T	25

1952

Willis Beal	T	13
Fred Bird	T	20
Fred Byl, Jr.	T	38
Jorden Daniels	T	13
Ronald Davis	T	77
Jerry Deck	T	18
John Duncan	T	28
Bruce Eberhard	T	77
Rodney Ervin	T	10
Francis Freener	T	13

1952 cont.

Name	Pos	No
Lawrence Helfter	T	77
James R. Hoxsie	T	20
Ned Joslin	T	84
Melvin Larson	T	25
Salvatore Marvaso	T	5
Donald Nolte	T	13
Jack Patterson	T	16
James Pizzo	T	6
Paul Schrader	T	25
Mel Sommer	E	38
Elmer Stone	T	48
Donald E. Thompson	E	26
Bill Wilson	T	77

1953

Name	Pos	No
Ronald Bureas	T	16
David Delwiche	T	53
James Edwards	T	5
Stuart Hippler	T	38
Tommy Laker	T	13
John Livingstone	T	18
Louis McKeown		
Michael Shea	T	18

1954

Name	Pos	No
Leon Beeler	T	53
John Bentley	T	25
Raymond Castello	T	53
Johne Crone (A)	A	1
George D'Artenay	T	66
John Havey	T	41
Jerrold Henley	T	28
Arthur Hill	T	28
Mike King (A)	A	1
William O'Brian	T	66
Tom West	T	13

1955

Name	Pos	No
John Bird	T	20
Richard Bricmont	T	66
Danny Brown	T	10
Jackie Cooper	T	83
H Lee Davis	T	20
Ronald DeRuise	T	25
Rodney DeRuise	T	25
Robert DeVries	T	20
Tom Doak	T	53
Roger Fremier	T	12
Michael Gill	T	20
John T. Golden	T	52
Glen Hoskins	T	20
Edwin Hoxsie	T	20
Peter Hunt	T	13
Dennis King	T	10
David Larson	T	25
Doug Lawrence	T	20
Alan Malyon	T	13
Curtis Mehlhoff	T	53
Bill Moore	T	10
Dick Moore	T	10
Dennis Nichols	T	20
John Ozbun	T	10
Norman Pasqual	E	77
Jerry Reeher	T	25
Russel Riech	T	83
John Salamida	T	66
Robert Schulenberg	T	25
Richard Stechalin	T	10
Lawrence Summers	T	20
Wayne Thomas	T	10
Tommy Weaver	T	14

1956

Name	Pos	No
John Amiot	T	42
Eugene Andres	T	28
Kenneth Bone	T	13
Frank Bria	T	80
Larry Daubeck	T	46
Judd Fuller	T	77
Gary George	E	84
Jim Jessup	T	8
Wayne Meyer	E	84
Kenneth Parker	T	23
Robert Pendley	T	83
Bill Powell	T	31
Leonard Rubino, Jr.	T	10
Leslie Seacrist	T	38
Kent Smith	T	13
Troy Smith	T	83
Harold Sparry	T	13
Jim Sweeney	T	13
Gary Tozer	T	23
George Ulledalen	T	38

1957

Name	Pos	No
Ned Altman	T	52
Harold Anjo	T	67
Gilbert Barnabe	T	66
Tom Berger	E	84
John Bissell	T	38
Richard Carrol	T	46
Richard Chew	T	14
Joseph Cronin	T	42
Dick Dietrich	T	38
John Eggers	T	89
John S. Falconer	T	31
Paul Farrell	T	47
Jack Herbert	T	47
Gordon Hunter	T	40
Lonnie Hunting	T	39
Kenneth Koga	T	23
Philip Krozak	E	84
Michael Kuhn	E	84
Robert Larson	T	43
Stephen Mercer	T	57
David Nelson	E	84
David Phillips	T	88
Terry Raine	T	14
Ross Reager	T	14
John Schulem	T	25
Bob Schulenburg (S)	T	25
Gary Shippam	T	26
Gilbert Solis	E	84
John Sparry	T	13
Louis Stutz	T	14
Donald Swenson	T	20
Charles Thome	T	94
Dick Townsley	T	14
Gabriel Vega, III	T	11
Burton Walter	T	47
Roger Wiley	T	80
Robert Wirtz	T	38

1958

Name	Pos	No
David Abildgaard	T	20
Roger L. Bridges	T	65
Albert Craig	T	101
Daniel Deis	T	71
David A. Devine	T	35
Steve Falconer (S)	T	31
Leon P. Fox, Jr.	T	41
Wayne W. Glass	T	65
Ralph H. Graves	T	25
Dean Hodges	T	20
Kenneth E. Jenks	T	17
Rainer McCown	T	88
Craig Pace	T	17
Nathan L. Pace	T	17
Ernest Pitts (S)	S	79
Richard Prater	T	65
Edward Quick (S)	E	84
James Ramsay	T	130
Jerry Rose	E	47
Paul Schraeder (S)	E	25
Paul Sweet	T	13
Keith Waters	T	14
Larry Waters	T	14
Don Wilson	T	44

1959

Name	Pos	No
W. J. Baird	E	6
Bruce Barton	T	31
Larry Brager	T	23
Oscar W. Burford	T	37
Clive E. Dorman	T	32
Michael Doughty	S	79
Bill Ford	T	11
David Freeman	T	84
Dann Gerblick	T	25
Gary Gray	T	25
W. Alfred Hartman	S	46
James Hiatt	T	84
John Hoskinson	T	72
Dick Lawrence	T	20
Larry Leedom	T	25
Robert Liden	T	25
Tom Madson	T	88
Warren Mercer	T	35
Donald Mills	T	130
John Mills	T	130
David O'Neil	T	39
Randy Reagan	T	20
Jerry Schell	T	88
Stephen M. Schneider	E	3
Harry Shehtanian	T	25
Donald Solari	T	62
Eddie Sutcliffe	T	84
Robin Wainwright	T	39
William J. Watson	T	13
Bruce Wilhelm	T	400
Larry Williams	E	3
Charles Yazel	T	25
John Yazel	T	25

1960

Name	Pos	No
Byron Berger	E	424
Leonard Campbell	T	20
Jeffrey Campen	T	213
Stephen Campen	T	213
David Chamberlain	T	43
Wayne Doran	T	33
Bob Ebright	T	32
Bill Gillespie	T	16
Tom Hartman	T	95
Harold Judd	T	481
Michael Kelly	T	488
David Kjar	E	6
Rusty Larsen	T	38
John J. Licursi	E	6
Jim MacInnis	T	225
Ted Mathewson	T	38
Ralph McDougall	E	480
Bill Neuroth	T	38
Vaughn Nixon	T	38
Carlos Ogden	T	38
Davis Popkins	T	38
John Quinn	T	38
Wayne Rogers	E	424
Richard Scariano	T	310
Alan Seacrist	T	38
Jim Sidey	T	498
Dan Steiling	T	210
Burns Woodward	T	310
Herbert Young	T	38
Howard Young	T	38

1961

Name	Pos	No
Steve Amdahl	T	484
Walter Baird	T	400
Warren Belisle	T	484

1961 cont.

John C. Benz	T	237
Larry Betten	T	38
Roger Bradley	T	38
Robert Browning	T	406
Gregory P. Burke	T	476
Jack Burleson	E	6
James Chouinard	E	6
Terry P. Daubek	T	46
Barry Davis	T	38
Donald G. Davison	T	17
Duane Denman (S)	S	470
Russell H. Downing	E	346
Larry Forman	T	498
Stephen Fredkin	T	38
Gary Heath	T	565
Duncan Herring	T	539
Tom Hollenhorst	T	406
Howard Jeffrey	T	498
Tom E. Johns	T	310
Kirke Jorgensen	E	540
Michael Layne	T	209
William Maire	T	564
Dan Malone	T	443
Michael Martin	T	6
Don Mikiska	T	540
Alan Miller	T	14
Douglass Morris	T	233
Richard Newfarmer	T	38
Dennis Northon	T	37
Jay O'Brian	T	341
Val O'Kane	T	400
John O. O'Leary	E	74
Ronald Pahl	E	540
Gregg Patrick	T	370
Robert N. Phillips	T	406
Mike Roa	T	476
Steve Scharf	T	400
Curtis Smith	T	498
Larry Stanley	T	220
George R. Stanton	T	483
Richard Stark	T	209
Robert Summers	T	130
Tommy Thompson	T	23
Mark Vining	T	38
William C. Webb	T	497
Robert Wilhelm	T	400

1962

J. B. Anderson	T	484
Tim Anderson (S)	S	470
Tom Baer	T4	50
Anton P. Ballek	E	347
Robert Bechen	T	38
Eugene Belogorsky	T	549
Frederick M. Bock, IV	T	535
Kenneth Bontadelli	T	203
Bruce Bowling	T	208
Robert Busma	T	497
Patrick Clowers	T	489
Douglas Crask	T	332
Dean Cromwell	T	233
David DeWitt	T	498
William Elliot	T	484
James Garrett	T	372
Mickey Glover	T	203
Philip S. Green	T	450
Robert Griffin	T	341
Harvey Hailer	E	313
Wendell Hammon	T	540
Timothy Hamsher	T	539
William Holmes	T	549
Jim Holt	T	488
Charles Jellison	T	23
Robert Johnston	T	426
Jared Jones	T	309
Locke Jorgensen	T	540

David Kessler	T	203
Kurt Klippel	T	540
Calvin Lansdowne	T	131
Relie F. Lawyer	E	466
Rodger Linquist	T	46
Robert Livingstone	T	370
Harold Malone	T	309
Arnold Mazotti	T	203
Neil McIntosh	T	555
Paul Miller	T	373
David Morris	T	233
Ralph Ogden	T	38
Dennis Pate	T	233
Richard Peltz	E	6
Stephen Peltz	T	46
Terrell A. Poland	T	335
James Prater	T	373
Dick Quinn	E	38
Mike Raven	T	540
William Robertson, Jr.	T	475
Ralph Scariano	T	310
Ron J. Scariano	T	310
Robert Sjolie	T	484
Ed Stevenson	T	483
Bob Steward	T	210
James C. Sturrock	E	460
William Taber	T	497
Jim Teal	T	549
Jim Triplett	T	38
Bruce Tufts	E	466
Dave Weyers	E	346
Steve G. Weyers	T	372
Richard Williamson	T	332
Terry Wood	E	540

1963

Andrew Allan	E	111
Tom Allan	E	111
Robert B. Ankeny	E	404
Jeffrey Armstrong	E	549
Charles E. Barkis, III	T	335
Val E. Barton	T	555
Michael Beard	T	535
Joe Benz	T	237
Thomas J. Breckon	T	418
Robert A. Buck	T	498
Gary L. Cannon	T	122
Kipp C. Crew	T	481
Walter J. Damkroger	T	77
David H. Edgar	T	490
Robert S. Elmore	T	213
Michael L. Elrod	T	375
Jim E. Ernest	T	294
Richard W. Evans	T	213
B. J. Fitzgerald	T	476
Roland E. Fitzgerald	T	476
Timothy Fitzgerald	E	564
Dale M. Follas	E	347
Keith G. Freeman	T	565
Michael E. Gunion	T	131
James E. Hahn	E	466
Richard C. Hall	T	484
Steven P. Hardman	T	341
William C. Heath	T	43
Glen Hollenhorst	E	466
David Hubin	T	237
Larry W. Hulberg	T	498
Patrick W. Jackson	T	220
Fred L. Jones	T	309
William B. Kincaid	E	346
Paul Kirkwood	T	404
Pat Kolstad	T	375
Michael Laurance	T	77
Craig L. Leventon	T	6
Thomas M. Lindon	T	418
Stephen Lowell	E	466
James D. McGill	T	426

John F. McKittrick	E	404
Malcolm Pace	T	220
Barry D. Patrick	T	370
Dennis Peebles	T	426
Richard T. Penrose	E	466
Lance Reebe	E	412
Roger T. Reed	T	68
Jim Rush	T	130
Robert A. Schramm	T	309
Albert G. Seid	E	466
Jon F. Spencer	T	38
James F. Stafford	T	426
Patrick S. Tansey	E	346
Tom M. Thompson	T	294
Steven H. Wilhelm	T	400
Michael Wolyn	E	549
Dale A. Youngman	E	347

1964

Ralph A. Accola	T	122
John P. Adams	T	6
John M. Allen	T	38
Gregory J. Anglemyer	T	497
David M. Bakke	T	466
Bruce K. Barnes	T	295
Douglas Bergtholdt	T	443
Ralph Boggs	T	233
Marvin D. Bottum	T	425
Harry Bradbury	T	203
Russell D. Brutsche	T	501
Earl S. Burke, Jr.	T	490
Tom D. Burke	T	490
Donald W. Burt	T	43
Thomas F. Carolan, III	T	466
Logan C. Chamberlain	T	77
James G. Cooper	T	540
Ed R. Cordia	T	127
John H. Cowgill	E	404
Willis D. Damkroger	T	77
Robert D. DuBoise	T	350
Jeffrey D. Edgar	T	490
Tom N. Ellis	T	480
Mark Enright	T	234
Lenard Favorite	T	233
Richard C. Floyd	T	440
Dennes B. Fogarty	T	414
Robert J. Fusto	T	295
Arthur J. Giles	T	335
Robert R. Hammer	T	425
David J. Hartesveldt	T	373
Frank R. Hastings	T	294
John E. Herschbach	T	233
Barry S. Hewlett	T	77
Paul M. Hoque	T	310
Don W. Jillie, Jr.	T	400
Jeff L. Johnson	T	484
Larry R. Johnson	T	233
Daniel R. Jones	T	233
Dwight L. Jones	T	233
Keith B. Judd	T	444
Jon Laporte	T	440
William M. Laupp	T	350
Robert A. Loehr	T	213
Joseph D. Longbrake	E	216
James R. Maberry	T	471
Robert Mancuso	T	213
Eugene Marcoccia	T	220
Thomas P. McMullen	T	484
Michael T. McVey	T	440
Michael E. New	T	77
John M. Page	T	370
Mark D. Papenhausen	T	127
Kenny Pate	T	233
Stan Praisewater	T	332
Robert A. Prentky	E	564
Gary D. Ross	T	437
Paul E. Ryon	T	201

1964 cont.		
Steve A. Schnoebelen	T	373
James A. Schulte	T	293
Timm A. Slater	E	347
Bruce J. Solari	T	294
John E. Sugar	T	6
Don Summers	T	130
Michael B. Teel	T	225
Wayne Torigoe	T	233
Donald A. Trimmer	T	404
David W. Weller	T	201
Scott L. White	T	130
David P. Williams	T	418
William M. Wilson	T	373
Joseph F. Wiseman	T	466
Randall D. Wright	T	201
Wayne L. Wright	E	30
Jack K. Young	T	488
Donn A. Youngman	E	347
1965		
Steve G. Anderson	T	484
Michael C. Atkinson	E	334
Bruce A. Bailey	T	411
Derek M. Becker	T	349
James L. Becker	T	294
Johnnie L. Beebe	T	616
James Belogorsky	T	549
Gary B. Bergtholdt	T	443
David Bishop	T	373
Michael B. Bowyer	E	74
John E. Sugar	T	6
Don Summers	T	130
Michael B. Teel	T	225
Wayne Torigoe	T	233
Donald A. Trimmer	T	404
David W. Weller	T	201
Scott L. White	T	130
David P. Williams	T	418
William M. Wilson	T	373
Joseph F. Wiseman	T	466
Randall D. Wright	T	201
Wayne L. Wright	E	30
Jack K. Young	T	488
Donn A. Youngman	E	347
1965		
Steve G. Anderson	T	484
Michael C. Atkinson	E	334
Bruce A. Bailey	T	411
Derek M. Becker	T	349
James L. Becker	T	294
Johnnie L. Beebe	T	616
James Belogorsky	T	549
Gary B. Bergtholdt	T	443
David Bishop	T	373
Michael B. Bowyer	E	74
Mitchel G. Buckingham	T	480
Kerry W. Burnham	T	41
Robert J. Carolan	T	466
Glenn C. Clukey	T	540
Mark W. Creighton	T	440
John B. Cummock	T	454
Matthew C. DeFreitas	T	539
Stanley L. Deller	E	626
Randy L. Ellis	T	480
James R. Forster, II	T	339
John G. Fox	T	43
Harold W. Griffith	T	375
Richard S. Griffoul	T	237
James T. Hackworth	T	150
William L. Hamilton	T	549
Douglas B. Hardie	T	479
Brent C. Harline	T	456
Thomas V. Heimsoth	E	77
Richard L. Henry	T	606
William J. Henry	T	606

Thomas L. Hinton	T	425
Duncan B. Hobbs	T	520
Paul G. Holman	T	476
Raymond A. Holme, II	E	549
John J. Holson, III	T	793
Don A. Holt	T	488
Stanley M. Holt	T	6
Bill Hurd	T	668
Randy B. Ingraham	T	295
Michael Irving	T	92
Gary W. Johnson, III	T	466
William L. Johnson	T	225
Robin L. Joy	T	442
Danial E. Kelley	T	442
Richard G. Kelso	T	6
Anthony L. Kiorpes	T	209
Joseph E. Librers	T	299
Michael T. McDonald	T	616
Paul G. Melicker	E	335
Kenneth C. Milind	T	425
Knut P. Niehoff	T	339
Jerry T. Okumura	T	74
Leon A. Panttafa	T	370
Jeff P. Pendergraft	T	334
Leonard Pinna	T	336
Hal R. Powell	T	480
Ross Rogers	E	466
Michael R. Rose	T	325
Rand B. Schaal	T	299
Gary T. Seidenkranz	E	74
Roland E. Shanks	E	30
William R. Shepard	T	373
Edward J. Sliger	T	616
James M. Spence	T	334
Daniel L. Stuart	T	443
Randall R. Talley	T	332
Kenneth L. Trammell	T	616
David D. Valentine	T	6
Steven Vandenbroeke	T	471
Michael S. Vanremortel	T	443
Mark R. Weisler	T	540
Brian R. Wood	T	540
Wilfred L. Wright	E	30
Gil S. Young	T	520
1966		
Creston G. Aldridge	E	77
Jeff C. Ashworth	T	236
Robert B. Bast	E	484
David R. Boles	T	74
William V. Brown	T	443
David K. Carl	T	564
Gary D. Chronert	T	478
Bruce S. Clair	T	43
Russell D. Clark	T	444
David R. Coleman	T	325
Geoffrey L. Collins	T	209
William D. Crowel	T	479
Timothy M. Cummins	T	373
Howard J. Davis	T	479
William D. DeHollander	T	201
Richard L. Dingey	E	363
Leo R. Domnick	T	92
Vaughn H. Duckett	T	332
Robert N. Ehmann	T	466
Charles F. Fulhorst	T	43
Gary R. Gabriel	T	407
Steve Gale, Jr.	T	43
Larry W. Gant	T	616
Steven P. Gardner	E	562
Leonard A. Gashler	T	616
R. G. Gilluly	T	325
Paul Grant	E	626
Richard D. Gray	T	305
Gary B. Hackworth	T	150
Roger L. Hahn	T	478
Larry V. Hall	T	489

Peter M. Harden	T	497
Melvin L. Ho	T	478
Paul S. Ingraham	T	295
John R. Jenson	T	76
Robert A. Johnson	T	603
Robert M. Johnson	T	38
Leland R. Jorgensen	E	563
Edward H. Kaler	T	335
Bradley W. Kinne	T	363
John C. Kirkish	T	500
Cary R. Kloes	T	339
Walter A. Lang, Jr.	T	497
Mark S. Lepiane	T	620
Guy M. Lohman	E	512
John J. MacDougall	T	76
Milton R. Mackay	T	336
Thomas D. Martinez	T	476
Alan L. Martini	T	501
James M. McLaughlin	T	441
Steven D. McVay	T	370
Tom O. Merrill	T	793
Ross A. Miles	T	495
Richard D. Miller	T	43
David P. Mollenhauer	T	51
John W. Morrison	E	549
Bruce D. Neuschwander	T	363
James T. Panttaja	T	370
John E. Parrish	T	476
David L. Patton	T	606
Stanley V. Perry	T	254
Keith D. Plottel	T	38
Lloyd L. Porter	T	616
Michael C. Rode	T	43
Charles A. Rogers	E	626
Keith A. Rogers	T	443
Robert W. Schmid	T	497
Richard J. Sciapiti	T	497
Matthew E. Sheedy, III	T	793
Larry H. Shoemaker	T	411
Mark D. Smith	T	549
Norman C. Spalding	T	500
Gregory D. Spence	T	334
Eric R. Stohl	T	437
Neil I. Swanson	T	488
Eugene D. Torrey	T	107
Thomas M. Werth	E	549
James C. White	T	130
Jeffrey L. Youmans	T	564
1967		
Steve F. Anderson	T	254
Dennis A. Andrade	T	336
Roger D. Andreen	T	12
Larry R. Anthon	T	444
Weldon R. Atteberry	T	495
Mark A. Baldwin	T	471
Lawrence P. Bergeron	T	48
George Blackburne	T	107
Kenneth I. Bode	T	471
Chris E. Bodenhamer	T	363
Jan P. Brandon	T	500
Robert E. Brandt	T	233
Robert D. Brown	T	363
Wayne C. Bushnell	T	471
Lee B. Bussey	T	237
Scott R. Butler	T	621
Stuart J. Butler	T	621
Bert M. Carmody	T	209
James D. Carpenter	T	130
Jerry C. Carpenter	T	12
Stephen A. Carter	T	76
Randall G. Casto	T	621
Richard A. Caulfield	T	225
Paul D. Cheim	T	620
John S. Cloud	T	74
Mike A. Cloyd	E	460
Gordon J. Coker	T	339

1967 cont.

David G. Cooper	T	540
Paul H. Daggett	T	371
Ronald C. Deller	E	626
Eugene D. Dingey	T	363
Michael D. Dingey	T	363
Mark S. Donnell	T	339
Carl G. Ehmann	T	466
Gregory J. Emery	T	535
Tom G. Erbes	T	478
Mark D. Eskeldson	E	369
Carl F. Ewert	T	365
William G. Fischer	T	535
Donald M. Follas	E	347
Douglas R. Forrester	T	466
Lawrence E. Furlow	T	76
Gregory R. Gabriel	T	407
David A. Garcia	T	620
William C. Gill	T	425
Michael G. Gilluly	T	325
Dave J. Goodman	T	318
Michael S. Gray	T	620
Montgomery B. Groves, Jr.	T	466
R. S. Guthrie	T	466
Mark H. Habermeyer	T	480
Bradley H. Hand	T	339
Gary A. Hansen	T	407
Daniel R. Harding	T	237
William C. Harkness	T	565
John B. Hart	T	466
William A. Headley, Jr.	T	616
John P. Healy	T	341
Scott T. Hector	E	520
Steve M. Henderson	E	466
Christoper A. Henry	T	480
Roger R. Hill	T	305
Jonathon R. Hulme	T	563
Charles E. Jeffries	T	495
Ken E. Jensen	T	375
Scot W. Kendall	T	207
Richard A. Kibler	E	606
James A. Koehn	T	480
Kurt L. Krizek	T	471
Steven M. Kuhlman	T	325
James N. LaBelle	T	466
Mike C. Leveroos	T	371
Richard E. Loehr	T	613
Edward J. Loss	T	480
Steven E. Lowery	T	74
Michael S. Malone	T	480
Paul Marcoccia	T	220
Michael L. Marquis	T	621
Laurence S. Masuoka	E	466
Paul E. McMeans	T	130
William V. Meyer	T	476
Thomas J. Mounts	T	225
Douglas E. Mullen	T	305
Kenneth R. Munson	T	365
William C. Murray	E	7
Brian W. Neuschwander	T	363
Quinn H. Parker	E	236
John R. Patty	T	210
Gary M. Pavusko	E	626
David M. Perham	T	480
Duncan L. Pollock	T	363
Jim J. Prandi	T	43
Chris B. Price	T	500
Edward C. Ramsay	T	308
Terry L. Randles	T	324
Cole E. Redmon	T	201
James W. Register	T	205
Larry A. Renshaw	T	620
William Y. Richardson, III	T	308
Michael W. Riddle	T	668
Paul A. Rode	T	43
Stephen E. Rose	E	369

Raymond L. Sandelman	T	363
David E. Sheldon	T	254
Howard W. Stanley	E	92
Kenneth L. Stewart	T	621
Randall R. Stringham	T	121
Howard Svigals	T	500
Richard H. Teel	T	225
Eric S. Torigoe	T	233
Gary M. Trimble	T	318
Jeff M. Uhler	T	130
John M. Walker	T	339
Fitzgerald O. Way	T	78
Joseph L. Weller	T	201
Roy L. West	T	620
Robert H. Wilson	T	373
Richard F. Wright	T	308

1968

William S. Alley	T	341
Richard P. Alter	T	799
David L. Anderson	T	476
Carl E. Avery	T	365
John D. Baker	T	348
Tom W. Baker	T	348
Reuel Jay Bawden	E	305
Scott G. Blackham	E	456
Stephen C. Boswell	E	290
Earl C. Bowling	E	346
Nicolas G. Bozovich	T	535
Bruce H. Brady	T	305
Daniel T. Brady	T	338
Ronald H. Brady	T	305
John R. Bretthauer	T	92
Jay M. Burcham	T	130
Patrick J. Burt	T	490
John E. Carpenter	T	444
Randall A. Christensen	E	456
Douglas Cole	T	12
Stephen F. Cook	E	497
Kenneth W. Cooley	T	237
Calvin W. Dawson	E	290
David C. Degiorgio	T	12
Steve H. Dewing	T	290
David L. Duerr	T	799
Patrick W. Duffy	T	114
Gregory J. Favorite	T	233
Lawrence D. Ford	T	549
Steven A. Foreman	E	373
Mark A. Gary	T	46
Leonard W. Gedenberg	T	210
Jerry H. Glass	T	120
Jack W. Goodwin	T	434
Douglas J. Hallock	T	107
Jeffery L. Hammill	T	434
John F. Hammill	T	434
Jock A. Heinrich	T	478
Jon K. Heinrich	T	478
James A. Hendrix	T	268
Charles R. Herbert	E	290
David W. Hittenberger	T	12
Alan B. Hoshor	T	467
Kenneth E. Isenberg	E	793
Laurence N. Jacobs	E	497
Milo A. Johnson, III	E	520
Jesse L. Judd	E	456
Daniel C. Killip	T	342
Robert F. Kincaid	T	346
Stephen P. Kissinger	T	418
Robert A. Kosten	T	426
Johnny W. Kreger	T	341
Lane J. Lance	T	708
Craig D. Lilly	E	520
Douglas Limbocker	T	148
Bret W. Logan	T	447
Fred J. Logan	T	447
Allan G. Lonzo	T	76
Darrell W. McNabb	T	374

Phillip E. Merritt	E	497
David J. Miller	E	497
Richard C. Miller	T	305
Kenneth L. Morgan	T	339
Steven D. Morgan	T	339
Mark Moriyama	T	210
Timothy D. Murray	T	426
Karl R. Neice	T	150
Robert C. Nessler	T	480
David A. Nile	T	418
Craig D. O'Connel	E	30
Thomas C. Onwiler	T	341
John W. Parker	T	18
Nathan R. Patterson	T	324
James D. Penrose	T	406
Ronald S. Poelman	T	444
David B. Prince	T	121
Willis W. Ritter, III	T	406
Thomas E. Roberts, III	T	549
Gary L. Ross	T	488
Jon E. Rudeen	T	497
John T. Salinas	E	346
Tim Salinas	E	346
Ray D. Schneider	T	12
David S. Scott	T	444
Mark R. Scott	T	455
Steven E. Scott	T	581
Paul A. Sheldon	T	254
Mark R. Shoemaker	T	478
Alan Curt Shufelt	T	121
Roger K. Sleight	T	120
James E. Smith	T	233
Daniel R. Southwick	T	305
Hugh R. Stahl	T	466
Claude L. Stanford	T	92
James E. Suffel	T	318
Everett P. Sullens, Jr.	T	395
James S. Szabo	T	406
David A. Thompson	T	549
Douglas W. Wacker	T	339
Wayne J. Waldorph	T	130
Leonard E. Ward	T	321
William C. Wells	T	120
Lee H. West	E	236
Christopher T. Westfall	T	478
Michael Weyers	T	318
Richard D. White	T	341
Mark C. Wilkinson	T	444
Bobby K. Williamson	T	74
Jimmy L. Withrow	T	403
Rick L. Woodland	T	321

1969

Douglas L. Abe	T	78
Mark W. Achziger	T	336
Robert G. Allen	T	148
Scott J. Ammon	T	150
Duane O. Anderson	E	488
Daniel A. Andreen	T	22
Douglas A. Andreen	T	22
David Archer	T	455
Richard P. Batchelder	T	225
David Biasotti	T	476
Frank E. Biehl	T	414
Daniel Blunk	T	325
David Buell	T	339
Mark S. Bull	T	205
Richard Cain, Jr.	T	233
Dugald B. Campbell	E	456
Eric Chalmers	T	447
David Cheim	T	120
Michael S. Clark	T	505
Louis J. Constanza	E	520
William R. Cronquist	T	211
Graig L. Cropper	E	470
Gregory S. Damon	T	211
Mark D. DeJarnette	T	346

1969 cont.

James Drennan	T	293
Gary L. Eck	T	260
Harold Ely	T	363
Richard B. Evans	T	447
Edward Fassett	T	412
Carmello N. Ferrigno	T	339
David Flanders	T	76
James C. Gessner	T	476
Charles G. Gibson	T	148
David A. Giroux	T	44
Robert D. Guthrie	T	434
David Habermeyer	T	480
Raymond L. Harkey	T	231
Gordon M. Henderson	T	480
George Hendrix	T	268
Kevin J. Henry	T	480
Carlton Ho	T	455
Sterling Hoskins	E	30
Robert Howell	T	434
Norman C. Hulberg	T	480
David M. Hulligan	T	107
Dennis P. Hultberg	T	321
Donald P. Jarrett	E	488
Lynn M. Jemison	E	2
Darwin D. John	T	346
Scott Jones	T	535
James Kirkwood	E	460
Stan T. Laegreid	T	481
Alan K. Lambson	E	456
Michael P. Lambson	E	456
Donald F. Lawrence	T	207
Michael Lozito	E	545
Michael T. Lucey	E	456
Hugh MacPherson	T	355
Jerald Martin	E	481
Michael R. Martinez	T	476
Gary McCauley	T	260
Jim C. McDonald	E	363
Christopher R. Meyer	T	476
Clyde A. Morris	T	476
Raymond W. Mounts	T	225
Gary Nakamoto	T	76
Craig B. Olsen	T	254
Creston T. Olson	T	120
Jeffrey C. Park	T	480
Mark Petersen	T	237
Mark M. Peterson	E	263
John T. Pfeifer	T	508
John A. Pinna	T	336
Albert Raithel, III	T	466
Matthew W. Raymond	T	500
Gregory C. Rimanich	T	30
Erik Rodts	T	495
Robert Rung	T	540
Donald Russell	T	563
James D. Sano	E	363
Lane A. Satterstrom	T	535
Brad C. Saville	E	305
Patric A. Sazama	T	476
Neil D. Scott	T	480
Cary Shufelt	E	121
Bruce Silva	T	339
Peter J. Stack	T	500
Robert Stamper	T	339
Robert A. Stancliffe	T	263
Chris Stanton	T	346
James E. Swartz	E	545
Tim Takahashi	T	205
William Taylor	E	230
Jon D. Ten Broeck	T	497
Robert Tope	T	221
Curtis L. Watson, Jr.	T	184
Timothy E. Way	T	78
Wesley Williams	E	497
David Wilson	T	205

Kevin C. Wood	T	540
Carl J. Woodland	T	321
Richard Workman	E	444
Bruse Worthen	T	254
Charles York	T	467
Robert Zeroun	T	150

1970

Victor L. Achziger	T	336
Craig Anderson	T	508
Terry E. Bailey	T	260
Ronald N. Bakke	E	466
John C. Barker	T	793
Clifford L. Barnwell	T	467
Steven F. Barth	T	406
Jay J. Beebe	T	325
Thomas E. Boenig	E	43
Bruce I. Bonfield	T	148
Mark A. Bosworth	T	500
Duane M. Bradley	T	48
Kent C. Cahill	E	494
Randall Calvert	T	230
David G. Carlson	T	443
John Carolan	T	508
Arthur D. Case	T	312
Kieth E. Claus	E	497
Mike Cook	T	582
Dane R. Cowan	T	313
Bruce K. Creager	T	500
Stuart J. Daley	T	349
James E. Darnell	T	308
Brian D. Dickerson	T	210
William J. Dimopoulos	T	148
Dennis Donithorne	E	456
Don A. Drake	T	374
Richard C. Dyer, Jr.	T	500
John R. Ehmann	T	466
Jonathan W. Evans	T	535
Jim S. Finnell	T	373
Gregory D. Fish	T	455
Eugene Foley	T	233
Jeffrey E. Friend	T	250
Joseph R. Gartner	T	148
Craig S. Gibson	T	221
John A. Green	T	374
Michael W. Gund	T	260
Gunnar B. Hafstad	E	520
Hugh Hall	T	481
Steven G. Harris	T	339
Timothy D. Harris	T	342
Scott A. Harrison	T	220
Edward R. Hawkins	T	343
Joel S. Hawley	T	564
Paul T. Hendrickson	E	43
Gregory W. Hildebrand	T	293
James G. Hill	T	535
Terry D. Hill	T	305
Charles Hindt, Jr.	E	460
Herbert W. Hoeptree, III	T	261
Donald Scott Houston	E	563
Jay R. Hoyt	E	488
Eugene R. Hurtig	E	520
Richard E. Jackson	E	230
David Jensen	T	374
Greg R. Jespersen	T	271
George H. Johnson	E	520
James Jones	T	233
Jim F. Kachur	T	490
Ronald I. Kanzaki	T	480
Christopher A. Keswick	T	434
Steven Kibler	E	606
Kevin C. Kmetz	T	374
George M. Kornievsky	T	76
Thomas M. Kroger	T	486
Phillip M. Kudenov	E	497
David B. Lang	T	497
Steven E. Leslie	E	497

Steve M. Lind	T	440
Patrick Lonzo	T	77
James Robert Malcolm	E	407
Wayne Marquard	T	211
Steve R. Masdon	T	14
Evan R. McCall	E	445
Barry G. McCorkle	E	497
Bill McEwen	T	582
Brain B. McGhie	E	456
D. Craig McKenna	E	312
Jerry P. McMillan	T	549
Richard V. Mettler	T	207
Brent Miller	T	481
Mike H. Mirovan	T	549
Richard M. Moore	T	409
Steve C. Morgan	T	312
William J. Morgan	T	46
Brent R. Moulton	T	321
Michael T. Murphy	T	342
Steve J. Narron	T	466
Thomas H. Neuman	T	414
Warren Scott Newkirk	T	373
J. Peter O'Bergin	T	793
Mark S. Orr	T	233
Paul G. Panelli	T	500
Mark F. Poelle	T	211
William J. Powell	T	347
Jonathan M. Prince	T	233
Delwin E. Quenzer	T	401
David M. Renner	T	478
Michael J. Rideout	T	346
Daniel L. Ritter	T	406
Roger M. Sadler	T	539
Michael P. Schmidt	T	210
Dave K. Schreiner	T	500
Mark Shoffner	T	582
Glenn K. Shore	T	539
Branden D. Simpson	T	44
Dairen C. Simpson	T	44
William F. Sirvatka	T	500
Kevin Slattery	T	433
Robert N. Smead	E	563
Gordon D. Stevens	T	471
John M. Stewart	T	325
Walter E. Stewart	E	30
James A. Sturges	T	339
Terry A. Teeters	T	233
Paul ten Zeldam	T	508
Gary Tibury	T	78
Wesley H. Toland	T	374
John G. Venerella	T	363
Kit A. Viale	T	318
Jeff W. Walker	T	339
Donald W. Wallace	T	470
Gary L. Walz	T	14
Michael E. Warant	T	401
David C. Warfield	E	106
Brian Way	T	78
Arthur C. Webster, III	T	408
Steve R. West	T	312
John S. Wiley	T	549
Tracy L. Williams	T	526
Rolland E. Windmueller	T	480
Kevin A. Wong	T	500
Gregory Wright	T	286
Roger A. Wright	T	408
Laurence G. Yaffe	T	406

1971

Buff Adams	T	367
Glenn R. Anderson	T	250
Travis T. Anderson	E	123
Thomas Armstrong	T	363
Martin J. Aubry	T	339
Derek N. Baker	T	536
Dustin B. Baker	T	536
Ryan H. Baker	T	536

1971 cont.

Mark S. Banta	T	221
Douglas G. Barth	E	406
Tony J. Bay	T	500
Michael E. Blount	T	478
Rene G. Boisvert	T	14
George W. Bonney	T	549
Russell S. Breed	T	535
Steven M. Brosnan	T	250
Gary L. Brown	T	408
Leonard M. Bruffett	T	144
Michael C. Brunt	E	456
Stephen T. Brunt	E	456
Curtis G. Buchanan	E	304
Jeff A. Byrne	T	535
Greg D. Chaba	T	404
William G. Chisholm, Jr.	E	520
Michael L. Clark	T	411
Bruce A. Coffman	T	347
Michael E. Cook	E	360
Craig A. Cowdery	T	363
David K. Crane	E	573
Craig C. Dahl	T	373
Armand E. D'Alo	E	14
Herbert W. Davis	E	293
Walter E. DeGear	T	237
Mark W. Dennin	T	408
Michael A. DesJardin	T	347
Andy H. Dorr	T	339
Fred M. Drennan	T	293
James R. Driggs	E	563
Harold C. Elrod	T	321
Benjamin L. Espiritu	T	104
Ernest H. Evans	T	582
Robert W. Fabini	T	130
Fred D. Ferrie	T	146
Stephen H. Fletcher	T	526
Karl F. Forsgard	T	478
Kenneth B. Gervais	T	505
Mark T. Giroux	T	44
Ron Gowen	E	573
James D. Graham	T	582
Dennis J. Green	T	433
Jeffrey P. Guill	T	327
Stephen W. Gum	T	237
Douglas D. Hamilton	T	233
Kimbal F. Hancock	T	230
Jeffrey S. Harris	T	480
Jacob E. Hartinger	T	535
Gary T. Hartwig	T	443
David C. Hatch	E	454
Charles D. Heist	T	403
Gerard R. Hepler	T	286
Stephen J. Hickey	T	104
Steven A. Hill	T	434
John M. Hillan	E	14
Carl B. Hinton	T	500
Eugene R. Hurtig	E	520
Steven D. Jacobs	E	497
Scott S. Johnston	T	363
Stephen A. Jones	T	409
Robert W. Jordan	T	230
Peter S. Joyce	T	293
John Kieser	E	14
Michael R. Kinser	T	14
Richard M. Kraynick	T	341
Ronald F. Kuka	T	14
Randy M. LaFrom	T	540
Daniel K. Lagasse	T	363
Ronald G. Lamica	T	406
Aaron J. Landsworth	T	293
Brian J. Leetham	T	230
Gregory W. Lind	T	440
Steven F. Marchesini	T	374
Eric J. Marler	T	230
Richard A. Masse	T	324

Nicholas J. Matulich	T	260
Richard J. Maze	T	266
Michael J. McCloskey	T	408
Jeff D. McDonough	T	130
Dennis C. McGuire	T	130
Theodore R. McKee	T	564
Larry S. Metivier	T	347
Phillip R. Miatech	E	407
Derek H. Mitvalsky	T	375
Douglas B. Morgan	T	301
William F. Morrison	T	582
Dennis J. Moulton	E	321
Kenneth R. Myatt	T	211
Christopher P. Nelson	T	266
Timothy F. Nelson	T	266
Brent A. Neuschwander	T	363
Robert G. Ney	T	266
Eric D. Nyberg	T	466
Kenneth M. Okazaki	T	339
Gregory M. Paape	E	14
Kevin D. Padrick	T	500
Ken B. Painter	T	14
Steve S. Painter	E	14
Bart M. Palmos	T	540
Franz L. Parik	T	443
Kenneth M. Pavloff	T	308
Dale Phelps	T	343
Frank A. Pierce, III	E	14
John W. Pierce	E	14
Jeffrey J. Potter	T	479
Brad M. Powell	T	347
Robert E. Pursel, Jr.	T	212
John L. Quilici	T	336
Craig H. Richins	T	230
John Riehl	T	336
David N. Robertson	T	508
David W. Rock	T	44
Charles C. Roland	T	286
Robert F. Routt	T	308
Charles W. Royer	T	481
Jeffry A. Ruhlin	T	144
Raymond J. Ryan, Jr.	T	37
Stan J. Sagi	E	2
Scott Sakaguchi	T	610
Bruce K. Salmond	E	562
Mark T. Schmidt	T	210
Glen Schuler	E	488
Richard E. Sessions	T	616
Fred Shumway	E	121
Mark F. Small	E	499
John A. Smith	T	230
Ray Robert Smith	T	363
Robert M. Stone	T	293
Scott V. Sutton	T	473
Barry K. Teopola	T	404
James J. Tesik	T	510
Robert D. Tingle	T	440
Michael L. Troiano	E	499
Dean C. Underwood	T	221
David R. Wahl	E	43
Douglas R. Wardian	T	77
Walter A. Weber, III	T	250
Stephen W. White	T	385
Craig Whitten	T	489
David S. Wiley	E	549
Kenneth A. Wirt	T	363
Harold S. Wood, Jr.	T	365
Craig R. Wuest	T	308
Bill G. Wullenjohn	T	433

1972

Peter L. Aberle	T	535
Brandon G. Ach'ee	T	535
Brenton B. Ach'ee	T	535
Keith A. Aplustill	T	362
Michael D. Avery	T	373
Vincent A. Bachanas, Jr.	E	500

Byron N. Bailey	T	363
Billy E. Balfour	T	616
Bryan C. Barrow	T	266
Mark H. Bennion	E	573
Terrance R. Berkley	T	539
Gary K. Biehl	E	545
Ira M. Bletz	T	327
John Bokelman	T	463
Michael Bonnie	T	260
Mark Boyer	T	470
Brian R. Boyle	T	476
Kevin E. Brooks	T	363
Daniel Brown	T	341
Mark W. Brown		
Brad A. Buell	T	339
Eric K. Bull	T	250
Valente V. Carrasco	T	323
Glen D. Cart	E	615
Phil V. Claussen	T	356
Carl Dais	T	323
Theodore W. Darnall	T	308
David A. Davis	T	490
Mark A. Deady	E	488
Jesse J. Dean	E	44
Chris Dennison	E	456
Gary Dewitt	T	222
Delane K. Donithorne	E	456
John C. Duncan	T	339
Bradley N. Dutton	T	233
Michael K. Dyer	T	363
Mark Early	T	476
Robert E. Eickmann, Jr.	T	404
James R. Evans	T	447
Jeffrey A. Favorite	T	233
David A. Finstrom	T	500
Craig Fischer	E	499
Scott Fletcher	T	371
Stephen W. Forbes	E	221
David M. Fullmer	T	221
David G. Geddes	E	563
Michael A. Gracie	T	222
Mark Greyson	T	266
Victor A. Groves	E	327
Kelley G. Guasticci	T	207
Bradley Hall	T	470
Brent R. Hancock	T	230
Matt J. Harline	T	430
Richard Hawkins	T	92
Dennis R. Heinsohn	T	411
Brent D. Helsop	E	454
Eric G. Henard	T	498
Geordy J. Henderson	T	480
Curtis B. Hill	T	221
Steven D. Hinde	T	454
Paul D. Hoff	T	375
Mark N. Holan	T	130
Richard K. Hulme	E	573
Mark T. Ivie	T	207
Stephen C. Jacobs	T	430
Kenneth E. Jordan	T	268
Jon W. Justice	T	341
Steve J. Kearns	T	494
Edward M. King	T	478
William D. Laidig	T	385
John Lamping	T	535
Dale Erik Larson	T	330
Robert Lawrence	T	207
Kent G. Leavitt	E	312
Steven H. Linder	T	566
Deward W. Loose	T	236
Christopher P. Mabey	T	582
Mike F. Maniates	T	145
James Leo Martin	T	6
Gary C. Mathis	T	488
Ricky E. McCalebb	T	610
Ryan R. McCardell	T	107
Glen B. McGhie	T	456

Name		
1972 cont.		
Steven J. McKenzie	T	476
Michael J. Mendizabal	T	222
James C. Mentink, Jr.	T	433
Jerome J. Millon	T	478
Mitchell L. Molling	E	615
John R. Montrose	E	500
Stephen Paul Murray	T	566
Blair Narog	T	499
Robert J. Naughten	T	500
Robert J. O'Haver	T	606
John C. Oravetz	T	323
Steven D. Oravetz	T	323
Joseph Osborne	T	339
Richard D. Otvos	T	470
Randy D. Patten	T	221
Richard B. Pickering, Jr.	T	206
Monty Pratt	T	145
Ian C. Purse	T	495
Steven R. Rice	T	122
Ed Ring	T	323
John D. Rockwood	T	481
Joe J. Santos	T	330
Lawrence B. Schubert	T	211
Brian A. Seller	T	385
Isidore A. Sevigny	T	371
Paul E. Sevigny	T	371
Samuel P. Shapiro	T	203
Gregory A. Sharp	E	44
Jon C. Skeels	T	130
James L. Smith	T	549
Steven L. Soares	T	78
Stephen Stewart	T	206
Gary E. Stribling	T	130
Gregory W. Stutz	T	500
David R. Swainston	T	454
Michael S. Trevisan	T	476
Marc K. Uhrey	E	445
David R. Vallett	T	563
Craig W. Verant	T	401
Mark S. Walker	T	339
Kirk W. White	E	314
Steve J. Wilburn	T	434
Dale M. Willden	E	615
Brian K. Williams	T	444
Douglas Williams	T	237
James D. Williams, Jr.	T	403
Mark A. Wright	T	308
Robert E. Wright	T	286
Robert W. Yuen	T	497
1973		
Bruce C. Achziger	T	336
Clifford D. Allen, III	T	494
Bill B. Anderson	T	394
Cameron L. Anderson	T	470
Jennings Apple	E	150
Kalman L. Apple	T	150
David M. Aquilina	T	361
Peter V. Badala	T	489
Christopher E. Bailey	T	286
Kevin S. Barney	T	471
John O. Barry	T	535
Gregory Baumann	T	144
Rocky D. Beckelman	T	164
Kirk G. Bettencourt	T	334
Jon C. Bianche	T	539
Keith L. Blaisdell	E	263
Jeff R. Bohn	T	233
Thomas J. Bommarito	T	336
William H. Boucher	T	443
John M. Brawn	T	498
Calvin L. Breed	T	535
Jeffrey J. Brown	E	212
Kevin N. Brown	T	148
Randy R. Brynsvold	T	260
Clair J. Buchanan	E	304
Terry J. Burr	E	204
Jim H. Burroughs	T	49
Gregg H. Bussey	T	237
Richard J. Byle	T	346
Michael J. Cabrinna	T	145
Robert L. Capp	T	365
Gerald K. Capps	T	799
William H. Carman	E	471
Jeffery W. Carty	T	411
Clifford D. Cayton	T	470
Ronald A. Cheney	E	470
Steve M. Chew	T	494
Brian Christensen	T	498
Roger W. Clemes	T	430
Randall L. Cobb	T	564
John R. Connell, III	E	616
Danny L. Conk	E	304
William Clay Cook	T	293
Robert G. Cosgrove	E	520
Robert C. Couch	T	325
Jon A. Cox	T	338
James B. Craver	T	411
Brian E. Cronquist	T	290
Cory M. Crosby	T	206
Matthew Curry	T	407
William Peter Daley	T	535
Kevin D. Dalley	T	327
Daniel M. DeGroot	T	78
Michael DeLeone	T	421
Jeff B. Delman	T	497
Gerry B. DeYoung	T	498
Thomas J. Dimopoulos	T	148
Dennis R. Early	T	411
Virgil E. Ellsworth	T	12
Marc D. Ely	T	363
Richard E. Farias	T	356
Doug W. Ferguson	T	535
Gary W. Fettig	T	394
Arthur W. Fisher	T	361
Jeffry J. Fitzsimmons	T	260
Michael K. Flake	T	294
Gary H. Fox	T	564
Kane S. Franklin	T	12
Dennis P. Fries	T	148
Boyd D. Fullmer	T	221
William G. Geis	T	104
David E. Gilbert	T	430
Michael L. Godwin	E	237
Beau Goldie	T	490
John B. Goodman	T	318
R. Bryan Graveline	T	508
Kevin D. Green	T	165
Matthew D. Griffon	T	237
Laurence T. Groves	T	405
Mark T. Grunau	T	148
Donald A. Guerland	E	434
Peter D. Gum	T	237
Glen R. Halliday	T	327
Kimbel Halliday	E	327
Dennis M. Hankel	T	480
Scott S. Havlick	T	270
Craig L. Henderson	T	480
Bryan Herpel	T	365
Gerard M. Hilgart	T	385
Glenn G. Hills	T	260
David W. Hitch	T	148
Gary A. Hitch	T	148
Scott Larrie Hobson	T	230
C. Edward Hoffman	T	471
James C. Hoffman, Jr.	E	470
Gary W. Holland	T	346
Fred Hollis	E	106
Mark H. Holt	T	454
Scott A. Holt	T	454
Dan L. Hopper	T	365
Frank E. Horst, III	T	480
John R. Huber	T	49
Douglas D. Hulme	E	562
Douglas J. Hulme	T	430
John Hunter	T	3
Raymond Hunter	T	3
Martin A. Hurt	T	375
Marshall F. Ignacio	T	150
Russ W. Irvin	T	343
Mark R. Isaacson	T	305
Dennis L. Jacob	E	207
Douglas S. Jain	T	330
Donald E. Jasmann	T	539
Thomas S. Johansen	T	346
David L. Johnson	T	446
Keith A. Johnson	E	211
Larry L. Kanzaki	T	480
Keith A. Kelly	T	230
Kevin D. Kemp	T	148
John W. Kent	T	343
Stephen M. Kimery	T	378
Richard C. Kindall	T	49
George T. King	T	207
Brian A. Kingsbury	T	430
Larry C. Knowlden	T	305
Jeff Labno	T	443
Scott L. Lance	E	708
Bryan T. Landreth	T	112
Robert S. Lang	T	497
Michael T. Leung	T	233
Jeffrey W. Lindgren	T	343
Brian C. Livingston	T	371
James P. Loweecey	T	363
Fred D. Lunday	T	535
John H. Lyle	T	535
John C. Macdonald	T	201
Lawrence P. MacNeil	T	146
Guy L. Marker	E	445
David E. McAdams	T	478
Andrew S. McClymont	T	566
Stephen A. McLaughlin	T	488
Scott R. McQueen	E	356
Mark L. Medland	T	346
Eric G. Miller	T	374
Ronald G. Miller	T	305
Michael Molerus	T	365
Paul E. Moore	T	406
David Mooring	T	37
Frank J. Morant	T	365
Bruce M. Morehead	T	442
David T. Mori	T	582
Mike T. Mori	T	74
William K. Moyer	T	375
Steve C. Myatt	T	211
Robert K. Nakamoto	T	74
Kenneth W. Newman	E	460
Brent J. Nicolai	T	210
Neal A. Nyberg	T	466
John Rick Oberg	T	375
Stephen C. O'Brien	T	479
Lawrence E. Ochoa	T	476
Raymond R. Ochoa	T	334
Scott B. Odell	T	478
Stephen R. Olney	T	421
Gilbert L. Olsen, Jr.	T	497
William M. Ordemann	T	434
Blain P. Owen	T	536
John R. Owen	T	536
Gregory S. Pape	T	489
Kirk H. Parker	E	304
DeLyle E. Perry	E	304
Todd A. Perry	T	346
Kenneth L. Peterson	E	304
Bruce H. Pownall	T	373
Gary M. Probert	T	260
John W. Pugmire	T	343
James V. Puzar	T	476
Stephen W. Rakich	T	476
Kenneth W. Ramirez	T	49

1973 cont.

Clayton M. Richardson	T	308
Douglas B. Rigby	E	221
Rod R. Riggen	T	233
David L. Robinson	T	488
Steve A. Rockhold	T	566
Robert P. Ross	T	233
James B. Rowe	T	365
Holland P. Rumph	T	582
Paul V. Sahakian	T	146
Thomas R. Sahakian	T	146
James S. Salisbury	T	144
Robert S. Sanders	E	51
Steve K. Sanders	E	51
James M. Scalet	T	488
Bruce A. Schmid	T	497
Robert A. Schmid	T	207
Steven G. Schmid	T	207
Robert B. Schott	T	440
Richard W. Scott	E	481
Steve S. Self	T	261
David Shearer	T	341
Brent A. Smith	T	498
Ronald C. Smith	T	286
Stephen R. Smith	T	470
Paul J. Spain	T	294
Daniel L. Sprague	T	470
John B. StClair	T	343
David E. Sturrock	T	308
Enock C. Taylor	T	230
John H. Taylor	T	230
John N. Thompson	T	375
William H. Thompson	T	375
Mark Treuhaft	E	456
Christopher E. Trevisan	T	476
Craig R. Uhler	T	130
Steven J. Vallett	T	563
Roy M. Vandoorn	T	488
Gerry B. Wallace	T	480
Michael P. White	T	293
Jeffery A. Wilkinson	T	470
John T. Wilkinson	E	573
Dean E. Williams	T	497
David R. Wilson	T	373
David M. Woodland	T	430
Michael J. Yamanaka	T	434
Michael A. Zarcone	E	43
Richard J. Zike	T	233

1974

David R. Akers	T	363
Christian M. Alexander	T	456
Karl S. Anderson	E	430
Mark J. Anderson	T	478
Roy Armstrong	T	106
Geralo F. Avery	T	346
James P. Bakke	T	406
Steven C. Barclay	T	456
Alan R. Bell	E	312
Michael G. Bennett	T	146
Blane E. Bergson	T	144
Mike J. Betz	T	433
Timothy J. Bigger	T	164
Michael Binkle	T	294
Gregory N. Bitter	T	430
Michael D. Black	E	254
Robert E. Blair	T	443
DeLyle W. Bloomquist	E	123
Phil J. Borgia	T	481
John C. Brewer	T	323
Kevin G. Bryan	T	315
Peter E. Bultman	T	385
Kevin G. Buttle	E	306
Kirk L. Buttle	T	305
Thomas L. Carlson	T	434
Paul Narr Carrier	T	305
Scott E. Cheim	T	139

Patrick D. Clemes	T	430
Paul W. Clenney	E	362
Michael D. Collins	E	212
Patrick D. Collins	E	212
Roger H. Cummings	T	139
Michael P. Dallas	T	139
Keith Davis	E	456
Robert B. DeLaGrange	T	139
Michael J. Delaney	E	191
Brian K. Deller	T	145
James T. Dopp	T	343
Norman O. Doyle	E	456
Spencer K. Dunn	E	456
Larry B. Edwards	E	573
Jimmy D. Eliot	T	74
Robert F. Fair	T	456
Mark C. Falcone	T	343
Douglas R. Finch	T	470
Erik E. Frerking	T	480
Ted S. Gagne'	T	566
Melchor B. Gascon	T	165
Leo A. Geis	T	104
Steven M. Gemar	T	792
Stuart C. Gemar	T	792
Richard K. Giroux	T	44
Brian L. Goetz	T	456
Mitchell Gohnert	T	263
Steven J. Gracie	T	222
Steven A. Greenacre	T	264
Michael J. Groves	E	327
Lester A. Gudger	T	433
Steven W. Gutke	T	404
William C. Hansen	T	130
Robert D. Harker	T	290
Mitchell C. Hart	T	165
David W. Heidmous	T	41
William D. Henderson	T	497
Matthew T. Hendrickson	T	320
Edward T. Hendrix	T	268
John P. Hinot	T	499
David J. Hohmann	T	436
Robert P. Hohmann	T	436
Randall E. Hold	T	535
Robert L. Holler	T	268
Michael J. Holstrom	E	221
Carl A. Horton	T	305
Michael H. Hover	T	148
Dino Imondi	T	77
Paul L. Isaacson	T	305
Scott C. Jankins	T	434
Bryan J. Jarvis	T	443
Alain H. Jensen	E	525
Thomas C. Johnson	T	260
Dana Scott Karren	T	456
John A. Kelly	T	230
Rod D. Kendrick	T	363
Jim K. Kenny	T	444
Paul D. Keswick	T	434
Jeffrey S. Kneisl	T	434
William R. Kraus	T	363
Theodore W. Kraynick	T	341
Forest P. Kreiss	T	466
Gregory T. Kremer	T	466
Nick R. LaHerran	T	456
Steven R. Lambson	E	456
William B. Langhorne	T	92
Mark A. Larson	T	535
Raymond P. Lazetera	T	145
Eric B. Leavitt	E	312
Loren D. Lee	T	434
Shannon Leso	T	799
Lyle E. Liden	T	345
Robert D. Lincoln	T	480
Kerry C. Loewen	E	470
Ed J. Loughrey	T	145
Clark N. Lovelady	T	250
Glenn A. Lovelady	T	250

Jedd M. Manson	E	430
James C. Marquis	E	191
Craig Mayne	E	456
Jeffery L. McAllister	T	107
Patrick J. McDonald	E	616
John R. McGhie	T	470
Michael D. McGhie	E	471
Gilbert M. McGuinness	E	499
R. Lee McKenna	E	312
Wayne N. McMahon	T	489
Donald McNeil	E	456
Michael E. Mentink	T	412
Craig A. Merlic	T	508
Kent E. Merlic	T	508
Anthony L. Molinaro	T	165
Geoffrey M. Moore	T	14
Terry L. Moore	T	14
Larry E. Morgenthal	T	266
Gregg E. Morioka	T	409
Eric M. Morita	T	611
Craig S. Moriyama	T	210
Joseph T. Mullens	T	286
Lee J. Myrick	T	320
Ron A. Nakano	T	611
Craig D. Nicolai	T	436
David Norris	T	120
Bill A. Northend	T	318
Bret W. Nyrick	T	320
Joseph C. Olsen, II	T	443
William K. Orr	T	323
James H. Overstreet	T	210
Michael K. Palmer	T	212
Jim J. Palmieri	T	41
Robert S. Pearson	E	470
Steven M. Petersen	T	536
Donald L. Pfluger	T	466
Brent N. Pingrey	T	508
Daniel M. Popylisen	T	566
Les G. Praisewater	T	233
Stuart W. Preston	T	363
Henry S. Price	E	254
Joseph A. Ramirez	T	478
David L. Ranck	T	497
Gerry H. Reynolds	E	434
John R. Reynolds	T	394
Tracy W. Riggs	T	41
Del A. Rio	T	146
Walter W. Ritt, III	T	510
Frederick A. Roberts	T	172
Duane M. Robson	T	374
Ronald S. Rosetta	T	346
Louis J. Royer	T	444
Reed A. Russell	E	573
Mark W. Sakamoto	T	611
David B. Schofield	T	407
William L. Schultz	T	103
Michael J. Score	T	325
David E. Seegmiller	E	314
Mark D. Shattuck	E	261
Mark O. Sheldon	T	254
David A. Smith	T	363
Guy E. Smith	E	312
Douglas E. Stevens	E	254
Robert W. Stevenson	E	304
Timothy K. Stiehr	T	606
James R. Stutz	E	563
Thomas Szabo	T	406
Frank J. Thompson	T	41
David M. Tilbury	T	78
David E. True	T	293
Neil Trueheart	E	456
John S. Unruh	T	295
John R. Vallett	E	563
Gregory H. Warnock	T	470
Kenneth V. Watkins	T	433
William J. Weaver	T	212
Steven Todd Weybrew	T	373

1974 cont.

Tracy G. Williams	T	444
Edward L. Wilson	T	99
Wayne P. Wilson	E	221
Loren P. Witherell	T	395
Glen Woods	E	314
Chris K. Yamashita	T	611

1975

Jerry B. Alden	E	13
Devon T. Anderson	E	194
Rickey A. Ando	T	611
David M. Artega	T	434
James W. Atherton	T	164
Michael G. Atkins	E	537
Mitchell C. Bandaza	T	260
Frederick C. Beall	T	262
John R. Beall	T	262
Scott B. Berglund	T	290
Bruce A. Bimber	T	373
Douglas A. Bloom	T	500
Dean W. Brennan	T	14
Ray Brooksby	E	457
David L. Burnham	E	537
Douglas V. Burnham	T	536
Brian P. Busalacchi	T	130
Jonathan R. Byrne	T	535
Ronald D. Capp	T	365
Norman O. Carpenter	T	12
Boyd L. Casselman	T	230
Frederick J. Christen	T	2
Michael A. Ciaffredo	T	77
Robert M. Clark	T	470
James R. Corridan	T	361
Mark J. Crowther	E	573
David R. Cutler	E	267
Gary Davis	T	456
Robert Davis, Jr.	E	222
Mark L. Dudley	E	456
Irwin R. Endelman	T	566
Allan Erbes	T	478
Brian S. Evans	E	573
Michael J. Fealy	T	466
John Brian Fitzgerald	T	488
Jeff Frost	T	250
Jonathan W. Fung	T	408
Gregory Hall	T	325
Paul J. Harvey	T	478
Lani J. Hatch	E	321
Mark A. Havens	T	374
Timothy J. Hawkins	T	268
Merel A. Heggelund, Jr.	T	12
Thomas E. Hoff		
Brian Hold	T	535
Carl Honore	T	49
Werner R. Howald	T	404
Jon E. Huber	T	563
Kenneth W. Humphries	T	339
Michael D. Jacobson	T	535
Jeffrey R. Judd	E	456
Douglas W. Kepler	T	375
Troy Kirk	T	500
Bradley W. Kurtz	T	49
Robert P. Leonardis	T	408
Jeffrey E. Lichtenstein	T	14
Daniel R. Lindsey	T	374
Rick S. Link	E	619
Jay E. Marler		
Steven R. Marquis	E	191
Chad A. Mayne	T	456
Emile A. Mestressat	T	346
Jimmie R. Mosley, III	T	112
Jeff Mullens	T	286
Todd T. Nakano	T	611
David Navarro	T	208
Richard W. Norris, Jr.	T	146

Greg Orzel	T	76
Phillip A. Parrish	T	799
David J. Peachey	T	470
Neil R. Picha	T	478
Raymond J. Renati	T	433
Steven W. Score	T	325
Kenneth E. Shaw	E	456
James D. Smith	T	250
Thomas E. Smith	T	621
Jay J. Sturges	T	172
Steven D. Stutz, Jr.	T	563
Martin R. Sweet	T	340
Thomas S. Templeman	T	293
David W. Thompson	T	254
Thomas E. Vancleave	T	262
Jeff M. Welliver	T	227
J. R. Wheelwright	E	267
Jonathan C. Wong	T	500
Colin C. Woods	T	312
Brian A. Yorke	T	488
Peter Yuen	T	501

1976

Mark Abrams	T	616
Jeremy K. Adamson	T	254
Michel B. Alberry	T	535
Jeff W. Alden	E	13
Lewis J. Alvernas	T	433
Richard F. Alyanak	T	497
Bradley C. Anderson	T	254
Clavell T. Anderson	E	194
Douglas D. Andrey	T	408
Alex N. Argo	T	74
Phillip J. Armstrong	T	535
Robert L. Avey	T	600
Robert D. Bates	T	339
Stephen L. Beveridge	T	564
Gary J. Blair	T	374
Borje Boklund, III	T	361
Roger K. Boucher	T	443
Kevin T.C. Bradshaw	T	211
R. S. Brock	T	206
Glen W. Brooksby	E	456
Mark Edward Cahn	T	260
Daniel Dennis Carter	T	305
Michael William Casey	T	710
Michael A. Cawood	T	447
Daryl A. Cheim		
Karl E. Christen	T	2
Gregory W. Clayton	T	227
Bradley S. Cobb	T	564
Robert Lawrene Comstock	T	293
Danny L. Connolly	T	616
Jerry L. Crosby, Jr.	T	290
Brian K. Dalley	T	326
Kenneth G. Danielson	E	457
Gary R. Davis	T	456
Tracy R. Davis	T	434
Thomas R. Dennis	T	145
Michael A. Dillon	T	549
Ronald L. Dotson	T	443
Scott P. Dunstan	T	339
James L. Eggleston	T	206
Steven L. Ellisworth	T	130
Leland T. Folsom	T	363
Leno N. Franco	T	191
Paul D. Fulhorst	T	14
James L. Fuller, Jr.	T	510
William Glen Gibbons	T	255
Jeffrey A. Gilmer	T	172
Jess A. Graham	T	112
William C. Guest	E	123
Robert N. Hamilton	T	41
Stephen G. Hansard	T	373
Kirk D. Harline	E	431
David J. Hart	T	14
Tony Hartinger	T	535

Scott G. Hartmann	T	307
William D. Hatch	T	406
Jeffery Ed Hayden	T	104
Bruce E. Haynes	T	535
Leonard C. Hayward	T	478
Robert G. Hepler	T	286
Howard A. Hodges	T	488
Kenneth B. Hoggan	E	707
William T. Hoggan	E	708
Peter W. Howald	T	404
Paul M. Howay	T	535
James S. Hunnewell	T	227
Reed T. Jacobs	E	431
Karl R. Jacobson	T	535
John Phillip Jenkins	T	526
William F. Johnson	T	233
Richard A. Jones	T	233
Ronald Martin Judd	T	326
David Kerr	T	478
James A. Kiessling	T	478
Todd D. Kingery	T	325
Darren M. Krommenhock	T1	10
Robert Lacey	T	330
Douglas Paul Lange	T	346
Jay P. Liggett	E	194
David A. Limberatos	T	470
John E. Limberatos	T	470
David Longaker	T	290
Robert C. Lowe, Jr.	T	497
Joseph P. Major	T	290
Rick I. Marimoto	T	345
Jeffrey A. Martin	T	255
Kenneth J. Masterenko	T	211
Scott D. McAllister	T	566
Scott G. McClellan	E	220
Donald McKenna	T	211
Michael S. McTighe	T	293
Brian S. Messenger	T	479
Timothy J. Moench	T	107
Kevin C. Monroe	T	294
Ron W. Morgan	T	363
Brent M. Morrow	E	281
Edwin H. Mortensen	T	107
David A. Nickson	T	307
Scott Norwood	T	549
William L. O'Brien	T	447
Ira B. Oldham	T	549
Paul E. Olson	T	385
Mark E. Pass	E	471
James Phillip Paulsen	T	107
Rob N. Pearman	T	566
Christen Pedersen	T	221
Burke B. Perry	T	253
James R. Pfluger	T	466
Rob W. Phillips	T	2
David R. Pickering	E	206
Harry Joseph Quimby	T	480
Kenneth A. Ragghanti	T	479
Fabian E. Ramirez	T	478
Drew R. Ramsay	T	165
Edward T. Ranck	T	497
Jeff P. Rehrig	T	107
Steve D. Reichwein	T	290
Kevin W. Reid	T	549
Harold E. Rhodes	T	312
Michael R. Rohwedder	T	221
David M. Roof	T	233
Bruce A. Ross	T	566
Michael H. Runyeon	T	508
David G. Russell	E	573
Ian M. Sandiland	T	377
Martin W. Sanner	T	363
Thomas C. Schmelzer	T	41
John E. Segale	T	254
Lance W. Servais	T	500
Thomas G. Sharp	T	44
Michael D. Slafter	T	361

1976 cont.

Tim P. Small	E	456
Jeffrey C. Smith	T	621
Gary R. Snell	T	294
Steven W. Snell	T	294
David C. Snider	T	294
David Snyder	T	456
Jeremy L. Speidel	T	210
James M. Staehs	T	294
Patrick Starr	T	13
Tom Steen, III	T	443
Frank R. Stewart	E	206
Kyle S. Stewart	E	470
Howard A. Stone	T	294
Peter R. Stone	T	294
Jay B. Thompson	T	254
Paul A. Thompson	T	374
David S. Tims	E	191
Matthew T. Vance	T	470
David W. VanOsdol	T	356
Christopher L. Walton	T	535
Michael P. Ward	T	466
Nick C. Weber	T	286
Gregory Scott West	T	321
John R. Wheeler	T	294
William E. Williamson	T	136
Gary A. Woffinden	E	562
Raymond Leslie Wolff	E	327
Michael B. Workman	E	13
Marke S. Wright	T	286
Donald M. Zinke	T	526

1977

Sandy H. Argabrite	T	462
Andy A. Arnes	E	451
Carlton J. Bailey	T	363
Paul A. Bakke	T	406
Brian E. Banner	T	321
Brent N. Barnes	T	172
John N. Baxter, III	T	104
Francis N. Beall	T	262
Kevin L. Beckstrand	E	304
Andrew N. Berney	T	799
Kenneth E. Blackburn	E	23
John F. Blanchard	T	233
Ed J. Booth	T	470
Joseph C. Bouchard	T	172
Russell C. Brent	T	240
Michael G. Brooks	T	510
Michael J. Brown	T	107
Kenneth S. Bryan	T	377
Richard A. Brynsvold	T	260
R. John Bull	E	470
Cory M. Burcham	T	130
Donald R. Burt	T	374
Henry P. Cate	T	221
Robert F. Cheim	T	139
Jeffrey V. Clemes	E	431
James D. Clinton	T	200
Matt S. Cogswell	T	456
George E. Comber	E	327
Arthur F. Coombs	E	470
Brian R. Corliss	T	262
Chris R. Cotterel	T	566
Jeffrey S. Criswell	T	260
Brian J. Crompton	T	290
Stephen M. Curulla	T	208
Harold S. DeMar	T	318
Thomas M. Dietrich	E	470
Stephen W. DiRito	T	466
Brian T. Donnelly	T	148
Michael J. Donnelly, Jr.	T	148
Patrick J. Donnelly	T	148
Chris Steven Dudley	T	456
Hyatt E. Dunn, Jr.	T	399
Scoww Andrew Dunn	T	107
Kevin Durst	T	434

Michael L. Evans	E	267
Dean L. Fortunati	T	373
Gregory L. Gilman	T	384
Russell R. Gilwee	T	433
Jay M. Giroux	E	44
Paul H. Grometer	T	374
Jeffrey D. Gunion	T	49
Robert A. Guth	T	290
Eric B. Hanlon	T	365
Charles K. Harvey	T	104
Frank E. Hawkins	E	303
James M. Healzer	T	221
Robert D. Hecocks	T	363
Robert F. Helms	T	294
Eric L. Henderson	T	44
Jonathan Mark Hoff	T	723
Vincent R. Hold	T	535
David Thomas Hollman	T	478
James Howell	T	434
Michael Howell	E	834
Mark W. Hubbard	E	834
Scott W. Isabell	T	312
Bradley D. Jensen	T	260
Peter I. Jepsen	T	339
Eric A. Johnson	T	233
Richard P. Johnson	T	743
Dennis L. Judd	E	537
David Allan Kenton	T	462
Glen A. Koutz	T	255
Mark A. Kurtz	T	330
Chris P. Lambson	E	457
Scott G. Larsen	T	236
Russell A. Ledwell	T	208
Brian A. Leete	T	221
Kevin C. Long	E	267
Richard B. Mackley	E	562
Clay P. Markley	E	194
Robert McCreight	T	330
Michael D. McKay	T	510
Chris Mousley	E	709
Steven Lynn Munyon	T	799
Paul T. Nakamoto	T	363
Mark R. Nall	T	2
Jay Todd Nilson	T	206
James A. Norris	T	172
Michael J. North	T	480
Paul M. Olsen	T	443
Robert Oxley	T	339
David G. Peck	T	488
Darryl S. Plumb	T	2
W. Scott Polland, III	T	466
Daniel Burton Pollard	T	500
Donald B. Prasek	T	463
Brian S. Prothero	E	537
Ronald David Prothero	T	537
James T. Quittner	T	267
Philip J. Rehkemper	T	373
Douglas M. Rodamer	T	266
David E. Ronco	T	172
Cary D. Schott	T	408
Craig D. Senzig	T	494
Robert K. Simonsen	E	537
Kenneth E. Slama	T	194
Kent S. Smith	E	573
Michael W. Smith	T	470
Tom E. Smith	T	480
Jeffrey L. Stolk	T	221
Robert T. Tobiason	T	500
Steve G. Townsend	T	478
John Eric Vogelgesang	T	501
Curtis D. Walton	E	220
Brian J. Ward	T	466
Criss R. Whalley	T	385
Dee J. Wheelwright	E	267
Robert L. White	T	408
Dan P. Wilkins	T	373
Donald A. Wilkinson	T	470

Roger L. Wise	T	363
Garth B. Woodland	T	321
Russell D. Woodmansee	T	227
L. Kenney Wright	T	330
Steven W. Young	T	610

1978

Brian A. Anderson	T	346
Richard Paul Anderson	T	456
Anthony T. Benevento	T	234
Ty N. Berry	T	218
Thomas L. Binford	T	470
David Bowman	E	222
Stephen Lincoln Brown	T	233
Cory Katsuki Butsuda	T	260
Robert M. Cahn	T	260
James V. Caines	T	211
Karl Marke Clinger	T	139
Michael L. Coombs	E	470
Craig Andrew Cornell	T	373
Douglas S. Crummey	T	375
Craig L. Dalley	E	326
Richard A. Davis	E	457
Frederick P. Dick	T	535
Darrin P. Donithorne	T	456
Douglas K. Dynes	T	564
Paul G. Farias	T	356
Robert E. Fish	T	463
Kenneth Lionial Fritz		
Lance M. Fung	T	408
Lawrence R. Gaffaney	T	260
Troy Val Garner	T	709
James Z. Gerlack	T	476
Gregg M. Giansiracusa	T	500
John W. Gill	T	535
John Joseph Gillio	T	218
David A. Goetz	E	451
Adam Ben Graham	T	112
Eric K. Gunther	T	447
Dale S. Haney	E	194
Mark Edward Hendrickson	T	320
Rololfo M. Hernandez	T	799
Matk G. Hilgart	T	385
Curtis B. Hoffman	E	471
Paul A. Hoffman	T	470
Mark A. Houde	T	566
Bret J. Hydorn	T	260
Scott A. Issacson	E	305
Jeffrey S. Jepsen	T	339
Michael D. Johnson	T	498
Greg A. Jones	T	539
Kurt Austin Jones	T	294
Nathan Elwin Lambert	T	408
Tharan Gregory Lanier	T	373
Ken J. Leetham	E	23
Keith G. Leong	T	462
Robert H. Lewis	E	305
Brian D. Lichtenstein	T	14
David D. Low	T	401
Terry J. Martin	T	505
Brian P. Mauldwin	T	234
Stephen V. Muller	T	377
Keith Erwin Murphy	T	476
Thomas A. Naylor	E	621
Curtis P. Nelson	E	326
Joel E. Nishida	T	233
Douglas M. Nordin	E	430
Gregory P. Nordin	E	431
Jeffrey R. Nordin	E	431
Eric A. Parnell	T	519
Joel W. Paulsen	T	107
Mark H. Peterson	E	303
David W. Pfluger	T'	466
Todd L. Quick	T	145
Kevin P. Remus	T	325
Ronald J. Renati	T	433
Christopher Nichols Rokas	T	262

1978 cont.

Name		
Duane J. Rothacher	T	172
Stephen Paul Russell	T	441
Terry K. Rutledge	T	114
Tim L. Sahagun	T	497
Dale R. Sahr	E	267
Craig J. Salmond	E	562
Scott F. Schilling	T	709
John E. Schuster	T	267
David C. Scott	T	478
Cameron W. Seitz	T	478
David A. Senzig	T	494
Bryan K. Shaw	E	457
Charles T. Shepperd	T	535
Timothy M. Sheridon	T	535
Benjamin A. Smith	T	148
Dana C. Smith	E	562
Derek E. Smith	T	709
David D. States	T	536
Douglas Andrew Stevens	T	426
Robert W. Stillwagon	T	365
Mark Hamilton Sutton	T	478
Charles Jeffrey Swanner	T	92
Robert B. Taylor	T	290
Loyd B. Treuhaft	E	457
Stevn H. Tyler	T	227
John T. VanArk	T	403
Mark A. Warren	T	408
Arthur R. Webb	T	208
Richard H. Webb	T	208
Christopher W. White	T	539
David L. White	E	123
Frederick A. Whitman	T	164
Jeffrey D. Williams	T	325
Jeffrey B. Wykoff	T	365
Eirc P. Zeitvogel	T	41

1979

Name		
Keith B. Almann	T	577
Doug W. Baer		
Marvin A. Bamburg	T	260
Michael W. Barbour	E	221
Christer J. Batchelor	E	305
Jeffrey C. Beckstrand	E	305
Kurt W. Berger	T	266
Mark S. Berkeland	T	373
Michael John Berryhill	T	92
Anson J. Call	T	255
William Arthur Callen, III	T	476
David M. Christensen	E	620
Kenneth Bryden Craib	T	340
Steven D. Crane	T	536
Bruce A. Cronquist	T	211
Gerald R. Curro	E	616
Eric Kenneth Dahlin	E	536
Ronald E. Davis	E	430
Kevin M. Dillon	T	549
Mark P. Duffy	T	535
Curtis D. Dunn	T	434
Todd J. Egan	T	233
Jay Matthew Eves	T	236
Douglas Scott Ewert	T	290
Douglas W. Franklin	T	74
Allen R. Frische	E	499
Nathan B. Furgeson	E	221
Robert M. Gaede	E	305
David P. Garner	T	706
Richard Dale Getz	T	799
Thomas D. Gilbert	T	107
Kevin J. Gray	T	535
Greg H. Gubler	T	536
Hugh D. Harline	E	431
Scott L. Harline	E	431
Peter A. Harthun	E	537
Gary L. Hawkins	E	305
Michael S. Heare	E	707
Glenn A. Hebel	T	421

Name		
Edward D. Hegstrom	E	537
Scott W. Helmers	T	566
Mark E. Huber	T	563
Jeffery F. Hughes	E	322
James W. Hulme	E	563
Lance A. Hulsey	T	510
Scott R. Hutchings	E	563
Eliot W. Jacobsen	E	563
John Gene Jelesko	T	260
Richard S. Johnson	T	365
Brian C. Judd	E	305
Randolph I. Judd	T	536
William L. Keck	T	535
Robert R. Lameira	T	262
Ronald P. Lameira	T	262
Jonathan R. Lance	E	707
Steven Larson	T	266
William S. Lewis	T	494
Lance Joseph Longaker	T	290
John R. Lyle	T	799
Robert C. Lyle	T	535
Russell V. Markus	T	233
Robin E. Martherus	T	441
Bryan L. Masters	T	434
John Henry Masters	T	505
Kevin E. Mayne	E	456
Shaun Patrick McCabe	T	304
Douglas M. McCroskey	T	233
Brian S. McMullin	T	536
Thomas J. Menard	T	505
Perry K. Merrill	E	305
David Ehly Miller	T	535
Stanley Mo	T	479
Tony A. Mohasci	T	51
Jeffery James Molno	T	112
George J. Moore, Jr.	T	260
William G. Murphy	T	476
Trevor Stanley Ngai	T	447
Sean L. O'Gwin	E	305
Kevin George O'Hara	T	148
Michael Jeffrey Ohlfs	T	535
Leo M. O'Neill	T	41
James F. Parker	E	563
Robert J. Pauley	T	260
David L. Pels	T	233
Daniel J. Pesta	T	212
Douglas Lee Peters	T	295
Bruce D. Piercy	E	305
Thomas J. Prout	T	494
Douglas E. Rittenhouse	T	51
Andrew E. Roberts	T	508
Steven R. Roof	T	233
Duncan P. Sandiland	T	377
Jerreld H. Schilling	E	470
Eric J. Shank	T	234
Kevyn Keith Smeltzer	E	305
Steven E. Smiley	E	709
James N. Smith	T	363
Michael F. Smith	T	535
Patrick D. Smith	T	535
Steven S. Switzer	T	447
Kirk H. Tamura	T	466
David R. Tanner	E	121
Daniel P. Ward	T	466
Dennis H. Watts	T	535
Matthew A. Weingart	T	363
Kenneth Michael Wood	E	237
Greg D. Wootton	T	708
David A. Wright	T	539
John O. Wright	T	330
Steven R. Wright	E	305

1980

Name		
William Scott Allen	T	488
David E. Anderson	T	280
George R. Apgar	T	711
Thomas G. Atkins	T	479

Name		
John S. Bakke	T	466
Brian Baumann	T	13
Michael R. Bench	T	192
Arthur E. Berg	E	230
Gus Bergsma	T	562
David E. Beverly	T	539
William Thomas Boothe	T	564
Russell S. Bowman	T	267
Stephen P. Byrne	T	535
David R. Carter	T	305
Daniel Marten Case	T	263
Vincent Aron Cate	E	221
Gregory Errol Chamitoff	T	325
Brian L. Colley	T	148
Jeffrey Stuart Crane	T	443
David J. DiRito	T	466
Peter S. Donnelly	T	148
Christian R. Dorst	E	563
John N. Douthit, Jr.	E	325
James Patrick Dowd	T	566
David A. Dumo	T	148
Michael J. Dyer	T	466
Michael E. Eng	T	479
Ronald C. Felder	T	406
David S. Ferrell	E	563
Kim L. Fortunati	T	266
Daniel T. Franklin	T	74
Thomas F. Goodwin	T	373
Gary D. Gubler	T	536
David R. Hall	E	471
Michael L. Hannah	E	545
Randal P. Hannah	E	836
Kendall S. Hansen	E	320
Mark H. Harrington	T	466
Richard A. Hart	T	14
David P. Hawranek	T	535
Ramon M. Hernandez	T	799
Eric Charles Heuck	T	307
Kevin L. Hing	T	407
James R. Hoggan	T	708
Gregory Alan Holmes	T	375
David C. Holt	E	121
Thomas W. Hughes	T	463
Clark A. Izu	T	172
Gregory Michael Jameson	T	123
Steen W. Jensen	T	375
Kurt L. Johnson	T	227
Mark J. Jorgensen	E	471
Arthur L. Jue	T	206
Gary T. Kanazawa	T	290
Scott R. Kirsch	T	295
Michael Walter Koop	T	408
Johann F. H. Krieger	T	264
Thomas P. Lackovic	T	564
Jared E. Lambert	T	536
Gregory P. Lamy	T	407
Christopher J. Lanier	T	373
Eric J. Linebarger	T	280
Gerald S. Litzelman	T	476
John C. Lundell	T	206
Russell A. Lundell	E	206
Henry R. Mahler	T	463
David L. Mariant	T	49
Richard A. Markus	T	233
David Lamar Martin	T	263
Michael Keith Mayes	E	151
George Robert McCarthy	T	208
Mark B. McKinzie	T	290
Patrick A. McTighe	T	211
Alan J. Minker	T	535
Andrew W. Minker	T	535
Robert L. Moya	T	233
Mark Douglas Newton	T	463
David C. North	T	480
Robert M. Nunes	T	505
Joseph R. Orrock	E	706
Scot R. Parks	T	488

1980 cont.

John Dewey Phillips	T	346
Wilbur R. Pierce	T	14
John J. Popylisen	T	566
Darryl L. Prince	E	191
Edward A. Pursley	T	290
David A. Rittenhouse	T	260
Paul C. Rokes	T	566
Mark E. Rose	T	488
Regis S. Rosetta	T	218
Adam J. Santos	T	330
Robert A. Schubert	T	211
Kirtis B. Shank	T	234
Brian A. Smith	T	41
Gerald D. Smith	T	363
Mark W. Smith	T	172
Michael J. Smith	T	480
Rand C. Smith	T	237
Russell K. Smith	T	621
Scott D. Smith	E	563
David M. Steele	T	407
Bret P. Stewart	T	441
Lee Fontela Story	T	549
Michael A. Story	E	537
John L. Sweet	E	508
Gregory Michael Thevenin	E	221
Scott William Thompson	T	294
Richard T. White	T	11
Matthew Merwin Williams	T	463
Todd L. Woffinden	E	562
James S. Wright	T	280

1981

David W. Andersen	T	148
Ted G. Arken	T	463
Samuel W. Asbury	T	215
Evan S. Bass	T	564
Edward P. Bendix	T	488
John E. Berney	T	799
Douglas D. Bodily	E	213
William B. Bonning	T	498
Michael W. Brown	E	563
Theodore L. Brown	T	566
Scott S. Carter	T	305
John R. Cerrato	T	148
John A. Chiorini	T	463
Doug L. Colby	T	447
Douglas Steven Cooper	E	470
Herbert F. Crane	T	443
Carl A. Dahlin	E	537
Ronald C. Darby	T	777
Raymond E. Debs	T	408
John D. Dillon	T	549
William Scott Edson	T	535
David L. Elggren	T	305
Thomas C. Ewert	T	290
Daniel B. Faulk	T	737
Joseph J. Ferranti	T	262
Brandt A. Foreman	T	211
Steven V. Gaffaney	T	260
Richard S. Gardner	E	121
Eric L. Goodrich	T	799
Darin P. Graves	T	267
John S. Griffin	T	375
Robert J. Gross	T	41
Philip T. Gruver	T	406
Howard H. Hall	T	233
William D. Hallahan	T	290
Roy D. Harline	E	430
Gregory E. Harrington	T	466
Steven L. Hayes	E	836
Scott L. Head	E	221
William M. Hoffman	E	47
Patrick S. Hoggan	T	708
Barton L. Hughes	E	238
Howard M. Itow	T	611
Christopher E. Jacobson	T	535

Damon V. Janis	T	706
Stanley C. Jones	T	463
Robert T. Kawashimi	T	611
Peter R. Keswick	T	434
Richard Kropp	T	295
Ronald D. Laflin	T	505
Daniel R. Larson	T	535
Michael L. Lawrence	T	404
Ronald F. Leedy	T	266
Paul A. Legasa	T	363
Steven W. Lowe	T	213
William A. Lowrey	E	238
David S. Lusvardi	E	221
James W. Lyon	T	564
Brian K. Maguire	T	476
Michael P. Maguire	T	476
Bruce A. May	T	49
Joseph F. Mayer	T	564
Bryan Patrick McCarthy	E	151
Douglas J. McGhee	T	711
Douglas McGill	T	463
Mark L. Meteer	E	563
Corbin K. Moots	T	266
Donald J. Morrison	T	237
Allen L. Morrow	T	255
Craig P. Mortensen	T	478
Eric L. Mortensen	T	478
Keith L. Mortensen	T	478
John M. Murai	T	566
Kenneth H. Murdock	T	479
Ronald R. Murphy	T	237
Jeffrey S. Nigra	T	208
Mark T. Norman	T	401
David T. Okamura	T	479
James R. Ramos	T	13
Sameer S. Rao	T	227
Daniel J. Reilley	T	441
Jeffrey Scott Richter	T	347
Gary K. Roberts	T	549
Douglas C. Rodenberger	T	294
Steven J. Roy	T	406
Jeffrey S. Savage	E	238
Brian A. Sechini	T	375
Michael Shearin	T	395
Edward A. Skidmore	T	488
Bryn T. Smeltzer	T	305
Gary C. Smith	T	294
Kenneth D. Smith	E	326
Thomas D. Stolk	T	221
David J. Story	T	549
Thomas K. Tilmant	T	41
Mark M. Urata	T	611
Allen J. Viarengo	T	792
Jeffrey D. Warner	T	148
Richard S. Weyland	T	799
Timothy P. Weyland	T	799
Michael D. Williams	T	51
William H. Winter, Jr.	T	330
Andrew J. Worth	T	325
Michael W. Yamate	T	611

1982

Michael J. Adamski	T	377
Daniel B. Alder	T	51
Peter J. Allen	T	488
David C. Allison	T	267
Peter S. Armstrong	T	799
Howard M. Baca	T	227
David R. Barlow	T	192
Darcy L. Bazzill	T	377
Jeffrey Hale Beckman	T	508
Paul M. Berg	T	777
Richard C. Bosley	T	295
Kenneth A. Bower	T	479
Allen B. Brockbank	T	777
Krit J. Buchmiller	T	280
Donald R. Call, Jr.	T	563

Jeffrey Chandler	T	747
Ri Pen Chou	T	466
Theodore E. Christensen	T	777
Evan D. Clayton	T	237
David R. Cloutier	T	463
John J. Cook	T	262
Robert A. Craig	T	363
Scott M. Cutler	T	709
Peter K. Dahlin	T	526
William A. Dawson	T	48
Albert T. Dayes	T	237
Gregory R. deVries	T	446
Stuart G. Donaldson	T	488
Daniel E. Donnelly	T	148
Lloyd Raymond Foster	T	112
Timothy J. Gaffaney	T	260
Gary J. Garay	T	215
Ronald B. Gardner	E	562
Christopher D. Greenwood	E	221
Jerry T. Hale	T	121
Terry T. Hale	T	121
William D. Hallahan	T	290
David A. Hamm	T	363
Stephen Henson	T	51
Mark G. Heron	T	799
Philip F. Hickenbottom	T	447
David R. Hill	T	526
Howard Fremont Hold	T	535
Dave A. Holmstrom	T	221
Jeffrey Marc Howlett	T	706
Bryan S. Hull	T	535
Alfred J. Hurt	T	535
Bradley Clark Jenkins	T	562
Scott D. Jensen	T	260
Gary D. Jungels	T	240
Eric Kendall	T	430
Michael A. King	T	488
Brian D. Leeper	T	233
Dennis Low	T	401
Jim Lyon	T	564
Kevin S. Marken	T	447
Bryan Y. Matsumoto	T	611
Christopher T. McCall	T	498
Thomas Anthony McCarley	T	539
Dudley E. McFadden	T	463
Kenn R. McFate	T	747
Craig E. Miller	T	535
Curtis K. Miyahara	T	611
Gary E. Morain	E	221
Geoffrey M. Morgan	T	799
Anthony D. Mosley	T	107
Mark Mushet	T	539
Robert I. Nakamura	T	611
Marco Y. Nakashima	T	478
Gregory H. Neher	T	441
Michael D. Nelson	T	711
Eric A. Nicolai	T	447
Timothy O'Brien	T	447
Shawn Michael O'Neill	T	621
Steve J. Orrock	T	706
James R. Perrault	T	305
Boyd G. Pett	T	236
Stephen J. Poulsen	T	206
David A. Pritchett	T	49
David R. Prolo	T	255
Darrell D. Provasek	T	377
John N. Roberts	T	549
Ty D. Rogers	T	211
Vincent Keahi Sa	T	51
Douglas W. Salmond	E	537
Ian K. Sandland	T	708
Jerry Santos	T	330
Mark T. Schreiber	T	633
Christopher M. Seniw	T	215
Vernon T. Sera	T	479
Richard A. Shepperd	T	535
Christopher D. Silva	T	139

1982 cont.

Michael F. Smith	T	535
Michael Scott Smith	T	172
William Mark Snow	T	227
Bruce E. Sommer	T	260
David B. Sommer	T	260
Scott A. Sommer	T	260
Paul E. Straubel	T	466
Russell R. Stringham	T	267
Billy Allen Taylor, Jr.	T	633
Donald S. Taylor	T	290
Joseph C. Taynai	T	401
Kyle D. Thomas	T	470
Brian D. Tsang	T	535
Larry G. Vallandigham	T	577
Lee C. Vassar	T	213
William C. Walters	T	219
Timothy F. Ward	T	466
Cecil Eric Webb	T	441
Robert E. Webb, Jr.	T	479
John R. Williams	T	172
Brian Wilson	T	255
Mitchell C. Wilson	T	221
Brent Lee Woffinden	T	562
Karl G. Wright	T	330
Ivan G. Yount	T	478

1983

William S. Adams	T	240
Neil C. Andersen	T	148
Matthew D. Bennett	T	124
Mark E. Bischoff	T	121
Tim W. Boothe	T	564
Thomas D. Bridenbaugh	T	295
George W. Brown	T	41
William A. Brown	T	280
Erik Buchmiller	T	280
Craig Burger	T	407
Brian B. Casby	T	339
Christopher Castillo	T	555
Richard Cawood	T	447
Arthur J. Chavez	T	434
Lonnie D. Chrisman	T	74
Matthew A. Cochran	T	633
Wayne L. Conley	T	212
Donald V. Cory	T	286
Jeffrey Dean Cosby	T	294
Douglas P. Cotton	T	212
Gregory W. Dalcher	T	510
Tracy R. Day	T	708
Robbie J. Dean	T	457
Lane P. Delano	T	498
Manuel Diaz	T	539
David M. Dietrich	E	470
Daryl J. Discher	T	498
Richard J. Doughty	T	172
William S. Dunton	T	549
Thomas V. Egan	T	476
Michael J. Emerson	T	510
William S. Frye	T	526
Russell C. Gaede	T	304
Nathan B. Gay	T	577
Aaron Gilbert	T	737
Michael C. Glew	T	577
Peter B. Griffin	T	373
Larry D. Guenther	T	539
Scott W. Harrington		
Todd A. Hauber	T	430
John R. Hill	T	526
James A. Hoff	T	799
Jeffery B. Holland	T	457
James M. Hornung	T	577
Edward A. Horsfall	T	172
Michael G. Ingalls	T	74
Darryl K. Itow	T	611
Blair E. Janis	T	707
Murray E. Johns	T	261

Marvin T. Jones	T	463
Paul E. Lambert	T	536
Robert E. Larson	T	266
Jeff H. Lewis	T	505
Jeffrey C. Lin	T	41
Devin R. Lindsey	T	407
David S. Makler	T	212
James Mansfield	T	233
John D. McDowell	T	400
Richard E. Meinzer	T	562
Steven L. Mitchell	T	312
James R. Moncrieff	T	212
Todd A. Morimoto	T	208
David O. Neville	T	255
Vincent J. Newman	T	347
Richard L. Niemann	T	14
Ken A. Nishimura	T	476
Robert J. Oxoby	T	434
Scott J. Parsons	T	170
Parag Patel	T	215
Timothy J. Plaubardo	T	219
Mark Polland	T	466
Douglas R. Prince	T	191
Paul A. Raftery	T	294
Denis M. Rittenberg	T	488
Robert W. Roba	T	234
Todd S. Rosenbaum	T	494
David Rowen	T	555
Michael W. Sarino	T	470
Steven W. Sarino	T	470
Scott R. Saunders	T	373
Christopher T. Shank	T	234
Alan Dale Siegwarth	T	264
Scott F. Sipple	T	563
David R. Smearden	T	286
Carl C. Snyder	E	457
David A. Swager	T	170
Steven R. Thoebald	E	12
Kip D. Thomas	T	470
David W. Thompson	T	447
Steve R. Thompson	T	14
Kevin C. Thurber	T	290
Jeffrey T. Tilman	T	41
Troy N. Warner	T	148
Darin T. Warnke	E	51
Reid L. Waterer	T	41
Ryan F. Waterer	T	41
Douglas A. White	T	123
Steven A. Wisbar	T	234
Thomas M. Wood	T	264
Robert D. Wright	T	294
Michael K. Yasui	T	611
Joel R. Yoder	T	172
Stephen W. Young	T	708
David W. Zehner	T	339

1984

James M. Alexander	T	172
Troy Duane Allen	T	441
Mark Alan Atkinson	T	286
Ronald Baker, Jr.	T	213
Alan W. Banks	T	708
Pasquale Barberi	T	498
John C. Bates	T	172
Scott Beckstrand	T	777
Matthew D. Bennett	T	129
George Bertram	T	51
Steve D. Bessler	T	799
Robert D. Bos, II	T	164
James Bradshaw	E	706
Christopher Buchanan	E	457
Jeffrey C. Burrows	T	777
John D. Catalana	T	564
Kenneth H. Chamitoff	T	290
William L. Chavez	T	41
Mark Christman	T	466
Tim S. Clark	T	234

Scott B. Cohen	T	498
James Cooper	T	708
Christopher J. Cota	T	41
Jerrold E. Creed	T	266
Jeffrey A. Crettol	T	406
John Czerniec	T	219
Christian L. Darby	T	777
Timothy Domke	T	74
Charles R. Donlon	T	363
Jeffrey Dorst	E	563
Clark R. Eller	T	280
Kenneth Kim Elsey	T	267
Reed Farnsworth	T	222
Bryan Dieter Fisher	E	457
Robert Florsheim	T	14
Bryan R. Foote	T	777
Nathan C. Fuja	T	747
Andrew J. Getzoff	T	564
Alan K. Gilbert	T	737
Michael Francis Gordon	T	148
Scott Gordon	T	322
David Gorman	T	535
Jonathan Grauel	T	711
Lonny Grow	T	777
Steve M. Grow	T	777
Gregory N. Habiby	T	407
Todd D. Hale	E	121
Reed S. Hansen	T	470
David Harmon	T	252
Richard Hill	T	479
Justin Brian Horner	T	342
Gary Hulme	T	563
Kevin W. Ihrig	E	221
David Isaac Jenkins	T	562
Matthew D. Jensen	T	260
Eric A. Johnson	T	266
Christopher Dumont Kimmel	T	505
Stuart Kraemer	T	711
Shawn Lance	T	708
Brian M. Lanier	T	373
Gary B. LeBaron	T	305
David Li	T	172
Patrick Li	T	172
Sean A. Lokey	T	67
Mark Manchester	T	215
David M. Marquis	E	191
Daniel Martinelli	E	457
Roger L. Mathis	T	233
Robert Kelly McAllister	T	339
Andrew McFadden	T	463
Brian E. McKinney	T	148
Kevin Meeker	T	406
James W. Metzler	T	227
Kevin D. Miller	T	286
Iain L. Morgan	T	347
Bruce Morley	T	535
Scott Morley	T	535
Craig A. Mulliner	E	238
Scott Nicholas	T	325
Robert S. Nishimura	T	611
Steven R. Osborn	E	326
James N. Poole	T	498
Craig A. Porter	T	708
Michael K. Potter	T	260
Geoffrey Pridham	T	295
David Ramos	T	14
Galen W. Ramos	T	13
Keith C. Rauchle	T	290
John G. Reynolds	T	466
Jeffrey M. Roy		
Sean P. Ryall	T	264
Craig A. Savage	E	238
James E. Scott	T	621
Christopher Shelley	T	363
Matthew Sherman	T	164
Christopher A. Shirley	T	41
Christian M. Sloane	T	347

1984 cont.

Charlie Smurthwaite	T	708
Craig M. Spring	T	233
Ben T. Stafford	T	219
David Sweet	T	508
Stephen R. Theobald	E	123
Royal Jay Toney	T	264
Kyle B. Topham	E	457
Michael J. Varozza	T	508
Lowell N. Voelker	T	539
William Welder	T	711
Todd E. Wells	T	373
Michael Bruce Whyte	T	466
Claude Alan Wiley	T	233
Charles Wilkinson	T	799
John J. Winter	T	330
Kevin D. Wood	T	737
Jeff Workman	T	711
Kevin J. Yeaman	T	330
Scott H. Young	T	566
Alan F. Zeitvogel	T	41

1985

Paul Andersen	T	148
David Balingit	T	67
Robert Barlow	E	193
Daniel Bogard	T	74
Harold Bogard	T	74
Matthew Bowman	T	267
Bryan Braithwhaite	T	577
Rustin Brynsvold	T	260
Brett Buchmiller	V	254
David Call	T	563
Timothy Carney	T	549
Stephen Cawelti	T	260
John Chavez	T	41
Neil Christensen	E	193
Kevin Cloutier	T	463
James Cooper	E	708
Donald Cortes	T	107
Karl Day	T	212
Scott Evans	T	476
Robert Felder, Jr.	T	406
Kenneth Ferber	T	290
Brian Ferry	T	266
Andrew Fletcher	T	371
John Foote	T	777
Daniel Ford	T	253
Todd Fouyer	T	213
Todd Galbraith	T	747
William Genske	T	711
Christopher Gill	T	172
Robert Gordon	T	148
Brian Grove	T	290
Christopher Grove	T	466
Robert Hallahan	T	290
James Harris	T	290
Mark Holland	E	457
Yuji Honma	T	611
Kenneth Howlett	T	407
Richard Hudnut, Jr.	T	74
Matthew Hungerford	T	139
Michael Ivanitsky	T	290
Jerry Izu	T	191
Scott Jackson	T	710
Kent Jamison	V	191
Matthew Johnson	T	563
John Jorgensen	V	191
Jeffrey Keck	T	476
Stephen Kelley	T	260
David Keyes	T	400
Mark Kilpatrick	T	330
Jonathan Kissane	T	407
Wilhelm Klaus	T	14
John Launder	T	330
Eugene Lee	T	169
Matthew MaClean	E	122

Eduardo Madrigal	T	286
Daniel Malone, Jr.	T	212
Andrew Mangney	T	463
Neil Markus	T	233
Stuart Matis	T	441
Stephen May	V	563
Paul Mayes	T	395
Wallace McLaughlin	T	508
Stephen Melz	T	262
William Mikesell	T	577
Larry Mistretta	T	447
Robert Miyahara	T	611
John Nakamura	T	611
Eric Neher	T	441
Gregory Nishimura	T	611
Keith Okabe	T	611
Steven Okano	T	611
Peter Olson	T	434
Rick Opp	T	234
Hans Orup	T	562
Mark Osburn	E	326
David Ott	T	255
Eric Paulsen	T	107
Scott Payne	V	256
Michael Pesta	T	219
Mark Pettit	T	330
Mike Pettit	T	330
Robert Powers	T	107
Norman Prokey, Jr.	T	479
Richard Proulx	T	320
Jonathan Raines	T	206
Charles Reynolds	T	466
Jeffrey Rose	T	172
Lindsay Ross	T	777
Steven Schilling	V	709
Peter Schmidt	T	170
Kenneth Schott	T	407
Jacob Shapiro	T	320
Thomas Slater	T	371
Darren Smith	V	236
Sidney Smith	V	709
Bradley Stephenson	T	202
Paul Stringer	V	191
Michael Su	T	221
Scott Szymanski	T	488
William Taylor	V	236
Todd Wikstrom	T	221
David Wood	T	263
James Wood	T	202
Carl Woodall	T	710
James Worledge	T	294
Sean Youngquist	V	236

1986

Michael Agostino	T	577
Eugene Ahn	T	211
Darin Albers	T	262
Jed Anderson	T	237
Michael Baker	T	294
Christopher Barton	V	237
Tyler Barton	V	237
Robert Beard	T	342
Jonathan Bennett	T	192
Tom Berry	T	212
Richard Blanton	T	107
Jeffrey Bloom	T	294
Eric Bowman	E	267
Kenneth Brady, Jr.	T	290
Gregory Bronstein	T	466
Derek Brown	E	267
Stephen Bryant	T	363
James Carney, III	T	339
Anthony Castelli	T	466
Robert Champion	T	494
Lars Claassen	T	799
John Clark	T	339
Gregory Crawford	V	236

Trevor Darby	T	777
Robert DeGaston	T	290
Cary Delano	T	498
Lawrence Demoss	T	294
Michael Draeger	T	321
Luke Dunbar	T	202
Erik Edler	T	407
Matthew Empey	V	563
Andrew Forristel	T	408
James Fox	T	330
Keith Franke	T	264
Peter Fry	T	510
James Gonzales	T	479
John Gonzales	T	479
Paul Hagelin	T	535
Steve Halter	T	202
Steven Hamm	T	363
Timothy Hardesty	T	400
Brian Harr	T	363
Tim Hearl	T	577
Scott Henry	T	203
Todd Hern	T	443
Alex Hill	T	479
David Horton	T	305
David Howell	T	407
Stephen Huff	T	203
Jeffrey Hufferd	T	290
Brian Itow	T	611
Kevin Izu	T	191
David Jenks	T	192
Douglas Johnson	T	494
Michael Johnson	V	237
Richard Johnson	T	564
Jeffrey Jolley	T	191
Douglass Judd	T	466
Daniel Jue	T	206
Grant Kappen	T	564
Christopher Kearns	T	494
Chrisopher Kemp	T	305
Jeffrey Kingsley	E	708
Prescott Knock	T	479
Andrew Lange	T	466
Robert Lewis	T	407
Jose Licea	T	633
Corbin Lindsey	T	407
David Loewer	T	264
Matthew Lorenzen	T	566
Kirk Loveland	T	505
Morgan Lynch	V	261
Eric Madren	T	510
Michael Mahlke	T	633
Patrick Malone	T	212
Carl Stan Matsuo	T	264
David McFate	T	709
Mark Miller	T	211
Scott Morgan	V	236
Rodney Morris	E	221
Cameron Murphy	T	236
Robert Nellis	T	494
Ronald Nelson	T	711
Kevin Nichols	T	266
Kevin Nolt	T	215
John Ogawa	T	611
Kevin Olser	T	295
Phillip Orton	V	236
Regan Patrick	T	479
Frank Penninger, III	T	711
Jeffery Place	E	526
Steven Ricci	T	164
Kevin Rice	T	219
Bryce Rockwood	E	536
Eric Ronsheimer	T	264
Erich Rummel	T	407
Jeffery Salisbury	T	407
Joseph Salisbury, II	T	407
David Schneck	T	233
Michael Seden	T	498

1986 cont.

Name		
Joseph Smith	T	169
Russell Smith	T	563
Jason Sowards	E	221
Kenneth Striebel	T	535
Scott Sullinger	T	535
Sean Sullivan	T	330
Gregory Sweet	T	211
Mark Taylor	E	526
Bryan Temmermand	T	407
Trevor Thomas	T	488
Richard Titus	T	107
Jeffrey Tsang	T	535
Theodore Turner	T	447
Steven D. VonDohlen	T	371
Robert Watt	V	256
David Wetzel	T	577
Matthew Whitaker	E	536
William Wiley	T	233
Bryan Williams	T	447
Gregory Williams	E	263
Kenneth Williams	E	263
William Wilson	T	711
Robin Wise	T	730
Jesse Woodnal	T	169
Steven Workman	T	13
James Wright	T	330
Eric Yeaman	T	330
Matthew Young	T	363

1987

Name		
Tom Adams	T	240
Donald Andrews	T	371
Stephen Bachman	T	466
Brian Ballek	T	294
Frederick Barberi	T	498
Alan Bell	T	169
Brian Blake	V	221
Scott Bone	T	290
James Boss	T	363
Darren Bowman	V	563
Brian R. Bretz	T	577
David Brittain	T	535
Adam Bullard	V	123
Troy Bullard	V	123
David Carlson	T	508
Kenneth Carlson	T	479
Paul Carvajal	T	48
James Castle	T	240
Lawrence Chan	T	407
Mark Chance	E	206
Gregory Chase	T	290
Robert Cook	V	122
William Cooney	T	260
Doug Cortney	T	227
Jason Covington	T	488
Christian Dobo	T	407
Matthew Downs	V	253
Brian Durbin	T	730
Guy Elliott	T	535
Jeffrey Faerber	T	305
Felix Fan	T	466
Devon Ford	T	463
Edward Galetti	T	373
Andrew Garrett	T	537
John Gaushell	T	466
Samuel George	T	123
Richard Gohl	T	74
Arthur Gomez	T	266
David Grandey	T	577
Stephen Griefer	T	227
Jarett Grimmett	V	51
Curtis G. Gubler	E	537
Bruce Gutman	T	290
Edward Hale	V	709
Alan Hamilton	T	406
Jonathan Hannum	T	401
Jeffrey Harris	T	777
Robert Hartley	V	121
Michael Hatch	T	621
Scott Hedberg	T	406
Thor Hendrickson	T	320
James Hillstead	T	221
Tyler Hofheins	E	526
Douglas Holley	T	74
Michael Holt	T	463
Donald Huckins	T	41
Steven Hudnut	T	476
Paul Jang	T	219
Michael Jolley	T	227
Jeffrey Jones	T	164
Brett Jorgensen	E	470
Chris Kanazawa	T	406
Jed Kaplan	T	466
Reed Kappen	T	564
David Kay	T	203
Dave Koon	T	240
Ethan Kutzscher	T	363
Glen LaBarber	T	498
Hyrum Lambert	V	537
David Langhart	T	233
Nathan Lawrence	T	305
Huan Le	T	310
Julio Licea	T	633
Terrence Liu	T	227
Glenn Livezey	T	434
Eric Lorenzen	T	566
Michael Luft	T	48
Michael Luna	T	577
David Mantelli	T	508
Edward B. Markus	T	233
David Marshall	T	236
Peter Martin	T	74
Richard Matsuura	T	342
Ronald Matsuura	T	342
Devan McCoy	T	264
Jeremey McFadden	E	537
Troy McFadden	V	537
Keith McGrew	T	215
Gregory Merritt	T	203
Craig Miller	T	466
Thomas Moyer	T	730
Kevin Mullaney	T	510
Christopher Nucci	E	750
Jeff Orr	T	49
John Owens	T	564
Ravin Patel	T	262
Mark Pesta	T	219
Timothy Plattner	V	563
Robert Potter	T	347
Matthew Powers	T	577
Alex Pranger	T	799
Joseph Prokey	T	479
Vikram Purohit	T	498
John Raftery	T	294
Scott Ranstrom	T	41
James Reilly	T	476
Steven Robbins	V	256
Kenneth Rogers	T	342
Bob Rosenfeld	T	407
Greg Rowe	T	41
Kevin Rummel	T	407
John Saunders	T	535
Joey Sayers	T	799
Andrew Seidel	T	466
Jeffrey Shane	E	737
James Smith	E	253
Ronald Smith	T	327
John Starkweather	T	777
Grant Takamoto	T	611
Thomas Takashima	T	611
Scott Taylor	V	236
Richard Unger	T	317
William Walley	T	535
Terrill Wantz	T	564
Jason Wells	T	777
Adrian Weyers	T	621
Mark Weyland	T	799
Gregory Wheeler	T	706
Robert Wiley	T	233
Jason Wilkinson	V	526
Alan Williams	T	260
Michael Winter	T	330
Anthony Wiseman	T	260
Kurt Workman	T	711
Daniel Worledge	T	294
Jesse Wu	T	221
Greg Yap	T	501
Stephen Young	V	121
Joseph Zuccaro	T	566

1988

Name		
Scott D. Adrian	E	206
Robert J. Aguinaga	T	792
Douglas M. Alder	E	51
Brett A. Anderson	V	312
John J. Arena	T	41
Andrew D. Bagby	T	508
Shannon T. Bahr	T	13
Bartholomew J. Bailey	T	170
Jonathan S. Barron	T	505
Allen Barth	T	510
Edward D. Basanese	T	41
Byron L. Beck	T	260
Morgan E. Bepristis	T	330
Patrick T. Blue	T	494
Leroy J. Brady	E	526
Steve M. Brandenburg	T	566
Jeffrey L. Braunstein	T	400
Michael W. Brown	V	709
Paul B. Brust	T	260
Michael J. Calvin	T	170
Christopher P. Candee	T	107
Justin Cassell	V	191
Daniel C. Chamberlain	V	312
John J. Cherry	T	312
Michael Clifton	T	436
Anthony D. Contreras	T	74
John A. Crus	T	260
Jeremy W. Dang	T	318
Lloyd Danon	T	290
Andrew C. Dauber	T	539
David A. Deardorf	T	564
Marc C. Doland	T	219
Kevin K. Donahue	T	260
Marcel R. Dubois	T	730
Clifford C. Dunn	E	457
Scott B. Eastridge	V	321
Jack W. Eldredge	T	266
David Andrew Eliason	V	321
Mark D. Emerson	T	203
Matt H. Emerson	T	203
Brent Field	T	401
Brad Fleury	T	219
John M. Foley	T	501
Daniel W. Frederick	T	107
Matthew W. Gallegos	T	535
Dennis Gansen	T	787
David W. Graul	T	325
Christopher P. Gruhn	T	260
Wesley W. Hansard	T	373
David Aaron Hansen	V	321
Michael Hanson	T	777
David C. Hartley	E	121
Craig M. Hiraki	T	611
James V. Hoffman	T	707
Jeffrey L. Hofmann	T	501
David A. Hudnut	T	476
Craig A. Hungerford	T	139
David W. Hunter	T	221
Charles R. Ingebrigtsen	T	633

1988 cont.

Brian T. Itaya	T	611
Jason D. Iverson	T	260
Richard G. Jespersen	T	441
Derek J. Johnson	T	498
Paul Joseph	T	294
Gregory Kaiser	T	14
Kent W. Kappen	T	564
Michael O. Kawamoto	T	611
Christopher B. Ketelsen	T	498
Eric T. Kodak	T	434
Brian Jeffrey Kovanda	T	787
Jeffrey P. Kuhlman	T	234
Michael M. Lam	T	227
Joseph W. Landucci	T	289
David H. Lea	T	505
Douglas W. Leonard	T	13
Darren S. Love	V	237
Todd M. Madigan	T	260
Gary L. Malick	T	373
James Ray Marshall	V	236
Mitchell Kunio Matsunaga	T	611
Daniel McAllister	T	74
Matthew W. McClelland	T	562
Samuel A. Meteer	V	563
Jeffrey L. Milde	T	290
Eric S. Miller	T	436
Kevin D. Mitchell	V	312
Douglas T. Mo	T	479
Iam A. Montgomery	E	193
David E. Morishige	T	260
Matthew C. Mouritsen	T	441
Micgael J. Newman	T	347
Darrel N. Nichols	T	266
Michael W. Niemann	T	14
Steven Minoru Oda	T	611
Peter C. Olson	T	510
Erik S. Orup	E	562
George T. Orwiler	T	14
Jonathan D. Panepinto	T	223
Avkash Patel	T	13
David A. Petersen	T	400
James P. Plummer	T	434
Matthew C. Plummer	T	434
Richard C. Potter	T	434
Scott M. Randall	V	321
Scott Rands	E	206
David E. Reimers	T	290
Daniel F. Robba	T	234
Timothy B. Roberts	T	317
Vincent E. Robinson	T	267
David A. Rokes	T	566
Michael Root	T	110
Scott W. Ross	T	777
Brian J. Rouleau	T	149
Gregory W. Sass	T	122
Mike Schneidereit	T	318
Darin Shintani	T	611
Phillip D. Shumway	T	14
Kent A. Shurtleff	T	312
David R. Smith	E	526
Edward A. Sobie	T	262
James P. Soboleski	T	476
Nathan D. Souza	T	164
Peter Stenseth	T	260
Chad T. Steward	T	436
David Stromfeld	T	260
Michael M. Swertfager	T	325

Craig S. Tanikawa	T	611
Todd M. Teresi	T	501
Darren Tokushige	T	312
Andrew M. Turner	T	294
Veko J. Vahamaki	T	312
James Valderama	T	621
Eugene John Vicknair	T	286
James J. Wanlass	V	470
Brian Watson	V	470
Ryan A. Watt	T	256
Jason W. Webb	T	441
Jarred Wells	T	787
Mark L. Williams	T	325
Aaron C. Wishnuff	T	750
Dwight R. Wood	T	737
Charles M. Yerry	T	234
Steven E. York	T	388
Mark R. Yuen	T	400
David R. Zinn	E	563

1989

James E. Abenroth	T	170
Garrett K. Akahosni	T	611
Todd Alan Baumgartner	T	227
Troy M. Bergstrom	T	227
John Robert Boyd	T	373
James C. Bronson	T	294
Charles David Broz	T	149
Bret J. Burkhart	T	566
Daniel Durrant Call	T	563
Christopher J. Calvin	T	170
John Gordon Campbell	T	505
Donald R. Cathcart	T	234
Mark Frankln ChuLin	T	463
James P. Cicen	T	488
William D. Clapham	T	535
Andrew Collins	T	566
James L. Coombs	T	466
Jeffrey Dansie	E	121
Jefferson Rich Davis	V	267
Nathaniel Clinton Denig	T	373
Eric Scott DePriest	T	234
Frank Dias	T	240
James Bradley Dickson	T	441
Douglas E. Erickson	T	566
Gregory S. Francis	V	563
Richard Garcia	T	262
Ernest F. Geigenmiller	V	709
Adam Gilbert	E	737
Carlton Barr Greenwalt	T	212
Stephen Edward Grove	T	290
Matthew A. Guch	T	566
Daniel B. Gunyan	V	253
David John Haskin	T	206
Mark Thomas Hegland	T	407
Arthur Katsuyi Hiranara	T	611
Kendall B. Holt	V	267
Allan Stewart Hoyland	T	212
John Sungjin Jang	T	219
Richard S. Johns, III	E	267
Scott J. Jorgensen	T	470
Daniel Katz	T	466
Christopher M. Kay	T	363
Stephen S. Kelly	T	260
Christopher Kiessig	V	221
Anthony Robin Kilmer	T	400
Quinten Klingonsmith	V	253
Evan Koutz	T	255

Peter Lackovic	T	564
Matthew David Lanier	T	373
Scott Leeman	T	51
Troy Jon Lenger	T	219
Ryan James Loesch	T	708
Douglas R. Londgren	T	711
Aaron William MacDonald	T	430
Jeff W. Mansur	T	74
Christopher A. Marshall	T	264
Matthew C. Martin	T	363
Jeffrey Nathan McBride	T	710
Michael McConagny	T	363
Michael Charles Meyers	T	400
Clinton Moore	T	139
John Thomas Moore	T	212
Matthew Leon Morris	T	267
David M. Moyer	T	730
Lon Mullaney	T	510
Patrick Munnerlyn	T	466
Christopher M. Murphy	T	371
Christopher Byron Nakaishi	T	407
Derek Felix Nalewajko	E	750
Khoa Nhu Nguyen	T	310
Khuong Dang Nguyen	E	216
Mark Nishimura	T	611
Leif Erik Nordstrom	T	787
Stephen Parks	T	498
Andrew D. Penn	T	294
David A. Petersen	T	400
Kyle William Pickett	T	363
David S. Place	T	240
Jason Reed Powers	T	577
Jess B. Rabourn	T	260
Kevin Ramirez	T	149
Mike V. Reinschmidt	T	505
Edward A. Rieve	T	373
Eric Martin Roesch	T	48
Mike Rosenbaum	T	494
David Wayne Schuck	E	255
Jason William Smiley	T	312
Adam Bunta Smith	T	566
Dellon T. Smith	T	236
Kevin James Smith	T	263
David James Stenseth	T	260
Eric E. Stephens	E	305
John Dale Stewart	V	221
Alan Su	T	221
Jeffrey Kiyoshi Tanaka	T	611
Daniel Andrew Theopalo	E	193
Keith Thompson	T	170
Alan James Tidwell	V	237
Dean G. Tsai	T	508
Sharad Verma	T	463
Jerry James VonDohlen	T	371
Andrew A. Voss	T	290
Dylan Shea Wade	V	305
Bradley R. Watson	'T	74
William B. Whitehead	V	123
Barry G. Wilson	T	289
John C. Winkleman	T	436
Ryan Tyler Wong	T	264
Keith Patrick Wright	T	535
Ryan Wright	V	708
Wynn T. Yamami	T	611
Stuart Kenji Yamatake	T	494
John Alexander Young	E	194
Mark R. Yuen	T	400

13. *Silver Beaver/Silver Fawn Recipients*

(Reference Chapter V, Page 107)

1934
Andrew M. Mortensen
1935
John O. Hansen
John E. McDowell
1937
Irvin C. Copple
R. J. Jungermann
Dr. Dorsey A. Lyon
1939
Anthony Amori
Marcus J. Vertin
1940
Ernest A. Abbott, D.D.S.
Claude Smith
1943
Russell R. Crane, D.D.S.
Hon. Marshall S. Hall
1944
Milton P. Ryder
1947
Sewall S. Brown
Hon. William F. James
Forrest Owens
1948
H. H. Hallin
Richard G. Wells
1950
Fred Hilton
1952
Robert F. Benson
Stanley B. Ellis
Morris F. Kaplan
1955
Sen. Clark L. Bradley
Lyndon Farwell
Laurence Hill
August Ricard
1956
William S. Powell
Kenneth Robinson
Dennis Tedford
1957
Jack Harvey
Dr. Vinton S. Matthews
Charles Mitchell
1958
Russell G. Hoxsie
Dr. O. S. Hubbard
Leon Maus
1959
Victor Chernoff
Harold Sparry
Austen D. Warburton

1960
Fred Byl
Dr. John E. Cox
William J. Fuller
William Sutcliffe
1961
Harry B. Hunter
Carlos C. Ogden
R. R. Stuart
J. Eric Thorsen
1962
Edgar Jackson
Archie McKellar
Wilmot J. Nicholson
Hugh Phillips
1963
Dr. Frank S. Bernard
Walter Cooley
Allen Gerblick
O. N. Hansen
Greg MacGregor
1964
E. Jerry Collins
Donald Hines
Robert Richardson
James P. Sturrock
Terry Worden
1965
Byron Favorite
Bev Freeman
Severance Hauck
Ed N. Stelling
1966
Shirl Burton
A. D. Coffman
Max Nigl
R. N. Stark
Wayne Wright
1967
Lyman O. Ash
Edward R. Gunion
John Ittner
K. Allan Mahugh
Robert B. Morris, Jr.
J. Winter Smith
1968
John Espinoza
Floyd Hobbs
Roy Hurtig
Charles Orr
Matthew Sheedy
E. J. Warne
1969-1970
William J. Adams, Jr.
John D. Crummey
Stephen H. Goodman
Ted Hall

1969-1970
Albert Herschback
Fred Logan
Joseph A. Rose
1971
Harry Buchalter
Walter D. Chronert
Bob Ellington
Gene Ellsworth
A.M. Ernat
Richard Hurt
Jules Schneider
1972
James Anderson
Eileen Brutsche
Carroll Favorite
Dale Follas
Jack Goodman
Richard Harline
Elaine Ho
Kon Fon Ho
John C. Howay
Helen Hurt
Vickie Jones
Janice Lewis
John McCloud
Charles N. Munger, Jr.
Vi Schneider
Ralph Storti
Robert Wilson
Gertrude Wright
1973
C. Donald Allen, Jr.
William L. Beck
Joseph Brown
Thomas Cardona
Frank Catalano
Dr. Joseph Evers
George Talley
Phil Tucker
Charles Wallin
Wesley Williams
1974
Jack Brittain
Frank Filer
Robert Holt
Joseph A. Jackson
Max Jenkins
Jane Reed
Joan G. Reynolds
Rudy Tokiwa
Mike Troiano
Ann Warfield
1975
John Alden
David LeRoy Badal
John Berney
Dick H. Berry
Andrew J. Bonfield

1975
Richard J. DeVilbiss
Ralph Ellington
Ronald Fitzgerald
Alice Helberg
Robert Herring
Loyce L. Holt
John Hopson
Jerry Millon
Robert O' Harver
W. William Ritt, Jr.
Loren E. Sheldon
Henry J. ten Zeldam
Alan Warner

1976
Ray L. Byrne
Kenneth N. Curzon
Malcolm R. Gaddis
Ralph W. Gray, Sr.
Arthur S. Green
Larry J. Herpel
Nick M. Milichevich
Herb Quick
Robert M. Reynolds
James P. Staehs
R. Maurice Tripp
Ronald H. Workman

1977
Michael Antonacci
Burton A. Corsen
Jerry L. Crosby, Sr.
James L. Devine
C. R. Gordon
Lyman B. Hitch
Ronald D. Irvin
George H. Martin
Robert C. Quincy
Knowlton Shore
Thomas A. Smith
Richard E. Trevisan
James R. Wall
Paul Ward
George C. Wise

1978
Earl S. Burke, Jr.
Michael J. Brady
Dr. Jeffrey S. Crane, Sr.
John P. de Heras, D.C.
Donald Eugene Denk
John A. Enslen
Jean Goodman
Kendon R. Jensen, Jr.
Patty M. Martin
Carolyn Minker
John Minker
Thomas F. Robinson
Frederick Duane Southard
Kay Ward

1979
Wilma Ruth Adams
Robert S. Anderson
Sam E. Case
James O. Daulton
Dennis L. Hatch
Joseph A. Hendrix
Donald R. Lundell
Mary O'Neill
Loretta C. "Nikki" Shank
Walter J. Stephenson, Jr.
Dan L. Stuart
Charles J. Swanner
May Tindall

1980
Leroy T. Adams
Elizabeth M. Crane
Jack M. Currie
Raymond R. Doying
Ian H. Graham
J. Richard House
Judy A. Griffin
Verle M. Shank
Albert B. Smith

1981
James D. Brent
Nessie E. Chesebrough
Paul Chesebrough
Elvera Chronert
Rod Diridon
Raymond J. Ewan
Glen E. Fitzsimmons
Dorothy Gatjen
Sharon Getz
Edward H. Goddard
Willis C. Hannah
Margaret Limberatos
Noboru Masuoka
John H. Mortensen
Thomas Zeitvogel
Winifred Stuart

1982
Robert Hoggan, D.V.M.
Norman Eamon
Jan W. Passmore
Glen Cantrell
Thomas P. Reilley
Ed Kent
Ken Henry
John Newman

1983
Glenn A. George
Charles Ingebritsen
Darrel D. Jensen
Dr. Harold H. Klepfer
William H. Winter

1984
Robert W. Gross
George Imokawa

1984
Janette Lawson
Richard McGhee
Glen McLaughlin
Donald Simpson
Robert Webber
William L. Wegner
Donna Wood

1985
Shirley Adams
William Adams
Enide Allison
Randy Christensen
Fr. Joseph Geary
Fr. John Geary
Gen. Robert E. Huyser
Helen Keyes

1986
Gary Citti
Glenna V. Corsen
Brent Dickson
Gale Ross Gordon
Wayne P. Keyes
Hans Krieger
Gerald Marks
Grace Matthews
Gary Swager
Douglas A. Velberg
Bobby Yount

1987
Chuck Carlstrom
Ronald Jungles
Chuck Kocher
Thomas Lackovic
John B. Lochner
Ray Silva
Lynn Sheldon
Diane Stalions

1988
Theodore Brown
Robert Kraemer
Robert Lacey
James Lyon
James McDonough
Sam Messina
Ken Myers
Lanna von Dohlen

1989
Goldia N. Barclay
Howard Davis
Jerome J. Dvorak
Raymond Jue
Hung Le
Stanley Matsuo
John E. Partanen
Charles J. Schmidt
Carleton K. Stalions
Lawrence Summers

oy Scout Memorial Foundation   -   Santa Clara County Council, Boy Scouts of America

DEDICATION CEREMONY

- - *Open House* - -

CHARLES E. MOORE MEMORIAL BOY SCOUT BUILDING

Sunday, February 7, 1954

2:00 to 5:00 P. M.

ACKNOWLEDGEMENTS

The Boy Scout Memorial Foundation Board acknowledges with sincere thanks the following Business Firms, Individuals and Labor Organizations who assisted in the building and equiping of the Administration Building.

The contribution of time, material and money is an expression of their faith in Youth and their belief in the effectiveness of the "CHARACTER BUILDING AND CITIZENSHIP TRAINING PROGRAM" of Scouting in the lives of Boys.

Craftsmen from the following
Labor Unions:
    Bricklayers' Union No. 10
    Carpenters' Union District Council
    Hodcarriers' Local 234
    International Brotherhood of
    Electrical Workers, Local 332
    Painters' Union, Local 507
    Plumbers' & Steamfitters
    Local No. 393
The American Legion,
    Memory Post No. 399
American Seating Company
Anthony Amori, Grading
American Can Company
Mrs. Gordon Ainsley
Ainsley Corporation
American Machine Tool Co.
George W. Baker, Jr.
Harry Barnes, Appliances
Barnes Drill Company
J. M. Bloom
Frank H. and Lillie Benson
Mr. and Mrs. John Boden
Ralph H. Bollard
Borchers Bros., Concrete
Mr. and Mrs. Roy Bronson
Butcher Electric Company
Oliver E. Brown
Blake, Moffitt & Towne
C. F. Bulotti Machinery Co.
Robert Benson
Beall Refrigeration (Al Beall)
Bernard Food Industries
James Boccardo
Carlton Machine Tool Co.
Cascade Metals Corporation
Cagny's Painting
Cangi Bros. Tile
Cobbledick-Kibbe Glass Co.
Leonard Coates Nurseries
Coastline Maintenance Company
California Dry Wall Taping Co.
Chase Lumber Company
Cheim Lumber Company
Central Concrete Supply Company
California Pacific Title Ins. Co.
California Packing Company
Chevy Chase
Coca-Cola Company
Grace Crim
John Crummey
Continental Can Company
Charles Dull
Harry L. Dull
Disabled American Veterans
Doud Lumber Company
Ditz Bros. (Rye Tractor)
Fred Drew
Robert M. Eberhartt
Stanley B. Ellis

Erickson Van & Storage
Engfer Iron Works
Economy Lumber Company
L. P. Edwards
Ralph Elsman
Morse Erskine
A. M. Erickson
Alice M. Everett
Owens-Corning Fiberglas Corp.
Fairbanks Building Supply Co.
Raymond W. Fisher, Engineer
Food Machinery Corp.
Fletcher Motor Company
Fibreboard Products, Inc.
Joseph George
H. E. & Doris Gray
H. C. Guenetti
Giacomazzi Bros. Transportation Co.
General Electric Company
Gladding Bros. Manufacturing Co.
Judge and Mrs. Louis E. Goodman
Harron, Rickard & McCone Co.
A. J. Hart, Jr.
Ray W. Harvey
Elystus L. Hayes
I. W. Hellman
Hunter's Office Equipment Co.
Phillip Hammer
International Business Machines
Judge Wm. F. James
Mr. and Mrs. I. R. Jarman
Cora H. Johnston
Kaiser Community Homes
Kaiser Company
Mr. and Mrs. Fred Kruse
Kearney & Trucker Corp.
Ladies' Aux. Major Randolph T. Zane
    Post No. 344, V. F. W.
C. W. Laird
Lion's, Furnishings
Robert I. Locke
Los Gatos Telephone Company
Dr. James Lovely
Martin LeFevre
Madsen's Linoleum
O. C. McDonald Co.
W. H. McLaughlin
Midstate Roofing Company
A. O. Mize
George W. Miller
Employees Moore Industrial
Monarch Machine Tool Co.
National Machinery Co.
Made-Rite Manufacturing Co.
Charles E. Moore
Mundell Paper Co.
Modern Ice & Cold Storage Co.
Muirson Label Co., Inc.
Norton Company
Fred Oehler
A. M. Ott

Ray O'Connor, Masonry Equipment
Pacific Manufacturing Co.
Pacific Coast Aggregates
Pacific Floor Products
Pacific Can Company
Pacific Electric Mfg. Co.
Mr. and Mrs. K. E. Parker
Plfuegar & Barnwald
R. A. Powell
Pratt Lowe Preserving Co.
Pittsburgh Des Moines Company
Marjoria K. Quonta
Quaker Pacific Co.
Rotary Club of Santa Clara
A. J. Raisch Pacing Company
L. D. Reeder Co., Installation
    Accoustical Tile
Al Reest, Painting
Rent-Rite Equipment Company
E. H. Renzel & Co.
Harry S. Robinson
Loreen C. Robertson
Richmond-Chase Company
Rankin, Oneal, Luckhardt & Hall
The Rosicrucian Press, Ltd.
San Francisco Machinery Dealers
San Jose Blue Print Company
San Jose Steel Company
San Jose Hardware Company
San Jose Brick & Tile, Ltd.
San Jose Shade Company
Shaw Insulation Company
Sobey & Green, Architects
Carl N. Swenson Company, Inc.
Serpa & Shanrock
Sunlite Bakery Co.
Sutherland Paper Company
Santa Clara Packing Company
Schuckel & Co., Inc.
Salvation Army Fund (Los Gatos)
San Jose Abstract & Tile Ins. Co.
San Jose Clearing House Assn.
Santa Clara Frosted Foods
San Jose Water Works
Security Warehouse Company
Douglas Sim
St. Claire Motor Company
Technical High School,
    Carpet, Linoleum and Soft Tile
    Apprentice Class
Thoeny Bros., Building Materila
United States Products Corp.
Mrs. M. D. Weill
Albert Wright
Thomas F. Wallace
West Coast Steel Company
Williams & Russo, Building Supplies
Wilmars, Inc., Lumber
Western Gravel Company
Will Weston
Sanborn Young

Index